THE BRITISH CINEMA BOO

Glenna Forster-Jones and Genevieve Waite in *Joanna* (Mike Sarne, 1968)

THE BRITISH
CINEMA BOOK

Edited by

Robert Murphy

BRITISH FILM INSTITUTE

bfi

BFI PUBLISHING

First published in 1997 by the
British Film Institute
21 Stephen Street, London W1P 2LN

Reprinted 1999

The British Film Institute exists to promote
appreciation, enjoyment, protection and
development of moving image culture in and
throughout the whole of the United Kingdom. Its
activities include the National Film and Television
Archive; the National Film Theatre; the Museum of
the Moving Image; the London Film Festival; the
production and distribution of film and video;
funding and support for regional activities; Library
and Information Services; Stills, Posters and
Designs; Research, Publishing and Education; and
the monthly *Sight and Sound* magazine.

British Library Cataloguing-in-Publication Data
A catalogue record for this book is available from
the British Library

ISBN 0–85170–640–1 (hbk)
     0–85170–641–X (pbk)

Cover design: Andrew Sutterby
Cover stills: Julie Christie in *Darling* (John
Schlesinger, 1964); back cover, Diana Dors in *Yield
to the Night* (Lee Thompson, 1956).

Typeset by Fakenham Photosetting Ltd, Fakenham,
Norfolk
Printed by St Edmundsbury Press Ltd,
Bury St Edmunds, Suffolk

for Lesley

Contents

Acknowledgments

I would like to thank my contributors for their positive responses to the sometimes startling criticisms I made of their manuscripts. I count it a major achievement that I am still on speaking terms with them all. Thanks are due to my editors, Ed Buscombe and Dawn King, who have staunchly backed this ambitious project; to David Wilson for his judicious copy-editing; and to Hilary Cunliffe-Charlesworth, Angela Wilson, Stephen Broadbridge, Pete Todd, Sheila Johnston, Pius Hume, Gerry Coubro and Steve Moore for their encouragement and support. I would also like to thank my children – Edward, Leo, Sophie, Joe and Josh – for putting up with me when pressure of work made me even more grumpy and bad-tempered than usual; and Lesley Glaister for her warmth and generosity.

Notes on Contributors

Charles Barr is the author of *Ealing Studios* (revised edition: Studio Vista, 1993), and editor of *All Our Yesterdays: 90 Years of British Cinema* (BFI, 1986). He has books in progress on *Vertigo* (BFI Film Classics series) and on *English Hitchcock*. He is Professor of Film Studies at the University of East Anglia in Norwich.

Sarah Street is a lecturer in Film and Television Studies at the University of Bristol. She is co-author with Margaret Dickinson of *Cinema and State* (BFI, 1985) and of *British National Cinema* (Routledge, 1997).

Tom Ryall teaches Film Studies at Sheffield Hallam University and is the author of *Alfred Hitchcock and the British Cinema* (Athlone Press, 1996) and *Blackmail* in the BFI Film Classics series (BFI, 1993).

Lawrence Napper gained an M.A. in Film and Archiving at the University of East Anglia. He currently lives and works in London.

Linda Wood is a freelance researcher with a special interest in British cinema.

Ian Aitken is Senior Lecturer in Film and Media Studies at the University of the West of England. He has written widely on British cinema, film theory and European cinema and is author of *Film and Reform: John Grierson and the Documentary Film Movement* (Routledge, 1990).

Robert Murphy is the author of *Realism and Tinsel* (Routledge, 1989), *Sixties British Cinema* (BFI, 1992) and *Smash and Grab* (Faber and Faber, 1993). He is Senior Research Fellow at De Montfort University, Leicester.

Marcia Landy teaches Film Studies at the University of Pittsburgh. Her publications include *British Genres: Cinema and Society 1930–1960* (Princeton University Press, 1991), *Film, Politics, and Gramsci* (Minneapolis University Press, 1995), and *Cinematic Uses of the Past* (University of Minnesota Press, 1996).

Raymond Durgnat is Visiting Professor at East London University after a Cloister-and-the-Hearth alternation between the film industry and the groves of academe, having been Visiting Professor at UCLA, UC Berkeley and Columbia University, and sometime Staff Writer at the Associated-British Picture Corporation, Literary Adviser for MGM-British, Iris TV, Elstree Distributors, etc.

Kevin Gough-Yates teaches at the University of Westminster. He has recently completed a book for I. B. Tauris on film exile and British cinema in the 1930s and 40s.

Tim Pulleine is on the editorial staff of the *Guardian* and has written extensively on the cinema for that newspaper and for various publications, including *Sight and Sound, Monthly Film Bulletin* and *Films & Filming*.

Vincent Porter is Professor of Mass Media Studies at the University of Westminster. He is co-editor of *British Cinema History* (Weidenfeld and Nicolson, 1983), author of *On Cinema* (Pluto Press, 1985) and a number of other books and articles.

Sue Harper is a Reader of cultural history at the University of Portsmouth. She has published widely on British cinema and is the author of *Picturing the Past: the Rise and Fall of the British Costume Film* (BFI, 1994).

Andrew Spicer has recently completed a PhD about the representation of masculinity in British cinema 1943–1958 at the University of Westminster. He teaches part-time in Film, Media and Cultural Studies at the University of the West of England.

Christine Geraghty is Senior Lecturer in Media and Communications at Goldsmiths College, University of London. She is the author of *Women and Soap Opera* (Polity Press, 1991) and has written a number of articles on constructions of masculinity and femininity in British cinema.

Jeffrey Richards is Professor of Cultural History at Lancaster University, author of *Films and British National Identity* (Manchester University Press, 1997), and co-author of *Britain Can Take It* (Edinburgh University Press, 1993).

Erik Hedling is a lecturer at the Department of Comparative Literature, Lund University, Sweden. His *Lindsay Anderson: Maverick Film-maker* is forthcoming from Cassell.

Geoff Brown is film critic for *The Times*. His studies of British cinema include *Walter Forde* (BFI, 1977) and *Launder and Gilliat* (BFI, 1977). He is a contributor to *Michael Balcon: The Pursuit of British Cinema* (New York: Museum of Modern Art, 1984), and author with Tony Aldgate of *The Common Touch: The Films of John Baxter* (NFT dossier, 1989).

Richard Dacre has written and lectured widely on British cinema and is the author of *Trouble in Store: Norman Wisdom: a Career in Comedy* (T. C. Farries, 1991). He is the owner of *Flashbacks*, London's film memorabilia shop and archive.

Jim Pines teaches Media Arts at the University of Luton. He is editor of *Black and White in Colour* (BFI, 1992) and co-editor with Paul Willemen of *Questions of Third Cinema* (BFI, 1989).

Allen Eyles is a film historian who edits the Cinema Theatre Association magazine *Picture House* and formerly edited *Focus on Film* and *Films & Filming*. He has written numerous career studies, including *Humphrey Bogart* (Sphere, 1990) and *The Complete Films of the Marx Brothers* (Citadel Press, 1992), as well as many books on cinemas, including *London's West End Cinemas* (Keytone Publications, 1991), *ABC: The First Name in Entertainment* (CTA/BFI, 1993) and *Gaumont British Cinemas* (CTA/BFI, 1996).

Ian Conrich teaches film studies at Nottingham Trent University and has contributed to a number of recent publications: *Liberal Directions: Basil Dearden and Post War British Film Culture* (Flicks Books, 1997); *Trash Aesthetics* (Pluto, 1997) and *A Handbook to Gothic Literature* (Macmillan, 1997).

Alan Lovell teaches Media Studies at Staffordshire University. He is co-editor with Jim Hillier of a study of British documentary, *Studies in Documentary* (Secker and Warburg/BFI, 1972), and has written articles on a number of British film and television topics, including Lindsay Anderson, Karel Reisz, British television drama and the contemporary independent film and television movement.

John Hill is Professor of Media Studies at the University of Ulster. His publications include *Sex, Class and Realism: British Cinema 1956–63* (BFI, 1986), *Cinema and Ireland* (Croom Helm, 1987), *Big Picture, Small Screen: The Relations Between Film and Television* (John Libbey, 1996) and *British Cinema in the 1980s* (OUP, 1999).

Introduction

Apart from a brief upsurge of interest between 1942 and 1947, British cinema has been disparaged and despised for most of its existence. In the silent period audiences deserted British films for more adventurous French and American films, and though the 1927 Quota Act boosted production it also muddied the waters by fostering the Quota Quickie. During the Second World War, British films did become genuinely popular, but as the decade wore on there was a widening divide between the realist films favoured by the critics and the escapist melodramas which attracted audiences. British cinema's box-office success continued with war films and comedies in the 50s and the American-backed films of the 60s, but by this time critical attention had turned away, returning only for occasional laments about the poor quality of British films.

In the 1950s the French critics around *Cahiers du Cinéma* had combined contempt for French cinema with passionate enthusiasm for Hollywood. They expressed their views in polemical writing and energetic and innovative films. *Room at the Top* and its kitchen-sink successors in the early 60s seemed to offer the chance of a British 'new wave'. But in the first editorial statement of the film journal *Movie*, Victor Perkins resolutely denied that anything new or significant had occurred, complaining that: 'There is as much genuine personality in *Room at the Top*, method in *A Kind of Loving* and style in *A Taste of Honey* as there is wit in *An Alligator Named Daisy*, intelligence in *Above Us the Waves* and ambition in *Ramsbottom Rides Again*.'[1] The talent histograms drawn in the same issue listed fifty-eight American directors in the top four categories and only five 'British' directors: Joseph Losey, Hugo Fregonese, Robert Hamer, Seth Holt and Karel Reisz. Hamer and Holt were soon to die, Fregonese never made another film in Britain, and Reisz fell from favour after *Night Must Fall* (1964). The *Movie* critics didn't put themselves forward to replace them; they were writers with no inclination to make films. In France the argument that Hollywood films were better than French films led to a surge of new talent into the industry and a radical revitalisation of French cinema. In Britain the argument that Hollywood (and European) films were better than British films led to an inferiority complex and an unhealthy divide between film-makers and film critics. Film Studies developed as an academic discipline around the study of American Westerns and melodramas, European art films and the semiotics of film language. British cinema hardly merited a backwards glance. When Alan Lovell wrote his 1969 BFI seminar paper, he called it, without irony, 'British Cinema: The Unknown Cinema'.

Though the industry declined rapidly in the 70s, the decade did produce a crop of books which took up Lovell's challenge to explore this unknown cinema. Raymond Durgnat's *A Mirror for England* emerged in 1970 and Rachael Low's 1918–1929 volume of *The History of the British Film* in 1971.[2] Alan Lovell and Jim Hillier's *Studies in Documentary* followed in 1972; David Pirie's *A Heritage of Horror*, Dennis Gifford's *The British Film Catalogue* and Ian Christie's *Powell, Pressburger and Others* in 1973;

Alexander Walker's *Hollywood England* in 1974; Elizabeth Sussex's *The Rise and Fall of the British Documentary* in 1976; Geoff Brown's *Walter Forde* and *Launder and Gilliat* and Charles Barr's *Ealing Studios* in 1977; and Roy Armes's *A Critical History of British Cinema* in 1978. Only the Armes book retained the orthodox tone of weary disappointment with the performance of British cinema. The other books, disparate though they were in style and attitude, laid the foundation for the serious study of British cinema.

Several books have been published subsequently and courses on British cinema have proliferated. The purpose of this book is to bring together different generations of scholars and different approaches to British cinema into a useful introductory volume. As editor I have stressed the importance of clarity and accessibility but I have not attempted to dragoon contributors into adopting a uniform or a particularly neutral style; nor have I tried to iron out their differences and disagreements. This is still a fresh field and, though my brief has been to concentrate the book on already cultivated areas, I have not restrained contributors who have insisted on straying into virgin territory. The first fifteen essays deal with historically specific issues, ranging from the British Documentary Movement in the 30s to women in 60s films. The second section is made up of more general essays dealing with censorship, realism, art cinema, horror, comedy, exhibition and, in two very different contributions by Alan Lovell and John Hill, attitudes to British cinema and its role in British cultural life. My concluding chapter concentrates on ten films which seem representative of the period in which they were made.

Notes

1. Victor Perkins, 'The British Cinema', *Movie*, no. 1, June 1962.
2. The History of the British Film project was set up in 1947. Volumes appeared at irregular intervals until *Film-Making in 1930s Britain*, published in 1983, after which Dr Low retired. The BFI is pledged to carry the series through to completion, though only the volume on the 60s has so far appeared.

PART ONE

1

Before *Blackmail*: Silent British Cinema

Charles Barr

To most people other than specialist academics and historians, British silent cinema is an unknown country. No British feature films from the silent era belong to an internationally known repertoire, or to a national tradition that is absorbed by, or at least known to, later generations of film-makers and cinephiles. Our film culture has no roots in, and no memory of, the formative silent period. For a country which was to become a major producer in the sound period, this is extraordinary.

It is now common to divide pre-1930 film history into three main stages: 1) early or primitive cinema, from 1895 to around 1907; 2) a period of rapid transition, at the level both of film form and of production methods; 3) a more settled period, starting around 1916, by which time certain standardised patterns of production and marketing were in place. During the transitional second stage, or early in the third, all the obvious rival countries to Britain managed to produce at least one set or strain of films whose national character was distinctive and attractive enough to make a strong, lasting impact, abroad as well as at home. When America came to dominate the world market, it continued to import films from Europe and to learn lessons from European countries, and often to sign up their directors, like Lubitsch and Murnau from Germany and Sjöström from Sweden. No British film of this time made any significant impact, nor was any British film-maker head-hunted by Hollywood. If Britons worked and prospered there – Chaplin for instance – it was not because of any experience in their native film industry.

The balance of power was different in the early years of cinema. The medium was a novelty. Films were cheap, short, and varied in form. If they told a story it was only a rudimentary one: they might just as well present a view, or a joke, or a brief record (or restaging) of a public event. Production was a small-scale local enterprise. Films were shown by the men who made them, or else copies were sold outright to showmen. They were shown not in special buildings but in fairgrounds or shops or lecture halls, or as part of music-hall programmes.

There was no such thing yet as a 'national cinema', because nothing was organised or standardised or marketed on a national scale. But we can claim that the new medium was explored as energetically and imaginatively in Britain as anywhere in the world.

Already, by the time of the first Lumière show in London in February 1896, a range of English experimenters were active. There are even British candidates for the title of 'inventor' of the moving picture: Augustin Le Prince, who disappeared mysteriously in 1890 soon after making some successful experiments in Leeds, and William Friese

Greene.[1] Two London-based collaborators, Birt Acres (still photographer) and R. W. Paul (scientific instrument maker), seem to have worked more or less in parallel with the Lumières, constructing their own equipment and shooting actuality material; they could immediately exploit the interest aroused by the Lumière show, by programming their own films in the West End. A variety of photographers, lantern-slide men and other showmen now diversified into moving pictures, seizing the moment energetically.

There seem to have been three main centres for sustained production in these early years: London and its suburbs; Brighton, or more accurately its affluent neighbour, Hove; and Yorkshire.

A lot of films from this period survive. Since prints were then sold outright, not rented, many copies of popular films were disseminated; and when the British Film Institute was founded in 1933 and launched a National Film Library, it was able to get hold of plenty of early material. These early film-makers, notably the Brighton School, were given the status of important pioneers. British cinema might, for much of its history, be a subject of embarrassment, but we could take pride in the period (albeit before cinema took on a 'national' dimension) when our men led the world.

Standard histories of the medium went on dutifully acknowledging these pioneer British films, without showing or inspiring any great interest in them. For a long time, the early years of cinema constituted a minority antiquarian concern. Film scholarship and film education, as they developed in the 1960s and 1970s, preferred to deal with the medium in its more accessible maturity. Silent films were not easy to see or to contextualise. When they were shown, they were generally in poor condition and lacked any sound accompaniment.

In the late 1970s this changed rapidly. The reasons are complex, but the key factor is a convergence of interests on the part of three separate groups: film archivists, academics, and popular historians like Kevin Brownlow.[2] While Brownlow and his collaborators began to create a new market, in cinema and on television, for the experience of mature silent film, archivists and scholars put equal energy into exploring the medium's pre-history and early years. The landmark event was the 1978 conference mounted in Brighton by FIAF (the International Federation of Film Archives), which showed all the material it could find in the world's archives from the period before 1906. For the first time, historians looked systematically, analytically, comparatively, at early material from all over the world. The event itself generated a flood of scholarly publications and has led to additional conferences and research projects.[3]

One might expect the British film pioneers to have been put in a humbler place by this sort of event, this new scholarly assessment – decentred and even debunked. And yet they were not. Scholars as diverse in their methods and ideologies as Barry Salt, Noël Burch and the American team of David Bordwell and Kristin Thompson continue to give the early British film-makers a privileged place. Like other exponents of the 'new film history', they make abundant use of the British pioneers in tracing the early material development of the medium.

These early films express a native eagerness to embrace and explore the new medium, and a craftsmanship in handling it, that flourish briefly and then are blocked off, before surfacing again in different forms, a long way in the future, in British film and television.

All the new histories refer to *The Big Swallow*, made in around 1900 by the Hove chemist/photographer James Williamson. A man is out walking, catches sight of the camera (i.e. the camera that is shooting the film), and advances menacingly towards it, then opens his mouth to swallow it. We see a camera, a tripod and an operator fall into a black hole; the man moves away, munching in triumph. This can be read as a visionary playing out of the aggression inherent in the camera-subject relation; at the same time (and the two things are not mutually exclusive) it's a brilliant little joke in the manner of a Monty Python TV sketch of around 1970, designed for inclusion within a similar *programme* of short, distinct items, each constituting an independent 'attraction'. The Monty Python slogan, 'And Now for Something Completely Different', echoes the way in which the short early films seem habitually to have been yoked together.

Cecil Hepworth made a comparable *tour de force* of aggression in *How It Feels to be Run Over* (1900). A car advances along a road from extreme long shot to, indeed, run us over; almost subliminally, the words 'Oh Mother Will Be Pleased' flash on the screen. There is a great abundance of early one-joke films, generally done in a single shot (like the many one-view films in the actuality mode). It might be inferred that film-makers in Britain exploited the medium effectively at the level of isolated effects or attractions but were left behind when representations became less bitty and the medium started to acquire a 'grammar' – to move towards the 'classical narrative' model that America was destined to impose and dominate. But this is not so at all. The early British film-makers are pioneers at this level too. Those early years are an island not just of Monty Python inventiveness but of an editing ingenuity that looks ahead, in its way, to the craftsmanship of a David Lean.

A consummation of all this early ingenuity, and possibly the high point historically for cinema in Britain relative to the rest of the world, is marked by a short narrative made by the Cecil Hepworth company in 1905.

Rescued by Rover

The baby of a well-off couple is looked after by a nanny. Out in the park, she flirts with a soldier, and the baby is stolen from its pram by a gypsy woman. While she is explaining this to the mother, the family dog, Rover, senses what has happened, speeds through the town, and locates gypsy and baby in an attic room. Rover then returns home and persuades the baby's father to come back with him. Father retrieves the baby, leaving the gypsy to swig from her gin bottle. The family is happily united, Rover included.

What is remarkable about the film is its systematic organisation. The camera scarcely moves, and there are no intertitles: a story of some seven minutes is told through a lucid succession of visual images.

There are four basic locations: the opulent family home, the park, the tenement block where the gypsy lives, and the route from the family home to the tenements. Setting the narrative out in tabular form enables the structure to be clearly read. There are eleven separate camera set-ups, here designated by the letters A to K (in the horizontal plane); and twenty-one shots, designated by successive numbers (in the vertical plane). The Time column gives the approximate length of each shot, in seconds.

In more detail, the camera set-ups are as follows:

Park	A and B: adjacent angles	
Family home:	C: close shot, living room.	D: wider shot, living room
	E: father's study	F: exterior, window
Route:	G: street, long shot	H: street corner
	I: river (with boat)	
Gypsy home:	J: exterior, street door	K: attic interior, with bed

7

PARK		FAMILY HOME				ROUTE			GYPSY HOME		time	
A	B	C	D	E	F	G	H	I	J	K		
		1									8	Rover and baby
2											16	nanny with pram: spurns gypsy
	3										42	– flirts: gypsy steals baby
			4								25	nanny tells mother: exit Rover [R]
				5							4	R out of window
					6						8	R runs towards/past camera
						7					4	R likewise
							8				20	R swims river, passes camera
								9			12	R pushes open street door: in
										10	63	gypsy/baby: R in, sees, exits
								11			5	R exits by street door
							12				15	R away from camera, swims river
					13						5	R away from camera
				14							4	R in through window
			15								22	father depressed, R in: exeunt
					16						11	father led by R ...
							17				30	... across river (in boat)
								18			13	... to the right door: in
									19		22	father takes baby, gypsy drinks
		20									20	bereft mother joined by all three
	21										10	happy family group

The analysis lays bare a pattern of repetition and symmetry which is pleasurable in itself, in the way that metre and rhyme can be in a poem. The action moves in a linear way from house to attic across a series of locations (shots 4 to 10), then back to the house (11 to 15), and thence back again to the attic (16 to 19). Repetition and variation – the variation comes from what is shown (dog coming, dog going, then dog and man coming) and from the unobtrusive shortening of the sequence: the street-corner shot (7) is missed out of the second journey, and the window shot (5/14) is missed out of the third. A fourth journey would be one too many, and is elided.

Form and content are beautifully matched. The confidence of the shot-by-shot construction is an ideal vehicle for the confidence of the narrative, as it moves in the classic manner from equilibrium to disruption to restoration of equilibrium in the happy ending; and, in turn, for the ideological confidence it expresses. Man is the hunter, women are transgressive or subservient; gypsies are menacingly other. Middle-class family values rule.

It's easy to see why this film became so celebrated and so widely imitated. So many copies were made for sale at home and abroad that the negative twice wore out, necessitating shot-by-shot remakes. I have neither seen nor read about any other film from this period that is constructed with this machine-like efficiency. It's a clear precursor of the short films made by D. W. Griffith for the Biograph Company in America between 1908 and 1913, based on the same structural principle of repetition and variation, of permutations worked upon a limited number of camera set-ups. Griffith is likely to have seen *Rescued by Rover*, and it may be no coincidence that his own first film, *The Adventures of Dollie*, tells of the loss and rescue of a small child.

What Griffith would soon make into his trademark was parallel editing, a dimension that *Rescued by Rover* lacks. Looking at the narrative chart, we can see that the movement is purely linear, following a single path. The Griffith of 1909 would assuredly have kept cutting back and forth between two and probably three centres of interest: Rover's journey, the helpless baby, the anxious mother.

It's not surprising Hepworth didn't go this far in 1905: *Rescued by Rover*, for its time, is extraordinary enough. Among other things it is a visionary model of economy in film-making. A complex narrative can be constructed on the basis of a limited number of fixed camera set-ups. The system lends itself to advance scripting and to unproblematically delegated editing. In theme, tone and organisation, *Rescued by Rover* seems the very model of the way mainstream popular cinema was destined to develop.

The question that does arise, though, is what happened to Hepworth and to the pioneer spirit in British film-making, after 1905. Why was it Griffith and not Hepworth himself who developed the system further, using it for films of greater range and depth? Why was it America and not Britain that built a production system on this model of structural economy? Hepworth continued as a director and producer for some twenty years; to judge from the films I have seen, he effectively turned his back on the line of development represented by *Rescued by Rover*. It's as if he and Smith and Williamson and the others ran the first lap, passed on the baton to the Americans, and then stopped exhausted.

Rescued by Rover may point the way to the future but it also belongs firmly to the primitive years. First, it was a cheaply shot family affair. The family are the Hepworths, and Rover is their dog, even though the other parts are played by actors hired for the day. Second, copies were still sold outright. Third, for all the claims one may make for it, it does undeniably have the childish quality that its title implies.

Momentous changes were taking place in cinema, with more organised patterns of production, renting of films, and exhibition – and an increase in production values. This is the point at which the British input falters: the stage when cinema begins to acquire genuinely national dimensions.

The next two decades were depressing ones. British production ceased to have much of an export market, except to some extent in the countries of the Empire; even in the home market, it supplied only a minor – and decreasing – proportion of the films shown. By the start of the First World War, the figure was around 15 per cent; by 1926, it was down to 5 per cent. The reputation of British films among audiences and critics had sunk to a low level, and remained there in spite of intermittent efforts by the film trade to promote them and to mount special events and campaigns.

The 'cottage industry' which produced *Rescued by Rover* could not survive the new developments in the international film market. The American industry organised itself in 1908 to form the powerful oligopoly of the MPPC (Motion Picture Patents Company), laying down a system that would enable it to service its own very large home market and to set strict controls on foreign imports. Williamson and Hepworth were among the film-makers who had relied on selling a lot of prints in America. Hepworth did manage to survive, and stayed active until the mid-1920s. Other pioneers, Williamson included, soon abandoned production and went back to their day jobs. But in other countries likewise, most of the early innovators had dropped out around this time, and dynamic new people took over, to work within the new structures. There seems no obvious reason why British production could not have organised itself in such a way as to serve its home market more effectively, and to do better in countries other than America. But it failed either to match the dynamism of American production, or to find an effective alternative style that could give it a distinctive niche in the world market. Not for the last time, British cinema was caught awkwardly between American and European modes of operation.

9

Square on, tableau-like shooting. Cecil Hepworth's Comin' Thro' the Rye *(1924).*

Tantalising as it is to see D. W. Griffith taking over the baton from Hepworth, and extrapolating ruthlessly and prolifically from the *Rescued by Rover* model of construction, it is pointless to regret that Hepworth himself did not go on in that way, or that no other British film-maker emerged to do so. Griffith's success resulted not just from his own talent but from a framework unavailable in Britain: a combination of the size of the American market, the security of the investment behind him, and other things about the history, landscape and culture of the nation. The 400-plus films that Griffith made for the Biograph Company between 1908 and 1913 are not much longer than *Rescued by Rover* and its British successors, but they have a stunning dynamism, maturity and range (from Westerns to domestic dramas). They are the dramatic equivalent of the comic energy and fertility of early American comedy. The most sensational of the comedians, Charlie Chaplin, was of course British, and moreover had learned his comic craft in the British music hall – as had Stan Laurel. Britain could supply not only 'talent' like these two, but the popular forms that fostered them. What it evidently could not do was to provide an appropriate cinematic framework for them, either institutionally or formally.

But if Britain could not compete with America, it might have operated in the manner of, say, Sweden. As Thompson and Bordwell remind us in their global survey of *Film History*:

> The Swedish cinema initially had little impact abroad, and so its film-makers were working without the larger budgets made possible by export. Sweden was among the first countries to create a major cinema by drawing deliberately upon the particular traits of its national culture. Swedish films were characterised by their dependence on northern landscapes and by their use of local literature, costumes, customs, and the like.[4]

There were indeed many attempts in Britain to capitalise on the indigenous landscape, literature and general 'heritage'. But to compare the silent British versions of Shakespeare, Dickens, etc., with the Swedish adaptations from stage and literature, notably the novels of Selma Lagerlöf, is to understand why they had such different status and staying power. According to a Swedish film historian, these Lagerlöf films

> became national events and drew the public to the cinema on a scale previously undreamed of. Victor Sjöström's film version of *Ingmarssönerna* (*The Sons of Ingmar*) was seen by 196,000 in Stockholm, a city which at that time had only 400,000 inhabitants. The picture ran for twenty years in the capital and surpassed both Douglas Fairbanks and Charles Chaplin in popularity.[5]

The Hepworth company's one-hour film version of *Hamlet* in 1913, in contrast, had some warm patriotic reviews but limited box-office appeal. Like many early British adaptations, it presents 'scenes from' the original, trading on the prestige appeal of the text and the performers, rather than, like the films of Sjöström and his colleagues, reworking the play in film terms. And the landscapes are a backdrop rather than an organic part of the work. The Swedes had carefully acquainted themselves with international developments in film style, absorbing what was appropriate rather than imitating. The equivalent British efforts are insular in comparison.

What, in more precise terms, was wrong with British films in these two decades, what made them so consistently unsuccessful? Commentators have identified a variety of reasons. James Park puts most emphasis on the script:

> Writing, it's true, isn't thought of as one of the problems of British cinema. It's the one thing the nation that produced Shakespeare thinks it can do rather well. But writing *screenplays* is something the British do very badly indeed.[6]

For Park, this failing goes right back to the years before the First World War. Rachael Low puts particular emphasis on the crudity, for most of the silent period, of the British approach to film editing and to film acting. Editing was all too often seen as a purely technical process of joining scenes together, while the dominance of stage work in the lives of most film actors meant that 'there was neither motive nor opportunity for actors to adapt themselves to the silent screen and discover a suitable style'.[7] Alfred Hitchcock, discussing with François Truffaut the low opinion he formed of British films as a consumer in the 1910s, singled out the unvaryingly flat quality of British lighting and photography.[8] Finally, Iris Barry, looking back in 1926, was exasperated by a regular directorial failing:

> the one, common in England, of using the screen as though it were a stage with exits left and right, the actors free to move only across a circumscribed oblong area, with a low skyline and the movements all parallel to the plane of the screen, not, as they should be, for the sake of depth-illusion, at angles to it.[9]

Writing, editing, acting, lighting, directing – that covers just about everything. The complaints fit together to create a sense of a total filmic *system* that is ponderous and literal-minded. The common criticism is of a failure to rethink material in film terms, or to consider what 'film terms' amount to. Material is mechanically transcribed or condensed from a stage or literary original: the actors act it, the camera shoots the scene, the editor joins the scenes together, and you have a film. And the audience endures it, perhaps thinking of it as a patriotic duty. Or it stays away.

But by 1926, the year of Iris Barry's book, things were starting to change on several fronts:

1. A new and more businesslike body of film-makers was emerging. It's as if enterprise and innovation had skipped a generation, but now returned. These are some of the people who came on the scene after 1920: Michael Balcon, Victor Saville, Herbert Wilcox, Graham Cutts, Anthony Asquith, Alfred Hitchcock, Ivor Montagu, Adrian Brunel. All of them combined ambition, and generally a degree of idealism, with a realistic knowledge of the film world, and an awareness that that world stretches beyond Britain. Balcon and Saville started as film distributors in the Midlands, Montagu and Brunel made their name as editors. Apart from Balcon, all of them were – or would at some point become – directors. Though many of them initially met obstacles from producers and exhibitors, they persevered.

2. The Film Society was founded in London in 1925, to show important new films from abroad as well as significant revivals, and to act as a forum for discussion. Again it met some opposition, from the established film trade, but it too persevered. Many of the new generation of film-makers belonged to it. Alongside this, belatedly, the medium started to get more sustained and informed critical attention in print – in Iris Barry's book, in the specialist magazine *Close Up* (from 1927), and in a few newspapers and magazines.

3. There was growing awareness of the existence of a branch of film-making which Britain might be in a position to lay a special claim to. Barry referred to 'documentary films' as 'a department of cinematography in which England is still unbeaten'.[10] Throughout the barren years from 1908 Percy Smith had been turning out, for a succession of companies, his studies of plant life, using close-up and slow motion. Entitled *Secrets of Life* or *Secrets of Nature*, these films appealed both to popular and to highbrow audiences; and there had been much more in the broad documentary mode. This work did not, yet, have a very high profile, but a young Scot named John Grierson was spending 1926 in America, studying the role of the mass media in influencing public opinion. Soon he would return to extend the role of documentary film considerably, and to attract a lot of publicity both to it and to himself.[11]

4. The British government was at last sufficiently disturbed by the hegemony of American films on British screens to prepare some protective legislation: the first Cinematograph Films Act was passed in 1927.

These four factors between them set an agenda for the 1930s, and indeed beyond. Committed film-makers, looking to make an effective career in an unstable industry. A strong critical and intellectual discourse about cinema. A concern for documentary and the realist film. And an involvement, however uncertain, on the part of the government.

One of the recurring debates around British cinema is between the concepts of the national and the international. British producers had already begun to toy with the strategy of aiming directly at the international market by bringing over American stars. Balcon did so for his first British feature, *Woman to Woman*, in 1922; the strategy was successful, but didn't work so well when repeated. After burning his fingers a few times like this, Balcon was to argue that 'we shall become international by being national'.[12] But it seems more plausible to rework the terms of this opposition: the lesson of the silent period is that we became national by being international. It was only when Britain became intelligently open to international influences that it began to be able to find a strong, meaningful, national identity for its own production.

Grierson needed to go to North America in order to formulate his ideas about the role documentary film could play in British society and British cinema. Michael Balcon made some of his early productions in German studios. Anthony Asquith spent six months on a study trip in Hollywood, before returning to make the sharp and precocious *Shooting Stars* for British International Pictures in 1927; set partly in a film studio, it's one of the few British silent films that would stand up to revival with full orchestral honours. Ivor Montagu travelled in Europe and in the young Soviet Union, and brought Eisenstein and Pudovkin, both in person and through their films, to the Film Society in London. The Society itself was a major medium for the dissemination of ideas from abroad.

This international dimension is crystallised in the person, and the work, of two young directors of the time. One is Michael Powell, who served an intensive European/American apprenticeship in the Victorine Studios in Nice, working mainly with two directors from Hollywood, Rex Ingram and Harry Lachman, and then came back to England, initially working as stills photographer on the Alfred Hitchcock film *Champagne*. The other is Hitchcock himself.

No one could be more obviously, tenaciously English than Hitchcock. At the same time, no one could be more international. He had gone to work, as a teenager, not for a British company (having a low opinion of British standards), but for the London office of an American firm. The films he remembered being impressed by were mainly American and German. When his first employers pulled out of London, he moved to a British company (Balcon's Gainsborough), worked on their German-based productions, and watched Murnau shooting *The Last Laugh* at the UFA Studios in Berlin. The first two films he directed were again shot in a German studio, as well as on Italian, French and Austrian locations. One of his main early colleagues was Ivor Montagu, the friend of the Soviet directors, and Hitchcock encountered them and their work at the Film Society. And his films are, unmistakably, the meeting place of stylistic influences from America, Germany and the Soviets. Hitchcock made no secret of this. He would always refer, in articles and interviews, to the impact made on him by Soviet montage editing and to the satisfaction he took in using devices drawn from Pudovkin and Kuleshov. For the magazine *Close Up*, reviewing *Blackmail*, he was already notorious for his use of 'the almighty German technique', at the level of image composition.[13] And early in his career he wrote an article in the *Evening News* expressing a shrewd sense of his own relation to the dominant American cinema.

> The American directors under their commercially minded employers have learned a good deal about studio lighting, action photographs, and telling a story plainly and simply in moving pictures. They have learnt, as it were, to put the nouns, verbs and adjectives of the film language together. . . . It is obvious that what we must strive for at once is the way to use these nouns and verbs as cunningly as do the great novelists and great dramatists, to achieve certain moods and effects in an audience.[14]

Nouns, verbs and adjectives. I think one can interpret the linguistic analogy at three levels. 1. The basic grammar of cinema: the way shots are composed and combined. 2. The grammar of narrative: economical and coherent story-telling, moving purposefully from beginning to middle to end, with no loose ends. 3. What one might call the grammar of story psychology: motivation, relationships, particularly between couples, and between parents and children, worked out across the narrative. Between them, these constitute the grammar of what historians now describe as the 'classical

Hollywood system': a highly purposeful and consistent model of film-making, seen as the basis of Hollywood's success in, at one end of the process, organising its production methods efficiently, and, at the other, appealing to wide audiences.

Long before the concept of classical Hollywood was named and analysed, Hitchcock had formed his own understanding of how it operated; and the film he was making at the time is a fine example of the judicious application of its principles to British material. *The Farmer's Wife* might sound unpromising: a film of the long-running West End comedy by Eden Philpotts, much of it shot on rustic locations. It could easily, in other hands, have been stagey in all the wrong ways, with the occasional insertion of picturesque bits of local scenery. Hitchcock (who here takes a rare screen credit as scriptwriter) is not disrespectful of the original, but reworks it deftly in terms of the 'nouns, verbs and adjectives' of popular cinema.

The grammar of narrative: sub-plots and diversions are cleared away, along with most of the dialogue, to give a lucid central story line – the quest by the newly widowed farmer Samuel Sweetland to find a second wife. Story psychology: a quite new emphasis is put on Sweetland's relationship with his only daughter (there are two daughters in the play). The death of the wife is quickly (in film time) followed by the daughter's marriage. Lonely after hosting the wedding feast and seeing her depart for her new home, he at once starts the search for a new wife. The ultimate choice will be his housekeeper, who is aligned both with the first wife (through her job) and with the daughter (through her youth – she is much younger than any of the other women whom Sweetland considers). The drama is thus given a clear though delicate Oedipal dimension, of a kind that was already thoroughly familiar in Hollywood narrative.

A stage play reset with the nouns, verbs and adjectives of popular cinema. Hitchcock's The Farmer's Wife *(1927).*

Finally, the grammar of film language. The intensity of feeling between father and daughter is conveyed not in intertitles but by visual means: point of view, and the shot/reverse shot construction. They exchange looks across the crowded scene of the wedding feast: shots of him are intercut with shots from his viewpoint of daughter and son-in-law, at the other end of the table. The pattern is repeated when the couple depart from the house (and thus from the film).

These linked devices – point of view, shot/reverse shot, and matching of eyelines – have been convincingly identified by historians as the cornerstone of 'classical' Hollywood's spatial system. It is a radical break from the mode of direction criticised by Iris Barry as typical of retrograde British films (square-on, tableau-like shooting). It doesn't simply 'open up' the play technically, make it more cinematic: it affords a new level of intimacy between audience and characters. Interestingly, it is a strategy against which Cecil Hepworth explicitly held out, to the end of his life. See the notorious passage in his memoirs of 1951:

> Smoothness in a film is important and should be preserved, except when for some special effect a 'snap' is preferred. The 'unities' and the 'verities' should always be observed, to which I should add the 'orienties'. Only the direst need will form an excuse for lifting an audience up by the scruff of the neck and carrying it round to the other side, just because you suddenly want to photograph something from the south when the previous scene has been taken from the north.[15]

It may seem ironic that this is the same Hepworth who in 1905, in *Rescued by Rover*, had offered such a precocious model of a cinematic system. In 1924 his most ambitious film, *Comin' Thro' the Rye*, helped to bankrupt his company. Although revisionist claims have been made on behalf of this film, it signally failed to make an impact with critics and audiences, or to carve out any sort of niche for its version of a national cinema. On his way out in the mid-1920s Hepworth passes Hitchcock coming in.

Notes

1. For Augustin Le Prince, see Christopher Rawlence, *The Missing Reel* (London: Collins, 1990); also his film of the same title broadcast on Channel 4. For Friese Greene, see especially Michael Chanan, *The Dream that Kicks* (second edition, London: Routledge, 1985).
2. Brownlow has had a remarkable influence at three levels: a) as author of books on the silent period, starting with *The Parade's Gone By* (London: Secker & Warburg, 1968); b) as co-director, with David Gill, of many TV series about silent cinema, starting with the 13-part *Hollywood: the Pioneers* (for Thames Television, 1979); c) as (again with Gill) restorer and exhibitor of silent film prints, with orchestral accompaniment, in cinemas and then on television. It's ironic, and symptomatic, that while these activities are based in Britain they have virtually ignored the British cinema of the silent period, although their recent series *Cinema Europe: The Other Hollywood* (Channel 4, 1995) does devote one programme to it. None of their choices for orchestral presentation has been a British film.
3. Details of the conference are given in *Cinema 1900–1906* (edited by Roger Holman, Brussels: FIAF, 1982). Some of the scholarly work directly and indirectly inspired by it is collected in Thomas Elsaesser and Adam Barker (eds.), *Space Frame Narrative: Early Cinema* (London: British Film Institute, 1990).
4. Thompson and Bordwell, *Film History: an Introduction* (New York and London, McGraw-Hill, 1994), p. 65.
5. Bengt Idestam-Almquist, *Nar Filmen Kom Till Sverige* (Stockholm: P. A. Norstedt, 1959; Swedish text, with summary in English), p. 608.
6. James Park, *British Cinema: The Lights That Failed* (London: Batsford, 1990), p. 14.
7. Rachael Low, *History of the British Film 1918–1929* (London: George Allen and Unwin, 1971), p. 301. On editing, see pp. 267ff.
8. François Truffaut, *Hitchcock* (first English edition, London: Secker & Warburg, 1968), p. 27.

9. Iris Barry, *Let's Go to the Movies* (New York: Arno Press, 1972), p. 233 (original publication in London, 1926).
10. Ibid., p. 220.
11. See Forsyth Hardy (ed.), *Grierson on Documentary* (London: Collins, 1946, and subsequent editions). Other important books written from within the documentary movement, by early collaborators of Grierson, include Paul Rotha, *Documentary Diary* (London: Secker & Warburg, 1973), and Basil Wright, *The Long View* (London: Secker & Warburg, 1974).
12. Michael Balcon, *A Lifetime of Films* (London: Hutchinson, 1969), p. 61.
13. *Close Up*, vol. 5, no. 2, August 1929, p. 134.
14. *Evening News*, London, 16 November 1929, cited in Donald Spoto, *The Life of Alfred Hitchcock: The Dark Side of Genius* (London: Collins, 1983), p. 102.
15. Cecil Hepworth, *Come the Dawn* (London: Phoenix House, 1951), p. 139.

Bibliography

Balcon, Michael, *A Lifetime of Films* (London: Hutchinson, 1969).
Barry, Iris, *Lets Go to the Movies* (New York: Arno Press, 1972).
Burch, Noel, *Life to Those Shadows*, (London: British Film Institute, 1990).
Chanan, Michael, *The Dream That Kicks*, (London: Routledge, 1983).
Elsaesser, Thomas and Barker, Adam (eds.) *Space, Frame, Narrative: Early Cinema* (London: British Film Institute, 1990).
Hepworth, Cecil, *Came the Dawn* (London: Phoenix House, 1951).
Higson, Andrew, *Waving the Flag: Constructing a National Identity in Britain* (Oxford: Clarendon Press, 1993).
Low, Rachael and Manvell, Roger, *The History of the British Film 1896–1906* (London: Allen and Unwin, 1948).
Low, Rachael, *The History of the British Film 1906–1914* (London: Allen and Unwin, 1949).
Low, Rachael, *The History of the British Film 1914–1918* (London: Allen and Unwin, 1950).
Low, Rachael, *The History of the British Film 1918–1929* (London: Allen and Unwin, 1971).
Salt, Barry, *Film Style and Technology: History and Analysis* (London, Starword, 1992).

2
British Film and the National Interest, 1927–1939

Sarah Street

Only by creating a centre, a home for the industrial art of the cinema, will it be possible by study and experiment to try out the economic, aesthetic and technical issues and the social, political and moral values implicit in them.... To place the industry on a footing of equality with its foreign competitors we must contribute something of our own.... There can be no national tradition of the film until there is an ideological nucleus.[1]

During the 1920s the financial health of the British film industry was examined by official and quasi-official groups who reached a consensus that a film industry was such an important component of national culture that the government must protect it. There was considerable debate as to how this protection and concern could best be achieved, but there was agreement on the need to reduce Hollywood's domination of Britain's cinema screens. These debates on the protection of the British film industry raised, but did not always answer, fundamental questions about the role of film as an expression of national identity.

The Cinematograph Films Act (1927)

The Cinematograph Films Act (1927) was the first case of the government intervening to protect the commercial film industry. Its intention was to foster production so that a larger percentage of screen time would be devoted to the exhibition of British films. It did not do this by providing a subsidy for producers, or by ensuring that they received a larger share of box-office receipts, but instead imposed a statutory obligation on renters and exhibitors to acquire and show a minimum 'quota' of British films out of the total number they handled, British and foreign. Up to 1927 the majority of films exhibited in Britain had been American. In 1914, 25 per cent of the films shown were British, but by 1923 this had dropped to 10 per cent and by 1925 it was only 5 per cent. In 1924 the total number of British films 'trade shown' (films shown to exhibitors before hiring) was 56. In 1925 only 45 were shown, and in 1926 the figure had slumped to 37.[2] It was this state of affairs that the first Films Act aimed to rectify.

The Act provided that in the first year the renters' quota should be 7.5 per cent, and the exhibitors' 5 per cent. The renters' quota was higher because exhibitors wanted to be offered an adequate selection of films. Both quotas were to increase by stages to 20 per cent in 1936, and remain at that level until 1938 when the Act expired. A British film was defined as one made by a British subject or company. The definition did not specify that control had to be in British hands, but only that the company had to be constituted in the British Empire and that the majority of the company directors should be British. All studio scenes had to be shot in the Empire, and not less than 75 per cent of the labour costs incurred in a film production, including payments for copyright and to one foreign actor, actress or producer, had to be paid to British subjects, or to persons domiciled in the Empire. The 'scenario' – a term never clearly defined, so that the provision became a dead letter – had to be written by a British subject. The Act also regulated booking practices in an attempt to open up more of the home market to British films. The Board of Trade, whose Industries and Manufactures Department was responsible for the film industry, was to register the films, and to consult with an Advisory Committee consisting of trade and independent members.

The Films Act was passed before Britain adopted a major programme of general protective industrial tariffs in 1931. In the late nineteenth and early twentieth centuries a policy of free trade had been pursued, even though Britain's share of the world export trade in manufactured goods fell from 35.8 per cent in 1890 to 28.4 per cent by 1900, and in 1921–25 was only 23.8 per cent.[3] The rise of competing industrial economies meant that Britain gradually lost its traditional role as the 'workshop of the world' to Germany and the United States, who protected their newly developed industries and began to supply markets previously dominated by British goods. Britain's trade deficit widened and by 1929 the leading export trades were suffering high levels of unemployment. It is in this context of gradual but limited pressures for protection that the Films Act should be seen.

Competition from Hollywood was overwhelming, and consolidated by booking practices which favoured the distribution and exhibition of American films in Britain. With British production at a low ebb in the mid-1920s, exhibitors were forced to rely on a plentiful supply of cheap and popular Hollywood films: as British production declined, exhibition boomed. In the 1920s the outstanding development in the structure of the film industry was the growth of the circuits. Whereas in 1917 there were ninety circuits (429 cinemas), by 1926 there were 139 (856 cinemas).[4] The optimism created by the prospect of quota legislation accelerated the trend towards vertical integration – the grouping of small companies into a combine which amalgamated the three main sectors of the film business: production, distribution and exhibition. By 1933 two combines dominated the British scene: the Gaumont-British Picture Corporation (GBPC) controlled 287 cinemas, and the Associated British Picture Corporation (ABPC) had 147 cinemas.[5] Financed by Maurice and Isidore Ostrer, GBPC was registered as a public company in 1927. It was an amalgamation of several important concerns: Gaumont, Ideal Films, the W & F Film Service, the Biocolor circuit, Denman Picture Houses and the General Theatre Corporation; the large Provincial Cinematograph Theatres (PCT) circuit was purchased in December 1928. ABPC was formed by John Maxwell in 1928 and consisted of his production company, British International Pictures, Wardour Films, First-National Pathé and the Scottish Cinema and Variety Theatres. The major advantage enjoyed by vertically integrated companies was that their studios were able to launch more ambitious production programmes, secure in the knowledge that the films would be shown in their cinemas and that box-office profits would finance subsequent productions. State protection was therefore responsible for a fundamental change in the structure of the industry and a revival in production.

Despite complaints that the Films Act encouraged 'quota quickies' (cheap British films financed by American renters to satisfy quota regulations while not affecting the number of American films they handled), British films increased their share of the market from 4.4 per cent in 1927 to 24 per cent by 1932.[6] British exhibitors consistently exceeded their quota requirements well into the 1930s, which would appear to contradict the view expressed by many at the time and subsequently by critics and film historians that British films were universally unpopular. Undoubtedly many poor-quality films were produced in the post-quota boom and in the awkward period of adjustment to sound, but 'good' British pictures, usually produced by highly capitalised companies like GBPC or ABPC, were welcomed by exhibitors, and many directors, technicians and actors gained valuable experience by working on British films, cheap or expensive. As John Sedgwick's statistical work has shown, by 1934 the industry was doing well, with British producers achieving 'comparable performance results per film product as their more renowned Hollywood counterparts', which supported the case that Britain could create a 'viable national cinema'.[7]

The 'Talkies'

The rush to exploit the novelty of the 'talkies' encouraged many companies to extend themselves beyond their means. While the arrival of sound attracted capital to the industry and hastened the trend towards vertical integration, it also caused confusion and panic. It is clear that some of the companies which had been formed in the immediate post-quota boom went under because of the coming of sound. Costs escalated – the average cost of a silent film production was £5–12,000, whereas a 'talkie' cost £12–20,000. Many of the new companies did not have the capital to produce on that scale and sound recording equipment was expensive. The quota helped the larger companies adjust to sound, but could not save the smaller, more precarious companies which had been set up between 1927 and 1930. Despite the expense of equipping cinemas for sound, exhibitors fared better. Britain was the first European country to convert its cinemas: 22 per cent of UK cinemas were wired by 1929, and by 1930 the figure had risen to 63 per cent;[8] that is, 980 cinemas by 1929, but as many as 3,151 by the end of the following year.[9]

The Americans thought it was the coming of sound, more than the quota, that rescued the British film industry. They thought particular types of film were more suited to British audiences, especially comedy-farces. One study in 1931 revealed that a higher proportion of farces and murder mysteries made by British companies were shown in Britain than similar American films. The report went on to say: 'The farces were among the most successful of British pictures, while most of the American were relatively unsuccessful ... Farce is a form of humor more appreciated on its native heath than elsewhere.'[10] American Westerns and dramas were still very popular, but clearly sound gave British producers the opportunity to develop certain types of film that audiences found more acceptable than has been supposed.[11] The quota helped in the process of adjustment to sound because the influx of capital which it encouraged enabled the larger companies to equip their cinemas and studios for sound. This required a considerable capital outlay, and it is doubtful whether the industry, in its moribund state before the quota, could have attracted the finance necessary for the changeover.

Korda and film finance

The revival of the British film industry in the early 1930s enabled Alexander Korda to

Alexander Korda's The Private Life of Henry VIII *(1933): showing the world that Britain could produce internationally successful films on British subjects.*

develop one of the most important British film companies, London Film Productions. Korda was an experienced Hungarian film-maker who came to England in 1931 after working in Vienna, Berlin and Hollywood. In 1933 he made *The Private Life of Henry VIII*, an irreverent historical comedy starring Charles Laughton, which raised the question of whether the goal of encouraging indigenous 'British' film styles and themes was compatible with achieving box-office success at an international level. *Henry VIII* certainly scored as far as the latter was concerned: it broke box-office records in America, taking over £7,000 in its first week at the Radio City Music Hall in New York and over £500,000 on its first world run, and was praised for showing the world that Britain could produce internationally successful films on British subjects.[12] But it was also accused of dictating an expensive style (it cost £93,710) and giving other producers and their financiers false optimism about the type of films which made money and the accessibility of the lucrative American market.

In the wake of *Henry VIII*'s success, production boomed and Korda was able to build lavish studios at Denham. Between 1935 and 1937 new studios mushroomed. In 1928 there were nineteen stages in British studios with a total area of 105,650 square feet; by 1938 there were seventy with 777,650 square feet.[13] Korda's success inspired others to make films for the American market. This was a dangerous policy, because if a film failed to recoup its production costs losses could be catastrophic, especially if the picture was a lavish venture intended to appeal to British and American audiences. *World Film News* anticipated problems in July 1936 when it commented: 'It is generally admitted in the film trade that a collapse is imminent and that it may come any time within the next six months.' By January 1937 there were signs that the bubble would burst. Julius Hagen's Twickenham group of companies went bankrupt after an attempt to make pictures for world release. Hagen claimed that he had been promised £40,000 for the American sales of *Scrooge* (1935), but had received only £1,200.[14] In March 1937 Gainsborough published a loss of £98,000 for 1936, and it was announced that the Gaumont studios at Shepherd's Bush would close. In the summer of 1936 Gaumont-British had an overdraft with the National Provincial Bank of £1,149,785, of which £247,904 was in respect of film production. By May 1936 Korda's London Films showed a loss of over £330,000.

It was clear that in a space of months the industry had passed from boom to bust.[15] In July 1937 the *Financial Times* declared that production losses were likely to be over one million pounds and that financial support would be withdrawn from film production.[16] Since film production was a speculative venture, especially in Britain where the producer received by far the smallest share of box-office receipts, ordinary channels of finance were wary of investing money. Although costs had risen and producers had lost money when their films failed in America, the root of the problem in 1937 was the unstable method of film finance that had developed in the boom period. In the first six months of 1937 over £4 million was borrowed by production companies, mainly by short-term financing. *Money Behind the Screen*, an exposé written by documentary film-maker Stuart Legg and Marxist art historian F. D. Klingender, concluded that:

> One of the most striking features of this expansion from a financial point of view is the fact that on the production side it is based almost entirely on *expectation*

Hagen claimed that he had been promised £40,000 for the American sales of Scrooge *(Henry Edwards, 1935) but he had received only £1,200.*

without any concrete results to justify that optimism ... the expansion has with few outstanding exceptions been financed not by increases in the companies' own working capital, but by a spectacular increase in *loans*.[17]

The financial crash of 1937 exposed the industry's weak foundations and company after company went into liquidation. Between 1925 and 1936, 640 production companies had been registered: by 1937 only twenty were still operating.[18]

The Cinematograph Films Act (1938)

In 1936, with only two years to go before the 1927 Films Act expired, amidst widespread criticism of 'quota quickies' and discussion of Korda's international strategy, an official Committee chaired by Lord Moyne reported on the film industry's affairs. In 1932 Britain had abandoned Free Trade for a system of Protection and Imperial Preference. Henceforth politicians, businessmen and civil servants began to show more enthusiasm for state intervention in industry, and many hoped that this mood would be reflected in the new Films Act. The Moyne Committee's report highlighted the strengths and weaknesses of the 1927 Act and made some key recommendations, some of which reached the statute book in 1938.[19] The ones that did not are extremely interesting and pinpoint some of the industry's fundamental problems in the 1930s. One recommendation was that the government should encourage the formation of a Films Bank to bring order to the chaotic world of film finance, and that it should keep a close watch on transfers of interests in British film companies 'to prevent control passing abroad'.[20] However, the published minutes of evidence to the Moyne Committee did not indicate that American companies had substantial interests in the British film industry, except in the renting sphere. R. D. Fennelly, who gave evidence for the Board of Trade, said that apart from Twentieth Century-Fox's holding in Gaumont-British there was little foreign capital invested in British production.[21] Warners and Fox had studios at Teddington and Wembley, but the only recent financial deal between a British and an American company mentioned was Universal's decision to distribute its films in Britain through General Film Distributors (GFD). GFD was controlled by the General Cinema Finance Corporation (GCFC) which had been established in March 1936 by J. Arthur Rank. As a result of the deal, which gave GCFC a 25 per cent interest in Universal, GFD was the main distributor of Universal's films in Britain, and the growing Rank group hoped the link would facilitate better exploitation of British films in America.

The 1938 Films Act was surprisingly modest. Quotas were set for another ten years and short films were protected as well as features, but despite support from the press a 'quality test' to ensure a certain standard of British film was rejected. Instead the 1938 Films Act tried to resolve the 'quickie' problem by insisting that quota films cost a certain minimum sum. The most curious aspect of the Act, however, was that it eased rather than increased quota burdens for American renters. Special 'multiple quota' concessions were available to those who wanted to make fewer, but more expensive, quota films which, it was hoped, would be distributed abroad. To register for renters' quota a film had to have cost a minimum of £1 per foot in labour costs, with a minimum total of £7,500 per film. If a film cost three times the minimum – at least £3 a foot with a total of not less than £22,500 in labour costs – it could count twice its length for renters' quota. A film of over £37,500 or £5 a foot in labour costs could count three times. Why was the Board of Trade prepared to do this when there had been so much agitation for tougher legislation, criticism of lavish, Kordaesque productions aimed at foreign markets, and anxiety about the dangers of a further wave of Hollywood domination?

Since the government was unprepared to commit itself to a policy of state subsidy for film production, finance had to be found elsewhere. Still recoiling from the shock of the 1937 crash, the City was unprepared to burn its fingers again. At the same time American companies were showing an interest in establishing production units in Britain. MGM was making bold plans for its new unit headed by Michael Balcon, and Warners First-National continued to produce at Teddington. Paramount announced plans for a series of films for the world market.

In February 1938 the Foreign Office sent a telegram to the British Ambassador in Washington, Sir Ronald Lindsay, disclosing that 'certain amendments' (triple quotas and reciprocity) would be introduced when the Films Bill was in Parliament to meet some of the American demands. This was designed to appease the Americans, and the telegram stressed the importance of secrecy:

> It would be extremely embarrassing if news of these proposals reached either the industry here or the press before the President of the Board of Trade has had an opportunity to mention them. . . . Any suggestions here that HMG were in receipt of formal representations from the US Government on the subject of the Bill while it was still under consideration by Parliament might well destroy any sympathy in Parliament for the proposals.[22]

The pro-American clauses were designed to lure more American dollars to Britain as a means of injecting capital into the ailing industry. It was hoped that American production in Britain would provide employment for British technicians and encourage production standards which would appeal to international audiences. Links with American companies also promised favourable distribution contracts in the USA. At the risk of threatening the British film industry's independence in financial and, possibly, aesthetic terms, the Board of Trade therefore welcomed American finance as a tempting solution to its chronic financial problems.

Apart from the financial argument, the international situation and British anxiety about Germany and Japan would not allow the British to be too hard on Hollywood. As the 1927 Films Act had played a major role in the Free Trade versus Protection controversy, the 1938 Act was in the forefront of discussions about Anglo-American economic and political relations. The debates on the new Bill coincided with negotiations for an Anglo-American Trade Agreement, and both sides were anxious not to allow a dispute over film to prejudice more important issues. The US Secretary of State, Cordell Hull, launched a trade agreements programme as part of his campaign to reduce international tension via 'economic appeasement' and an agreement with Britain was considered to be a cornerstone of this policy. On the British side, the situation was delicate because politicians, particularly Foreign Secretary Anthony Eden, were keen to court American support against fascism.

Britain was Hollywood's most lucrative overseas market, especially since the coming of sound and the virtual exclusion of American films from Soviet Russia, Germany and Italy. American producers culled as much as 30 per cent of their income from Britain and Will Hays, representing Hollywood's major producers, encouraged Cordell Hull to use the film dispute as a lever in the wranglings over trade. The State Department backed Hollywood's bid to make the 1938 Films Act as innocuous as possible. Hays even threatened the State Department with an anti-British press and newsreel campaign based on the injustices of the film quota, to be conducted by the major film companies. Hull was receptive to such tactics because his trade agreements programme was already being severely criticised in Congress: the last thing he wanted was for Hollywood's plight to provide his opponents with ammunition against greater Anglo-American co-operation. In March 1938, while the Films Bill was being debated in the House of Lords, Oliver Stanley, the President of the Board of Trade, had a crucial meeting with Joseph P. Kennedy, the new American Ambassador. Stanley promised to secure the pro-American amendments to the Bill, an astonishing move, especially since he had just made a speech in the Commons professing: 'I do not want our defences to be made in Hollywood. I want the world to be able to see British films true to British life, accepting British standards and spreading British ideas.'[23] Even so, Hollywood did not have things entirely its own way. Hull wanted film quotas to be discussed in the trade negotiations, but this time the Board of Trade dug in its heels and insisted that the topic should be excluded because film was an internal cultural responsibility rather than an ordinary industrial commodity. The Board of Trade argued that Britain did not intend to discriminate against American films, but wanted

> only to ensure a certain percentage of English films being shown for cultural reasons. The American film industry expects to have things too much its own way. Unfortunately ... the US Government continues to look on films as a purely commercial item in the trade negotiations ... while we regard them partly at least as a cultural responsibility.[24]

Using this argument the British succeeded in keeping film out of the discussions on trade, though the Americans tried to introduce it on several occasions. From the way the Board of Trade legislated for the film industry it is hard to imagine that it took cultural arguments seriously; but in the negotiations it was found expedient to present a cultural face.

The new Films Act became law in March 1938. The quotas for long films were to be 15 per cent for renters and 12.5 per cent for exhibitors. In the Lords they had been raised by Lord Moyne to 20 per cent and 15 per cent, but Stanley made sure, after considerable pressure from both the Americans and the exhibitors, that they were brought down again in the Commons. The quota for 'shorts' was 15 per cent for renters and 12.5 per cent for exhibitors. Studio wages and labour conditions were safeguarded in the Act, and other provisions included the multiple quotas; the reciprocity clause; the inauguration of the Cinematograph Films Council to 'keep under review the progress of the British film industry and report to the Board of Trade'; and a stipulation that the Board could vary, within limits, the quota percentages and the cost test. The new Films Act followed the lines of the 1927 Act, but revealed the government's willingness to rely on American finance rather than try to reorganise the industry. The Association of Cinematograph Technicians' (ACT) Annual Report commented that the new legislation was 'fundamentally unsound in that the basis of the Act is not primarily concerned with the development of a flourishing British film industry independent of foreign control'.[25]

The industry's crucial infrastructure had been established and it is inconceivable that the film industry would have made such strides in the 1940s if its basic foundations had not been laid in the 1930s. As far as the government was concerned, it is remarkable that despite the orthodoxy of Free Trade there had been a response to the 'Hollywood invasion' which involved a degree of protection for the British film industry, albeit limited. British cinemas still needed Hollywood's movies and the US majors had the support of the State Department in their quest to 'Americanise the world'. In the late 1930s, with the shadow of war just around the corner, Britain was not in a position to be Hollywood's reluctant and ungrateful customer. By 1939, therefore, the *ideal* of a strong British film industry had been compromised by complex economic and political realities, realities which did not go away but remained firmly on the agenda of subsequent debates about the protection of the film industry.

Notes

1. *The Times*, 25 February 1926.
2. *Parliamentary Debates* (Lords), vol. 69 (1927), col. 272, and R. Low, *The History of the British Film 1918–1929* (London: George Allen & Unwin, 1971), p. 156.
3. W. A. Lewis, 'International competition in manufactures', *American Economic Review*, Papers and Proceedings, XLVII (1957), p. 579, and S. Pollard, *The Development of the British Economy, 1914–80*, 3rd edition (London: Arnold, 1983), p. 116.
4. Low, *History of the British Film 1918–1929*, pp. 40–1.
5. *The British Film Industry* (London: Political and Economic Planning, 1952), p. 56.
6. US Department of Commerce reports, 1927–32.
7. John Sedgwick, 'The Market for Feature Films in Britain, 1934: a viable national cinema', *Historical Journal of Film, Radio and Television*, vol. 14, no. 1, 1994, pp. 28–9.
8. Douglas Gomery, 'Economic Struggle and Hollywood Imperialism: Europe converts to sound', *Yale French Studies*, no. 60, 1980, p. 92.
9. US Department of Commerce reports, 1929–31.
10. US Department of Commerce report, 1931, p. 8.
11. See Tony Aldgate, 'Comedy, Class and Containment: The British Domestic Cinema of the 1930s', in James Curran and Vincent Porter (eds.), *British Cinema History* (London: Weidenfeld and Nicolson, 1983).
12. Although in his book *Hollywood's Overseas Campaign: The North Atlantic Movie Trade, 1920–1950* (Cambridge University Press, 1992) Ian Jarvie urges us to distinguish *Henry VIII*'s fame from its profit, arguing that 'close analysis of the career of the film in the US would ... show that it had in fact a limited release, confined to major cities, and that it gained, by Hollywood standards, a modest return' (p. 144).
13. *The British Film Industry* (1952), p. 67.
14. *Morning Post*, 15 January 1937.
15. Karol Kulik, *Alexander Korda: The Man Who Could Work Miracles* (London: W. H. Allen, 1975), p. 170.
16. *Financial Times*, 13 July 1937.
17. F. D. Klingender and S. Legg, *Money Behind the Screen* (London: Lawrence and Wishart, 1937), p. 54.
18. *Kinematograph Weekly*, 13 January 1938, p. 139.
19. *Report of the Committee on Cinematograph Films* (1936), Cmd. 5320.
20. This recommendation was rejected largely because an inquiry into the film industry's affairs conducted by the Bank of England in 1937 warned the government against subsidising producers. See Margaret Dickinson and Sarah Street, *Cinema and State: the Film Industry and the British Government, 1927–84* (London: British Film Institute, 1985), pp. 81–8.
21. *Minutes of Evidence to the Committee on Cinematograph Films* (HMSO, 1936), 5 May 1936, p. 5, para. 39.
22. Public Record Office: Foreign Office records, FO 371 21530/A 791.
23. *Parliamentary Debates* (Commons), 4 November 1937, vol. 328, col. 1173. For a full account of the interaction between American diplomacy and the Films Bill, see Sarah Street, 'The Hays Office and the Defence of the British Market in the 1930s', in *Historical Journal of Film, Radio and Television*, vol. 5, no. 1, 1985.
24. Public Record Office, Foreign Office records, FO 371 21530/A175, minute by Beith, 10 January 1938.
25. *Kinematograph Weekly*, 5 May 1938, p. 29.

Bibliography

Dickinson, Margaret and Street, Sarah, *Cinema and State: The Film Industry and the British Government 1927–84* (London: British Film Institute, 1985).
Hartog, Simon, 'State Protection of a Beleaguered Industry', in Curran, James and Porter, Vincent (eds.), *British Cinema History* (London: Weidenfeld and Nicolson, 1983).

Klingender, F. D. and Legg, S., *Money Behind the Screen* (London: Lawrence and Wishart, 1937).

Kulik, Karol, *Alexander Korda: the Man Who Could Work Miracles* (London: W. H. Allen, 1975).

Low, Rachael, *The History of the British Film, 1918–1929* (London: Allen & Unwin, 1971).

Low, Rachael, *The History of the British Film, 1929–1939: Film Making in 1930s Britain* (London: George Allen & Unwin, 1985).

Murphy, Robert, 'The Coming of Sound to the Cinema in Britain', *Historical Journal of Film, Radio and Television*, vol. 4, no. 2, 1984.

Murphy, Robert, 'A Rival to Hollywood? The British Film Industry in the Thirties', *Screen*, vol. 24, no. 4–5, July–October 1983.

Political and Economic Planning, *The British Film Industry* (London: PEP, 1952).

Sedgwick, John, 'The Market for Feature Films in Britain 1934: a viable national cinema', *Historical Journal of Film, Radio and Television*, vol. 14, no. 1, 1994.

Street, Sarah, 'The Hays Office and the Defence of the British Market in the 1930s', *Historical Journal of Film, Radio and Television*, vol. 5, no. 1, 1985.

Street, Sarah, 'Alexander Korda, Prudential Assurance and British Film Finance in the 1930s', *Historical Journal of Film, Radio and Television*, vol. 6, no. 2, 1986.

Wood, Linda (ed.), *British Films, 1927–1939* (London: British Film Institute Library Services, 1986).

This essay reworks material which first appeared in Sarah Street and Margaret Dickinson's *Cinema and State*, British Film Institute, 1985

3

A British Studio System: The Associated British Picture Corporation and the Gaumont-British Picture Corporation in the 1930s

Tom Ryall

The 1940s are conventionally regarded as the 'golden age' of British film whereas the interwar years have been more a matter of cultural embarrassment. Despite the fact that the British film industry was effectively constructed in the 1930s out of the ruins of the 1920s, the cinema of these years was harshly judged by contemporary commentators, as it has been subsequently by film historians. It has been dismissed as trivial and escapist, unduly dependent on the West End theatre for its sources, inattentive to social realities, dominated by cheaply made pictures and, at best, a pale copy of Hollywood. Above all, despite modern purpose-built studios, generous production funding and guaranteed exhibition outlets unavailable to earlier British film-makers, a distinctive national cinema did not emerge. Sometimes this failure was explained in xenophobic terms and laid at the door of the numerous foreigners – Hungarians, Germans, Americans and others – who came to England during the period and exerted a considerable influence on the course of British cinema. Sometimes it was attributed to the shortage of entrepreneurial and creative skills necessary to the business of creating art in the cinema and possessed in abundance by the Hollywood production bosses. 'Unless we find our Schulbergs and Thalbergs it is no use having our millions,' wrote one commentator as production funds – 'our millions' – began to flow into the industry following the passage of the Cinematograph Films Act of 1927.[1]

The Act, designed to stimulate an ailing production industry, included a requirement for exhibitors to screen a quota of British-originated films, beginning at 5 per cent but rising to 20 per cent by 1937 and offering protection to a production industry almost extinguished by American competition. Production firms mushroomed in the wake of the act, and although many of these were short-lived, two large production bases were established by the Gaumont-British Picture Corporation and the Associated British Picture Corporation (British International Pictures until 1933), along with smaller though significant companies such as London Films, British and Dominions and Associated Talking Pictures. New studios were built at Ealing, Shepperton, Pinewood and Denham, while the Elstree complex was expanded and the Shepherd's Bush studio rebuilt.[2] The main British renter firms merged into two large distribution networks, and a third important firm – General Film Distributors – was set up in 1936.[3] The number of cinemas increased from just under 4,000 in the mid-1920s to just under 4,500 in the mid-1930s, with many of these organised into circuits; and the period also saw the emergence of a new influential force in exhibition – Oscar Deutsch's Odeon chain.[4] A modern film industry had emerged with two large vertically integrated 'majors' with interests in production, distribution and exhibition, a string of medium-sized production companies, and a number of small firms specialising in low-budget films designed to meet the quota requirements of the powerful American distributors. The 1927 Act was responsible for the emergence of a 'studio system' not dissimilar to that of Hollywood with its interrelated cluster of major, minor and 'B' picture companies.

During the years following the 1927 Act the industry moved from a total of 34 British-produced films in 1926 to over 200 a year by 1936 – equivalent to about 40 per cent of the American industry's output.[5] In addition, a British film – *The Private Life of Henry VIII* (1933) – was a box-office success in the USA, and its star, Charles Laughton, won the Oscar for the best actor of 1933. The ten-year life of the Act saw a dramatic increase in the number of British films, with some 1,600 films produced and Britain becoming the most substantial source of production in Europe.[6] Critical judgment of the British entertainment cinema of the 1930s, however, has been severe. Although production expanded dramatically during the period, it has been estimated that 'approximately half the enormous number of films turned out by British studios up to 1937 were produced at minimum cost simply to exploit the protected market or, at worst, to comply with the law.'[7] These cheaply made films were sometimes made outside Britain – in Australia, Canada and India for example – and they were often designed simply to fulfil the distribution and exhibition quotas as they increased during the decade. 'Quota quickies' – as such films were called – sometimes remained unscreened, and in general these low-budget pictures gave the British cinema a poor reputation with both critics and the cinema-going public.[8]

When it came to the character and quality of the films actually produced it was argued that too many films – whatever their budget – were based upon middle-class, middlebrow stage plays and failed to reflect social reality. According to many it was a trivial, escapist cinema in a volatile social and political period; Michael Balcon, who had presided over the Gaumont-British output, reflected in his autobiography that hardly 'a single film of the period reflects the agony of those times'.[9] The strict codes of the British Board of Film Censors effectively inhibited social and political comment in the entertainment film, and consequently the British cinema failed to 'bring to the screen something of the life, tradition and culture of Britain and its Empire' which many considered a vital objective of the quota legislation.[10]

Studio formation

The two film combines set up in the late 1920s consolidated operations in the different branches of the industry into unified enterprises, a process the Hollywood film industry had undergone some years earlier. British International Pictures (Associated British Picture Corporation) and the Gaumont-British Picture Corporation grouped together specialist firms from all branches of the industry into companies that were to produce just over 20 per cent of the feature films made between 1928 and 1937, establishing distinctive and contrasting profiles both as powerful forces in the indigenous industry and as international film companies.[11] British International Pictures is often seen as an unambitious company exploiting the outlets for its pictures guaranteed through vertical integration with a production schedule based on modestly budgeted programme-fillers. Gaumont-British, by contrast, is usually seen as an ambitious concern with a programme of high-budget quality pictures aimed at breaking into the US market and establishing Britain's credentials in the international film industry.

British International Pictures amalgamated John Maxwell's Wardour Films (distribution), British International Pictures (production) and subsequently Associated British Cinemas (exhibition), and in 1933 the group set up a new concern – the Associated British Picture Corporation – as a holding company for the group's various interests. Despite the subsequent image of the company as a medium or low-budget producing concern, when first established British International Pictures had the ambition to match its size.[12] The company employed some of the most important British directors – Alfred Hitchcock, Victor Saville and Thomas Bentley – but, true to its international aspirations, also recruited directors from overseas, including the Americans Harry Lachman and Tim Whelan, the Germans E. A. Dupont and Arthur Robison, and an Italian who had acted in Hollywood and was to become a prolific director in the British cinema of the 1930s, Monty Banks. The company signed up the major British stars such as Betty Balfour, but more important were the foreign stars – Maria Corda, Syd Chaplin, Tallulah Bankhead, Lionel Barrymore and Anna May Wong from Hollywood, Carl Brisson, Anny Ondra, Olga Tschechova from continental Europe – who seemed to guarantee access to the international market. The company's international aspirations were also reflected in the setting up of an American distribution base – World Wide Pictures – together with companies in Germany and Austria for both production and distribution purposes. In addition, BIP pioneered the 'multiple-language version' production technique in which different language versions of a picture were shot, usually simultaneously with a change of director and/or actors as appropriate.[13] The head of production at BIP was Walter

Anna May Wong in Dupont's Piccadilly *(1928), guaranteeing access to the international market.*

Mycroft, critic for the *Evening Standard* and a member of the Film Society Council. He was also a screenwriter, and started at the company as scenario supervisor.

The Gaumont-British Picture Corporation was formed in 1927 from the Gaumont Company – originally an agency for the famous French firm but since 1922 a British-owned production/distribution concern – and two of the leading British distribution firms, Ideal and W & F Film Services. Subsequently the company acquired exhibition interests, and its underwriting of the public flotation of Michael Balcon's Gainsborough Pictures brought in additional production facilities. This enterprise was financed by the Ostrer Brothers merchant bank, which had organised the British buy-out of the original Gaumont Company. Gaumont-British had a production pre-history at both Gainsborough and the Gaumont Company, but the decision in 1929 to rebuild the Shepherd's Bush studios meant that output from the newly formed combine was small and it was not until the opening of the new studio in 1932 that the corporation was able to mount its ambitious export-oriented programme of around twenty films a year.

The arrival of sound

In October 1927, the release of *The Jazz Singer* in America ushered in a period of profound change in the global film industry. In Britain, production expanded dramatically to meet the demands of the 'quota' Act, but by early 1929 it became clear that there had to be a shift to expensive sound production as well.[14] However, many in the industry were cautious, judging sound pictures to be passing fashions. John Maxwell, head of BIP, predicted their co-existence with silent films, suggesting that 'there will arise the general principle of showing one sound picture and one silent picture wherever there is a two picture programme'.[15] Despite Maxwell's caution, the BIP company report for 1928–29 announced that plans for the installation of 'sound-proof studios for the production of talking pictures' had been agreed during 1928.[16] The critical and commercial success of BIP's first 'talkie', Hitchcock's *Blackmail*, released in June 1929, confirmed that the future lay in sound pictures – although the film was also made in a silent version for cinemas not yet equipped for sound.[17]

The Gaumont-British combine was not as quick off the mark, although Gainsborough, its associate production company, began adding sound to silent films and preparing part-talking pictures towards the end of 1929. Its first two full-talking pictures – *Woman to Woman* (1929) and *Journey's End* (1930) – were made in America in conjunction with the small Tiffany-Stahl studio. Neither of the corporation's studios was suitable for the production of sound films. Gainsborough's Islington studio was a converted power station; Gaumont's Shepherd's Bush studio dated from 1915 and, since it was surrounded by housing, the only way of expanding it was to build upwards.[18] A further complicating factor was the combine's ownership of a sound equipment company, British Acoustic, which meant pressure to equip from within despite the superior technology available from the American companies. Balcon resisted this, with the result that the Islington studio, which handled the combine's production while Shepherd's Bush was out of action, was not ready for sound production until late in 1929 when American RCA equipment was installed. A studio fire at Islington early in 1930 brought further problems and production was shifted on a temporary basis to Elstree.

The commercial and critical success of *Blackmail* appeared to give BIP the edge over its rival and in this transitional period 1928–31 BIP released more than twice as many features as Gaumont-British/Gainsborough.

Divergent paths in the 1930s

In 1931 BIP presented itself in the trade press as 'the first company to establish a film producing organisation capable of becoming an international force in the film business and worthy in scope and dignity to rank with the great concerns in other industries and in other countries.'[19] In its formative years, the company had recruited an impressive roster of experienced creative and technical staff. They included directors such as Dupont, Robison and Hitchcock, the art director Alfred Junge, who had worked on some twenty films in Germany, and the cinematographer Charles Rosher, who had shot Murnau's *Sunrise* (1927). The studio's artistic ambition was demonstrated by the European sophistication of Dupont's *Moulin Rouge* (1928) and *Piccadilly* (1929) and Hitchcock's boldly experimental *Blackmail*. According to Low, the studio 'spent money in something like the Hollywood manner', allocating £150,000 to six productions in 1927–8, including Hitchcock's *The Ring*, Dupont's *Moulin Rouge* and the Betty Balfour vehicle *A Little Bit of Fluff*.[20] Prestige production continued into the early 1930s with adaptations of stage plays by Shaw (*Arms and the Man*, 1932), Galsworthy (*The Skin Game*, 1931) and O'Casey (*Juno and the Paycock* 1929), together with ambitious pictures such as *The Informer* (1929, directed by Arthur Robison), the espionage tale *The W Plan* (1930), and the historical drama *Dreyfus* (1931).[21] However, these films represented the tail-end of BIP's production strategy of balancing 'prestige and profit', and as early as the middle of 1929 the trade press was carrying news of impending staff cuts at the studio and suggestions of retrenchment.[22] The investment in sound production had been considerable and the company needed a 'pause in production while economies were made to recoup the expense of converting to sound'.[23]

It was a pause that led to a significant reorientation of the studio's production strategy and thereafter, despite its name, the company concentrated upon the domestic market, operating 'a policy of cut-price window dressing, trying to make cheap films which looked like expensive ones'.[24] From around 1932, the studio's production schedules were dominated by comedies, musicals and crime films. BIP drew extensively on the established popular formats of variety theatre and musical comedy, and much of their output featured comedians and musical performers such as Leslie Fuller, Ernie Lotinga, Stanley Lupino and Lupino Lane. But their films never achieved the critical or commercial success of the comparable offerings of Gracie Fields, George Formby, Jessie Matthews, Jack Buchanan and Tom Walls. The company also developed a thriller/horror strand of low-budget film-making, utilising its second-string studio at Welwyn, but it no longer had a Hitchcock to bring these to the attention of the critical establishment. There was a foray into big-budget production in the middle of the decade with a small number of musical and historical costume pictures: *Blossom Time*, starring the Austrian tenor Richard Tauber; *Mimi*, a version of Puccini's *La Bohème*; *Drake of England*, *Royal Cavalcade* and *Abdul the Damned* (all 1935).[25] But such ventures were uncharacteristic and the predominant strategy was to make modestly budgeted productions, to supply the needs of the company's growing cinema circuit. BIP's sustained though variable profitability during the 1930s was based mainly upon the earnings of its cinemas, and the shift in emphasis from production to exhibition was marked in 1933 when the company was reorganised as the Associated British Picture Corporation, the new name highlighting the ABC cinema chain rather than the BIP production arm.

In contrast to BIP, Gaumont-British, with Balcon established as 'general manager of film production', moved in the opposite direction, pursuing an explicitly internationalist policy during the period 1932–6 while its chief rival was in the process of retrenching.[26] With studio facilities rebuilt at Shepherd's Bush, and Gainsborough fully integrated into the combine, the studio recruited extensively within Britain and from continental Europe and Hollywood. Indeed, a description of Gaumont-British in this period sounds a little like that of BIP in the late 1920s. It can be argued that one of the key differences was that in Michael Balcon Gaumont-British had a very skilled and experienced producer at the helm. By contrast, Maxwell had entrusted supervision of production to the uninspiring Walter Mycroft. From the start of his career Balcon had been an internationally oriented film-maker, targeting films at America and organising European co-productions. During the 1920s he had established a team of colleagues which included Hitchcock, Victor Saville, Ivor Montagu and the scriptwriter Angus Macphail, and many of these joined Gaumont-British in the 1930s, together with a number of figures previously at BIP.[27] Hitchcock rejoined Balcon in 1934 to make his best-known British films – *The Man Who Knew Too Much* (1934), *The 39 Steps* (1935), *Secret Agent* (1936), *Sabotage* (1936), *Young and Innocent* (1938) and *The Lady Vanishes* (1938); Jessie Matthews, whose first starring role had been in *Out of the Blue*, made at Elstree in 1931, moved to Shepherd's Bush and became one of the most popular British stars of the time; and Alfred Junge brought a Germanic sensibility to the design of many of the best-known Gaumont-British pictures of the period.

In his autobiography, Balcon divides Gaumont-British output into vehicles for its most popular stars – Jack Hulbert, Jessie Matthews and George Arliss – Hitchcock's thriller sextet, Anglo-German films, and epics 'made with an eye on the American market'.[28] The Gaumont-British comedies and musicals, like their BIP counterparts, drew upon theatrical traditions and turned stage performers like Jack Hulbert and Cicely Courtneidge into film stars. Jessie Matthews came from the world of the West End musical revue and, after appearing in dramas such as *The Good Companions* (1933) and *Friday the Thirteenth* (1933), established herself with *Evergreen* (1934), a stylish musical combining elements of Edwardian music hall, the Warner Bros backstage musical and the art deco *mise en scène* of the Fred Astaire/Ginger Rogers films.[29]

Anglo-German co-production began in 1932, as part of an international co-production strategy which included English-language versions of successful films from France (*The Battle*, 1934) and Italy (*The Divine Spark*, 1935). Anglo-German pictures like *Happy Ever After* (1932) and *FP 1* (1933) were filmed abroad (though with largely British casts), but they were not a success and Balcon preferred to remake German films such as *Sunshine Susie* (1931) and *Marry Me* (1932) in England.[30]

Hitchcock's thrillers – now the studio's best remembered contribution to British cinema – were part of a vigorous tradition which included Walter Forde's *Rome Express* (1932), the first thriller to use an international train journey as its setting; early horror films such as *The Ghoul* (1933) and *The Man Who Changed His Mind* (1936), both starring Boris Karloff; and Berthold Viertel's *The Passing of the Third Floor Back*, which in its combination of mid-European sophistication and English realism prefigured the collaborations of Michael Powell and Emeric Pressburger.[31]

Gaumont-British made a much more determined attempt on the international market than BIP, and films like *Jew Suss* (1934), *The Iron Duke* (1935), *Rhodes of Africa* (1936), *King Solomon's Mines* (1937) and *The Tunnel* (1936) had budgets of £100,000 or more. In the tightly controlled American market these films fared badly, but they should not necessarily be dismissed as extravagant follies. A large-budget British film like *Jew Süss*, costed at £125,000, was not much more expensive than the routine standard-budgeted A-features of the big American studios, and much cheaper than the top-budget (a million dollars and more) American films.[32] American producers, of

Gaumont-British goes international. Leslie Banks and Richard Dix prepare to cross the Atlantic in The Tunnel *(Maurice Elvey, 1935).*

course, with an internal market several times larger than the British market, could afford to spend a great deal more on production.

Michael Balcon, along with Alexander Korda, was probably the nearest British equivalent to the prominent Hollywood production chiefs such as Schulberg and Thalberg, but despite its relatively successful production policies, Gaumont-British, along with Korda's London Films and others, had to curtail production and close down studios in 1937. However, production did continue at Gainsborough, and whereas BIP's Elstree studio was requisitioned during the war, Gainsborough – relocated at Shepherd's Bush – developed a strong studio identity and enjoyed considerable commercial success.[33]

British films of the 1930s: appeal, popularity and critical success

The view that the films of the 1930s failed to win favour with the ordinary cinema-going public or to construct a distinctively British cinema has come under scrutiny recently in two different ways. Firstly, statistical information from the period has been used to argue that quality British films – those made for reasons other than simply quota requirement – were in fact popular with audiences.[34] British audiences may have preferred American films but this did not preclude approval of British films.[35] The exhibitors' quota in the years 1932–6 was exceeded, indicating that 'the cinemas were showing of their own volition [and no doubt because the demand was there] a good deal more British films than the 1927 Act required of them'.[36] Secondly, film historians have argued that national cinematic specificity can be located in the less respectable areas of British cinema, in non-realist genres such as horror, comedy and melodrama,

33

in an introspective self-reflexive cinema of fantasy rather than a realist cinema of observation. This reorientation, although based largely on the 1940s and after, on Gainsborough melodrama and Hammer horror, invites a critical reconsideration of the British cinema of the 1930s. It can be argued that the vigorous strands of popular culture evident in the music hall-based comedies of Gracie Fields, George Formby and Will Hay, in Hitchcock's thrillers, in the Jessie Matthews musicals and in horror/fantasy films such as *The Ghoul* (1933), *The Ghost Goes West* (1935) and *The Clairvoyant* (1934) do constitute a distinctive cinema of national identity. It would not have been one to find favour with intellectual and socially committed critics who searched in vain for the direct reflection of social realities more common in the documentary films of the time, but it might be equally valid.

The legacy of the 1930s

Although much work remains to be done, particularly in the analysis of the films of the decade, effective traditions were established in the popular generic cinema of the 30s, often in the shape of low-budget thrillers, and comedies with a largely domestic and even specifically regional appeal. Despite the financial crises and the poor reputation that the industry derived from quota production, the foundations for the subsequent 'golden age' of British cinema in the 1940s had been laid. As Linda Wood has observed:

> By 1939 Britain possessed the necessary facilities and personnel with the relevant expertise to produce the kind of quality films which could not have been made in this country ten years previously and on a sustained basis. For many film-makers, the Thirties provided the apprenticeship which made possible the flowering of British production in the Forties.[37]

The large combines formed a substantial infrastructure for the industry and the old Gaumont-British empire with its studios and cinemas became the core of the Rank Organisation in the early 1940s. Numerous film-makers – Anthony Asquith, Michael Powell, David Lean, Frank Launder, Sidney Gilliat, Ronald Neame, Charles Frend, Arthur Crabtree and Leslie Arliss – emerged from Elstree and Shepherd's Bush, from Islington and Welwyn. By 1939 the ground had been prepared for 'the appearance of a British cinema that was original and free from influences from Hollywood'. The historical costume pictures, the popular musicals and comedies, the 'quickie' productions that drew their material from the indigenous popular culture focused on crime, fantasy and horror, together constitute a rich cluster of traditions in which a number of the key film-makers of the 1940s were nurtured and out of which the post-war British cinema emerged.

Notes

1. *Kinematograph Weekly*, 6 January 1927, p. 99.
2. See Patricia Warren, *British Film Studios* (London: Batsford, 1995).
3. General Film Distributors was the foundation of the Rank Organisation, which was to dominate the British cinema in the post-World War Two period.
4. Statistics on the number of cinemas are drawn from James Curran and Vincent Porter (eds.), *British Cinema History* (London: Weidenfeld and Nicolson, 1983), p. 375. It is worth noting that the figure for the 1930s probably represents a significant increase in seating capacity as the small 'penny gaffs' were replaced by 'picture palaces'.
5. Political and Economic Planning, *The British Film Industry* (London: PEP, 1952), p. 41.

6. Film statistics are approximate and derived from Denis Gifford, *The British Film Catalogue 1895–1985* (Newton Abbot and London: David and Charles), and an unpublished digest of British film statistics by Simon Davies. See also Simon Hartog, 'State Protection of a Beleaguered Industry', in Curran and Porter (eds.), *British Cinema History*, p. 65.

7. Rachael Low, *Film Making in 1930s Britain* (London: George Allen & Unwin, 1985), p. 115.

8. Films made in countries under British imperial rule were regarded as 'British' for the purposes of the quota.

9. Michael Balcon, *A Lifetime of Films* (London: Hutchinson, 1969), p. 99.

10. See Jeffrey Richards, 'Controlling the Screen: The British Cinema in the 1930s', *History Today*, March 1983, p. 12.

11. Only one other company – British and Dominions – approached the level of production of the two large combines, but it operated solely as a production concern.

12. The name itself with the word 'international' implies this, as did the company trademark displayed at the beginning of a BIP film – Britannia seated in front of a revolving globe.

13. See Ginette Vincendeau, 'Hollywood Babel', *Screen*, vol. 29, no. 2, Spring 1988, for a discussion of this phenomenon in Hollywood and Europe.

14. For a detailed analysis of the way in which sound was introduced in Britain see Robert Murphy, 'Coming of Sound to the Cinema in Britain', *Historical Journal of Film, Radio and Television*, vol. 4, no. 2, 1984, pp. 143–60. See also Tom Ryall, *Blackmail* (London: British Film Institute, 1993).

15. See John Maxwell's comments in *Kinematograph Weekly*, 25 April 1929, p. 21.

16. *Kinematograph Weekly*, 27 June 1929, p. 30.

17. See Charles Barr, 'Blackmail: Silent and Sound', *Sight and Sound*, vol. 52, no. 2, Spring 1983, for a comparison of the sound and silent versions.

18. Warren, *British Film Studios*, pp. 138–9.

19. Advertisement in *The Kinematograph Year Book 1931*, quoted in PEP, *The British Film Industry*, p. 68.

20. Rachael Low, *The History of British Film 1918–1929* (London: George Allen & Unwin, 1971), p. 278.

21. Around half the films made at the studio between 1928 and 1937 were based on theatrical sources and even a 'cinematic' director like Hitchcock based six of his ten features for the company on plays.

22. For example, *Kinematograph Weekly*, 29 August 1929, p. 18.

23. Low, *Film Making in 1930s Britain*, p. 117.

24. Ibid., pp. 116–17. *Abdul the Damned*, in particular, seems to be a departure from BIP's cost-conscious budgeting policy, but it was a co-production and the then large budget of £500,000 was partly met by co-producer Max Schach.

25. See ibid., p. 142.

26. *Kinematograph Weekly*, 19 May 1932, p. 19.

27. See Geoff Brown, 'A Knight and His Castle', in Jane Fluegel (ed.), *Michael Balcon: The Pursuit of British Cinema* (New York: Museum of Modern Art, 1984), p. 17.

28. Balcon, *A Lifetime of Films*, pp. 62–3. As at BIP, a high proportion of Gaumont-British films came from the three most popular genres: comedies, *c.* 31 per cent; musicals, *c.* 16 per cent; crime, *c.* 15 per cent.

29. See Andrew Higson, *Waving the Flag: Constructing a National Cinema in Britain* (Oxford: Oxford University Press, 1995), ch. 4, for an extended analysis of *Evergreen* in the context of British production strategies of the 1930s.

30. See Low, *Film Making in 1930s Britain*, p. 133.

31. Powell made a number of films at Gaumont-British, including *The Fire Raisers* (1933), *The Night of the Party* (1934) and *The Phantom Light* (1935).

32. The budget figure for *Jew Suss* is taken from Sue Harper, *Picturing the Past* (London: British Film Institute, 1994), p. 31, although both Balcon and Low suggest a lower figure of £100,000.

33. As indicated by his subsequent appointment to head the new MGM-British set up in 1936. However, a number of the key studio decisions, including the internationalist policy and the acquisition of performers and stars such as George Arliss, were taken at board level by the Ostrers and C. M. Woolf rather than by Balcon himself. See Geoff Brown, 'A Knight and His Castle', in Fluegel (ed.), *Michael Balcon*, pp. 19–22.

34. See John Sedgwick, 'The Market for Feature Films in Britain, 1934: a viable national cinema', *Historical Journal of Film, Radio and Television*, vol. 14, no. 1, 1994. Sedgwick's paper is based partly on Simon Rowson's 1936 paper 'A Statistical Survey of the Cinema Industry in Great Britain in 1934', *Journal of the Royal Statistical Society*, vol. 99.

35. See Jeffrey Richards and Dorothy Sheridan, *Mass-Observation at the Movies* (London: Routledge & Kegan Paul, 1987), pp. 33–4, for survey material on audience preferences during the period.

36. Tony Aldgate, 'British Domestic Cinema of the 1930s', in Curran and Porter (eds.), *British Cinema History*, p. 262.
37. Linda Wood (ed.), *British Films 1927–1939* (London: British Film Institute Library Services, 1986), p. 6.

Bibliography

Balcon, Michael, *A Lifetime of Films* (London: Hutchinson, 1969).

Durgnat, Raymond, *A Mirror for England* (London: Faber & Faber, 1970).

Fluegel, Jane (ed.), *Michael Balcon: The Pursuit of British Cinema* (New York: Museum of Modern Art, 1984).

Gifford, Denis, *The British Film Catalogue 1895–1985* (Newton Abbot and London: David and Charles, 1986).

Grierson, John, 'The Fate of British Films', *The Fortnightly*, July 1937, p. 5.

Harper, Sue, *Picturing the Past* (London: British Film Institute, 1994).

Higson, Andrew, *Waving the Flag: Constructing a National Cinema in Britain* (Oxford: Oxford University Press, 1995).

Landy, Marcia, *British Genres: Cinema and Society, 1930–1960* (Princeton, New Jersey: Princeton University Press, 1991).

Low, Rachael, *The History of the British Film 1918–1929* (London: George Allen & Unwin, 1971).

Low, Rachael, *Film Making in 1930s Britain* (London: George Allen & Unwin, 1985).

Political and Economic Planning, *The British Film Industry* (London: PEP, 1952).

Richards, Jeffrey, *The Age of the Dream Palace* (London: Routledge, 1984).

Richards, Jeffrey and Sheridan, Dorothy, *Mass-Observation at the Movies* (London: Routledge & Kegan Paul, 1987).

Rowson, Simon, 'A Statistical Survey of the Cinema Industry in Great Britain in 1934', *Journal of the Royal Statistical Society*, vol. 99, 1936.

Sedgwick, John, 'The Market for Feature Films in Britain, 1934: a viable national cinema', *Historical Journal of Film, Radio and Television*, vol. 14, no. 1, 1994.

Warren, Patricia, *British Film Studios* (London: Batsford, 1995).

Wood, Linda (ed.), *British Films 1927–1939* (London: British Film Institute Library Services, 1986).

4
A Despicable Tradition? Quota Quickies in the 1930s

Lawrence Napper

The most curious result of the quota war has been the new orientation in British film values. Before it, our eyes were focused on Denham and the 'bigs'. Today the big pictures, like the dinosaurs, appear to be too big to be economic and are heading for extinction. We are all interested now in what can be done with fifty thousand pounds ... we are even interested in what can be done with twelve thousand pounds. The record of these cheaper pictures is a lot better than the more pretentious ones. I do not mean better in production values, I mean better in essence ... without any pretensions to those values, some of the cheaper pictures have a vitality which the luxury ones lack. My theory is that this vitality comes almost invariably from the English music hall, and this is true British cinema's only contact with reality.

John Grierson, *World Film News*, 1937

Film criticism has viewed quota quickies as an anomaly in British film history, their existence only worth recognising in the context of the industry's relationship to the state or as the 'primitive' forerunners of the mature British cinema of the war years. My own interest in the 'quota quickies' is not that they were sometimes made by directors who later went on to make more 'interesting' films, but rather that they represent almost half of the British film output of their period. Their fate at the hands of critics is indicative of a more general problem that has pervaded thinking and writing about British films since the 1920s, and I would argue that it is these traditions of thought, unable to accommodate specifically British films in a meaningful way, which are responsible for the poor reputation of the British cinema. Before undertaking a reassessment of quota production, it is perhaps necessary to lay these critical ghosts to rest.

Since its inception with *Close Up* in 1927, serious film criticism in Britain has displayed an almost unseemly passion for denigrating the British film. This tradition can be seen as the result of various concerns operating on the critical community itself, rather than a reflection on the films which they saw. From the 1920s to the 1970s the paramount tendency was to judge British films not in terms of British culture, but in the light of international movements stemming from Europe and America. Internationalism on the part of critics led them to bemoan British cinema partly because it was so very British, because it retained the popular culture of Britain as its inspiration rather than aspiring to the cinematic culture of Russia, Germany or

America. A consensus emerged that an expression of the British national identity must necessarily make for bad cinema.[1]

In this essay I wish to take a different tack, looking at British films not in terms of their poverty in relation to British film criticism, but rather in terms of their richness as a reflection of the society and culture that produced them. This approach appears to be particularly suitable with regard to the 'quota quickies' produced as a result of the 1927 Films Act.

The Films Act hoped to provide a space in the distribution monopoly of the American majors for a genuinely national cinema to emerge – one which dealt with British issues and retained or created a sense of national identity in opposition to what was seen as a cultural onslaught from America. The domination of this space by low-budget British films funded by American distributors led to claims of a deliberate attempt by the Americans to sabotage the British industry. However, despite the financial interest of the American majors, their influence on the content of the 'quota quickies' was minimal, and it is possible to argue that these films did present a British national identity which was appreciated by certain sections of the audience. While figures such as Balcon and Korda strove to produce a British cinema that was international in outlook and appeal, the 'quota quickie' producers were content to make small-scale productions with limited and purely national appeal.

Given the significance of the cinema as a site of mass consumption in Britain during the inter-war period, it is worth considering what kinds of consumer attitudes American films (which still constituted 80 per cent of all films shown) themselves contained. The startling glamour and wealth visible in American films is often accounted for by critics and historians simply as a function of their 'escapism'. However, I would argue that the differences run deeper than this. The American films, not only in their more fantastic mutations, but also at their most realist, presented a kind of consumer society that British audiences could barely even dream about. Sue Bowden has shown that by 1939 in the United States 60 per cent of households owned a washing machine, whereas in Britain the figure was a paltry 3.5 per cent, which even by 1958 had not risen above 25 per cent. In the same year, 56 per cent of American households owned a refrigerator; the figure in Britain was 2.4 per cent and did not rise to 25 per cent until 1960. Most significantly, in 1939 70 per cent of American households owned a car, whereas even by 1956 the figure was only 25 per cent in Britain.[2] Given the starkness of these contrasts, it is hardly surprising that British commentators were concerned about the messages audiences might receive from American films.

The connection between American films and mass consumption was seen as an alarming phenomenon. As V. F. Perkins states:

> For some British commentators, the image of the popular audience as threateningly other was matched by the foreignness of popular films, overwhelmingly American. If the clients were an undiscriminating class, their supply came from a whole society which was held to lack class and culture.[3]

The specific threat was that the Americans might import this classlessness, with its corrupting influences, into British society. Advertisers were quick to realise the potential of linking their products to the popularity of American – and even British – stars. Advertisements in magazines such as *Picturegoer*, *Film Weekly* and *Women's Film Fair*, claimed, for example, that 'beautiful Binnie Barnes, now playing Catherine Howard in the film *The Private Life of Henry VIII*, finds "Sphere Oval-octo" suspenders "thoroughly reliable"'; or that 'Jessie Matthews says her love for OVALTINE is EVER-GREEN'.[4] The most galling thing for many commentators was the spectacle of the wage-earning classes wearing the styles, buying the goods and adopting the manner-isms associated with American movie stars. This presented a threat not only to the British way of life but, as a result of the introduction of sound, to that most sacred of cows, the English language. Jeffrey Richards, writing about a campaign to regulate cinemagoing in Birmingham in the early 1930s, quotes G. A. Bryson, the deputy chair-man of Birmingham Justices: 'We don't want our children to go about saying "Oh yeah" and "OK kid" and there is no doubt a tendency to Americanise the English lan-guage throughout the film that is, I think, deplorable.'[5]

Such attitudes reflected important concerns amongst that section of the cinema audience who had an interest in maintaining the nuances of class in British society. For other sections of the audience, however, the American cinema, and the cheap clothing and cosmetics that went with it, represented a welcome relief from the con-stant process of demarcation and judgment which the British class system entailed. As Jerry White suggests: 'This borrowed "style" was a self-conscious identification with a more democratic discourse than anything British society (including the Labour move-ment) had to offer them.'[6] Unfortunately for these filmgoers, their very attempt to es-cape meant they were marked out as contemptible in certain eyes. In 1933, a journalist from the *Islington and Holloway Press* visited 'Islington's most notorious café' and re-ported that: 'Nearly every girl there was acting a "hard-boiled Kate" role. Nearly every youth with a very long overcoat and a round black hat on the rear of his head, was to himself a "Chicago nut".'[7] Cinema became the symbolic focus, both economically and culturally, of fears of the American threat to Britain's national life and her inter-national status. On the one hand, the British film was expected to represent an in-digenous and unchanging version of British National Identity, specifically distinct from the alternative presented by Hollywood. On the other it was to export this mess-age, gaining a place for itself in the competitive domestic and international markets by becoming more efficient and versatile, but without compromising its essentially British nature by taking on the characteristics of its foreign competitor.

Throughout the early 1930s, the British cinema was the subject of competing dis-courses in the trade papers and amongst popular critics. It was criticised for being too parochial and too internationalist; for its primitive style and its 'slavish imitation' of Hollywood; for being too reliant on stage and literary adaptation, and for its inability to draw on the richness of British literature and history; for being too slow and pic-turesque, and for failing to use the setting provided by the British landscape; for being too reliant on foreign stars and technicians, and for the poverty of its native talent.

The 1927 Act was certainly successful in giving the British production industry the boost it so badly needed. Only 34 films were made in 1926, but in 1928 production leapt to 131 films. After the difficulties of converting to sound had been overcome, production rose again, with a boom in film-making around 1934–5 which reached a peak in 1937 with 228 films.[8] The industry of this period is often portrayed as con-sisting of two irrevocably separate halves: on the one hand, quality producers such as Balcon, Wilcox and Korda making ambitious films for international markets, and on the other the notorious 'quota quickie' companies which came into being as a result of the sudden demand amongst the big American majors for British films to fulfil their quota obligations.

The legend of 'quota quickies' is that they were so much dud footage, unwatched and unwatchable. Margaret Dickinson and Sarah Street consider that the films are 'best forgotten', and Michael Balcon claimed that they were shown early in the morn-ing when only the cleaners were in the cinemas.[9] In the mid-1930s the 'quota quickie' seemed to represent an even greater threat to British national pride than Hollywood, since while Balcon and co. were struggling to provide a bona fide quality British cinema, the quota producers were operating to 'bring the name of British films into disrepute' through their production of cheap, unambitious films.[10]

The success of Korda's *The Private Life of Henry VIII* in late 1933, and the resultant release of a large amount of finance capital, enabled producers such as Balcon, Korda and Herbert Wilcox to aim at a wider international market, and in the years that followed they strenuously sought to distance themselves from the quota section of the industry. However, before 1934 the situation was less well defined. During the early 1930s many companies operated a dual policy – Wilcox's British and Dominions attempted to make quality pictures, but also ran a quota department under Richard Norton, producing twelve 'quickies' a year for Paramount.[11] Other companies which have since been identified as quickie producers also made more ambitious films intended for an export market. Julius Hagen ran such a policy at Twickenham, operating under two different brand names: Real Art for his quickies (sold to Radio and Fox), and Twickenham Film Productions for more ambitious 'supers', distributed variously by United Artists, Gaumont and Wardour.

The annual round-ups in January editions of *Kinematograph Weekly* for the early years of the decade are remarkably free of negative references to the 'Quota' Act. The main concerns of the exhibitors were not to do with the unpopularity of the British film, but rather with the question of Sunday opening and the Entertainments Tax. In discussions of British production by producers and critics, no distinction is made between quota and quality producers, although concern is expressed over the quality of the British product as a whole and its perceived inability either to portray national life effectively or to appeal to the majority of filmgoers over and above the product of Hollywood. By the summer of 1934, however, controversy over 'quota quickies' filled the pages of the trade papers and the fan magazines. A leading article in *Film Weekly* complained that:

> For over six years the British film industry has borne the brunt of these pictures with great fortitude, regarding them as necessary evils. But at last the time has come for plain speaking . . . as long as the present quota regulations remain in force [the British filmgoer] is in danger of having his time wasted and his patience exhausted by inferior British pictures which have been produced, not to stand on their own merits as entertainment, but to enable some American film company to fulfil its legal obligations.
>
> In his own interests the filmgoer should learn to recognise such pictures – to know them for what they are – and to voice his disapproval of them so forcefully that the authorities who framed the obsolete quota law will be compelled to make sweeping reforms.[12]

What is interesting about this article is that it creates the 'quota quickie' in the mind of the filmgoer. It calls for filmgoers to 'learn to recognise' such films, connecting them explicitly to the American distributors. Only a month before it denounced the 'quota quickie', *Film Weekly* had carried stories in its 'In British Studios' column – with no sense of outrage – about productions at Twickenham being filmed through the night for American distributors.[13] And in *Picturegoer*, E. G. Cousins had written an approving column entitled 'Putting England on the Screen' which praised (albeit faintly) the efforts of John Baxter and Bernard Vorhaus. Cousins argued that low production values enabled some British producers to 'turn aside for a moment from his proper employment of slavishly imitating Hollywood, and to put on British screens British themes in British scenes.' And he went on to argue that Baxter's *Say It With Flowers* was as English as 'tripe and onions'.[14] What he appears to be suggesting is that the much-despised quota section of the industry held the key to the problem of 'putting England on the screen'.

I would argue that as a direct result of their stringent finances and the limited re-lease patterns open to them, the quota producers sought to portray England for two specific markets: the lower-middle class and the older generations of the working class. Both were defined by their reluctance to partake in the optimistic visions of a consumerist society embodied in Hollywood and 'quality' British films. The lower-middle classes were ambivalent about consumption, as they were about the cinema. The 'cloth-cap' working class looked back nostalgically to music hall. As a result of their portrayal of sections of British society which identified themselves not through processes of consumption but through British notions of class and community, the 'quota quickies' produced for these markets responded exactly to the intentions of those who had created the Films Act of 1927.

The specific audiences for 'quota quickies' are often difficult to identify because sur-veys of cinemagoing during the period are usually skewed towards the more numer-ous young working-class film fans in the bigger cities. However, close attention to their likely release patterns suggests that an audience for these smaller British films was there. In 1937 a report in *World Film News* about a symposium on box-office appeal suggested that audiences generally appreciated films 'dealing with people like them-selves whose lives they can understand and whose reactions they can appreciate'.[15] While amongst younger working-class film fans Hollywood remained king, Richard

As English as tripe and onions. George Carney and imprinted soubrettes. John Baxter's Music Hall (1934).

41

Carr noted of the East End of London that 'middle-aged and elderly men continue to find their main relaxation in pigeon clubs, in darts, and in their working men's clubs'.[16]

Here, Carr said, 'music halls have vanished', but this was not so in the North. Leslie Halliwell recalled that in Bolton in the 1930s the Grand Theatre was still operating successfully as a music-hall venue, attracting crowds with great names such as 'George Robey, Frank Randle, Gillie Potter, Old Mother Riley . . . and Florrie Forde'. While the young Halliwell and his mother were devoted cinemagoers, his father preferred to patronise this music hall, and when he did go to the pictures it was significantly 'to see one of the broader Comics'.[17] The *Bolton Standard* of 1934 reveals that the Grand booked George Formby (then virtually unknown outside Lancashire) as a top biller twice during the year, and Florrie Forde appeared at the top of the bill during the summer. When these stars appeared in their respective 'quota quickies' (*Boots! Boots!* and *Say It With Flowers*), the cinema advertisements and local reviews made the most of their music-hall connections. While it is true that in predominantly working-class areas such as Bolton, which boasted no less than forty-seven cinemas, the more middle-class 'quota quickies' were often used as programme supports to American films, this was not always the case. In September 1933 the Queen's Cinema in Bolton showed *The Shadow*, with Henry Kendall, as its main feature, and in June 1934 *The Ghost Camera*, also with Kendall, was the main feature at the Rialto, unashamedly publicised as a British film with 'English scenes and English humour'.[18] In other areas the middle-class 'quota quickies' fared even better, for outside the big cities, in places where there were fewer cinemas, the culture of the young film fan was not so dominant.

Between them the three largest cinema circuits in Britain – Odeon, ABPC and Gaumont-British – accounted for the exhibition of the four more celebrated producers of 'quality' British films.[19] Their cinemas were the sites we usually associate with filmgoing in 1930s Britain – the opulent picture palaces with 2,000 or more seats situated in and around large cities. Because of their status and their situation in populous areas, the large cinemas were able to get big features quickly after their release and run them in popular 'double feature' programmes, often pairing British and American films. However, despite their high visibility, these cinemas were in fact in a minority, as Simon Rowson points out:

> The general view of the cinema has been formed and is maintained by the large, brightly coloured, brilliantly illuminated picture palaces, built and building, which are the constant experience of those who live in London and the large provincial towns. To all, the surprise must be profound when asked to credit the information that more than one half of the seating accommodation in the cinemas throughout the country will be found in houses containing less than 100 seats, and that the number of these houses is more than 70% of the total.[20]

For these smaller independent cinemas the situation was very different. Unable to get the 'quality' British films from British distributors, either because they could not afford them or because they were in competition with a large picture palace which had already screened them, the independent exhibitors were reliant on the American renters for their British quota. Furthermore, Rowson's figures on opening hours seem to suggest that while a double feature was the norm in the large houses, which opened at midday and ran a three-hour programme three times, the smaller house could only afford to open at about 6 p.m., running its programme twice with a length averaging two and a quarter hours. Despite the fact that feature films were shorter in the 1930s, it seems unlikely that a full programme lasting only two and a quarter hours could accommodate two features (even if one was only a sixty-minute 'quickie').

This evidence suggests that, although *Kinematograph Weekly* regularly recommended British quota productions as fillers 'suitable for programme material in large popular houses', many exhibitors would be showing them as their main feature. This is confirmed by research into cinemagoing in the rural areas and coastal towns of Norfolk in the 1930s, where the *Norfolk Gazette* advertisements for programmes at cinemas in Sheringham, Holt and Cromer show a pattern of single-feature programmes changing twice a week and frequently centring on British films made by quota producers. If Balcon's claim that the British cinema as a cinema of 'disrepute' amongst picturegoers is correct, one would have expected these cinemas to play down the British aspect of what was on offer. Instead the opposite is the case – 'British to the backbone', says the Regent Hall cinema in Sheringham of *East Lynne on the Western Front*, while of Julius Hagen's *The Crooked Lady*, the Central Cinema in Cromer says, 'Thrilling, romantic, dramatic, and humorous by turns, it boasts one of the greatest casts of British stage and screen personalities ever seen.'[21]

Discovering a small independent cinema in Tooting in 1937, Richard Carr could hardly conceal his incredulity at what appeal it might offer:

A small and rather depressed audience visits this cinema. One fancies them lost, hovering helplessly between the cinemas they knew in the ill-lit novelty days, and the new 'supers'. These are neither the simple, easily satisfied audiences of the pre-war days, nor the sophisticated movie fans of today. Perhaps too old or tired to go further than just round the corner to the pictures, or too conservative to accept change, or too dazed and bewildered by the luxury of the 'super' and the speed and complexities of the modern film. Some are people from small provincial towns and villages who find the less luxurious cinema more like home.[22]

Despite Carr's disparaging image, it is important not to underestimate the intelligence or the values of the audiences of such houses. Carr's experience was repeated at Lyme Regis. It appears that in spite of the dominance of the young film fan, the 'quota quickies' did find an audience, not necessarily as sad as Carr imagines, who may have constituted that section of the public, whom Simon Rowson thought 'there must be in considerable numbers', who visited the cinema 'once every fortnight or even less frequently'.[23]

While the fever for exporting British film lasted, the 'quota quickies' were seen as irretrievably contemptible. It was not until 1937, when Gaumont-British, sustaining a loss of £97,000 for the previous year, finally accepted the failure of their international policies, that cheap, indigenous culture once more became acceptable.[24]

Formally, 'quota quickies' are defined by their lack of high production values – sophisticated editing, emphasis on action, economic storytelling. Instead they use slow narratives told through dialogue rather than editing, and styles of acting and presentation taken from the theatre and the music hall. These characteristics enabled 'quota quickies' to appeal to that section of the British audience which felt ill at ease with American films. In their thematic concerns 'quota quickies' dramatise the fears of a threat to indigenous British cultural values. This 'threat' is characterised as being to do with the modernity, classlessness and instability implied by the impetus towards social mobility which was an increasingly visible aspect of Britain in the 1930s.

The two most significant genres of quota production (indeed of British production generally) during this period were the comedy and the crime picture, comprising 38

Another threat to the class structure averted. Tangled Evidence *(George Cooper, 1934).*

per cent and 26 per cent of total output respectively.[25] In the hands of British quota producers these developed into genres which were distinctively different from their Hollywood counterparts. In contrast to the Hollywood gangster film, British crime pictures were sedate English country house detective stories. British comedy films drew substantially on the music-hall tradition.

Of the fifty-six films made at Twickenham between 1932 and 1934, half are 'crime dramas' such as *The Shadow* (George Cooper, 1933), *Shot in the Dark* (George Pearson, 1933) and *Tangled Evidence* (George Cooper, 1934). They portray upper-class families, homes and manners, and structure themselves around the creation and resolution of a threat to that class. Their likely audience was the lower-middle or salaried class who, having made the leap of social mobility, had a vested interest in cementing their new status, which they expressed through a fetishisation of the unchanging class order embodied in Stanley Baldwin's rural idyll. It is within this idyll that the whodunit films are situated, providing a spectacle of traditional upper-class wealth and manners, and narrating the threatened destruction, but final reaffirmation, of that world through the story of a murder.

All these films portray a wealthy family; however, in contrast to the wealth and cosmopolitanism defined by consumption portrayed in, for example, Jessie Matthews musicals, this is a wealth which is directly in opposition to modernity. The money is old money, and wealth is portrayed not through the spectacle of consumption but rather through that of tradition, specifically signified not by fashionable clothes or expensive goods but in James Carter's sets (described by Baynham Honri as 'miracles of plasterwork') denoting the English country house. These films open on a moment of crisis over inheritance, precipitated by the murder (or in the case of *The Shadow*, the threatened murder) of the family patriarch. The various family members gather to resolve this crisis, both literally through an inquest and the reading of a will, and symbolically by defining who are legitimate carriers (and inheritors) of class status and who is the impostor – the murderer who precipitated the crisis. The murderer is characterised quite literally as a threat to the class structure, though since all the members of the cast are suspects they are all connected in different ways with that threat. Working-class barbarity and female sexuality unsettle the established order, but the most serious threat stems from modernity, urbanity and consumption.

In all three films the villain is represented as an interloper. While he is part of the family, his influences are not those of the tradition, stability and insularity valued in the rural idyll, but rather those of fluidity, sophistication, cosmopolitanism and consumption represented by the urban scene which he occupies. Significantly, in both *The Shadow* and *Shot in the Dark* (and to a lesser extent in *Tangled Evidence*), he is represented by the fey young man, conspicuously well-dressed and 'debonair'. This figure is defined by his acts of impersonation, most importantly by his construction of himself as 'a very modern young man', who in a phrase used by Beverley Nichols (constructing himself in the same vein) has 'seen through things'.[26] It is this modernity and cynicism with regard to the old class structure that mark him out as such a potential threat. Both *Tangled Evidence* and *The Shadow* contain strong blackmail plotlines, in which the villain turns conservative respectability (which he himself flaunts) to his own profit. In *Tangled Evidence* the villain steals the manuscript of a novel written by his victim, which he then proceeds to pass off as his own with great success and profit. Significantly, the title of the novel is *Tradition*.

Thus the whodunits reveal the urban consumer society as the most potential threat to the British class system, even as they recontain it by the final exposure and capture of the killer. Perhaps the most important characteristic of the threat represented by this figure is the fact that he is disguised as a member of the family and economically as a member of the right class, for he is certainly rich. The minor threats which have been assigned to other suspects, particularly those to do with the working-class characters (for instance the chauffeur in *Tangled Evidence* and the criminal son of the butler in *The Shadow*), are easily containable because they are clearly visible. It is the interloping consumer who must be most vigorously resisted. His capture enables the resolution of the crisis of inheritance and the reinvestment of tradition and stability with the value that they hold as the most privileged indices in the construction of middle-class identity.

The semantic struggle over 'value' is also a characteristic of the films dealing with music-hall performances. Music-hall artists and acts formed the main attraction in many 'quota quickies' of the period, as is shown by the numerous shorts made by Widgey Newman, the Max Miller films made at Teddington, the films made by Stanley Lupino, Lupino Lane, Flanagan and Allen, Sandy Powell, and Arthur Lucan. They operate in roughly similar ways in their negotiation of the thematic issues of consumption, in that they organise themselves around themes of work and leisure, consistently privileging production over consumption in both areas.

This is most explicitly stated in *Music Hall* (John Baxter, 1934), which tells the story of a music hall which has fallen on hard times as a result of the competition of other, newer, more commercialised entertainments – cinemas and dance halls. The backstage staff decide that it is up to them to save their jobs by revitalising the hall, making it popular once more. They identify the recent failure of the hall with a new manager who has been attempting to run it on more commercial lines by turning it into a business. Stage staff turn instead to the previous manager, now an old man, whose attitude to entertainment is far more emotive: 'I've put a lot into that place,' he says, 'and I've drawn something more than money out of it.'

Throughout *Music Hall* and *Say It With Flowers* (John Baxter, 1934), the music-hall tradition is privileged precisely because its relationship with its audience is emotional rather than commercial. It is a crucial signifier of class identity which is inward-looking rather than outward-looking. Whereas Hollywood films represent a culture of aspiration, music hall, it is implied, represents a culture of affirmation. Its performers are of the same class as the audience, and the whole activity is one of production. This is represented by the community singing which forms the highlight of several of the films, and also by the fact that music-hall gags are told 'spontaneously' throughout the film and constructed as being part of the conversation patterns of their 'real' charac-ters. This connection is portrayed as aggressively indigenous, arising from the diffi-culties of living a life defined by the inability to consume because of poverty. The problems implied by poverty are solved through the productive activity of the music hall. Thus the plot of *Say It With Flowers* revolves around the flower seller Kate, whose illness can only be cured by a holiday at the seaside. She is too poor to be able to af-ford that luxury and so her friends at the market and in the halls conspire to put on a benefit concert to raise the money to enable her to go. This is only possible because the music-hall performers are 'our own people'. As one of the characters observes, 'They have always looked after our class.'

It might be argued that the 'crime' whodunits and the music-hall 'comedies' consti-tute, in both their formal and thematic concerns, narratives of resistance to American values of mass consumption in exactly the ways intended by the 1927 Films Act. They addressed their audiences with an intimacy and intensity unavailable to American films. Unable, because of their minuscule budgets, to construct worlds of glamorous fantasy or protagonists defined by conspicuous consumption, they relied on portray-ing the spartan worlds of the British defined by class.

'Quota quickies', contrary to their traditional reputation, represent a corpus of British films which are constantly surprising in their ability to entertain, intrigue, engage and fascinate any historian with a little imagination and a passion for the popular culture of the 1930s.

Notes

1. Charles Barr, 'Amnesia and Schizophrenia', in Charles Barr (ed.), *All Our Yesterdays* (London: British Film Institute, 1986), pp. 1–29.
2. Sue Bowden, 'The New Consumerism', in Paul Johnson (ed.), *Twentieth Century Britain: Economic, Social and Cultural Change* (London: Longman, 1994), p. 247.
3. V. F. Perkins, 'The Atlantic Divide', in Richard Dyer and Ginette Vincendeau (eds.), *Popular European Cinema* (London: Routledge, 1992), p. 197.
4. *Film Weekly*, 4 May 1934, and *Woman's Filmfair*, July 1934.
5. Jeffrey Richards, 'The Cinema and Cinema-going in Birmingham in the 1930s', in James Walton and John K. Walvin (eds.), *Leisure in Britain 1780–1939* (Manchester: Manchester University Press, 1983), p. 46.
6. Jerry White, *The Worst Street in North London* (London: Routledge & Kegan Paul, 1986), p. 166.
7. Quoted in ibid., p. 166.
8. Tom Ryall, *Hitchcock and the British Cinema* (London: Croom Helm, 1986), p. 48.
9. Margaret Dickinson and Sarah Street, *Cinema and State* (London: British Film Institute, 1985), p. 42, and Michael Balcon, *A Lifetime of Films* (London: Hutchinson, 1969), p. 16.
10. Balcon, *A Lifetime of Films*, p. 16.
11. Rachael Low, *Film Making in 1930s Britain* (London: George Allen & Unwin, 1985), p. 188.
12. 'Plain Speaking About Quota Pictures', *Film Weekly*, 29 June 1934, p. 3.
13. Stephen Watts, 'In British Studios', *Film Weekly*, 11 May 1934, p. 18.
14. E. G. Cousins, 'Putting England on the Screen', *Picturegoer*, 23 June 1934, p. 28.

15. 'Conflicting Tastes of British Filmgoers', *World Film News*, February 1937.
16. Richard Carr, 'People's Pictures and People's Palaces', *World Film News*, January 1937.
17. Leslie Halliwell, *Seats in All Parts* (London: Granada, 1985), p. 31.
18. This material is taken from issues of the *Bolton Standard* (a local evening newspaper) for 1934, held in the British Newspaper Library at Colindale.
19. Namely Gaumont-British, ABPC, British and Dominions, and London Films.
20. Simon Rowson, 'A Statistical Survey of the Cinema Industry in Britain in 1934', *Journal of the Royal Statistical Society*, vol. 99, 1936.
21. This material is taken from various local papers held in the Norwich Central Library.
22. Richard Carr, 'Cinemas and Cemeteries', *World Film News*, May 1937, p. 18.
23. Rowson, 'A Statistical Survey'.
24. Low, *Film Making in 1930s Britain*, p. 143.
25. Denis Gifford, *The British Film Catalogue 1897–1970* (Newton Abbot and London: David and Charles, 1973).
26. See Beverley Nichols, *Are They the Same at Home?* (London: Jonathan Cape, 1927), p. 191. Nichols is defending himself against an attack on the 'modern young man' by the Baroness Clifton in the *Daily Express*.

Bibliography

Barr, Charles, *All Our Yesterdays* (London: British Film Institute, 1986).

Branson, Noreen and Heinemann, Margot, *Britain in the 1930s* (London: Weidenfeld & Nicolson, 1971).

Brunel, Adrian, *Nice Work* (London: Forbes Robertson, 1949).

Dickinson, Margaret and Street, Sarah, *Cinema and State* (London: British Film Institute, 1983).

Gifford, Denis, *British Film Catalogue 1895–1970* (Newton Abbot: David & Charles, 1973).

Halliwell, Leslie, *Seats in All Parts* (London: Granada, 1985).

Higson, Andrew, *Waving the Flag* (Oxford: Clarendon Press, 1995).

Johnson, Paul, *Twentieth Century Britain: Economic, Social and Cultural Change* (London: Longman, 1994).

Jones, Steven, *Workers at Play* (London: Routledge & Kegan Paul, 1986).

Low, Rachael, *Film Making in 1930s Britain* (London: George Allen & Unwin, 1985).

Nichols, Beverley, *Are They the Same at Home?* (London: Jonathan Cape, 1927).

Pearson, George, *Flashback* (London: George Allen & Unwin, 1957).

Powell, Michael, *A Life in Movies* (London: Heinemann, 1986).

Richards, Jeffrey and Sheridan, Dorothy, *Mass-Observation at the Movies* (London: Routledge & Kegan Paul, 1987).

Richards, Jeffrey, *The Age of the Dream Palace* (London: Routledge, 1984).

Walton, James and Walvin, John K. (eds.), *Leisure in Britain 1780–1939* (Manchester: Manchester University Press, 1983).

White, Jerry, *The Worst Street in London* (London: Routledge & Kegan Paul, 1986).

Wood, Linda, *Low-Budget Film Making in 1930s Britain* (M.Phil. thesis, Polytechnic of Central London, 1989).

Wood, Linda, *The Commercial Imperative* (London: British Film Institute, 1987).

5
Low-budget British Films in the 1930s

Linda Wood

The Cinematograph Films Act (1927), which came into effect on 1 January 1928, made it compulsory for all cinemas to show a quota of British films, starting at 5 per cent in 1928 and eventually rising to 20 per cent by 1936.

For many, the very fact that legislation reached the statute book was interpreted as a *de facto* acknowledgment by the government of the importance to the national interest of an indigenous film production industry. Unsurprisingly, the initial call for protection had come from British film-makers, perturbed by the danger of imminent collapse facing their industry, with British screens throughout the 1920s being monopolised by a relentless stream of films from Hollywood.

However, the film production sector itself lacked the necessary economic clout to strongarm the government into action, and it is unlikely that anything would have happened had not producers successfully wooed the imperialist/nationalist lobby into their corner. This lobby had powerful friends both within the government and among Conservative backbench MPs. That trade followed film was an article of faith reinforced by US success in both. Business leaders were convinced that if they could show off British wares in British films this would go a long way to fight off US competition. But for the Imperialist lobby it was not simply a matter of trade; the need to promote British cultural values was considered of equal importance.[1]

This background is important when looking at the reaction to the films produced in the post-legislation era. If British films were to fulfil the roles used as the justification for legislation, there would appear to be an implicit commitment to the production of quality films. Poor films would fail to attract audiences overseas, and the association of 'British' with inferior products would not help in the promotion of the nation. Yet the Cinematograph Films Act did not incorporate a quality threshold, despite repeated calls for the inclusion of such a measure. While the imperial/trade lobby exerted immense influence, a number of counter-pressures were operating on the government. There was the opposition of the film trade: both the exhibition and the distribution sectors did very nicely out of American films, which had long since proved more popular with audiences than British films. The American film companies had hinted that they were ready to boycott Britain if the burden placed on them was too onerous.

The prevalent political ethos made the Board of Trade keen to avoid any measures that might require a day-to-day involvement in the film industry. Accustomed to dealing with easily quantifiable matters such as weights and measures, it was wary of setting 'quality' guidelines and making value judgments. Since very large sums of money would be needed to build up the film industry and any provision of government finance was rejected from the outset, the Act deliberately excluded anything which might discourage private investment.

However, the government's bland assurances that it was fully behind the efforts to establish a British film industry, and the rhetoric of the production lobby, fostered the illusion that legislation would instantly result in the creation of a British Hollywood. When this didn't happen, blame was laid at the door of the Films Act. In the years that followed it was derided for giving rise to the heinous practice of the 'quota quickie' while failing to help 'legitimate' producers such as Alexander Korda and Michael Balcon who were trying to produce the sort of film envisaged by the Act's promoters.

Quickies were films made at minimal cost – generally £1 a foot – which enabled distributors to comply with the letter of the Films Act while flouting its spirit. The cost of a 60-minute film (with 35mm film running at ninety feet a minute) would be about £5,400, many times less than that of even a modest British feature production. Criticism of the American companies – widely perceived as being responsible for these films – might not have been so virulent had it not been for the large discrepancy in cost between their British and their Hollywood films. According to Howard T. Lewis, around this time the US companies were spending between $170,000 and $250,000 (£40,000–£65,000 at the then exchange rate) on their Hollywood films.

Because of the distributors' quota – set 2.5 per cent higher than that for exhibitors – an American company like MGM with a slate of forty or fifty of its own films on its books would also have to offer exhibitors four or five British films when the quota was 10 per cent, and eight or ten by the time it was 20 per cent. In order to fulfil these quota requirements the American renters quickly and unanimously adopted the strategy of producing low-cost films of the second-feature class. As early as June 1928, within months of the Act coming into force, the trade press was commenting on the poor-quality films being acquired by the American renters. *Kine Weekly* observed: 'American distributing houses are making arrangements to make British pictures at a low cost incompatible with good quality. These films are doomed to be "duds" before they start.'[2]

Looking at the production schedules for the years that followed, it is possible to pinpoint a handful of films which fall outside the low cost category: in 1933, for example, Gloria Swanson came to Ealing Studios to make *Perfect Understanding*, whose £70,000 budget exceeded the combined cost of all the other films made at the studio that year. But these were the exceptions that proved the rule, one-offs that never formed part of any coherent policy to produce quality production.

What is less clear, however, is to what extent these cheaply produced films were booked to cinemas. While initially some American distributors seemed prepared to shelve the worst examples and write off their cost as a straight loss, it would appear that others were including them in packages of films being block-booked to cinemas. And as the percentage of British films required to be screened increased with each year, the more these films were shown. In 1932, Seton Margrave, who regularly argued the need for 'quality' British films to save the Empire from disintegrating, pointed out in an article severely criticising American distributors for acquiring substandard films that 'now with the quota at 15 per cent this buying – registering – shelving dodge has become too expensive.'[3]

Because the US distributors had become the only significant source of finance for the independent producer the policies they followed acquired a crucial importance. In 1933, for instance, they were responsible for 53 per cent of British films. This key role was not one which they had sought, or welcomed.

The attitude of the American distributors to the Films Act was understandable: they were commercial organisations who owed no loyalty to the British film industry. From their standpoint, they were being forced to use their resources on helping foster a rival to their home industry. Moreover, Britain was just one of many markets in which the US majors came under attack for undermining the local industry; and they were very aware that concessions made in one territory were liable to be demanded in others.

In the post-legislation euphoria a large number of film production companies were floated on the stock exchange. Of these, only two had any real success, Gaumont British and British International Pictures. They were larger than other British companies, and with their own cinema chains they could guarantee that their productions reached an audience. The remaining companies soon found themselves facing severe financial problems, and bankruptcy became commonplace: it had been drastically underestimated just how much reviving a dormant industry would cost. In the wake of large losses on investments in film, funds from City institutions dried up.

In 1933 the Board of Trade, faced by a well-organised and unrelenting campaign attacking the quality of British films produced under the Films Act, set up an internal inquiry. Its findings, based on British films produced in 1932, provide firm evidence that the vast majority of low-cost films could be laid at the door of the American distributors: 60 out of 83 American-sponsored films, compared with 15 out of 73 British films, cost less than £75 per 100 ft (and only 8 out of 83 American-sponsored films cost over £125 per 100 ft). But the inquiry was not just concerned with cost; it also attempted to assess the entertainment value of films, adopting the points system used by the CEA, the trade organisation representing exhibitors (every film trade-shown was marked on a scale from 1 to 10: the 'better' the film, the higher the mark). Surprisingly it found that as many as 45 per cent of the pictures handled by US distributors were 'good programme pictures'.

When looking at the performance of individual companies operating specifically within the low-budget context, the committee discovered considerable variation. United Artists and Paramount had on the whole 'acquired better pictures than most US renters ... Although their expenditure has been by no means lavish, they can certainly be regarded as doing their share.' Fox, Radio and Warners had 'a definite policy of producing second features of about 4,000 ft which vary in quality but some of them are acceptable second features for the ordinary cinemas.' Warner Brothers–First National and Fox had both recently set up their own production units with mixed results. MGM was taken to task: 'They have acquired at times good pictures and at others sheer rubbish.' Given that only two out of nine of their films were marked by the CEA at 8 points and above, the rubbish appeared to predominate. Universal was castigated as a black spot. 'So far as films made in this country are concerned, they only acquire rubbish.'[4]

Although with the proper resources it is easier to turn out a watchable film, money in itself does not guarantee a 'good' film, nor a low budget automatically result in a 'poor' one. For instance, the MGM film which obtained the company's highest CEA marking was made by Sound City for only £1,100. The CEA points system also reveals that the entertainment value of certain companies' films was far higher than would be expected, given the level of expenditure: at Radio, seven out of ten films were marked 8 points or over; at Paramount, all films were $7\frac{1}{2}$ or over; at Fox, seven out of eleven films received 8 or over. Interestingly only three films out of twenty made by Warners were marked at 8 points and over, and 'although their films cost more money than Fox's, they are not nearly so good'.

Though warning of the need for continuing vigilance, overall the committee found the progress made by the British film industry to be satisfactory and that the quality of British films was improving. In fact, remarkable progress had been made in the previous five years. Despite the unwillingness of the City to make funds available for film production and despite the unenthusiastic response of the US distributors to their quota obligations, production was expanding rapidly. In the year ending September 1932, while the quota requirement was only 15 per cent, 25 per cent of the films registered were British. A revitalised production sector exuded confidence and was eager to take on new challenges.

1933 marked a turning point in many ways for the British film industry. Certainly from that year on it became possible to detect a greater effort being put into their quota production by the US companies. Whereas in the early years films had been contracted out to a wide range of independent producers, from this point the American companies either set up in-house production operations or became closely tied to one producing outfit. 20th Century-Fox made major improvements to its recently acquired Wembley Studios and instituted a training programme. Warner Brothers–First National upgraded its Teddington Studios and brought over the energetic young producer Irving Asher to run the operation. In October 1935, the trade press carried the story that Universal was to have its own studios at Sound City (Shepperton). In November 1935, Sam Eckman, head of MGM (UK), announced that MGM was to produce 'quality' films in Britain. As adept businessmen, the company chiefs recognised that the time had come to adopt a new strategy.

The situation they faced had drastically altered. The City was once more making finance available to independent British producers. British technicians had learnt their

Dramatic scenes and the chance of becoming a Hollywood star. Ida Lupino in The Ghost Camera *(Bernard Vorhaus, 1933).*

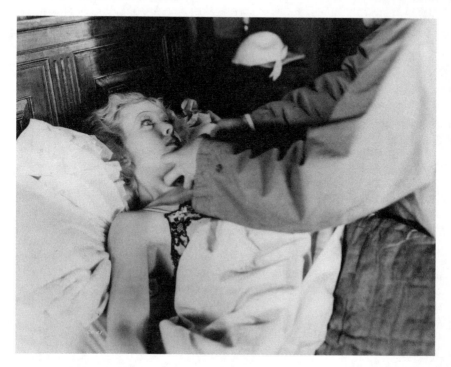

trade and were being supplemented by top European film-makers fleeing the Nazi threat. As the general quality of British films improved, the US distributors could no longer blame any shortfalls in the standard of their quota films on the incompetence of British film-makers. Moreover, the period had witnessed the growth of strong British circuits which were less willing to take the poorer type of quota films. Also, as the quota requirement increased, it made little commercial sense to spend money unproductively and there was an incentive to put the films to better use. A final factor associated with the new vigour displayed by the US companies towards their quota obligation was the imminent expiry of the 1927 Films Act. With good cause to fear what might replace it, the American companies made a belated effort to convince the Board of Trade that they were committed to making good British films.

Up to the mid-1930s, if the independent producer was to survive he had little alternative than to take on the making of quota films for the American distributors. Anthony Havelock-Allan, who produced Paramount's quota films at British and Dominions, recalled that their films were usually made for a flat fee:

> The profit to the maker was whether we could supply them to Paramount at a price that enabled us to make a profit. Sometimes if something was especially good we would try and bargain for a little more money than the £6,500. But in the main what we were doing was making them for about £5,000, £5,500. Somehow we managed to make an average of £625 or £500.[5]

The flat-rate system of payment seemed to remove any incentive to make better films – there was no reward for effort or penalty for the lack of it. As Norman Loudon, who ran Shepperton Studios, pointed out: 'The producer hands over the picture to the American distributor with no thought of making additional money and that is what makes a quickie.'[6] Though the system actively encouraged producers out for a quick profit there were few instances of this occurring. Most producers took the only work they could get, the production of low-cost films, and used this as a means of building up their operation, with the long-term objective of moving on to something better.

While the producer would often have liked to make more money available for his productions – after all, it was his name that went on the credits and his reputation which suffered if a film was substandard – he faced the problem of convincing a sceptical and unsympathetic American distributor that spending a little more to produce a better film might boost its box-office takings.

Richard Norton typifies the enthusiasm of quota producers at this time, and his experience at United Artists demonstrates the generally negative response to anyone pursuing their duties over-zealously: he was called in to see his boss, Murray Silverstone, who suggested he might be happier with another company. In his autobiography Norton recalled:

> I knew, of course, that Murray wanted to get rid of me. I had got obsessed with the idea of doing something for British films: and of course to Murray, a middle man entirely interested in distribution, and unwillingly saddled with a Quota Act, I was simply a continual nuisance. Every time he looked round, there I was making another picture.[7]

George Pearson, one of Britain's foremost silent directors who during the 30s directed many quota films, observed:

To make a talking film with £6,000 only to meet the cost of studio space, subject, script, director, technicians, film stock, lights, artistes, overheads, and end up with a profit needed a spartan economy and a slave-driving effort. All vaunting ideas of film as an art had to be abandoned; only as a capable and speedy craftsman could one survive in that feverish and restless environment.[8]

The need for economic stringencies had a range of practical implications for film-makers. Only stories which could be made cheaply were used. The most popular types were comedies, crime/detective stories and domestic melodramas, which required few sets, small casts and no elaborate costumes. There was also a tendency to be conservative in the choice of subject matter as producers wanted to avoid having their films rejected by the American distributors, or a censor quick to ban anything vaguely straying in the direction of sex, violence or politics.

Films were often adaptations of novels or plays which could be quickly converted into film scripts. Terence Rattigan, for instance, wrote a screenplay for Paramount British. But according to Norman Lee, 'quota quickies' proper made wide use of original scripts since these could be bought from unknown writers more cheaply – purportedly for as little as £25 – than the rights of a West End play.[9]

The need to cut financial corners frequently resulted in inadequate preparation time being allowed. John Paddy Carstairs, later a director but at that time a scriptwriter, recalled working on a Columbia picture called *Boomerang*:

> They were in a frightful hurry and simply had to have a complete shooting script; that is the whole picture cut up into screen terms and dialogued all within a week as they had booked studio space. I agreed to take on the job provided I was given every kind of clerical assistance – a relay of girls for dictation and typists available at all hours of the day and night to bat out the stuff. The picture was no world beater, but the reviews were favourable and I had the satisfaction of doing the whole job within three days.[10]

There are innumerable references in accounts of film-making during this period of writers sitting in a corner and changing the script as filming proceeded. While the situation was not an ideal one, there comes across a sense of pride in the ability to do a good job of work under difficult circumstances.

Although economic expediency meant that directors rarely had the opportunity properly to rehearse their casts, good performances could markedly reduce the damage arising from other deficiencies. Consequently producers were usually prepared to be a little more generous in their budgeting for casts than for other areas. Bernard Vorhaus, who directed a couple of quota quickies at Twickenham, recalled that studio boss Julius Hagen

> left me completely free to choose who I wanted so long as it wasn't wildly expensive. One thing they were quite ready to pay money for was to engage good actors. You had to shoot with them damn fast. He didn't mind them getting a lot of money a day as long as there were only a few days involved.[11]

Indeed producers were fortunate in that they could turn to the rich array of talent provided by the theatre, and stage actors were relatively cheap to hire. Jack Hawkins recalled the time he was making *The Lodger* in 1932: 'When I was drawing my £8 a day during the month I was filming, I little thought that in future years I would be earn-

A rich array of theatrical talent. A. W. Baskomb and Barbara Everest in Maurice Elvey's The Lodger *(1932).*

ing £100,000 a year. After all, at a time when the average wage in Britain was £2.10s, £8 a day was a princely sum indeed.'[12]

Because of the high stakes at play when it came to big-budget film-making, producers would generally try to reduce their risk by using established stars, and it was exceptional for an unknown to be given a lead role. Producers of low-cost films were prepared to be a little more experimental – apart from anything else they could not afford the salaries commanded by the top players. Consequently many British actors and actresses – for example Jack Hawkins, Jessica Tandy, Merle Oberon, Geraldine Fitzgerald, John Mills, James Mason and Margaret Rutherford – gained valuable experience and exposure early in their careers by appearing in low-budget films. Ida Lupino from Twickenham studios, Richard Greene and Roddy McDowell from Wembley and Errol Flynn from Teddington were given Hollywood contracts on the strength of their performances in low-budget British films. There were many more. Editor Peter Tanner recounts that while he was at Wembley the studio was always experimenting with young actors, and all the pictures went to Fox in America. Low-budget production played the vitally important role of allowing the industry to find out whether particular actors photographed well or came across sympathetically. The players themselves were very much aware of the possibility of being asked to appear in 'quality' films if they were seen by the right person. John Mills recalls of his part in *The Ghost Camera* (1933):

> I liked the script and I thought my part was outstanding – dramatic scenes, accused of murder, wrongly of course – and felt I had a chance of really making a mark. By this time I was fascinated by the new medium and decided that, as I'd turned down the chance of becoming a Hollywood film star, nothing was going to stop me from becoming an English one.[13]

The introduction of a quota requirement had resulted in a substantially increased demand for film personnel, both on and off screen. When it came to finding their actors, producers could call on theatre, music hall and radio. While they still needed to learn how to adjust to working for the camera, these actors were relatively skilled before they passed through the studio gate. However, there was no equivalent pool of trained and experienced technicians in Britain. The shortfall had to be met through the importation of personnel, initially from Hollywood, subsequently in the shape of émigrés from Hitler's Germany and elsewhere in Europe.

Most British technicians accepted that they would have to go through a training period, and the expansion in production brought about by the 1927 Films Act provided them with the opportunity to be trained by film-makers of international standing. When making the transition to editor, cameraman, etc., they would hone their skills on low-budget productions. Oscar-winning cinematographer Oswald Morris recalled of Wembley:

> During those two or three years at Fox I was promoted from assistant to operating. But what we did was that we alternated. On one picture I was allowed to operate and the assistant, he'd assist, and on the next picture he would operate and I would assist. They insisted we did this but it was quite good training.[14]

Among the directors who got their initial directing experience through working on films commissioned for quota purposes were Anthony Asquith, Michael Powell and Walter Forde. Other directors who first learnt about film-making from working as technicians on low-budget productions included Michael Relph, Thorold Dickinson, Guy Green, David Macdonald, Ronald Neame and Leslie Norman. Frank Launder worked on BIP's low-budget *Josser* films and was briefly in charge of the script department at Shepperton. Adrian Brunel concluded:

> For most British film-makers it was this or nothing ... many technicians and artists got continuity of employment for the first time and became expert performers in their field, a number of them graduating to big productions. Quickies became a training ground for film-makers.[15]

Although British films of this period were widely disparaged, many people – from glamour seekers to intellectuals – were attracted to the idea of working in film-making. A few dilettantes found their way in, but the work was demanding and only the tough and the dedicated were able to stay the course. Working conditions were unpleasant. Studios were icy-cold in winter and unbearably hot in summer. The producers' need to maximise studio resources resulted in very tight shooting schedules which often involved working into the early hours of the morning. Indeed, many of studios on the outskirts of London had sleeping facilities for those who were needed to work after public transport had closed down. Yet despite strenuous working conditions, all the evidence indicates that those working in films were capable, committed and even enthusiastic. Director Bernard Vorhaus recalled:

> At Twickenham it was extraordinary that the crews had considerable enthusiasm. I say that because they were so overworked. The films were knocked out in a ridiculously short time. When a director finished one of these films, certainly terribly exhausted, he could have a rest; next morning the crew were immediately on to another. It was extraordinary they made the effort they did. If they saw a director

was trying to make something good and not just churn out footage they responded marvellously.[16]

Although there were grumbles, mainly about the absence of overtime payment, most film workers knew that, while the producers made a better living, they were on the whole unable to make better resources available because they could not afford to, not because they were milking the system. Many who worked in films at the time have stories of the ingenious ways they got round problems created by working with very basic equipment: home-made attachments to cameras, makeshift fog machines, dubbing from gramophones, wall sections which could be slotted together and rearranged to create whatever set effect was required. Low-budget films benefited enormously from the dedication of the people working on them.

At times it seems that all British films made in the 30s that fall outside a handful of prestigious titles get lumped together under the designation quota quickie. And were it not for the pejorative undertones of cheap and nasty, it would be a very useful banner to cover what turns out to be a wide and complex continuum within the low-cost spectrum. Early quota films suffered from the fact that they had been made by fledgling film-makers in inadequately equipped studios who were trying to come to terms with the new medium of sound, but the later ones were far more technically assured. Throughout the 30s some dreadful films continued to be made: renters discovered a sudden shortfall and deliberately went out to buy something as cheaply as possible; producers with commissions for six films found that by the time they reached the sixth most of their fees had gone, so they knocked out the last film with minimal resources. Some of these films got shelved, to the relief of all concerned; others deserved to be shelved but were screened, to the detriment of the reputation of British films. But this was a minority; more typical were the solidly made second features, and judged as such they were of a reasonable standard. In the era before television when there was little by way of home entertainment, the supporting feature was a welcome addition to the programme. And it often incorporated distinctively British elements, such as popular music-hall and radio performers.

While the American companies deliberately pursued a policy of producing low-cost films which offered no competition to their own first feature, they did not maliciously cut costs to the core. Certainly they paid their staff better than the British majors: Oswald Morris recalled that when he left BIP for Wembley his salary as a camera assistant doubled. Similarly Ronald Neame remembered that when he moved to Wembley 'they offered me the fantastic salary of £25 a week'.[17] Once they set up their own in-house production operation, the American outfits set about making their quota films with the same professionalism that they applied to their Hollywood films.

The quota quickie officially came to an end with the passing of the Cinematograph Films Act (1938), which introduced a minimum cost requirement. The government, guided by interest groups primarily interested in promoting the production of 'quality' films, omitted to include measures necessary to safeguard the 'bread and butter' end of the film production industry and production slumped.

Although the Cinematograph Films Act of 1927 had failed to incorporate the full scope of measures envisaged by its supporters, it had provided a major stimulus to British film production. In 1927 only 27 films were made in Britain; by 1936 there were over 200. In 1928, the average cost of films produced in Britain was £5,374; by 1932, it was £9,250; and in 1936 it was £18,000. Average figures disguise the wide variation in costs between films but do give an indication of the steady increase in the general quality of British films during these years. While giving birth to the quota quickie, the Films Act was also responsible for building up the kind of infrastructure required to support first-feature production on a regular rather than an *ad hoc* basis.

It had been unrealistic to expect the outcome of political intervention to be the transformation of the British film industry from being one of the most backward in Europe into becoming one which could instantaneously rival Hollywood. But as Anthony Havelock-Allan has pointed out, 'On the basis of these small pictures, a sort of industry grew up.'[18]

Notes

1. Fifteen years later the ideological importance of film was still being put forward as a reason for government involvement: 'A film production industry is essential to this country both in peace and war for purposes of direct and indirect propaganda, commercial advertising and prestige.' Public Records Office, BT64/61/17793/1941.
2. *Kine Weekly*, 21 June 1928, p. 83.
3. *Daily Mail*, 1 April 1932.
4. Public Records Office, BT64/97.
5. Anthony Havelock-Allan, BECTU History Project.
6. Evidence to the Moyne Committee, 12 May 1936.
7. Richard Norton, *Silver Spoon* (Hutchinson, London, 1954), p. 184.
8. George Pearson, *Flashback* (London: George Allen & Unwin, 1957), p. 193.
9. Norman Lee, *Money for Film Stories* (London: Pitman, 1937), pp. 71, 75.
10. John Paddy Carstairs, *Honest Injun* (London: Hurst and Blackett, 1942), p. 85.
11. Interview with author, 23 October 1986.
12. Jack Hawkins, *Anything for a Quiet Life* (London: Elm Tree Books, 1973), p. 49.
13. John Mills, *Up in the Clouds – Gentlemen Please* (London: Weidenfeld and Nicolson, 1980), p. 117.
14. Oswald Morris, BECTU History Project.
15. Adrian Brunel, *Nice Work* (London: Forbes Robertson, 1949).
16. Interviewed, 23 October 1986.
17. Ronald Neame, BECTU History Project.
18. Anthony Havelock-Allan, BECTU History Project.

Bibliography

Ackland, Rodney and Grant, Elspeth, *The Celluloid Mistress* (London: Allan Wingate, 1954).
Brunel, Adrian, *Nice Work: The Story of Thirty Years in British Film Production* (London: Forbes Robertson, 1949).
Carstairs, John Paddy, *Honest Injun* (London: Hurst and Blackett, 1942).
Dean, Basil, *Mind's Eye* (London: Hutchinson, 1973).
Klingender, F. D. and Legg, Stuart, *Money Behind the Screen* (London: Lawrence & Wishart, 1937).
Kulik, Karol, *Alexander Korda – The Man Who Could Work Miracles* (London: W. H. Allen, 1975).
Lee, Norman, *Log of a Film Director* (London: Quality Press, 1949).
Low, Rachael, *The History of British Film 1929–39: Film Making in 1930s Britain* (London: George Allen & Unwin, 1985).
Moyne Committee, The, *Cinematograph Films Act 1927: Report of a Committee appointed by the Board of Trade* (London: HMSO, 1937).
Pearson, George, *Flashback* (London: George Allen & Unwin, 1957).
Powell, Michael, *A Life in Movies* (London: Heinemann, 1986).
Richards, Jeffrey, *The Age of the Dream Palace: Cinema and Society in Britain 1930–39* (London: Routledge & Kegan Paul, 1984).
Robinson, Martha, *Continuity Girl* (London: Robert Hale, 1937).
Shafter, Stephen Craig, *Enter the Dream House: the British Film Industry and the Working Classes in Depression England 1929–39* (University of Illinois at Urbana-Champaign, 1982).
Wilcox, Herbert, *25,000 Sunsets* (London: Bodley Head, 1967).
Wood, Alan, *Mr Rank* (London: Hodder & Stoughton, 1952).

6
The British Documentary Film Movement

Ian Aitken

In many respects the British documentary film movement can be considered a touchstone for debates on the nature and achievement of British cinema. If, as many have argued, one of the central paradigms of British national film culture is realism, then the documentary film movement is one of the principal sources of that tradition. However, despite this apparent record of achievement the movement has often been the subject of criticism, even condemnation, both for the role which it is perceived to have played in the 1930s, and for the influence which it is perceived to have had on contemporary film and broadcasting practices. This essay will attempt to address these criticisms and also try to assess the value of the documentary movement's achievements.

The founder of the documentary movement, John Grierson (1898–1972), believed that film, and documentary film in particular, could play a crucial role within society by providing an effective medium of communication between the State and the public. Grierson's views on the cinema were formed against the background of the economic slump and the slow build-up to war in the 1930s. In this context of mounting national and international instability he felt it was vital for relatively new mass communications media such as film and radio to play a role in helping to stabilise society. He was, therefore, concerned to a considerable extent with questions of the civic and social purposiveness of film. However, this did not mean that he ignored questions relating to the aesthetic qualities of film. On the contrary, part of Grierson's importance for film theory lies in the fact that his ideas on documentary can be traced back to a complex set of systematic aesthetic theories.

In 1927 Grierson joined the Empire Marketing Board, a government organisation whose brief was to publicise trade links between Britain and the countries of the Empire. Grierson's job involved the development of a programme of publicity films for the Board, but his first film, *Drifters* (1929), became a far more ambitious project than the Board had originally envisaged. The film quickly became a critical success, and its combination of naturalistic images and formative editing has influenced traditions of documentary film-making in Britain ever since. *Drifters* also illustrates what was to become the central strategy of the documentary movement during the 1930s: to seek sponsorship from government bodies with limited remits, and then, whenever possible, to make films which went far beyond those remits.

Following the success of *Drifters*, Grierson founded the documentary film movement as such, by establishing the EMB Film Unit and by appointing young directors such as Basil Wright, Arthur Elton, Edgar Anstey, Harry Watt and Paul Rotha. Grierson and the Unit remained at the EMB until it was was abolished by Act of Parliament in 1933. After this the Film Unit moved to the Post Office, where they were re-established as the GPO Film Unit. New film-makers were also appointed, the most prominent of whom were Humphrey Jennings and Alberto Cavalcanti.

In 1936, frustrated by the restrictions increasingly imposed on the film unit by the GPO, Grierson left in order to establish other documentary film units and a co-ordinating body called Film Centre. In 1938 he left Britain to become first Film Officer of the National Film Board of Canada. In the meantime, following the outbreak of war, the GPO Film Unit was transferred to the Ministry of Information, and was renamed the Crown Film Unit. After the war the movement's importance diminished, and its personnel and ideas were dispersed into the cinema, and into the burgeoning industries of public relations and television.

In order to fully understand the documentary film movement it is essential to view it within its historical context: that of Britain in the 1930s. The period has frequently been characterised as one in which radical politics were widespread, and several histories have painted a picture of the 'red decade'. However, this is misleading. Although radical political movements and organisations certainly existed in Britain during the 1920s and 1930s (and one of them – the 'Red Clydeside' movement – had a direct influence on Grierson) none of them developed into a genuine mass movement. In fact, throughout the decade conservative ideas dominated social and political discourse, and Conservative-dominated National Governments continued to be elected. Had war not intervened in 1939, the Conservatives would have been re-elected in the coming election.

This conservative hegemony was not absolute, however, and from 1931 to 1939 various strands of opinion gradually converged to form a social democratic consensus which eventually achieved political ascendancy in 1945. It is this strand of political and cultural discourse, described by one of its Conservative proponents, Harold Macmillan, as 'the middle way' between unfettered capitalism and a nationalising socialism, with which the documentary film movement, and Grierson in particular, must be associated.[1] Although radical and Communist figures such as Paul Rotha, Ralph Bond and Ivor Montagu were associated with the movement, its overall political profile was in fact similar to that of other pressure groups of the period, such as The Next Five Years Group and Political and Economic Planning, who were concerned to build up support for a new social democratic corporatist consensus. The documentary movement is best understood, then, as social democratic and reformist in relation to the dominant conservatism of the inter-war period, but not as occupying any explicitly socialist position.

Grierson

John Grierson was concerned with the potential which documentary film had as a medium for communicating social information, but he was also interested in exploring the aesthetic qualities of the medium.[2] The first formulation of his theory of documentary film, in an official memorandum written for the EMB in 1927, argued for the creation of a new genre: films of 30–40 minutes which through creative editing of actuality footage would enable stories to be 'orchestrated into cinematic sequences of enormous vitality'.[3] This first definition of the 'Griersonian documentary' contained both formalist and naturalist elements, but it is the former which have the ascendancy. Grierson believed that these films, the first of which would be *Drifters*, would 'mark a new phase in cinema production'.[4]

A film of considerable aesthetic interest. John Grierson's Drifters *(1929).*

The documentary movement is sometime accused of being too close to the establishment. Grierson was strongly influenced by forms of neo-Hegelian philosophy which placed considerable importance on the value of the State and corporate institutions. He believed that the institutions of State possessed intrinsic merit because they were the culmination of long-drawn-out historical attempts to achieve social integration and harmony. This led him to the view that the proper function of documentary film was to promote an understanding of social and cultural interconnection within the nation.[5]

These views led Grierson to place great emphasis on notions of duty and service, and to argue that documentary film-makers should not merely follow their own individual predispositions and inclinations, but should also devote themselves to the social duty of revealing and describing social interconnection. He also argued that ideologies which promoted social integration were 'good propaganda', whilst ideologies which promoted social division were 'propaganda of the devil'.[6] Consequently, he believed that documentary film-makers must discipline themselves to work within what he called 'the degree of general sanction': the sphere of consensual discourse generally circulating within society. This 'discipline' of consensual practice inevitably worked against the development of a radical, critical documentary film culture.

Grierson's beliefs about cinema and society can be described as corporatist and consensual, and the theory of documentary film within which they are contained can be characterised in the same terms. However, this is not the whole story. Grierson made a fundamental distinction between what he called the 'institutions of State' and the 'agents of State'. Whilst the institutions of State possessed intrinsic historical value, he believed that circumstances could exist in which the agents of State could subvert those institutions for sectional, class purposes.[7] In these circumstances it was permissible for documentary film-makers to oppose the State, and to make radical, critical films. Grierson believed that, in the 1930s, rather than working for the benefit of the nation as a whole, the establishment was encouraging processes of unregulated capitalist development which reproduced its own interests and threatened social stability. Consequently, he argued, documentary film had to play a role in promoting social reform and, above all, in providing positive images and stories of working-class individuals and communities: in Grierson's own phrase, the documentary film must 'put the working man on the screen'.[8] In relation to the historical context of the inter-war period, then, Grierson's ideas on social change and documentary film can be characterised as reformist and progressive.

The films and film-makers

The films made by the documentary movement from 1929 to 1939 fall into a number of categories. On the one hand there were routine films commissioned in order to publicise government services – films such as *Cable Ship* (1933), which dealt with the laying of submarine telephone cables. On the other hand there were more ambitious projects, such as *Night Mail* (1936), which attempted to realise Grierson's objectives for the documentary film more fully. During the EMB period of 1930–34 the most important films made were Grierson's *Drifters*, and *Industrial Britain* (1931), a film shot and partly edited by Robert Flaherty, the Canadian film-maker who had made *Nanook of the North* (1924). When the documentary movement moved to the GPO in 1934 two other major projects begun at the EMB – Arthur Elton's *BBC Voice of Britain* (1934) and Basil Wright's *Song of Ceylon* (1934) – were continued and completed. The latter film, which won first prize at the 1935 Brussels Film Festival, remains one of the most technically and aesthetically accomplished films made by the documentary movement.

Paul Rotha was one of the most important of the young film-makers employed by Grierson. Rotha was rather semi-detached from the movement, coming and going over the period and occasionally at odds with Grierson. In general, Rotha can be characterised as politically to the left of Grierson, and as an individualist who experienced difficulties in working under Grierson's omnipresent tutelage. He was opposed, in particular, to Grierson's encouragement of 'group' film-making, a practice first employed during the editing of *Industrial Britain*. In addition to his work with the documentary movement, Rotha also made a number of films with the commercial documentary film company British Instructional Films, including *The Face of Britain* (1934), inspired by a reading of J. B. Priestley's *English Journey* (1933). His most important film for the documentary movement was *Today We Live* (1937), about the social hardship caused by unemployment in a Welsh mining community. He was also the author of one of the first major English-language books on cinema history, *The Film Till Now* (1930).

One of the aims of the documentary film movement was to influence the production of socially purposive and aesthetically innovative art across a range of artistic fields. To this end relationships were established with many individuals and organisations during the period, and several artists and film-makers, later to become prominent in their own right, worked on films made by the documentary movement. These included the poet, W. H. Auden, the composer Benjamin Britten, the writer J. B. Priestley, and film-makers such as Robert Flaherty, Carl Dreyer and Ernst Meyer. Others associated with the movement during the period included H. G. Wells, Julian Huxley, Graham Greene and the painter/designer László Moholy-Nagy. This attempt to connect with other cultural movements of the period was also fostered by the house journals of the documentary movement: *Cinema Quarterly* (1932–36), *World Film News* (1936–38) and *Documentary Newsletter* (1940–47), all of which regularly featured articles written by those mentioned above.[9]

A number of the movement's best known films emerged from this context of association with artists and intellectuals of the period. *Coal Face* (1935), with music composed by Britten, employs modernist techniques such as non-synchronous sound and montage editing, in conjunction with a critical commentary on harsh working conditions within the mines. *Night Mail*, although conventional in terms of its overall narrative structure, contains the well-known sequence in which the poetry of Auden and the music of Britten accompany close-up montage images of racing train wheels, as the postal express journeys to Edinburgh.

Most of the films made by the documentary movement were collaborative projects, sometimes involving as many as six people, each engaged in several activities. This was a practice strongly encouraged by Grierson because it helped to foster and disseminate production skills. Grierson also placed less importance on the emergence of individual 'auteurs' from the ranks of his film-makers than he did on using them to promote the ideals and aspirations of the movement as a whole.

Perhaps because of this, few important film-makers emerged from within the documentary movement, and few managed to sustain a high level of achievement throughout their careers. Grierson himself directed only one film, *Drifters*, after which he became a producer. Paul Rotha's best work was carried out in the 1930s and 1940s, with *Shipyard* (1935), *The Face of Britain*, *Today We Live*, and *World of Plenty* (1943),

Modernist techniques in conjunction with a critical commentary on harsh working conditions within the mines. Cavalcanti's Coal Face *(1935).*

but he did not produce or direct any important films after the war. Basil Wright's career followed a similar trajectory. His best film is *Song of Ceylon* and he also made a contribution to *Night Mail*. *The Country Comes to Town* (1931) and *The Face of Scotland* (1938) are also interesting, but like Rotha, Wright neither produced nor directed anything of significance after 1946.

Two major film-makers who did emerge from the documentary movement were Alberto Cavalcanti and Humphrey Jennings. Cavalcanti, who was Brazilian, had worked with the French avant-garde of the 1920s, alongside directors such as René Clair and Jean Renoir. He brought much needed technical and aesthetic expertise to the movement, as well as a knowledge of recent developments in the pictorial arts. He was appointed head of the GPO Film Unit in 1936, when Grierson left to form Film Centre, and during the war joined Ealing Studios, where he made *Went the Day Well* (1942), *Champagne Charlie* (1944), *Dead of Night* (1945) and *Nicholas Nickleby* (1947). Along with Harry Watt, Cavalcanti can also be credited with helping to develop the documentary-drama form which had such an influence on the British cinema of the Second World War, and which first appeared in Watt's *North Sea* (1938).

Humphrey Jennings began work with the GPO Film Unit in 1934. During the late 30s he became involved with Mass-Observation, and brought the study of popular culture associated with that organisation to bear on his film-making activities. His *Spare Time* (1939) and *Listen to Britain* (1941) remain impressive, marked by a lyrical humanism and a sensitivity to the ordinary which stands out from the often stereotyped representations of working-class people found in some of the films made by the documentary movement. Indeed, Jennings' ability to portray the working class literally and authentically often put him at odds with Grierson, who preferred more idealistic images of working-class people.[10] Jennings went on to make a number of important films in the 1940s, including *Fires Were Started* (1943) and *A Diary for Timothy* (1945). His career was cut short by a fatal accident in 1950.

The critical reputation of the documentary film movement

Over the decades the reputation of the British documentary film movement has fluctuated considerably in debates on its role in and influence on British cinema and society. Initially, the movement was promoted as a heroic struggle by gifted and principled film-makers against both the banality of the commercial industry and the interference of corporate bureaucrats. The early literature on the movement reflects this position, particularly Paul Rotha's *The Film Till Now* (1930) and *Documentary Diary* (1973). Other works in this tradition include Elizabeth Sussex's *The Rise and Fall of the British Documentary Movement* (1975), James Beveridge's *John Grierson: Film Master* (1986), Harry Watt's *Don't Look at the Camera* (1975), and Forsyth Hardy's *John Grierson: A Documentary Biography* (1979). In two edited collections of essays by Grierson, *Grierson on Documentary* (1946) and *Grierson on the Movies* (1981), Grierson's official biographer, Forsyth Hardy, has also attempted to promote a conception of the movement as principled, socially purposive, and successful.

By the 1970s new traditions of film theory were emerging in Britain, influenced by work in the fields of semiotics and structuralism, and by translations of early Russian and German writings on film – writings which advocated an anti-realist and formalist aesthetic. The new film theory was often critical of Grierson's ideas on documentary naturalism and the need to work within 'the system'. Writing in 1983, Alan Lovell argued that the 'basic thing was to break open the prison of Griersonism', and in 1980 Paul Willemen summed up the prevailing attitude:

Official film culture has enshrined the documentary film movement as the high point of the British cinema.... Consequently, criticism of the documentary movement and of the Griersonian ideology runs the risk of being regarded, not only as heresy, but as an attack on great artists and film-makers.[11]

The criticisms levelled at the documentary movement during the 1970s and early 1980s can be divided into three main categories. The first consists of opinions to the effect that the movement's reputation has obscured the achievements of more progressive film-making traditions in the 1930s. Critics holding these opinions gradually turned their attention away from the documentary movement in an attempt to recover these lost traditions. In *Traditions of Independence*, published in 1980, an attempt was made to reassess the work of radical organisations such as the Workers Film and Photo League, Kino, the Progressive Film Institute and the Workers Film Association; and to consider the achievements of radical film-makers such as Ivor Montagu, Norman McLaren and Ralph Bond.[12]

However, this view that the documentary movement was of less consequence than other, supposedly more valuable documentary traditions in the 1930s is problematic. The films made by the organisations and film-makers mentioned above were seen by far smaller audiences than the films made by the documentary movement. The evidence which we have suggests that they were largely consumed by minority audiences already committed to the political views which the films expressed. The documentary movement's films, on the other hand, were seen by a much more extensive and varied audience, and therefore had the potential to alter opinion across a far greater spectrum.[13] Distinctions made by critics such as Claire Johnstone and Paul Willemen between the documentary movement and leftist documentary organisations during the 1930s are overstated. In fact, there was a great deal of interaction at the time between the movement and leftist film-makers such as Ivor Montagu, Norman McLaren, Ralph Bond and Sydney Cole. These film-makers did not see the documentary movement as the enemy, but on the contrary as an ally, and as a progressive oppositional film practice.[14]

A second major criticism of the documentary movement to emerge during this period was that the reputation and ideology of the movement had been used by a conservative media establishment to reinforce consensualist ideas. Stuart Hood, for example, has argued that Grierson's belief in working within the general sanction helped to institutionalise doctrines of 'balance' and 'due impartiality' in British television, and led to the establishment of a politically toothless current affairs media, unable to carry out critical, investigative work.[15] Whilst there is some justification in this criticism, it also needs to be set against an understanding of the historical context from which the documentary film movement emerged. It is necessary to understand the politics of the movement in relation to the 1930s, rather than to judge those politics from the standpoint of political problems and criteria in the late 1970s and early 1980s.

The third major criticism of the documentary movement to emerge during the 1970s and early 1980s revolved around questions of aesthetics. In 1976, writing in *Screen*, Bill Nichols associated Grierson's ideas with various forms of naturalistic cinéma-vérité film-making.[16] Two years earlier, Andrew Tudor had argued that Grierson's theories were based on an ideology of social persuasion, and had no implications for an aesthetic of film.[17] In a similar vein, Alan Lovell, writing in 1983, argued that Grierson had subordinated aesthetics to social persuasion.[18]

These criticism are largely unfounded. A close study of Grierson's writings reveals that his theory of documentary film did not imply the subordination of aesthetics to social and political instrumentality. Grierson himself makes the point well: 'Most people ... when they think of documentary films think of public reports and social problems.... For me it is something more magical. It is a visual art.'[19]

The documentary movement's reputation suffered further damage in a body of work which emerged from the history and communication departments of some British universities during the late 1970s and early 80s. This work was primarily (though not exclusively) concerned with the exploration of film as a form of historical record rather than as an aesthetic object. Within this tradition the work carried out on the documentary movement was based on the empirical analysis of archival records held at the Public Records Office and elsewhere, rather than on the application of critical theory to the movement. These archival documents, generally written by middle-ranking civil servants and political figures during the 1930s, furnished an account of the movement as a group of well-meaning but politically naive individuals who frequently frustrated the attempts made by enlightened civil servants to create a permanent State film unit. Historians writing in the 1980s, who accepted this version of events because it was inscribed within archival sources of evidence – conventionally regarded as the most 'objective' form of evidence – then began to rewrite the history of the documentary movement, placing lesser emphasis on the achievements of the film-makers and greater emphasis on the role of largely forgotten government officials.[20]

There is some truth in this account of the documentary movement. Grierson, for example, was an extremely dogmatic and obsessive individual who often generated friction with the officials for whom he was supposed to be working. Similarly, the film-makers around Grierson had little experience of how to work within bureaucratic government organisations like the EMB and the GPO, and often incurred official displeasure through their naivety. Nevertheless, there is no real evidence to suggest that, even had Grierson and the film-makers been paragons of civil service propriety, a permanent and influential State documentary film unit would have been established in the 1930s. The historical context remained that of an establishment which was hostile to any substantial amount of reform-oriented film-making taking place within government organisations. Given this overriding context, Grierson's tactics at the time seem justified, and the view that he should have let the civil servants just get on with it seems faintly absurd.

The most recent reconstructions of the documentary movement's reputation have taken a number of different directions. In *Film and Reform* (1990), I have argued that it is of primary importance to understand Grierson's ideology, and to relate the documentary movement to the context of Britain in the inter-war period. I have viewed the movement as progressive in relation to the dominant conservatism of the period, and I have argued that Grierson's ideology was related to a sophisticated and liberal branch of continental idealist philosophy. I have also argued that this relationship to a philosophical tradition of real substance distinguishes Grierson – in a positive sense – from any other figure within British film culture.[21] Some recent commentators, mainly in Canada, have attempted to argue that there was a relationship between Grierson's ideas and various totalitarian philosophies prevalent in Europe during the inter-war period.[22] This is a misconception. Grierson was neither a fascist nor any other sort of totalitarian: he was a democratic corporatist, whose ideas can be related to other corporate, centre-progressive political ideologies of the period.

Finally, what is the legacy of the British documentary movement today? The movement is no longer a focus of debate in the way that it was between 1975 and 1990. Few new publications on the movement have appeared since 1990.[23] With many of the film-makers themselves now dead, the sources of biographical information have been significantly reduced.[24]

Nevertheless, one can still trace the influence of the movement on contemporary film culture in a number of ways. One result of the work done on Grierson and the movement in the late 1980s has been to emphasise the modernist nature of both Grierson's ideas and the films produced within the movement. Grierson's theory of documentary film is now of more interest to film-makers and film theorists. It is a complex theory, informed by several strands of early modernism, as well as by various philosophical positions. With this in mind, the films themselves can be looked at anew. What emerges from such a reappraisal is a realisation that, despite the difficulties which the movement experienced, the films are of considerable aesthetic interest and quality. *Drifters, Song of Ceylon* and *Listen to Britain*, in particular, stand as major achievements of the British cinema.

Notes

1. Paul Addison, *The Road to 1945* (London: Quartet, 1977), p. 29.
2. John Grierson, 'I Derive My Authority From Moses', (Grierson Archive papers, University of Stirling, 1957–72) G7A.9.1. p. 3. Cited in Ian Aitken, *Film and Reform: John Grierson and the British Documentary Film Movement* (London: Routledge, 1990), p. 7.
3. John Grierson, 'Notes for English Producers', Memorandum to the EMB Film Committee (April 1927), PRO BT 64/86 6880, p. 2. Cited in Aitken, *Film and Reform*, pp. 97–9.
4. Ibid., p. 22. Cited in Aitken, *Film and Reform*, p. 98.
5. John Grierson, 'The Challenge of Peace', in Forsyth Hardy (ed.), *Grierson on Documentary* (London: Faber and Faber, 1946), p. 174.
6. John Grierson, 'Preface', in Paul Rotha, Richard Griffith and Sinclair Road, *Documentary Film* (London: Faber and Faber, 1952), p. 2.
7. John Grierson, 'Byron and his Age' (Grierson Archive papers 1898–1927) G1.2.10.p. 9. Cited in Aitken, *Film and Reform*, p. 190.
8. John Grierson, 'The Course of Realism', in Hardy, *Grierson on Documentary*, p. 77.
9. Forsyth Hardy, *John Grierson: A Documentary Biography* (London: Faber and Faber, 1979), p. 84.
10. Aitken, *Film and Reform*, p. 147.
11. Paul Willemen, 'Presentation', in Don Macpherson (ed.), *Traditions of Independence* (London: British Film Institute, 1980).
12. Macpherson (ed.), *Traditions of Independence*.
13. Precise information on the audiences for the documentary films is unobtainable. An EMB Film Committee memorandum of 19 March 1932 suggests an audience of 1.5 million by that date at the Imperial Institute Cinema alone. By October 1932 bookings had been received across the country for 4,380 film screenings. A fairly conservative estimate, based on these figures, would suggest a possible audience of between 10 and 15 million by 1939, although the actual figure could well be higher.
14. Ivor Montagu, *Film World* (Harmondsworth: Penguin, 1964), p. 281.
15. Stuart Hood, 'A Cool Look at the Legend', in Eva Orbanz (ed.), *Journey to a Legend and Back: The British Realistic Film* (Berlin: Edition Volker Spiess, 1977), p. 150.
16. Bill Nichols, 'Documentary Theory and Practice', *Screen*, vol. 17, no. 4 (Winter 1976–7), p. 35.
17. Andrew Tudor, *Theories of Film* (London: Secker and Warburg/British Film Institute, 1974), p. 75.
18. Alan Lovell, 'The Grierson Influence', *Undercut*, no. 9, Summer 1983, p. 17.
19. John Grierson, 'I Remember, I Remember' (Grierson Archive papers 1957–72), G7.17.2. pp. 10–11. Cited in Aitken, *Film and Reform*, p. 11.
20. See, for example, the work of Paul Swann, including his *The British Documentary Film Movement 1926-1946* (Cambridge: Cambridge University Press, 1989).
21. See Ian Aitken, 'Grierson, Idealism and the Inter-War Period', *Historical Journal of Film, Radio and Television*, vol. 9, no. 3, 1989; and Aitken, *Film and Reform*.
22. See, for example, Peter Morris, 'Re-thinking Grierson: The Ideology of John Grierson', in Pierre Verronneau, Michael Dorland and Seth Feldman (eds.), *Dialogue Canadian and Quebec Cinema* (Montreal: Mediatexte, 1987), pp. 25–56.
23. A collection of writings by members of the documentary movement will appear in *The Documentary Film Movement*, Ian Aitken (Edinburgh, Edinburgh University Press, 1998).

24. Brian Winston's *Claiming the Real: The Griersonian Documentary and its Legitimations* (London: British Film Institute, 1995) makes the point – repeatedly – that the documentary movement was not radical enough. It seems odd that this argument should still be thought tenable, following the detailed historical work on the movement carried out in the 1980s. Winston also makes a connection between Grierson's ideas and nineteenth-century French realism, without offering any convincing grounds for such a connection. Grierson was influenced by ideas emanating from the German, not the French, intellectual tradition and made no reference to French nineteenth-century realism in any of his writings or reported conversations.

Bibliogaphy

Aitken, Ian, *Film and Reform: John Grierson and the Documentary Film Movement* (London: Routledge, 1990).

Beveridge, James, *John Grierson: Film Master* (London: Macmillan, 1979).

Hardy, H. Forsyth (ed.), *John Grierson: A Documentary Biography* (London: Faber and Faber, 1979).

Hardy, H. Forsyth (ed.), *Grierson on Documentary* (London: Faber and Faber, 1946).

Hardy, H. Forsyth (ed.), *Grierson on the Movies* (London: Faber and Faber, 1981).

Hillier, Jim and Lovell, Alan, *Studies in Documentary* (London: Secker and Warburg/British Film Institute, 1972).

Jarvie, Ian and Pronay, Nicholas, 'John Grierson A Critical Perspective', *Historical Journal of Film, Radio and Television*, vol. 3, no. 3, 1989.

Macpherson, Don (ed.), *Traditions of Independence* (London: British Film Institute, 1980).

Orbanz, Eva (ed.), *Journey to a Legend and Back: The British Realistic Film* (Berlin: Edition Volker Spiess, 1977).

Rotha, Paul, *The Film Till Now: A Survey of World Cinema* (London: Cape, 1930).

Rotha, Paul, *Documentary Diary: An Informal History of the British Documentary Film, 1928–1939* (London: Secker & Warburg, 1973).

Sussex, Elizabeth, *The Rise and Fall of the British Documentary Movement* (London: University of California Press, 1973).

Swann, Paul, *The British Documentary Film Movement 1926–1946* (Cambridge: Cambridge University Press, 1989).

Watt, Harry, *Don't Look at the Camera* (London: Elek Books, 1974).

Wright, Basil, *The Long View* (London: Secker and Warburg, 1974).

7
The Heart of Britain

Robert Murphy

Patriotism and the Brains Trust, fighting the Nazis and lunchtime concerts were different expressions of the brief period when the English people felt that they were a truly democratic community.[1]

It is easy to look back on the Second World War with a rosy glow of nostalgia, particularly when considering films such as *The Way Ahead*, *In Which We Serve* and *Millions Like Us* which seem to capture that ethos of people pulling together, sacrificing class boundaries in the common effort to defeat the enemy. The good-heartedness and optimism, the striving towards a better society, make it all seem so admirable that it is easy to forget the boredom, the queues, the shortages, the general inconvenience of life under the blackout and the blitz. 35,000 members of the merchant navy, 60,000 civilians and 300,000 servicemen and women lost their lives in the war and if these numbers look insignificant compared to the millions of Russians killed or the millions of Jews massacred in concentration camps, they are still huge enough to leave a deep scar. Most people lost neighbours, friends, family, and bombing brought the war home to everybody except the few who escaped to quiet little hotels in Cornwall and the Lake District. Yet for many people the war was a highpoint of intensity and excitement when things seemed possible which wouldn't normally be possible. And these wartime films are something more than empty propaganda: the characters wrestle with difficult moral and physical problems, and when they win through it is at some cost.

Several of the films deal with the transforming effect of the war, turning timid, ineffectual civilians into warriors and war workers, as if the war were a blessing which enabled people to realise their potential. The protagonists of *Millions Like Us*, *Perfect Strangers*, *The Gentle Sex*, *The Way Ahead*, *The Bells Go Down*, *The Lamp Still Burns*, *English Without Tears* become more confident and capable, more mature and fulfilled, even when they have to endure tragedy and loss. Films like *Ships with Wings*, *We Dive at Dawn* and *The Rake's Progress* have characters who redeem themselves through heroic self-sacrifice. But more typical of the later war films is the stoical, unmelodramatic death of Jacko the newsagent in *Fires Were Started*, holding the ladder steady so that his injured colleague can be saved, or of Tommy in *The Bells Go Down*, sharing a fag with the fire chief who reprimanded him for smoking on the job, before they both plunge to a fiery death.

The war opened up a range of experiences – travel, the use of complex machinery, meetings with people from different regions and backgrounds – which would not have been open to most people in peacetime. The normal patterns of family life were disrupted, but the war made possible a greater range and availability of sexual liaisons. The separation from regular partners, the removal of the restraining influence of parents and neighbours, the opportunities for chance meetings at dances and improvised get-togethers, the cover of the blackout, the feeling of 'live now, for tomorrow we die', worked a profound change in sexual mores.[2]

British wartime films reflect these changes, though, in chaste and diluted forms. Chance meetings lead to romance in *Piccadilly Incident* (an air raid), *In Which We Serve* (a crowded train), *Millions Like Us* (a dance organised for the factory women and the men from the nearby RAF base). But caring, committed relationships, not brief sexual flings, grow out of these meetings. The war effort tends to nudge romance out of its central position in the narrative, and wartime films either under-romanticise their lovers, making them ordinary, decent and not very glamorous, or mark their relationship as passionate but impossible, using the war as a device to hurl them away from one another.

In several films, harmonious, friendly relationships between men and women are stressed. Maggie (Rosamund John) and her exhausted colleagues in *The Gentle Sex* find their already crowded railway carriage invaded by noisy, inquisitive soldiers, but she quickly makes friends with them and berates the sourpuss who complains that they are loud and disruptive. Alison (Sheila Sim), threatened by the 'glueman' in *A Canterbury Tale*, forges solid, non-sexual friendships with her fellow 'pilgrims' Bob and Peter. When romantic relationships do develop they are easily confused with friendship. In *Perfect Strangers*, Robert (Robert Donat) and Cathy (Deborah Kerr), separated by the war and transformed into dynamic, successful people, both think they have found someone more suitable to their new selves. But when they finally meet again and realise that they have both grown and changed, their marriage is redeemed and their new romances downgraded into friendship. In *Waterloo Road*, Tilly (Joy Shelton) is vulnerable to seduction precisely because she thinks smooth-talking Ted Purvis (Stewart Granger) is a sympathetic friend whom she can trust and confide in.

Though the war brings lovers together in films, it is also endangers their happiness: the ever-present threat of death, the separation that leads to misunderstandings and new temptations, the injuries (Gordon Jackson's blindness in *The Captive Heart*, for example) that cast doubt on the viability of a relationship. Here ordinariness is no guarantee against tragedy, as Celia (Patricia Roc) in *Millions Like Us* and Walter Hardy (Bernard Miles) in *In Which We Serve* discover. The possibility of relationships between working-class men and upper middle-class women is explored in *Millions Like Us*, where the antagonism between languid, lazy Jennifer (Anne Crawford) and her dour, pipe-smoking foreman (Eric Portman) flowers into something akin to love; and in *English Without Tears*, where very posh Penelope Dudley Ward is united with her ex-butler (Michael Wilding), whom the war has transformed into an officer and a gentleman. GIs are also shown as acceptable partners for respectable English women in *I Live in Grosvenor Square* and *The Way to the Stars*, but in both cases they are fliers whose planes are shot down, enabling them to die heroic deaths before any cross-cultural complications set in.

British wartime cinema is characterised by realism, but as Sidney Bernstein points out:

> Story films ... are bound to concentrate for their subjects to a large extent on violence and passion, because such is the raw material of drama. Except for isolated attempts to break the rule, as with *Millions Like Us*, films deal with the exceptional

in life rather than the usual. It is the unusual which exercises a strong appeal to the sense of curiosity which is innate in us.[3]

During the war even the most mundane people could find themselves involved in life-endangering adventures, and the exceptional *was* the usual. Films which dealt with such wartime adventures had to pay attention to detail if they were not to offend the credulity of a knowledgeable audience. Realism was an appropriate method for telling the story of the war – though the popularity of films like *Dangerous Moonlight* and *Mrs Miniver*, which present a blatantly romanticised view of the war, showed that audiences were not averse to a degree of glamorisation.

Gainsborough's popular melodramas, with the exception of *Love Story* and the framing story of *The Man in Grey*, ignore the war and were critically disparaged for their escapism. But their star-crossed lovers torn apart by conflicting demands are subject to the same burdens of sacrifice and loss as the protagonists of war films. William Whitebait, film critic of the *New Statesman*, wrote warmly about *Western Approaches*, a flagship of the new documentary realist cinema, before turning to *Madonna of the Seven Moons*, one of Gainsborough's most improbable melodramas, starring Phyllis Calvert as the wife of an Italian banker who periodically changes identity and becomes the gypsy mistress of a Florentine bandit. He complains that 'we slip back almost as far as it is possible to slip. It is notably bad. . . . Everything in *Madonna of the Seven Moons* is treacly: characters, dialogue, situation.'[4] *Madonna* certainly has none of the virtues of *Western Approaches* (meticulous attention to detail, a believable set of characters, an exciting but authentic-seeming story), but despite being a farrago of impossible events it deals with deep and disturbing issues of sexual identity and the expression of seemingly inexpressible desires.

Andrew Higson argues that 'Under the unique circumstances of World War II, the documentary idea came to inform both much commercial film-making practice and the dominant discourses of film criticism.'[5] But this is more true of film criticism than of commercial films: what was 'realist' was assumed mistakenly to be 'documentary'. Realism was not simply transfused from the documentary movement to the commercial industry; it was something which came from greater involvement with the real world by film-makers from both sectors. Humphrey Jennings, writing to his wife from Wales where he was making *The Silent Village*, told her:

> I really never thought to live to see the honest Christian and Communist principles daily acted on as a matter of course by a large number of British – I won't say English – people living together. Not merely honesty, culture, manners, practical socialism, but real life: with passion and tenderness and comradeship and heartiness all combined. . . . On this I feel at least that we have really begun to get close to the men – not just as individuals – but also as a class – with an understanding between us: so they don't feel we are just photographing them as curios or wild animals or 'just for propaganda'.[6]

The movement towards realism was part of a more general feeling that it was right and necessary for the cinema to show people from all walks of life pulling together for the common good. This ethos penetrates such disparate films as *The Bells Go Down* and *Fires Were Started*, *Millions Like Us* and *In Which We Serve*. People felt this way – that differences and difficulties could be overcome – at least some of the time during the Second World War. Undoubtedly there was betrayal, injustice, abuse and exploitation, but people were fighting a cruel and oppressive enemy and they gained knowledge and self-respect in that struggle. If this was truly a 'people's war', then films can be seen to reflect, as much as they helped to create, the mood of populist pulling together.

With the survival of Britain at stake, it became possible to ask fundamental questions. In his BBC 'Postscript' broadcast on 21 July 1940, J. B. Priestley invited his audience to consider whether the concept of private property wasn't now outdated; and George Orwell was convinced that 'We cannot win the war without introducing Socialism, nor establish Socialism without winning the war'.[7] In 1941 Orwell saw this as a winnable struggle: 'Everywhere in England you can see a ding-dong battle ranging to and fro – in Parliament and in the Government, in the factories and the armed forces, in the pubs and the air-raid shelters, in the newspapers and on the radio.'[8] In December 1942 the government published the Beveridge Report, which outlined plans for a comprehensive welfare scheme: children would be financially supported by means of a family allowance; a national health service would be provided; and the unemployed would be eligible for benefits until they could return to work. The report sold 635,000 copies, and a Gallup poll two weeks after its publication reported that nine out of ten people thought its proposals should be carried out. The most popular policy of a new political party, Common Wealth, launched in July 1942, was full and immediate implementation of Beveridge's proposals. Priestley, who had helped to create the party, resigned in the autumn, but Common Wealth won its first by-election victory in April 1943 and continued to harry and embarrass the government until it was swamped by the Labour landslide in July 1945.

Anthony Howard, writing in 1963, thought that:

> 1945 was not merely a political watershed: it had at least the potentiality for being a social one too. The war had not only buried the dinner jacket – it had reduced famous public schools to pale, evacuated shadows, it had destroyed the caste system in the Civil Service, it had eroded practically every traditional social barrier in Britain.[9]

But the new Labour government was saddled with a grossly distorted economy, a huge American debt, and an empire it could no longer afford to police, and social change proved more difficult to sustain than had been hoped. Howard concludes that 'Far from introducing a "social revolution" the overwhelming Labour victory of 1945 brought about the greatest restoration of traditional social values since 1660'.[10] However, his judgment may have been coloured by the impatient desire for political and social change prevalent in the early 1960s, after more than a decade of Conservative government. Fifty years on from the end of the war, the post-war Labour government can be seen to have worked a massive transformation of British society. The post-war desire for tranquillity and affluence may have slowed things down, but there was no return to the rigidly class-divided society of the 30s.

The struggle between traditionalism and radicalism – often ending up as an odd mixture of both – can be seen in the ways film-makers attempted to represent Britain on the screen. As Antonia Lant explains, the way in which British society, character and culture should be portrayed was not something which could be easily agreed upon:

> War produced the need for images of national identity, both on the screen and in the audience's mind, but British national identity was not simply on tap, waiting to be imaged, somehow rooted in British geology. 'National characteristics' could not simply be 'infused into a national cinema', however much later writers wished that

The England of unemployment, misery, deprivation and squalor. John Baxter's Love on the Dole *(1941).*

version of the story to be true. Instead, the stuff of national identity had to be win-nowed and forged from traditional aesthetic and narrative forms, borrowed from the diverse conventions of melodrama, realism, and fantasy, and transplanted from literature, painting, and history, into the cinema.[11]

Film-makers were very aware of these problems. Ian Dalrymple, the producer of *The Lion Has Wings*, a propaganda film rushed out by Alexander Korda in the early months of the war, tried to give some durability to the film by concentrating on abstract virtues: 'I opened our film with the suggestion that there was a British ideology aris-ing from our national character; that it was valuable to the world; and that it should not be lost.'[12] Merle Oberon's final speech – 'We must keep our land, darling. We must keep our freedom. We must fight for what we believe in: truth and beauty and fair play and kindness' – which she declaims to her snoozing husband under an oak tree, now seems risible. But the picture of Britain conjured up by the film's documentary footage is certainly effective.

The new flats, happy people, swimming pools and health centres seen in *The Lion Has Wings* belie our view of the 30s as a depressed and demoralised decade. The evils of unemployment, the Jarrow March, the Means Test, were an important part of the 1930s, but so too were economic growth and rising living standards for those in em-ployment. J. B. Priestley, in his 1933 *English Journey*, discovered three Englands, one of which was something like that depicted in *The Lion Has Wings*:

This is the England of arterial and by-pass roads, of filling stations and factories that look like exhibition buildings, of giant cinemas and dance halls and cafés, bungalows with tiny garages, cocktail bars, Woolworths, motor coaches, wireless, hiking, factory girls looking like actresses, greyhound racing and dirt tracks, swimming pools and everything given away for cigarette coupons.[13]

This England was confined to prosperous pockets of the country, however, and could not properly represent the nation. A national identity which attempted to build upon it would contradict the reality of most people's lives in England, not to mention the rest of the United Kingdom. Priestley's second England was

nineteenth-century England, the industrial England of coal, iron, steel, cotton, wool, railways; of thousands of rows of little houses all alike, sham Gothic churches, square-faced chapels, Town Halls, Mechanics' Institutes, mills, foundries, warehouses, refined watering-places, Pier Pavilions, Family and Commercial Hotels, Literary and Philosophical Societies, back-to-back houses, detached villas with monkey trees, Grill Rooms, railway stations, slag-heaps and 'tips', dock roads, Refreshment Rooms, doss-houses, Unionist or Liberal Clubs, cindery waste ground, mill chimneys, slums, fried-fish shops, public houses with red blinds, bethels in corrugated iron, good-class draper's and confectioners' shops, a cynically devastated countryside, sooty dismal little towns, and still sootier grim fortress-like cities.[14]

This is the England of unemployment, misery, deprivation and squalor, the England depicted in John Baxter's adaptation of *Love on the Dole*, but in precious few other British films. During the war full employment, high wages, factories working to full capacity brought it back to life. But it still seemed grim, the Dark Satanic Mills of Blake's 'Jerusalem', not something to celebrate. Humphrey Jennings' *The Heart of Britain*, which in contrast to most wartime documentaries is set in the industrial north, concludes with a warning: 'Out of the valleys of power and the rivers of industry will come the answer to the German challenge, and the Nazis will learn once and for all that no one with impunity troubles the heart of Britain.' But the film's fiery furnaces and smoking factory chimneys are far outweighed by images of concert halls and cathedrals. If there was an England worth fighting for, it seemed more likely to lie in the countryside – in what was left of England's green and pleasant land.

Priestley had seen rural England in 1933, and had not been impressed:

Old England, the country of the cathedrals and minsters, and manor houses and inns, of Parson and Squire; guide-book and quaint highways and byways England ... we all know this England, which at its best cannot be improved upon in this world. That is as a country to lounge about in; for a tourist who can afford to pay a fairly stiff price for a poorish dinner, an inconvenient bedroom and lukewarm water in a small brass jug.[15]

He concludes that 'It has long since ceased to earn its living.' But the myth of an idyllic rural England was important to both right- and left-wing ideologies. Conservative nostalgia for a stable, hierarchical society where everyone knew their place ('the poor man with his yard of ale, the rich man in his castle', as Tommy Trinder mockingly sings in *Champagne Charlie*) had to be set against an equally powerful left-wing yearning for a time when every man had his acre of land and his pig. William Morris and the Arts and Crafts movement, Robert Blatchford's *Merrie England* (1894) – described by G. D. H Cole as 'the most effective piece of popular socialist propaganda ever written'

– led directly to the Clarion Clubs, the mass trespasses on the moors and mountains of the Peak District, and the innumerable working-class hiking and cycling clubs. One can glimpse this working-class enthusiasm for the countryside in *Love on the Dole*, when Larry asks Sally to come out with him on a Sunday ramble with the Labour Club. Relaxing on a hillside, she is overwhelmed by the beauty of the countryside, declaring, 'Oh, I never knew anywhere could be so lovely. It doesn't seem that this and Hanky Park can be same world.'

There was something for everyone in the countryside. Right- and left-wing versions of the myth were by no means mutually exclusive. Angus Calder draws a composite picture:

> The ideal village – it may be in Sussex or in the Cotswolds, or in Jane Austen's Hampshire – contains a pleasant Anglican vicar, an affable squire, assorted professionals, tradesmen and craftsmen, many of whom will be 'characters', plus a complement of sturdy yeomen and agricultural workers learned in old country lore. It has a green, on which the village team plays cricket, with the squire or his son as captain.[16]

The reality of country life between the wars was very different. The import of grain from North and South America meant that small-scale British farms could only compete in the most fertile areas. Some switched to livestock farming, but not enough to prevent a general agricultural depression between the wars. Farm labourers suffered unemployment just as urban workers did. When they were working, wages were low and picturesque thatched cottages concealed primitive and squalid living conditions. There was very little mechanisation of farming and many rural areas were still without gas and electricity in 1939. Drains, ditches and fences were neglected, water meadows fell into disrepair and disuse, and: 'In almost every part of Britain, there were large tracts of total dereliction, where bracken, gorse and briars had encroached on good grassland, or where fertile soil had been abandoned because it paid no one to cultivate it.'[17]

War transformed the countryside. The dangers to shipping and the need to preserve foreign exchange made it imperative that Britain grow its own food rather than import it. Farmers were encouraged (by a subsidy of £2 per acre) to plough up grassland. War Agricultural Committees ensured that derelict farms were brought back into production, forests were cleared, fenland drained. In 1939 there were 12 million acres of arable land; by 1944 this had increased to 18 million acres. Agricultural workers who were called up were more than replaced by the 80,000-strong Women's Land Army and the 40,000 Italian prisoners-of-war who were set to work on the land. Mechanisation helped too. The number of tractors increased from 56,000 in 1939 to 253,000 by January 1946. According to Angus Calder, 'A degree of modernisation had occurred in six years of war which might have taken decades in peacetime.'[18]

During the war the countryside became less remote, the divide between town and country less sharp. Army camps and RAF bases rapidly spread over what might once have been isolated rural areas. If most soldiers and airmen confined themselves to the local pubs, land girls and evacuees permeated the marrow of rural existence, and no film set in the countryside seems complete without them. In the towns, the blackout reclaimed the night, parks and waste ground were utilised for allotments, vegetables replaced flowers in gardens and pigs and chickens proliferated.

Angus Calder's caustic judgment that 'the more picturesque parts of Britain were inhabited by increasingly demoralised and often remarkably incestuous communities' was unlikely to have been true of many parts of the country in the latter days of the war.[19] But it does strike a chord with David MacDonald's *This England*, released in March 1941. In the present-day village where the film begins, the villagers seem servilely deferential to their squire, and flashbacks to key points in history – 1086, 1588, 1804 and 1918 – are unexpectedly gloomy. In the first episode the villagers murder the Norman lord, in the second a shipwrecked gypsy is hounded to her death, in the third the lord of the manor complains about 'this sticky, clinging, damnable creeper of an English past', and in the fourth the three central characters are too disillusioned to join in the jingoistic celebrations at the end of the First World War. Perhaps, with the threat of invasion imminent, it was impossible in *This England* to articulate a satisfying and convincing rural myth. A group of films made between 1942 and 1944 were much more successful.

In *Went the Day Well?*, directed by the documentary film-maker Alberto Cavalcanti for Ealing Studios, a platoon of soldiers who arrive unexpectedly in a typical English village turn out to be German paratroopers in disguise. The villagers are chirpy and do not seem to have incestuous relations. They appear to have adapted to the war and to the modern world but they are a little too comfortable in the security of their idyllic community. The Home Guard refuses to heed the warning of the church bell which signals that Germans have landed, and are shot down as they cycle along a leafy lane. The postmistress's distress call is ignored by chattering switchboard girls in the next village and she is bayoneted before they bother to answer. Most significantly, no one can bring themselves to believe that their genial squire could be a traitor – except the clergyman's daughter, who finally overcomes her romantic illusions about him, faces up to the truth, and kills him.

Tawny Pipit, directed by the actor Bernard Miles for Filippo del Giudice's company, Two Cities, is about a recuperating airman and his nurse who discover a couple of rare

A resolutely democratic rural community. Tawny Pipit *(Bernard Miles, 1943).*

pipits and mobilise a village community against an array of threats which might prevent the birds from successfully hatching their eggs. It is the sort of film which, if made in the 50s, would have been regarded as a typical Ealing comedy. But in 1943 there is something resolutely democratic in the way the whole community – from crusty colonel to Cockney evacuees – unites to protect the birds.

Like Anthony Asquith's *The Demi-Paradise*, *Tawny Pipit* was made at the height of pro-Russian feeling, when Mrs Churchill spearheaded fund-raising schemes to aid the Russians and elaborate pageants were held in the Albert Hall to celebrate Anglo-Russian friendship. But in contrast to Asquith's film, which uses its Russian hero (Laurence Olivier) as a conduit for celebrating the endearing eccentricities of the English character, *Tawny Pipit* uses the visit of a Russian woman soldier to suggest a new and better alignment of class and sexual relationships. Here, as in *Went the Day Well?*, with its land girls who gamely turn their hand to sniping, this is a countryside mobilised for war.

Even an upper-class country house comedy like *Don't Take It to Heart*, directed by Jeffrey Dell for Two Cities, was not immune to the new spirit. The lord of the manor happily doubles up as tour guide for visitors to his crumbling stately home, and his daughter is a socialist, determined to marry a boy from the village. In the event, the village boy prefers a parlourmaid and she is free to marry a middle-class lawyer. But since he is a radical who drinks with the locals and champions their cause against a *nouveau riche* incomer, this doesn't seem like a betrayal of her principles.

Don't Take It to Heart shows little respect for the countryside either as landscape or as the repository of true values. The villagers are rough and tough enough not to be demoralised but, at least until the lawyer has reclaimed their rights, they are poor and – as they are all part of an extended family called Bucket – probably incestuous. Energy and vitality come from the radical lawyer and the city-educated lady socialist. Powell and Pressburger's *A Canterbury Tale* is much more thoroughly immersed in the mythology of rural England.

A land girl, a GI and an English army sergeant meet in a village ten miles from Canterbury. After the girl is attacked they team up to unmask the local magistrate Thomas Colpeper (Eric Portman) as 'the glueman', a mysterious assailant who throws glue in women's hair. Colpeper is more complex and more sympathetic than the villainous squire of *Went the Day Well?* His motivation is to discourage women from going out at night with soldiers from the local army base, thus leaving them with nothing to do but come to his slide-show lectures on the English landscape and its significance for modern man. Logically weak though the plot is, there is an emotional resonance to the film which stifles rational objection. As Clive Coultass explains:

> The clue lies in an appreciation of the sense of the miraculous that attaches itself to the film. Perhaps only those who are antipathetic to British cinema can fail to recognise the ways in which Powell, in *A Canterbury Tale*, anticipates the surrealism of Italian film-makers like Fellini and Antonioni.... Its romantic, arguably parochial and certainly conservative, vision of the kind of country and society the British had been fighting to preserve from fascism is allied to the disturbing eccentricity and misogyny of a man like Colpeper, defender of the faith against the uncaring materialism represented by the military he has to educate at all costs.[20]

It is Colpeper's misogyny and eccentricity which makes the film so interesting. Is this a right-wing film showing that change is bad, women are trouble and only a return to traditional values can bring happiness? Or is it a left-wing film showing traditionalists as sexually disturbed psychopaths? It certainly confused the critics. Caroline Lejeune of the *Observer* set the tone of lip-pursed disapproval which would characterise much criticism of Powell and Pressburger's films henceforth:

> *A Canterbury Tale* is about a Kentish JP who believes so deeply in the message of his native soil that he pours glue on girls' hair in the blackout lest they distract the local soldiery from his archaeological lectures. That's the theme, and to my mind, nothing will make it a pleasant one. This fellow may be a mystagogue, with the love of England in his blood, but he is also plainly a crackpot of a rather unpleasant type with bees in the bonnet and bluebottles in the belfry. Only a psychiatrist, I imagine, would be deeply interested in his behaviour.[21]

Better reviewers, such as Richard Winnington, were more sympathetic, but the film was not commercially very successful and it was drastically recut for the American market. It was not until the National Film Archive issued a restored print in 1977 that *A Canterbury Tale* began to be seen as a peculiarly powerful and resonant evocation of wartime Britain.

Coultass, contrasting the elegiac nostalgia of Asquith's last war film, *The Way to the Stars*, with *A Canterbury Tale*, comments: 'Powell and Pressburger, in *A Canterbury Tale*, at least understood the potential power of the upheaval in Britain that the war had stimulated, and they tried to absorb it into the common stream of English culture.'[22] It is possible to discern a vision of the future in *A Canterbury Tale*, though it is an unusual one. As Priestley had forecast, his third England – of arterial roads and Woolworths and factory girls looking like actresses – spread out from the prosperous South-east, slowly absorbing the old Victorian England of grimy factories and red-brick terraced houses, which was modernised by continuing prosperity and full employment in the post-war period. Powell and Pressburger never had anything to say about industrial Britain. The only film Powell made which was supposed to be set in this industrial landscape was *Red Ensign*, one of the low-budget films he made for Michael Balcon in the mid-30s. It stars Leslie Banks (the traitorous squire of *Went the Day Well?*) as a progressive ship-builder who arouses the hostility of the workers by his cost-cutting methods. It is a potentially interesting film but has none of the vitality of Powell's other 'B' movies such as *The Love Test* and *Something Always Happens*, which are set among entrepreneurs and new industries, or *The Phantom Light*, which is set in an isolated Welsh lighthouse. Powell was perfectly at home in the urban world, and Pressburger ('I like a startling car, a startling film, a startling woman') was equally attached to the conveniences of modern living. Powell's idea of country life was to get the sleeper from London to Dumfries, spend the day visiting his mother in a shepherd's cottage and have a brisk walk in the fresh air before returning to the metropolis the following night.[23]

A Canterbury Tale's view of the countryside, despite the blacksmith and wheelwright and lyrically beautiful landscapes, is essentially a modern one. Its fusion of magic, mysticism and naive Freudianism (the glue-throwing, the moths eating away the contents of Alison's caravan) reaches beyond realism and simple moralities. And in its ending, where the three pilgrims finally get to Canterbury and are granted miracles which restore them to happiness and fulfilment, it realises that gift bestowed by the war of making the impossible possible.

Notes

1. A. J. P. Taylor, *English History 1914–45* (Harmondsworth: Penguin, 1970), p. 668.
2. See John Costello's impressively comprehensive *Love, Sex and War* (London: Pan, 1985).
3. Sidney Bernstein, *Film and International Relations* (Workers Film Association, 1945), p. 7, quoted in Robert Murphy, *Realism and Tinsel: Cinema and Society in Britain 1939–49* (London: Routledge, 1992), p. 96.
4. Quoted in Murphy, *Realism and Tinsel*, p. 51.
5. Andrew Higson, 'Britain's Outstanding Contribution to the Film: the documentary realist tradition', in Charles Barr (ed.), *All Our Yesterdays* (London: British Film Institute, 1986), p. 72.
6. Mary-Lou Jennings (ed.), *Humphrey Jennings: Film-maker, Painter, Poet* (London: British Film Institute, 1982), p. 33.
7. 'Near where I live is a house with a large garden, that's not being used at all because the owner of it has gone to America. Now according to the property view, this is all right, and we, who haven't gone to America, must fight to protect this absentee owner's property. But on the community view, this is all wrong. There are hundreds of working men not far from here who urgently need ground for allotments so that they can produce a bit more food. Also, we may soon need more houses for billeting. Therefore, I say, that house and garden ought to be used whether the owner, who's gone to America, likes it or not.' J. B. Priestley, BBC Radio 'Postscript', 21 July 1940. Quoted in Angus Calder, *The People's War* (London: Pimlico, 1992), p. 160.
8. George Orwell, *The Collected Essays, Journalism and Letters of George Orwell* (Harmondsworth: Penguin, 1970), vol. 2, 'The Lion and the Unicorn', p. 118.
9. Anthony Howard, 'We Are the Masters Now', in Philip French and Michael Sissons (eds.), *Age of Austerity* (Hodder and Stoughton, 1963, reprinted Oxford University Press, 1986), p. 18.
10. Ibid., p. 19.
11. Antonia Lant, *Blackout: Reinventing Women for Wartime British Cinema* (Princeton, NJ: Princeton University Press, 1991), p. 31. Her reference is to Dilys Powell, *Films Since 1939* (London: Longmans Green, 1947), p. 8.
12. Ian Dalrymple, *Cine Technician*, February/March 1940, p. 10.
13. J. B. Priestley, *English Journey* (Harmondsworth: Penguin, 1979), p. 375.
14. Ibid., p. 373.
15. Ibid., p. 372.
16. Angus Calder, *The Myth of the Blitz* (London: Jonathan Cape, 1991), p. 188.
17. Calder, *The People's War*, p. 485.
18. Ibid., p. 488.
19. Ibid., p. 484.
20. Clive Coultass, *Images for Battle: British Film and the Second World War* (London: Associated University Presses, 1989).
21. *Observer*, 14 May 1944.
22. Coultass, *Images for Battle*, p. 182.
23. Michael Powell, *A Life in Movies* (London: Heinemann, 1986), p. 445.

Bibliography

Aldgate, Anthony and Richards, Jeffrey, *Britain Can Take It: British Cinema in the Second World War* (Edinburgh: Edinburgh University Press, 1994).
Badder, David, 'Powell and Pressburger: The War Years', *Sight and Sound*, Winter 1978.
Calder, Angus, *The People's War* (London: Pimlico, 1992).
Calder, Angus, *The Myth of the Blitz* (London: Jonathan Cape, 1991).
Costello, John, *Love, Sex and War* (London: Pan, 1985).
Coultass, Clive, *Images for Battle: British Film and the Second World War* (London: Associated University Presses, 1989).
Hurd, Geoff (ed.), *National Fictions* (London: British Film Institute, 1984).
Lant, Antonia, *Blackout: Reinventing Women for Wartime British Cinema* (Princeton, NJ: Princeton University Press, 1991).
Murphy, Robert, *Realism and Tinsel: Cinema and Society in Britain 1939–49* (London: Routledge, 1992).
Orwell, George, 'The English People' in vol. 2 and 'The Lion and the Unicorn' in vol. 3 of *The Collected Essays, Journalism and Letters of George Orwell* (Harmondsworth: Penguin, 1970).
Ponting, Clive, *1940 – Myth and Reality* (London: Sphere, 1990).
Powell, Dilys, *Films Since 1939* (London: Longmans Green, 1947).
Richards, Jeffrey, 'Why We Fight: *A Canterbury Tale*' in Anthony Aldgate and Jeffrey Richards (eds.), *Best of British: Cinema and Society 1930–1970* (Oxford: Basil Blackwell, 1983).
Taylor, A. J. P., *English History 1914–45* (Harmondsworth: Penguin, 1970).
Taylor, Philip (ed.), *Britain and the Cinema in the Second World War* (London: Macmillan, 1988).

8
Melodrama and Femininity in World War Two British Cinema

Marcia Landy

Let's give in at least and admit we really are proud of you, you strange, wonderful, incalculable creatures. The world we shape is going to be a better world because you are helping to shape it. Silence, gentlemen, I give you a toast. The gentle sex.'

Leslie Howard, voice-over in *The Gentle Sex*

David Lean's *Brief Encounter* (1945) is one of the best remembered British films of the 1940s. Lean's film is set in everyday surroundings, and the focal point of the film is the disjunction between the protagonist's inner fantasy world and the world of domestic duties. Laura Jesson (Celia Johnson), a respectably married woman with two children, gets a piece of grit in her eye while waiting for a train after her weekly shopping trip to town. Alec Harvey (Trevor Howard), who removes the grit, is a doctor. They meet illicitly until she realises that she has neglected her familial responsibilities. Narrated in flashback by Laura, the film does not hinge on whether the relationship she is describing has ever actually happened. What matters is that life exists apart from her family. The implication is that women cherish a private fantasy life, that their lives are split between the romantic and the banal.

The repetition of Rachmaninoff's second piano concerto reinforces Laura's fantasies, accompanying her narration and prodding her memories. It is the music that arouses her – music accompanies her narration, evokes her memories – but the most disturbing sound in the film is the sound of laughter. Laura and Alec's relationship is linked to their common bond of laughter at a woman who plays the cello in the background while the couple lunch together. And when Laura talks to her husband, she laughs as she seeks to allay her feelings of guilt. Increasingly her laughter begins to border on tears and hysteria as she narrates her story, and it appears that laughter is the tell-tale sign of her inability to bring together her inner and her outer existence. Constrained by her marital and maternal responsibilities, she is forced to live in her mind and to talk to herself.

The film reproduces the plight of the feminine figure seeking a voice, while at the same time silencing her as the text constructs a world of conventional morality in which feminine desire is inhibited and silenced. In its use of memory and recollection, the film suggests that the telling is all: the enactment of the fantasy is superior to its fulfilment. Romance is engendered by deprivation. There is no question that the film portrays the feminine domain as stultifying, if not hostile, but in the final analysis the narration aestheticises the pain, making that pain the basis of pleasure – the pleasure of telling a story that would not be half as engaging if it had a 'happy ending'.

In its indirect allusions to the war, its yoking of realism and fantasy to its feminine protagonist, *Brief Encounter* is symptomatic of how the wartime cinema did not create new concepts of femininity; it enabled old ones to circulate. Melodrama is the medium through which these concepts travel, fused with and animating discourses of familialism, community and nation. However, melodrama is also a medium that exposes the problematic and tenuous nature of social constructions of femininity, and it is through their melodramatic style and forms of narration that the films shed light on conceptions of femininity circulating in the 1940s. My essay examines the value of the uses of various forms of melodrama as the unstable circuit through which social and political codes centring on representations of femininity erupted in the Second World War.

Sue Aspinall writes that 'the realist films of the early 1940s were trying to provide a more faithful reflection of common experiences than British fictional films had hitherto attempted'.[1] What the narratives promulgated and sought to valorise was fidelity to the common cause. Films such as *Millions Like Us, The Gentle Sex* and *2000 Women* are part of a concerted effort to portray contributions of women to the war effort, providing images of women's competence often in situations that parallel men's. While certain subjects still continued to be censored in accordance with pre-war guidelines, there was relaxation in some areas, particularly concerning the portrayal of workers and of women. An examination of the narrative strategies of these films reveals how the texts cannot contain a cohesive affirmative stance apropos of woman. The metaphor of mobility, often invoked as a means for describing the conscription of women and their assumption of new activities outside the home, exceeds its pragmatic uses, signalling conflicting responses to present exigencies.[2]

In speaking of *Millions Like Us* (1943), Frank Launder and Sidney Gilliat said, 'We were very impressed with the fate – if you like to call it that – of the conscripted woman, the mobile woman'.[3] A mixture of documentary footage and fictional narration, the film sets up a series of contrasts between home and work, abundance and scarcity, familial unity and separation, pre-war forms of leisure and relationships and changing wartime patterns of social life. The altering face of British society is conveyed through images of mobility, in the conscription of the women, the scenes of their training as they learn to do work that was formerly the province of men, and the portrayal of growing solidarity among women of different classes and backgrounds.

Millions Like Us alternates between scenes of work and scenes of leisure. The dances, the concerts, the pub scenes, and Fred and Celia's honeymoon trip to Eastgate dramatise accommodation to change within wartime constraints. The unstable parameters of the 'mobile woman' are measured by melodramatic affect, specifically by the incommensurability between desire and gratification. The film portrays romantic entanglements but the relationships serve to underscore the problem of balancing continuity and change. In one relationship, the man dies; in the other, he refuses to commit himself until he knows whether the changes wrought in class relationships by the war are permanent. The question of continuity or change extends to the patterns of women's lives. Is the war merely a temporary disruption, or will wartime experience have an impact on their lives – in the breaking of familial ties, moving out of the home, living collectively with others, and working at non-domestic labour?

The Gentle Sex (Leslie Howard, 1943) also focuses on the conscription, training and acclimatisation of women to a new and demanding way of life. The women form relations with other women and perform vital activities under stress in an efficient manner, though the film cannot resist including romantic entanglements with men. The women's separation from civilian life is handled through scenes of individual parting at the train station filtered through the commentary of Leslie Howard. In its focus on different women, the film breaks down the exclusive preoccupation with one dominant character so typical of pre-war films.

The women are representative of different classes in the same way that the male war films seek to provide a picture of cooperation across class lines. By introducing an older woman who was active during the First World War, the film indicates the historical antecedents of women's involvement in war as well as the sense that this involvement arises under exceptional circumstances. The question raised by this film, as articulated by several of the characters, in ways similar to *Millions Like Us*, concerns change – whether the world after the war will return to its former patterns or whether society will alter its direction, specifically in relation to feminine sexuality and woman's position. While the nature of the desired changes remains ambiguous, there is the implication that the war's promotion of greater equality in sexual and class relationships is of primary concern. This anxious question is one that will appear in many films of the period, though not always as explicitly as in this film and in *Millions Like Us*.

Two Thousand Women (1944), directed by Frank Launder for Gainsborough, explores personal relations among women. The film is set in an internment camp in France. Its female characters are of different ages and occupations – from nuns to nurses to stripteasers – and are portrayed in less stereotypical terms than usual. The women stand up to the enemy, outwit their jailers, and help two British fliers to escape, with a minimum of tears and hysteria. They organise entertainment, too: in a reversal of the usual female impersonation acts of the conventional prison camp drama, the women do male impersonations. They are also mutually supportive in the face of the privations of the internment camp. In the scene in which the arriving women are brought to their rooms and baths are prepared, the film avoids the temptations of voyeurism. The female body is not fetishised. In place of the conventional portrait of a masculine fascination with the vision of the feminine body, the women are seen through each other's eyes. Women's mobilisation is presented as an outgrowth of mutual assistance rather than an externally enforced service. The grapevine, usually presented as evidence of woman's garrulousness, is here presented as a survival strategy, as when the women warn each other of the spy in their midst. The text unsettles any unified sense of woman and by extension any coherent sense of national unity in relation to the role of femininity. The cross-dressing, the mimicry of male prison camp dramas, the suggestion of lesbian relations, all are tell-tale signs of excess that undermine realism's strategies of containment, revealing that in its reliance on the necessity of incorporating woman into the national scenario the film has inevitably introduced spectres of irreconcilable differences in gendered and sexual representation.

The highly stylised, anti-realist melodramas produced during the war by Gainsborough provide a complementary, not antithetical, perspective on woman in the 'realist' melodramas. The success of *The Man in Grey* (Leslie Arliss, 1943) was dependent on the creation of a definitive visual style, developed by the art department of Gainsborough, which 'viewed history as a source of sensual pleasures, as the original novels had done'.[4] The sets and the costumes were not produced with an eye to authenticity. As Sue Harper suggests, 'The affective, spectacular aspects of *mise en scène* are foregrounded, to produce a vision of "history" as a country where only feelings reside, not socio-political conflicts.'[5] Similarly, the costuming, make-up and coiffures of the characters were orchestrated, to enhance the affective elements.

The stars who appeared in these films were equally responsible for the films' popularity. Margaret Lockwood projected an 'image of a woman who was not part of the upper-class establishment. Although she was by no means working-class, she did not possess the kind of poise that comes from knowing one's place in the world and from expecting respect. There was an edge of bravado and insecurity in her personality as she appeared on film.'[6] Not only are women at the centre of these films, but the point of view appears more explicitly feminine. While the resolutions often appear to recuperate female domesticity, disciplining the women who violate social mores, the films are daring in their willingness to explore constraints on women. Unlike the historical films, which claim to re-enact the lives and actions of prominent individuals, the costume dramas are fictional and play loosely with historical contexts, transposing history into romance, The films' remote historical settings allow for greater latitude in dramatising departures from portraits of conventional femininity, portraying conflicts surrounding choice of partners, marriage, motherhood and female companionship. Like the realist dramas, the narratives depend on the existence of a dual discourse which sought to dramatise social changes affecting women while maintaining a continuity with traditional values.

The Man in Grey, the first of the Gainsborough melodramas, featured such Gothic elements as the old manor house with its brooding and cruel lord, the imprisonment of a high-born woman in this forbidding world, the presence of the supernatural in the form of a gypsy, and the animistic uses of nature. The film functions by means of polarisation and splitting. There are two female protagonists: Clarissa (Phyllis Calvert), who is high-born and privileged, and Hesther (Margaret Lockwood), who is poor but ambitious and worldly. Two types of masculinity are also represented: the unscrupulous Lord Rohan (James Mason) and the socially ambiguous but romantic Rokeby (Stewart Granger). Clarissa's world is a feminine world of acceptance and trust, whereas Hesther's world is a phallic one of seduction, aggression.[7] Clarissa is associated with social legitimacy, with marital and familial responsibility. Hesther is an adventuress. Bereft of social status, she attempts to usurp Clarissa's position. The upper-class Rohan prefers lower-class women. Marrying Clarissa because he must have an heir, he sees Hesther complementing his own aristocratic rejection of middle-class morality and sentiment. Their contacts are characterised by passion and physical aggression, leading finally to his beating her to death when he learns she has murdered Clarissa. The film is unrelenting in its portrayal of the component of cruelty inherent in masculine and feminine relationships. A big commercial success, *The Man in Grey* led to a cycle of films with similar ingredients.

Gainsborough's 1944 costume melodrama *Fanny by Gaslight*, directed by Anthony Asquith, is a female initiation drama. Fanny (Phyllis Calvert) is called upon to confront one obstacle after another in her path to self-discovery. As a child she discovers a brothel in the basement of her home and is dispatched to boarding school. On her return as a young woman she sees the man she looks on as her father trampled to death by Lord Manderstoke's horse. Her mother's death follows, and Fanny becomes the archetypal orphan of melodrama until she meets her real father, Clive Seymour (Stuart Lindsell), an MP and cabinet minister. Seymour's wife, Alicia (Margaretta Scott), unaware of Fanny's identity, takes her as a lady's maid and Fanny is initiated into Alicia's world of intrigue. Here Fanny again encounters Lord Manderstoke (James Mason), with whom Alicia is having an affair. When Alicia asks Seymour for a divorce so that she can marry Manderstoke, he refuses. Seymour commits suicide, and again

Fanny loses a father. Fanny thereupon falls in love with her father's solicitor, Harry Somerford (Stewart Granger). His mother and sister (he, too, is fatherless) are adamantly opposed to the marriage, warning him that it will ruin his career. For the sake of his future, Fanny disappears. Harry finds her on the verge of prostitution and takes her to Paris, where they accidentally encounter Manderstoke. Harry is provoked to a duel in which he kills Manderstoke and is himself seriously wounded. His sister arrives to tend Harry, forbidding Fanny to see him, but Fanny triumphs and, with the doctor's urging, dedicates herself to restoring Harry's health.

This film can be read as a straightforward legitimation of middle-class morality and the idealisation of the female as the stabiliser of familial values. The narrative presents female 'promiscuity' as a threat to the family. Fanny is the offspring of her mother's earlier sexual impropriety. The Hopwoods' comfortable Victorian house sits atop a brothel, suggesting the dangerous proximity of brothel to middle-class family. The Seymour family is similarly destroyed by the wife's extramarital affairs. Fanny's cousin, unlike Fanny, is also portrayed as sexually promiscuous. The film is not, however, as straightlaced as these examples of straying female virtue might suggest. Female suffering is traced not to the women's actions but to Manderstoke, the aristocrat. His sensuality, cruelty and indifference to social decorum are a source of fascination for the women he seduces, who are rendered completely helpless by his charms. He offers a striking contrast to the other masculine figures in the film, who are portrayed as vulnerable, if not ineffectual. While he represents the arrogant, lawless and sadistic side of masculine power, he is also attractive, and the women who associate with him are free from conventional constraints. Fanny resists him, preferring the more romantic, pliable and chivalrous Harry. Nonetheless, this film, like *The Man in Grey*, invests sexuality with power and, rather than marginalising it totally, allows it to be seen in attractive as well as destructive terms.

Madonna of the Seven Moons (1944), another Gainsborough melodrama directed by Arthur Crabtree, is a maternal drama, focusing on mother and daughter relations, not on marriage The film is structured around oppositions between past and present, traditional and modern attitudes towards sexuality, action and paralysis, respectability and nonconformity, and repression and sexuality. Competing conceptions of femininity are highlighted through the convention of split identity. In one identity, Phyllis Calvert's Maddalena is the wife of a respectable Italian banker; in her other identity she is Rosanna, the passionate lover of a gypsy thief, Nino (Stewart Granger). The protagonist's self-division is traced to her upbringing in a convent where she was raped by a peasant. She remains there until marriageable age, and the film picks up her story many years later when her daughter, Angela, is an adult. A contrast is set between the constrictions of the mother's life and the daughter's freer attitudes. The mother is excessively religious, her nun-like clothing exemplary of her sexual restraint and repression. Angela tries to bring her mother into her (modern) world, counselling her on clothing, make-up and jewellery. Maddalena suffers a breakdown, faints, and when she awakens assumes the identity of Rosanna. Dressed as a gypsy with peasant blouse and skirt, bracelets and long dangling earrings, like a seductive Carmen, Rosanna re-enacts an earlier disappearance and returns to her lover, Nino.

The daughter assumes an active role in the second part of the film, piecing together clues about her mother's disappearance and putting herself in danger in order to find her. In the vein of maternal melodrama, the mother sacrifices herself for her daughter. The conflict between desire and repression is represented by the final image of Maddalena-Rosanna's corpse with both the cross and the rose resting on her breast. The daughter, who has been closer to the father, is now free to pursue her life

Phyllis Calvert, changed from dutiful wife to passionate lover of gypsy thief Stewart Granger in Madonna of the Seven Moons *(Arthur Crabtree, 1944).*

untroubled by the question of her mother's identity. It has been argued that Angela is representative of a more progressive life-style for women than her mother, but Sue Aspinall finds that the film's 'proposal of a modern "enlightened" sexuality as the solution to the dilemma of the virgin/whore/mother/mistress dichotomy fails to satisfactorily resolve the contradiction. This new sexuality is still romantic marriage, dressed in modern, less class-bound clothes.'[8] Where the film more cogently captures the sense of feminine subjection is in its portrayal of Rosanna's hysterical symptoms. As in many of the woman's films, illness becomes the strategy for expressing antagonism towards or resistance to the physical, psychic and moral constraints on women's lives. In the case of Maddalena, her illness represents one way in which her body manages to elude the control of her husband and family doctor by becoming a text that can be read for its symptoms rather than as an object of erotic contemplation. The male protagonist's inability or unwillingness to interpret, explain or 'cure' these symptoms indicates the limits of control by social institutions of the feminine body.[9]

The transgressive and unstable nature of femininity is central to *The Wicked Lady* (Leslie Arliss, 1945). Margaret Lockwood's Barbara violates all the conventional expectations of women. She plays an adventuress who steals her best friend's fiancé, marries him, tires of him, seeks adventure disguised as a highwayman, has an affair with Jerry Jackson (James Mason), a notorious highwayman, poisons and kills a moralistic servant who has learned her secret, falls in love with another man, Kit (Michael Rennie), and dies at his hands after killing Jackson. Her 'wickedness' consists in her hedonism, her contempt for the law and others' private property, her lack of sentiment, and her flouting of prescribed notions of femininity.

The film is built on the classic melodramatic chain of unfulfilled desire. Caroline

(Patricia Roc) loves Sir Ralph (Griffith Jones), who loves Barbara, who loves Kit. The familiar Gainsborough strategy of polarising and splitting is evident in this film. The narrative makes clear-cut oppositions between Barbara and Caroline, between chaste and passionate femininity. Differences between the women are signalled by their wardrobes and hairdos. For Sue Harper, 'the film signals two sorts of female sexuality by carefully differentiating between the two wedding veils. Roc's has cuddlesome, kittenish "ears", whereas Lockwood's is a mantilla, redolent of passion.'[10] The film also contrasts the men. Ralph is assigned to the category of ineffectual, if not masochistic, masculinity; Jerry Jackson to the category of passionate, witty and unsentimental masculinity; Kit, like Rokeby in *The Man in Grey*, is the feminised masculine fantasy figure of romances, the tender rescuer.

While Barbara is also aligned with masculinity in her apparent lack of sentimentality and conventional notions of loyalty, she maintains an attachment to her dead mother. At first, she recklessly gambles away a brooch that had been her mother's, but then the brooch becomes the pretext for her to take to the highway and reclaim it during a raid. Sue Harper suggests that Barbara is 'identified with the mother – rather than the father – principle'.[11] Her identification with the 'mother principle' expresses itself in her protean behaviour, her disregard for rules, conventions and boundaries as opposed to the maternal virtues of service, sacrifice and commitment to home and family associated with Caroline. Having only the subversive dimensions of the mother principle, Barbara is eliminated from the narrative, rejected by all as the subverter of social stability, upper-class cohesiveness and domestic rectitude.

Competing definitions of femininity are central to *They Were Sisters* (1945), a Gainsborough melodrama in contemporary garb, directed by Arthur Crabtree. This film dramatises the impossible position in which women are placed by the conflict between their own desires and the expectations of others. The narrative apportions facets of femininity among three sisters, two of whom represent extremes while the third is a mediating figure. Charlotte (Dulcie Gray) portrays one face of woman: suggestibility, masochism, the absence of a strong ego: the Victorian middle-class woman who tries to be an angel in the house but becomes the madwoman in the attic. She is the totally abject woman who allows herself to be bullied, abused, humiliated and silenced by Geoffrey (James Mason), her husband, and when she seeks to escape, he cajoles her to remain only to repeat his cruelty. By contrast, Vera (Anne Crawford) is the modern independent woman who scorns conventional relationships. Brian (Barrie Livesey), the man Vera marries, is Geoffrey's opposite, earning her contempt for his pliability and permissiveness. If Charlotte overvalues marriage and overestimates her dependency on family, Vera undervalues and underestimates its importance. She is disciplined to proper familial attitudes through the temporary loss of her lover and her daughter. When she meets a man who is dominating, she settles down to domesticity.

The images of the two women unable to conform to the demands of family life sit uncomfortably with the film's formulaic solutions. But the film does dramatise, especially through Charlotte's situation, the impossible burdens placed on women in family life. The alternatives that the film has to offer – self-discipline, familial responsibility and maternal sacrifice – are in Charlotte's case clearly unworkable. Her husband's humiliation of her before the children, his toying with her sanity, his mockery of her behaviour, his refusal to relinquish her, her alcoholism, and her retreat into herself, all unbalance the tripartite structure of the film and call into question the third sister Lucy's role as successful intermediary between extremes of femininity.

The film's discourse seems to argue for a more enlightened attitude towards marriage. The alternative to the asymmetrical relations of both Charlotte's and Vera's marriages is presented through Lucy (Phyllis Calvert) and her husband William (Peter Murray Hill), but their desexualised relationship, signified by their lack of progeny, does not address the disrupting nature of unfulfilled feminine desire. Lucy's role in particular is illuminating for the ways in which she seeks to ameliorate Charlotte's dilemma, indicative of contemporary 'solutions' to feminine discontents. She enlists the aid of a psychoanalyst to protect Charlotte from Geoffrey; she also fights Geoffrey in court and publicly exposes his cruelty – thus breaking his hold over his eldest daughter, who now recognises his maltreatment of her mother – and she creates a conventional familial environment for the children of her sisters. Thus she enlists the major institutional forces in society to ensure the stability of the family. With the sisters eliminated, one dead and one banished to South Africa, the narrative abandons the schema of tripling and moves into the 'ordinary' world, leaving the one family – Lucy, William and the children.

The doctor is a pivotal figure in melodrama, serving to identify and cure the physical and psychic maladies of femininity. In *Madonna of the Seven Moons* and *They Were Sisters*, his role is understated. In *The Seventh Veil* (1945), he becomes central. Directed by Compton Bennett, the film copied Gainsborough's flamboyant style with an emphasis on extraordinariness, hysteria and exaggeration. Francesca (Ann Todd) is another of melodrama's orphan figures. Adopted by her uncle Nicholas, this unwanted female child is reared to become a great artist, like Nicholas's mother. Nicholas (James Mason), resentful of his mother's rejection, her running off with a lover rather than facing the responsibilities of marital life, displaces his rage onto his niece. In the name of art and excellence, he subjects her to his discipline until she is able to become a successful concert pianist. As in a fairy tale, an ugly duckling turns into a swan, wins acclaim, and chooses her Prince Charming among three suitors. Her attempted drowning becomes the means to her rebirth, for with the help of the magical figure of the psychoanalyst she is brought to a new definition of herself and of Nicholas. The film is replete with father figures – Nicholas, Francesca's suitors, and the psychoanalyst, all competing for Francesca. Maternal figures are absent except as they appear as surrogate figures in Francesca's childhood in the guise of her disciplinary schoolmistress and in allusions to Nicholas's mother.

The film problematises the relationship of femininity to language. Nicholas gives Francesca speech and direction, assumes her voice, and even harnesses her musical expression. Her refusal to speak and play after her accident and her separation from Nicholas portrays her as bereft of both verbal and non-verbal language in the absence of the masculine figure. When she seeks to express herself, she can only speak through the symptoms of her illness. Francesca is presented as the object of male doctors' scrutiny, exposed as helpless before their inquisition, but the doctors' omnipotent position is disrupted by her gaze at them, undermining the naturalness of her subordinate position. As intermediary, the psychoanalyst provides her with language and hence is instrumental in restoring her to Nicholas. Her choice of Nicholas does not, however, constitute a 'happy ending'. Rather it underscores the impossibility of other alternatives, since they would position her outside language and hence outside society.

The genre of the 'woman's film' features rebellious representations of femininity, foregrounding women who do not conform to models of supportive maternal or conjugal behaviour. They are at war with men and with domesticity, guilty of harbouring secret desires and of seeking to gratify their longings. While marriage and family life may be presented in *They Were Sisters* as woman's domain and as the guarantor of tradition and stability, many of the films, especially those produced in the postwar period, also reveal the constraints of domesticity. The home is a prison which head-strong women seek to subvert or escape. The popularity of domestic melodrama during this period is not surprising, given the emphasis on the privatisation of family life which came with rising incomes, changes in housing conditions, and increasing social mobility. According to John Stevenson, 'these tendencies reinforced ideals of domesticity and private life which, ultimately, frustrated the fuller emancipation of women'.[12] The melodramas portray the greater drive towards reinforcing personal relations within the family, but they also dramatise social forces that undermine the realisation of these ideals.

The mid and late 1940s provide striking instances of the transformation of the woman's film into film noir. *Bedelia* (1946), written by Vera Caspary, who also wrote the novel *Laura*, and directed by Lance Comfort, is a portrait of the *femme fatale*, the fascinating and dangerous disrupter of domestic harmony. The film stars Margaret Lockwood, who was breaking box-office records in the mid-1940s. *Bedelia* opens with a familiar film noir strategy: the image of a painting of a woman and a man's voice describing Bedelia as the film moves into a flashback. The voice says: 'This was Bedelia, beautiful and scheming. She radiated a curious innocence, eager to fascinate those she attracted like a poisonous flower.' The speaker is a detective intent on discovering Bedelia's whereabouts and her identity, and bringing her to justice.

The narrative portrays Bedelia as rising in the world by marrying men, poisoning them, and getting their insurance money. As she puts poison in the men's food, she uses the traditional woman's vehicle of nurture to wreak her revenge on men. The film begins in France in an urban setting, but ends in an English village where Bedelia

Margaret Lockwood as a fascinating and dangerous disrupter of domestic harmony. Bedelia *(Lance Comfort, 1946).*

comes to live with her latest husband, Charley (Ian Hunter). Transplanted to the English pastoral environment, she is represented as the proverbial snake in the paradisiac garden. She resents her husband's association with Ellen, a professional woman, but masquerades as the perfect wife – a good cook, gracious at parties, eager to help her husband – and provides no clue to her malevolent intentions. Pursued by the detective, posing as a painter, she is thwarted in her scheme to poison Charley; instead Charley forces her to take the poison intended for him.

On the one hand, the film can be read as a parable of housewifery run amuck. On the other, it can be read as an inevitable outgrowth of feminine resistance to domestication. In many ways, Bedelia's character seems to represent a reaction to conventional portraits of cultural expectations of femininity. For example, she resents being photographed and painted, which on the level of the narrative indicates her attempts to escape detection, but on a more culturally profound level signifies woman's resistance to being scrutinised and exposed. She admonishes Charley, 'Haven't you something better? You have me.' If Bedelia is 'a love story gone bad', it dramatises the 'impossible position of women in relation to desire in a patriarchal society'.[13] Reviewers objected to Lockwood's portrayal of the *femme fatale*, lamenting her lack of extreme villainy.[14] But Bedelia's ordinariness makes her 'sordid' domestic schemes typical rather than exceptional.

The 1940s preoccupation with the 'gentle sex' reveals a fusion of femininity with the national interest. In their narratives and styles, the films make visible the constructed nature of femininity, exposing it as multivalent, always circulating but subject to variation and permutation, sameness and difference. Femininity as a fabrication of mobility – rather than the idealised 'mobile woman' of wartime rhetoric – can be seen through the melodramas in the partial and contradictory subject positions the films assign to woman. Whether the films utilise realist or escapist scenarios, adopt accommodating or disciplinary strategies, the excess generated by the various figurations of woman reveal a continuing crisis – not a rupture – in representations of femininity.

Notes

1. Sue Aspinall, 'Women, Realism and Reality', in James Curran and Vincent Porter (eds.), *British Cinema History* (London: Weidenfeld and Nicolson, 1983), p. 280.
2. See Dana Polan, *Power and Paranoia: History, Narrative and the American Cinema, 1940–1950* (New York: Columbia University Press, 1986), p. 9.
3. Geoff Brown, *Launder and Gilliat* (London: British Film Institute, 1977), p. 108.
4. Sue Harper, 'Historical Pleasures: Gainsborough Melodrama', in Christine Gledhill (ed.), *Home is Where the Heart is: Studies in Melodrama and the Woman's Film* (London: British Film Institute, 1987), p. 178.
5. Ibid., p. 179.
6. Aspinall, 'Women, Realism, and Reality', p. 276.
7. Sue Aspinall, 'Sexuality in Costume Melodrama', in Sue Aspinall and Robert Murphy (eds.), *Gainsborough Melodrama* (London: British Film Institute, 1983), p. 33.
8. Ibid., p. 36.
9. Mary Ann Doane, *The Desire to Desire: The Woman's Film of the 1940s* (London: Macmillan, 1987), pp. 62–4.
10. Harper, 'Historical Pleasures', p. 184.
11. Ibid.
12. John Stevenson, *British Society, 1914–1945* (Harmondsworth: Penguin, 1984), p. 467.
13. Doane, *The Desire to Desire*, p. 122.
14. See *Time and Tide* review reprinted in Aspinall and Murphy, *Gainsborough Melodrama*, p. 77.

Bibliography

Aldgate, Anthony and Richards, Jeffrey, *Britain Can Take It: British Cinema in the Second World War* (Edinburgh: Edinburgh University Press, 1994).

Aspinall, Sue, 'Women, Realism and Reality', in Curran, James and Porter, Vincent (eds.), *British Cinema History* (London: Weidenfeld and Nicolson, 1983).

Aspinall, Sue and Murphy, Robert (eds.), *Gainsborough Melodrama* (London: British Film Institute, 1983).

Harper, Sue, *Picturing the Past: The Rise and Fall of the British Costume Film* (London: British Film Institute, 1994).

Higson, Andrew, *Waving the Flag: Constructing a National Identity in Britain* (Oxford: Clarendon Press, 1993).

Hurd, Geoff, *National Fictions: World War Two in British Films and Television* (London: British Film Institute, 1984).

Landy, Marcia, *British Genres, Cinema and Society, 1930–1960* (Princeton, NJ: Princeton University Press, 1991).

Lant, Antonia, *Blackout: Reinventing Women for British Wartime Cinema* (Princeton, NJ: Princeton University Press, 1991).

Murphy, Robert, *Realism and Tinsel, Cinema and Society 1939–1949* (London: Routledge, 1989).

This essay reworks material which first appeared in Marcia Landy's *British Genres*, Princeton University Press, 1991.

9
Some Lines of Inquiry into Post-war British Crimes

Raymond Durgnat

This survey of British Crime Films from 1945 to 1949 derives from a work in progress on British cinema in the Age of Austerity. The subheadings indicate, not *pigeonholes,* inside which the films mentioned would belong, but *ad hoc* groupings around selected themes. No genre *requires* or *imposes* stereotypes. No genre has unique themes, attitudes, moods, styles, or narrative structures, most of which are shared by many genres. Genres freely crossbreed, and generate hybrids and unclassifiables.

1. The crime genre(s) – and crimes in other genres
If the Crime Film is a genre (rather than a set of genres), it's difficult to define, for crimes abound in films of all genres. *The Wicked Lady* (Leslie Arliss, 1945) would qualify as a crime story, in so far as James Mason and Margaret Lockwood are highwaypersons, yet it's usually grouped with romantic/costume melodramas. *Carnival* (Stanley Haynes, 1946) climaxes with a *crime passionel*, as Bible-black farmer Bernard Miles shoots his wife, music-hall ballerina Sally Gray, for loving aristocratic sculptor Michael Wilding, but the film's major interests make it mainly a romantic melodrama. In *Kind Hearts and Coronets* (Robert Hamer, 1949), Dennis Price kills a whole family tree of Alec Guinnesses, but the film is conventionally thought of as an Ealing comedy. In *The Winslow Boy* (Anthony Asquith, 1948), a very young naval cadet's alleged theft of a 5-shilling postal order precipitates an elaborate courtroom struggle. It certainly revolves around the minutiae of a crime (which wasn't), but its main theme is not 'crime' but 'the law', and conflicts between 'Establishment' and 'private' attitudes. Rather less tangential is *For Them That Trespass* (Alberto Cavalcanti, 1949). Middle-class writer Stephen Murray is fascinated by a low-class girl, but finds her murdered, and to preserve his own respectability withholds vital evidence, thus sending lower-class Richard Todd to jail for fifteen years. Todd breaks out, hears Murray's 'fictional' radio play, recognises the case, and comes after him, to get the wrong righted. This *is*, I think, a Crime Film – even though crime does *not* subordinate its *other* interests, notably class injustice. As often, in films of our period, the upper classes wrong the lower (though the detail and reasons are beyond our scope here).

2. Criminals, lumpen, Ordinary People, populism

There's a large grey area, or rather overlap, between the Crime Film and the 'Ordinary People' genre. In *Waterloo Road* (Sidney Gilliat, 1945), John Mills, respectable lower-class, finds himself in a sort of 'deserters' network', and as he squares up to spiv Stewart Granger, Alastair Sim, the local GP (i.e. middle-middle-class), looks on, keenly and benignly. *It Always Rains on Sunday* (Robert Hamer, 1947) strikes some critics as an 'Ordinary People' film, a sort of East End cross-section. Others see it rather as a 'low life' film, and indeed most of its characters are criminals, or accomplices, or police-men. On the Ordinary People side, its love story can evoke *Brief Encounter*, for sharing the everyday anguish of an ordinary middle-aged housewife, while trains shriek by. On the other hand, John McCallum is a violent convict, on the run, and Googie Withers, by helping him, becomes a criminal too.

London Belongs to Me (Sidney Gilliat, 1948) is another genre 'amphibian'. It's a tale of the shabby pseudo-genteel (a very low middle class), in a drab boarding house, who falteringly and loosely get together to protest on behalf of a mucky-handed mechanic (Richard Attenborough), who has turned luckless spiv and bungled himself into a death sentence. Their demo is 'too little and too late', the sentence having been commuted anyway, but in the process barriers between the stiffly respectable, the common and the criminal classes crumble.

3. Traditional British miserabilism, and other feel-bad factors

The heavy weight, in post-war British movies, of guilt and gloom, and broodings about crime, is very surprising for a victorious nation busily constructing a kindly Welfare State. I'd diagnose not *one* reason, but a 'pluri-causal convergence' of factors, some long-term (like puritan pessimism and sobriety, some short-term, like war-weariness, widespread bereavement, and middle-class fears of Labourist egalit-arianism). Whereas Hollywood noir between 1945 and 1949 is driven by an optimism/cynicism split, the British mood owes more to a more gradual, uneasy shift of the balance between older, more traditional suspicions about human nature and more modern, lenient attitudes, spreading fastest among the middle classes, some of whom regarded Victorian harshness as a main cause of evil.

4. Middle-class noir. I: incomes and inheritances

Since the Great War (1914–1918), the upper-middle classes have experienced, or feared, a certain decline and fall. The Great War escalated their taxes. Slump and Depression decimated their dividends. The Second World War saw Britain bankrupt by 1941 (though US aid averted disaster). Now Austerity and Labourism threaten to finish them off. Death duties, which ravage inheritances, crucial to many middle-class people (especially women), are a very sore point. Two films ingeniously combine 'inheritance' themes with 'social rise' themes, thus appealing to spectators in *both* the threatened upper *and* the rising lower classes. In both *Jassy* (Bernard Knowles, 1947) and *Blanche Fury* (Marc Allégret, 1948), Jassy (Margaret Lockwood) and Blanche (Valerie Hobson) are female servants, with whose social ambitions we can sympathise and whose hard-ness of heart we can understand. Both marry into the gentry (brutal Basil Sydney, vulnerable Michael Gough) for security, wealth and property, but love another. Both, after being involved in one or two murders, *convey* this 'patrimony' to a more 'demo-cratic' character (Jassy to tenant farmer Dermot Walsh; Blanche to her son by co-employee Stewart Granger). Both films feature those *property-less* nomads, gypsies.

Whereas gypsy Jassy is 'rising lumpen', Blanche seems 'sunken middle-class'. Granger, Blanche's lover, is both a 'have' and a 'have not'. (1) As manager of this property, evicting gypsy lumpen, he's a 'have'. But (2) as *merely* its manager, whose duties often evoke manual labour, he's a 'have not'. He evicts the gypsies, not through 'middle-class' loyalty to its legal owners, the Fury family, but because he schemes to get hold of it. So he's (3a) *seemingly* servile middle-class, but actually (3b) graspingly ambitious middle-class. But he's *also* (4) a bastardised relative of its owners, i.e. 'sunken upper-class'. Whence his obsessive, bitter fury (!) at what he considers his *expropriation* into servility. So he can stand as metaphor for (5) a *proletarian resentment*. He's an omnibus, or portmanteau, of class furies, in all directions, and can attract diverse identifications from diverse spectators. Probably the *principal* tension is his 'have not' animus against the property-owners. It drives him to murder Blanche's husband, and father-in-law, and he'd kill the last heir, the little girl to whom Blanche was governess. After he's hanged, she dies giving birth to their child, who will inherit the stately home. All this evokes, in personal drama, some bitterness and sufferings in British social history – the passing of power to *lower-class democracy*. It's a positive end, though hardly a happy one, with the hero/villain hanged and the heroine dead! But most 1940s spectators well understand that movies are *not* moral instruction manuals to prove that sins are punished, that unhappy ends don't flow from sins whose avoidance would have brought a happy end, and that unhappiness can hit us as arbitrarily as a German bomb, or illness, or fatal complications in childbirth.

5. Middle-class noir. II: The Portman murders

Up to 1945, Eric Portman played a nice diversity of roles. In *Millions Like Us* (Frank Launder, Sidney Gilliat, 1943) he's a factory foreman, and his intellectual forehead, hooded eyes – now cloudy, now gleaming – and tight yet sensual mouth suggest Ordinary People thoughtfulness, J. B. Priestley-style. In *Great Day* (Lance Comfort, 1945) he's a demoralised country gentleman, whose moment of shame is stealing, while drunk, a 10-shilling note from a working-class woman (Kathleen Harrison). (Here's another upper-class 'trespass' against the lower …) From then on he's a one-man crime wave. In *Wanted for Murder* (Lawrence Huntington, 1945), he's the Hyde Park strangler, and attributes his murderous drives to his hangman forefather (hereditary tendencies? or morbid imagination? or both?). In *Daybreak* (Compton Bennett, 1948), Portman *is* the public hangman, and ingeniously frames, for his own murder, the bargee (Maxwell Reed) who seduces his wife (Ann Todd). But face to face in the condemned cell he can't hang him, and confesses (reprieved by censor?). In *Dear Murderer* (Arthur Crabtree, 1947) Portman kills Maxwell Reed again, for loving his wife again, though this time she's Greta Gynt.

These murders evoke *crimes passionnels*, in evolving sexual jealousy, but they smack even more strongly of offended vanity (egomania), or cold pathology, which are hardly 'passionate', in the usual sense of loving attachment to an individual. The films play on such confusions. Moreover, the Portman–Reed 'duos' upfront class tensions. Portman is middle-class: suave, supercilious, secretive, rational, deadly jealous. Reed is a hunk-cum-barrow-boy, virile, shifty, physically aggressive. *The Mark of Cain* (Brian Desmond Hurst, 1947) is different again. Portman's stifled, homicidal hatreds are 'all in the (upper-class) family'. To win Sally Gray, he poisons his manly brother (Guy Rolfe), and this time frames *her*, inadvertently, but gets sussed out by another virile admirer (Dermot Walsh). In *Corridor of Mirrors* (Terence Young, 1947) he's a rich mystical aesthete who thinks he murdered Welsh beauty Edana Romney in their previous incarnations. In effect, he frames, and then hangs, himself. But he's also goaded by his possessive housekeeper (and malignant mother-figure?) Barbara Mullen.

6. Middle-class noir. III: The Gentle Sex

Most ladies who murder prefer to quietly poison. In *Pink String and Sealing Wax* (Robert Hamer, 1945) Googie Withers is a battle-axe barmaid resolved to eliminate her husband. She coaxes poisons from a shy and innocent pharmacist's assistant (Gordon Jackson), whose religious fanatic father (Mervyn Johns) rules him with a rod of iron. In *Madeleine* (David Lean, 1950) Ann Todd is a Scottish banker's daughter resolved to preserve her respectability by poisoning her penniless French seducer when he threatens scandal. In *So Evil, My Love* (Lewis Allen, 1948) Ann Todd (again) is a missionary's widow who is seduced by immoral artist Ray Milland, with whom she schemes a convoluted path through old friendships, blackmailings and poisonings. Here, not just sexual love but *all* social relations, and religion, and art, become hypocritical, insidious, abusable. In *Bedelia* (Lance Comfort, 1946) Margaret Lockwood is a Riviera socialite who poisons her three husbands. In *The Wicked Lady*, as a Cavalier socialite, she poisons an oppressively puritanical old servant (Felix Aylmer) who cramps her hedonistic style. Her upper-class 'trespass' against a lower class is repaid, to another Margaret Lockwood, in *Jassy*, where her devoted mute maidservant (Esma Cannon), thinking to help her mistress, poisons brutal Basil Sydney, inadvertently framing her. In *This Was a Woman* (Tim Whelan, 1948) Sonia Dresdel humiliates and then poisons her husband, in order to get a richer one, and ravages her daughter's life, until her son the brain surgeon, whom she idolises, turns against her. If Dresdel is a bourgeois matriarch, Siobhan McKenna in *Daughter of Darkness* (Lance Comfort, 1948) is an outcast. A nymphomaniac Irish girl witch-hunted by the village wives, she's inclined to despatch her lovers during, or just after, her sexual excitations.

Where Portman seems coldly rational but seethes with mad emotion, these lady poisoners are more socio-materialistic, and in that sense rational-realistic. Money, or respectability, looms quite large in their motivations. Lockwood as the wicked lady wants to eat her cake *and* have it (by enjoying social status *and* untrammelled independence *and* her bit of rough). But not all the women are calculating. Esma Cannon's motive is platonic gratitude to her kindly mistress, and Sonia Dresdel is vulnerable through her successful son (though perhaps that's more 'Oedipal' than platonic). The missionary's widow's suicide in *So Evil My Love* suggests that her poisonings were for love of the artist, but then again, perhaps they're a case of *folie à deux*.

In these films woman's sexuality isn't generally the problem and where it is, in *Daughter of Darkness*, it is a *twisted* sexuality as distinct from normal and generally accepted female desire. The woman here is a switch on the (normally male) sex-murderers who proliferate in plays and films in our period: Portman repeatedly, and two charming lady-killers – Richard Greene in *Now Barabbas Was a Robber* (Gordon Parry, 1949) and Dennis Price in *Holiday Camp* (Ken Annakin, 1947), both possibly inspired by the Neville Heath case (1946).

7. Close pent-up guilts

On screen at least, the respectable middle classes commit more than their fair share of murders. In *The October Man* (Roy Baker, 1948), chemical engineer John Mills, to clear himself of a murder charge, must overcome his shyness, guilt, self-doubt, self-restraint, and low assertiveness – conventionally, middle-class traits. The film attributes much of this 'characterology' to a work accident and brain injury inducing amnesia, but the man's style and symptoms evoke the meekly worried middle-class character type. A similar weakness of spirit pervades three other English heroes. In *Take My Life* (Ronald Neame, 1947) another murder suspect (Hugh Williams) panics and runs for it, but is saved by the spunky detective work of his clever diva wife (Greta Gynt). In *The Small Voice* (Fergus McDonnell, 1948) Valerie Hobson tartly criticises the self-indulgent depression of her writer husband James Donald, and braces him to outwit (with her help) the escaped convicts who hold them hostage. Richard Todd in *Interrupted Journey* (Daniel Birt, 1949) is unfaithful to his wife (Valerie Hobson), thus getting drawn into a vortex of crime; it's only a dream, but the 'nightmare' is still *in his soul*. These inadequate protagonists anticipate a kind of 'anti-hero', or V.O.P. (Very Ordinary Person), much rarer in Hollywood. Maybe traditional English modesty and pessimism help audiences in Britain understand, and identify with, guilty weakness and failures rather better than American audiences do.

In *The Upturned Glass* (Lawrence Huntington, 1947) bitchy gossip Pamela Kellino is indirectly responsible for the death of the wife of brain-surgeon James Mason. He plans to kill her, and, backing away from him, she dies accidentally. Then he finds himself having to jeopardise his alibi to save an injured boy.[1] In *Obsession* (Edward Dmytryk, 1949), smooth Harley Street doctor Robert Newton outdoes Eric Portman in cool nasty crime. Each day he brings a hot-water bottle filled with acid into a blitzed house and pours it into an old bath beside which he has chained his wife's lover. *Although* it's a *crime passionel* he's so cruel, cold and gloating that, far from getting any sympathy from us, he's a powerful argument for capital punishment. On the other hand, hospital nurse Megs Jenkins in *Green for Danger* (Sidney Gilliat, 1946) actually does murder several patients and staff. She too uses a sneaky method (switching operating-theatre gasses), and has a deplorably trivial motive: to conceal from nasty neighbours that a relative of hers is a 'Lord Haw-Haw'. Yet Megs Jenkins is so poignant, with her plump motherly figure, high-pitched voice and generally distressed frailty, that we can't but sympathise with her fearful conformity, and the clinging to respectability that links her with Ann Todd in *Madeleine* and *So Evil My Love*, and Dennis Price in *Kind Hearts and Coronets*. On a lower level of the medical classes fairground quack Douglass Montgomery in *Forbidden* (George King, 1947) starts slow-poisoning his wife (Patricia Burke), and, just as he remorsefully desists, a chapter of accidents incriminates him.

Martha Wolfenstein and Nathan Leites point out that most Hollywood murders involve quick, brutal, impersonal methods, whereas British murderers have subtler ways of making you croak, like anaesthetic or gasfire poisoning, and a pseudo-reasonable approach.[2] Most such films involve us so closely with their murderers as to induce an involuntary identification with them, often coupled with a certain sympathy for their motives and an antipathy towards their victims. These stories acknowledge the hostilities pervading ordinary relations, and remind us how easily civilised and coldly barbaric attitudes may intertwine. They're more pessimistic (but also more sensitive) than Hollywood noir, with its relatively simple, sharp, good/bad distinctions. In *The Shop at Sly Corner* (George King, 1946), Kenneth Griffith as a sneaky and spiteful shop assistant threatens to blackmail his boss, Oscar Homolka, a foreign antiques dealer (and fence) unless he is given the hand of his musician daughter (Muriel Pavlow). Whereupon Homolka murders him (and so would I).

From one angle, this ready intimacy with criminals may de-demonise the criminal, apprise the 'honest' spectator of his own guilts, and even plead against capital punishment. But back in 1945 many spectators would react more traditionally, on lines like this. 'The more "naturally human" the act of murder is, the more strongly society must assert its disapproval and impose awesome deterrents, even if the dividing lines get tragically arbitrary'. Such crime films accommodate audience ambivalence about the slowly tilting balance, from Victorian severities to modern leniencies.

8. Whodunits

Whodunits are relatively rare among 'A' features, but among cheaper films they abound. Three star lady detectives. In *Penny and the Pownall Case* (Slim Hand, 1948) Peggy Evans is a model-cum-amateur sleuth who exposes her boss Christopher Lee as complicit with Fascists. In *Celia* (Francis Searle, 1949) Hy Hazell is a 'resting' actress who turns 'tec, 'plays' charwoman, and saves a wife from a homicidal husband. *My Sister and I* (Harold Huth, 1948) rather fumbles an intriguing idea. Set designer Sally Ann Howes finds herself uncovering a murderer, and a very closely pent-up guilt – incest – in the family of a patron of the arts (Martita Hunt).

The liveliest 'tec 'B' films, unlike films noirs, prefer brightly normal settings. There's a fashion salon in *Death in High Heels* (Lionel Tomlinson, 1947), the one London nude show sanctioned as respectable in *Murder at the Windmill* (Val Guest, 1949), and a BBC radio quiz in *The Twenty Questions Murder Mystery* (Paul Stein, 1950).[3]

9. Ladies in distress

Uncle Silas (Charles Frank, 1947) is a floridly Gothic piece, with rather beautiful (and expensive) decor. But, alas, its drama is limited to switches between sweetness and threats from the Victorian heroine's guardians (Derrick de Marney, Katina Paxinou), so it's a box-office flop. *Madness of the Heart* (Charles Bennett, 1949) bombs for the opposite reason: melodramatic overload. Margaret Lockwood hesitates between the convent life and marriage to a rich Frenchman, shrinks from his viciously snooty family, loses but then regains her sight, then feigns blindness to entrap her murderous rival (Kathleen Byron of *Black Narcissus*, on the rampage again). Between these two extremes, *A Man About the House* (Leslie Arliss, 1947) gets the mixture right (between domestic drama/suspense, melo/pathos). Spinsters Dulcie Gray and Margaret Johnston move into their Italian dream villa but slowly wonder if they're not at risk from their very obliging, very handsome major-domo (Kieron Moore). It's another master/servant plot, like *Jassy* and *Blanche Fury*, but with gender reversals and a softer touch.[4]

10. Thrillers: two-fisted/thick-ear/hard-boiled/tough/noir

By 1945 two-fisted English gentlemen like Bulldog Drummond seem a touch passé. This may be less to do with Britain's shaken self-image – appeasement having associated the toff class with weakness – and the English gentleman's socio-economic decline and fall, than with Yank private eyes having muscled in on the 'private justice' racket.

Nonetheless, the thrillers which most widely popularise American noir in France come from two British authors, specialists in faking pseudo-Yank tough thrillers. Peter Cheyney and James Hadley Chase start to churn them out in 1936. In 1948 two hit the screen, with a faint plop. In *Uneasy Terms* (Vernon Sewell, 1948) gumshoe Slim Callaghan (Michael Rennie) recces the murky intrigues of a Colonel's stepfamily (a soupçon of *The Big Sleep*?). In *No Orchids for Miss Blandish* American gangsters kidnap an heiress, dope her and rape her silly. But in the film (St John L. Clowes, 1948) she's saved from such a fate by romantically respectful gangster Jack La Rue, a good-bad guy (made even more sympathetic by a domineering mother). As the police burst in to rescue her, she realises they've killed him and joins him in death. Miss Blandish's rejection of rich respectable boredom for the sex-and-violence life means she's a soul-sister of two Gainsborough girls: Phyllis Calvert as schizo-mum in *Madonna of the Seven Moons* (Arthur Crabtree, 1944), and Lockwood's Wicked Lady. The Gainsborough films infuse their murky and morbid intimations with a robust energy, and balance them with healthy and heartily sensitive characters whose lively sexual promise goes with normal pleasures like horse-riding and grand balls. In contrast, *Miss Blandish*, with its sleazy, sensual faces and nasty air, paraphrases the novel's porno-philosophical Sadism, via visuals as bad as its prose.

11. Two gentleman criminals

As the Bulldog Drummond-type toff is in eclipse, so is the gentleman crook. By 1945 the confident individuality of Raffles and Blackshirt has gone the way of their class-mate Blimp's chivalry. Still, two films hark back. *The Spider and the Fly* (Robert Hamer, 1949) observes, wistfully but finally with saddened cynicism, a moral duel between a gentleman crook (Guy Rolfe) and a 'civilised' policeman (Eric Portman). They're both French, which enables Hamer to combine his 'French' leanings and his moral wry-ness/melancholy. In *Escape* (Joseph L. Mankiewicz, 1948), officer-class Rex Harrison, chatting to a 'Mayfair darling', accidentally kills an obnoxious bobby, gets sent to Dartmoor, breaks out, is helped by Peggy Cummins, but finally gives himself up, largely to protect a parson who has helped him.[5] It's a strange blend of Galsworthy's moral scrupulousness and Warners' man-on-the-run melo. It's hard to say how far play or film consider the fugitive's moral punctiliousness specific to *gentlemen* as a social class and how far it's a shining example of 'decency' generally.

12. Lyceum melodrama modernised

The Curse of the Wraydons (Victor M. Gover, 1946) and *The Greed of William Hart* (Oswald Mitchell, 1948) end a long line of George King 'B' films smacking of Victorian 'blood and thunder' melodrama. Both star Tod Slaughter (aptly named), a fine old trouper of live theatre and better, I'd say, on stage than in these films.[6] On screen, the lord of this genre is Derrick de Marney. He's juicily friendly-sinister in *Uncle Silas*; in *Latin Quarter* (Vernon Sewell, 1945), he's a mad sculptor whose work of art entombs his wife's body.

Some stories retain faintly Gothick overtones by using Bohemian milieux, like fair-ground or circus. In *Dual Alibi* (Alfred Travers, 1947) Terence de Marney (brother of Derrick) cheats trapezist twins (Herbert Lom × 2) of their lottery win. He's murdered, but *which* Lom dunnit? Witnesses, and justice, are baffled. Lom's smooth glowerings reconcile melo and deadpan. In *The Trojan Brothers* (Maclean Rogers, 1946) David Farrar is the front half of a pantomime horse, and enjoys an affair with society beauty Patricia Burke until she dumps him, whereupon he strangles her. It's a lively comedy-of-manners (what with insults hurled across the footlights, and backchat between the horse's mouth and its other end, Bobby Howes), set in the Bohemian world of the music-hall. *The Shop at Sly Corner*, a 'shopkeeper's tragedy', gives its contemporary set-tings Gothick inflections: exotically overripe acting (Oscar Homolka vs Kenneth Griffith), eerie antiques (an Oriental idol and an Eastern poison unknown to science).

Trapezist twins, Herbert Lom × 2 in Dual Alibi *(Alfred Travis, 1947).*

Backchat between the horse's mouth and its other end. The Trojan Brothers *(Maclean Rogers, 1946).*

It's Plain Clothes Gothickry, well adapted to what many think an old-fangled, doomed genre.

It shares a pride of place with two British National movies of 1948, both co-scripted by Dylan Thomas. *The Three Weird Sisters* (Dan Birt, 1948) rejoices in juicily Gothic performances by Nancy Price, Mary Clare and Mary Merrall, a trio of bitter crones out to kill their half-brother Raymond Lovell, and his pretty secretary Nova Pilbeam. Though Gothick, in a sense, it really derives from genres (or traditions) about rural evil. *No Room at the Inn* (Dan Birt, 1945) brings the idiom virtually up to date. Slatternly alcoholic Freda Jackson starves and brutalises wartime evacuees, and squanders the benefit money doled out by negligent social workers (*plus ça change ...*).

13. BBC thick-ear pulp
Surprisingly, the principal supplier of pulp tosh for British Bs, Cs and Ds is the supposedly high-minded BBC, whose radio thriller serials are lowbrow, boyish and smashingly popular. Its heroes star in cheapissimo Bs, mostly from Butcher's and Exclusive, like *Dick Barton – Special Agent* (Drummond's 'scrapper' successor), Paul Temple and his faithful wife Steve, *The Man in Black*, and Dr Morelle. Both *noir* man and mournful doctor are played by Valentine Dyall, whose dark mean voice well expresses (like, later, Edgar Lustgarten's and, recently, Dr Martin Vigo's) the mixture of libidinal fascination and moralistic gloating conspicuous in popular attitudes to crime and punishment.[7] It's not usually *just* morbid, and even where it is, it's an *authentic* pessimism, with a philosophical pedigree going back to the atheist Hobbes and the harsh puritan Calvin. For both of them, Man, like Nature, is nasty, brutish and morally stunted.

14. Tales of the criminous
This pessimism/severity imbues a very old, very morbid, pre-Victorian genre, the Criminal Chronicle. Here, a vicious criminal's career is retold, with no real 'interpretation' and with no real sympathy for anybody much: just archetypal, gut-instinct horror and punitiveness. It may seem Victorian but it goes much further back. It's there in the 'hanging' broadsheets, then in the Newgate Calendar, then in *Reynolds News*, which in Victorian times combined popular radicalism with sensationalism, then in the *News of the World*, and it gets into some early films, like *The Life of Charles Peace* (1905). It's soon pressure-grouped out of movies, and only fully resurfaces in *The Case of Charles Peace* (Norman Lee, 1948). But its spirit seeps into a whole range of films: *The Wicked Lady*, *Good-Time Girl* (though overall it's too soft-heartedly reformist), *Night and the City* (though it's more drama than chronicle); and *Brighton Rock*, set among the razor-slashing racetrack gangs of the 1930s.

15. Return to Civvy Street
More topical problems included demobbed servicemen finding post-war readjustment very difficult. It inspires many films in many genres, though only crime films concern us here. Most demob yarns concern the black-marketeers and spivs so useful to honest citizens throughout Austerity. In *Nightbeat* (Harold Huth, 1948) ex-commando pals sign on as bobbies: one stays straight, one goes crook. It's scripted by two ex-wartime 'Specials', Guy Morgan and Tommy Morrison, and they tackle that rare theme, the badly bent bobby. In *They Made Me a Fugitive* (Cavalcanti, 1947) ex-

officer Trevor Howard joins a gang of black marketeers; when they're revealed as dope-peddling torturers, he wants out, which they won't allow. In *Dancing with Crime* (John Paddy Carstairs, 1947) taxi-driver Richard Attenborough sets out to avenge army pal Bill Owen and summons a horde of brother cabbies to help round up dance-hall racketeers. In *Hue and Cry* (Charles Crichton, 1947), warehouse lad Harry Fowler sets out to help save a comic from crooks, and summons a horde of kids and chums to help round up dockland racketeers. In *Noose* (Edmond T. Gréville, 1948) ex-commando Derek Farr sets out to help crusading reporter Carole Landis and summons a horde of pugilistic pals to help round up night-club racketeers.[8] All hopefully populist, like *Man on the Run* (Lawrence Huntington, 1949), where decent deserter Derek Farr must live outside the law unless the government decrees an amnesty.

16. Rackets and gangs

On racetracks and in gambling clubs (the latter illegal until the 1960s), champagne-swish Society and organised crookery can meet and mingle. *The Calendar* (Arthur Crabtree, 1948) has a sneaking sympathy for racehorse owner John McCallum's shaky morality. Clever Greta Gynt helps get him off the hook. Casino gambling is not underworld exactly, but 'demi-monde', where feckless nobs, rich Mayfairites, bookies, harmless and otherwise respectable fun-lovers, and consenting victims rub elbows with criminals. The politer, pleasanter side of all this inspires *Adam and Evelyne* (Harold French, 1949), where orphan Jean Simmons charms professional gambler Stewart Granger into going straight. It's much less a crime film than a café society romance (with charmingly Oedipal overtones). The uglier, nastier side of all this inspires *Third Time Lucky* (Gordon Parry, 1949). Here Charles Goldner as an outraged gangster stalks Dermot Walsh as a professional gambler and Glynis Johns his mascot (*verb. sap.* for 'mistress'?). Alas, violence substitutes for the subtler disillusionments implied by the title of Gerald Butler's source novel, *They Cracked Her Glass Slipper*.

British screens swarm with spivs and black-marketeers.[9] In *Dancing with Crime* they infest the Palais de Danse, that beacon of pleasure that shines over mean streets. In *Noose* they run a Soho nightclub. The tougher screen gangs tend to mix Cockney with Mediterranean ethnic types (Italian, Sicilian, Maltese, Greek), represented by George Coulouris and Charles Goldner. A few conspicuous immigrants from these violent cultures did lead a widespread escalation from smuggling nylons to smuggling dope, from bouncing to poncing, and from fist and cosh to knife and shooter. Still, vile Brits dominate *Brighton Rock* (John Boulting, 1947), *They Made Me a Fugitive* and *The Blue Lamp* (Basil Dearden, 1950).

Tough-as-nails William Hartnell is a small-time gangster wreaking harsh vengeance for betrayal in both *Murder in Reverse* (Montgomery Tully, 1945) and *Appointment with Crime* (John Harlow, 1946), and a fat lot of good it does him. *Good Time Girl* (David MacDonald, 1948) traces, with too-distant compassion, a slum kid's sleazy rise and wretched fall.

In *Brighton Rock* the bare rooms, smelling of bugs and damp, stand as metaphor for empty, festering minds. Graham Greene, as a pessimist Catholic, can recognise evil – slate-eyed, unreformable, inexplicable – when he sees it. *Night and the City* (Jules Dassin, 1950) is a *ne plus ultra* of noir visual style, every frame a painting, every character a deep-sea monster, gritty or flabby, like noir Fellini. Its London makes Chandler's L.A. look like Surbiton. And yet this 'absolute' style somehow 'blacks out' the vulnerability of Gerald Kersh's characters. Richard Widmark's is the only 'rounded' role, and he's ruinously miscast, being always the clever, intelligent 'King Rat', never the ambitious, slightly cunning little git, quite out of his class.[10] So though Dassin (and photographer Max Greene) fully deserve the Gold-plated Cosh Award for the Harshest Atmosphere in Any Film Noir Ever, the Solid Gold Razor must go to a smaller, rougher, more uneven film, *They Made Me a Fugitive*. Its director, Cavalcanti, comes to noir from early French Poetic Realism, a tradition more sensitively melancholy than American deadpan Expressionism. Faces and voices are limned with a disabused sensuality (Sally Gray's sulky lips, hurt angry eyes and husky voice) or disgust (Griffith Jones's cruel, witty, irrational malice). Trevor Howard, as a cynic fallen amongst racketeers, is caustic, explosive, reflexive as Bogart. This sleazy brew of meanness and sadism is Cavalcanti's most poetic, gloomy mood piece since his avant-garde years. Even the advertising copy revs up into blank verse: 'Mayfair darling must have nylons, Park Lane lovely must smell sweet, But what price glamour when the guns go off, And that red smear ain't rouge!'[11]

17. Juvenile delinquency

Post-war moralists emphasise wartime's glorifications of violence, its family dislocations, notably the wartime absence of strong fathers, and the lure of black market profits. *Good Time Girl* adds sexual harassment (by Jean Kent's pawnbroker employer), overuse of Dad's belt, and Approved Schools as the most intense criminal environment of all. This brave criticism of social work has its producers very nervous, and the censors insist that they add a sermon from a kind but stern magistrate. So Flora Robson tells Jean Kent's sad story, in flashbacks, to young Diana Dors, who, deeply impressed, resolves to step off the primrose path to the condemned cell.[12]

A similar mix of tentative criticism and respect pervades *Boys in Brown* (Montgomery Tully, 1949). This motley bunch of Borstal boys aren't all bad lots, many of them more sinned against than sinning, but one must be tough on crime, especially the rotten apples who corrupt the merely weak, and it takes all Guvnor Jack Warner's fatherly sagacity to save Attenborough, R., from the sneaky influence of Bogarde, D. This paternalist Borstal for boys is paralleled by a matriarchal remand home for girls in *The White Unicorn* (Bernard Knowles, 1947). Here Matron Margaret Lockwood encourages young mum Joan Greenwood, who has attempted infanticide and suicide, by confiding her own sad story about irresponsible men.

18. Wickedness vs moral weakness

In *My Brother's Keeper* (Alfred Roome, Roy Rich, 1948) two convicts escape, handcuffed together: Jack Warner, cast against type, is the hardened criminal; George Cole is the innocent (simple-minded?) youth. Now wouldn't you expect some positive relation, with mutual hatred perhaps and as many complications as the scriptwriters can think of, to grow between them? But *The Defiant Ones* this is not. The old lag cuts free of his 'useless' companion, killing a farmer in the process. The horrified lad surrenders to the police, who promptly charge him with the crime. The loner keeps going and, when cornered, takes his chance in an uncleared minefield. He ends as a pillar of smoke in long-shot.[13]

This strange film is dissatisfying, yet disconcerting. The police go aggressively wrong, and the newspaper reporter on the case is David Tomlinson, bumbling fusspot of umpteen comedies. The biblical title suggests another angle, perhaps related to Rank's earlier tries at moral-religious messages, though this film puts it in noir negative: 'All you weak lads in the audience, *don't* trust your "big brother" criminal mates.'

The film allows a little pathos but otherwise moves in a mysterious, cold, non-identifying way – alienation by emptiness of explanation – though this could be quite inadvertent, in a 'dollar-crisis quickie' rushed into production from an under-developed script.

Now Barabbas Was a Robber sympathises, in various ways and degrees, with crooks of most classes (a bank cashier, an IRA man, a Cockney ticket-forger, a Negro matelot caught smuggling, a bigamist – but not the charming killer).[14] Far from rigidly distinguishing heroes from villains, or good girls from bad, British films routinely compare-and-contrast the wicked with the weak. In *Temptation Harbour* (Lance Comfort, 1947), railway signalman Robert Newton turns out to be a middle-way tangle of moral weakness and animal-natural ability to kill. For most of his life a considerate family man, he remains so even as temptation (weakness of will? strength of desire?) leads him ever more deeply into crime.

19. Cops and robbers and the moral order

A longing for '*popular* moral authority' can help explain the genesis of that classic homage to law and order, *The Blue Lamp*. It's produced by Balcon (a Labour voter in 1945), who buys the first script from Gainsborough (whose boss, Sydney Box, is another Labour supporter). Its major writers are Ted Willis (an authentically working-class ex-Comrade, from the left-militant Unity Theatre) and T. E. B. Clarke (an ex-policeman, whose other voices are distinctly mischievous about law and order). Jack Warner's PC Dixon emblemises – what? 'Labour's People now-in-authority'? Conformism? Working-class embourgeoisement? Petit-bourgeois authoritarianism? Working class as New Pillar of Society? The decent common man endowed with responsible authority? Whichever, as Dixon of Dock Green he'll become a figurehead of the 1950s, as spreading affluence reconciles ever wider sections of the lower-middle and the working classes.

The Blue Lamp may seem stodgily conformist and petit-bourgeois (there are worse things, dare one say). *Hue and Cry* may seem delightfully anarchic. But they're opposite poles of the same spirit. The very phrase 'hue and cry' suggests a sort of *populist citizenship*, a 'have-a-go' spirit, a 'citizen's arrest'. In *The Blue Lamp*, even crooks help hunt down the cop-killer: partly for selfish reasons (of course), but partly from an indignant, almost principled respect for *some* law and order. It's not so much Ealing being soft on crime, as part of Ealing's faith in 'the benevolent community'.[15]

20. Philosophical thrillers

The criminal world, with its solitudes, distrusts, guilts and despairs, its self-appointed tasks and projects, its *ad hoc* loyalties, and its emotive, precarious subculture of 'honour among thieves', lends itself to a certain existentialism. Though movies of this period can't yet pursue deep thoughts through the labyrinthine finesses, which need philosophical *writers*, they *can* flesh out some basic propositions in movie atmospherics like the near-expressionist idioms of two Carol Reed films, *Odd Man Out* (1947) and *The Third Man* (1949).

The Odd Man Out is James Mason, a patriotic terrorist, stripped, as he wanders dying through Belfast, of his 'terrorist' identity, but meeting precious little kindness from a cross-section of 'ordinary people'. Populism extends as far as visionary artist Robert Newton, who props the dying man on a model's throne to 'paint his soul' at the moment of death. Finally his girlfriend (Kathleen Ryan) pretends they're escaping together, so that he can die happy, but her loving kindness entails *another* betrayal. It's as if the human condition must always confuse terrorism/idealism, love/treachery.

The Third Man (scripted by Graham Greene) is a relatively simple narrative. What gives it popular classic status is its atmosphere: a chemistry of realistic locations + slanting shadow-throws + deeply diagonal night-streets + Dutch tilts (learned from Duvivier) + strong, insolent, secretive faces + charged acting + zithery-slithery vibrations tangling and unwinding our nerves, teasing and haunting us like a ghostly hurdy-gurdy, in the key of Kurt Weill. It's another meditation on the 'iron law' of betrayal. Orson Welles is the charming but morally ugly American – a racketeer, now bootlegging not hooch but penicillin, in cold, hungry, post-war Europe. Joseph Cotten as the innocent American becomes *culpably* innocent, in refusing to betray his old friend, and when at last he does his moral duty he's punished by Valli's silent rejection. If loyalty matches legality she's entirely right. Yet, as a racketeer's mistress, her moral authority is not exactly awesome. It's Trevor Howard, as a British army officer, who provides the necessarily harsh moral realism, to hold back the forces of chaos and black night. Greene and Reed share one inspiring obsession: treachery – malevolent, or righteous, or inadvertent – is the human condition. And isn't treachery (to neighbours, to society ...) what crime is all about?

Notes

1. As a rejection of intellectual elitism, *The Upturned Glass* matches *Rope* (1948). Hitchcock's Hollywood film has strong British connections. He co-produced it with Sidney Bernstein of Granada, and it's inspired by a British play (Patrick Hamilton, 1929).
2. Martha Wolfenstein and Nathan Leites, *Movies: a Psychological Study* (Illinois: Free Press, 1950).
3. The Windmill Theatre (whose nudes never moved) had already inspired *Tonight and Every Night* (Hollywood, 1945).
4. From another angle it foreshadows *The Servant*.
5. *Escape* was first filmed in 1930, with Gerald du Maurier (father of Daphne), the West End theatre's specialist supreme in suavely casual, understated gentlemen. He'd created Raffles on stage, and his gentlemen ranged from the casually sensitive to raffish nobs and rascally toffs.
6. For an attempt to evoke Slaughter's great stage role, Sweeney Todd, as it will evolve by the mid-50s, cf. Raymond Durgnat, 'A Salute to Slaughter', in *Ark* (Journal of the Royal College of Art), no. 30, 1961–2.
7. Dr Martin Vigo, *Murder After Midnight*, a long-running radio series about True Crimes.
8. *Noose*, being thick-ear comic noir, comes as a surprise after the same author Richard Llewellyn's soulful Welsh novel, *How Green Was My Valley* (1940). The missing link may be *None But the Lonely Heart*, about the casually-class drifter.
9. Cf. the chapter on 'The Spiv Cycle' in Robert Murphy, *Realism and Tinsel: Cinema and Society in Britain 1939–49* (London: Routledge, 1989).
10. Kersh's 'anti-hero' defies perfect casting, but umpteen British actors would have been more suitable, in one way or another: Attenborough (in his early, spiritually stunted period), Maxwell Reed (jumped-up barrow-boy/spiv, with a swagger, a punch and low cunning), George Cole (no, don't laugh; cf. *My Brother's Keeper*), Laurence Harvey?
11. These stresses and alliterations smack of Anglo-Saxon (Old English) patterns. Eerie atavism? Doggerel drumroll-and-rap?
12. Where, maybe, Eric Portman awaits, as in *Daybreak*. Come to think of it, his wife in that film (Ann Todd) has been a bit of a good-time girl in her delicate, mournful way, though she's relieved when he makes an honest woman of her.
13. This distant understatement is a British way to go – especially compared with James Cagney, in *White Heat*, a year later.
14. Its writer, William Douglas Home, aristocratic brother of a future Conservative Prime Minister, had been a wartime army officer, and had gone to prison for disobeying an order which he considered pointlessly inhumane. (Is this a crime story? Don't we admire the 'sin' he's punished for?)
15. Cf. Charles Barr, *Ealing Studios* (London: Cameron and Tayleur/Newton Abbott: David & Charles, 1977).

Bibliography

Durgnat, Raymond, *A Mirror for England* (London: Faber & Faber, 1970).

Durgnat, Raymond, 'Gainsborough: 'The Times of Its Time', *Monthly Film Bulletin*, August 1985.

Durgnat, Raymond, 'La Gainsborough e i suoi Cugini', in Emanuela Martini (ed.), *A Gainsborough Picture* (Bergamo Film Meeting, Italy, 1994).

McFarlane, Brian, *Sixty Voices: Celebrities Recall the Golden Age of British Cinema* (London: British Film Institute, 1992).

Murphy, Robert, *Realism and Tinsel: Cinema and Society in Britain 1939–49* (London: Routledge, 1989).

Oakley, Charles, *Where We Came In* (London: Allen & Unwin, 1964).

10
Exiles and British Cinema

Kevin Gough-Yates

European exiles dominated British film production in the 1930s. In his now notorious review of a Max Schach production, Graham Greene, then film critic of the *Spectator*, wrote in 1936 of 'the dark alien executive tipping his cigar ash behind the glass in Wardour Street, the Hungarian producer [Alexander Korda] adapting Mr Wells's ideas tactfully at Denham, the German director [Karl Grune] letting himself down in his canvas chair at Elstree', and asked whether *The Marriage of Corbal* could be considered an English film at all, directed as it was by 'Karl Grune and F. Brunn, photographed by Otto Kanturek, and edited by E. Stokvis [*sic*], with a cast which includes Nils Asther, Ernst Deutsch and the American, Noah Beery.'[1] Greene, grossly misrepresenting the Cinematographic Act of 1927, writes that the 'Quota Act has played into foreign hands ... there is nothing to prevent an English film unit being completely staffed by technicians of foreign blood. We have saved the English film industry from American competition only to surrender it to a far more alien control ... it is not English money that calls the tune, and it is only natural that compatriots should find jobs for each other'.[2] Greene argues that there are perfectly good 'English technicians capable of producing films of a high enough standard to take their place in the international markets', technicians who had made *Song of Ceylon, The Voice of Britain, The Turn of the Tide, Night Mail* and *Midshipman Easy*.

The sometimes acrimonious debate about aliens in the British film industry was not only about employment, it was concerned with the concept of national identity as expressed through the cinema. Documentary film-makers, perhaps self-servingly, have wanted to see Britain's national cinema as having its roots within films such as *Song of Ceylon* and *Night Mail*, made at the Empire Marketing Board and the GPO Film Unit in the 1930s. Basil Wright, for example, writes of how 'the great period of the British feature film, which was during and immediately after the Second World War, owes a tremendous amount to the influence and example of the documentary film'.[3]

This essay questions whether a national cinema can be constructed by following so narrow a trajectory. What is generally forgotten in writings about the development of British cinema, particularly those which focus on the documentary film movement as providing the inspiration for its 'classic period', is that for the ten years before the Second World War the production context outside of the documentary film movement was fashioned by film-makers – producers, writers, cinematographers, directors, and designers – most of whom had been driven out of Nazi Germany. Not only were they engaged in all capacities in the production of British films, they trained the future generation of native-born film technicians; they were, for the most part, not economic migrants seeking employment, but experienced film-makers who helped develop a fledgeling industry.

Alexander Korda made films in his native Hungary and in Austria, Germany, Hollywood and France before settling in England in 1931 and establishing himself as Britain's foremost independent producer. Although his career to this point was relatively undistinguished, with fifty films behind him his understanding of the international market was unique in Britain. He created London Film Productions and scrambled together the money to make *The Private Life of Henry VIII* (1933), which, by a stroke of good fortune, became a great success, the first British film to make a breakthrough into the American market. His achievement encouraged major financial investment in the industry and he was able to build Denham Studios with the financial backing of the Prudential Assurance Company.

Korda was a visionary with regard to British cinema, and set about correcting its fundamental weaknesses: underinvestment in equipment, studios and manpower, and inadequate distribution. He built Denham Studios along Hollywood lines and brought in leading technicians from abroad to work on such films as *Sanders of the River* (1934), *The Ghost Goes West* (1935), *Things to Come* (1936), *The Scarlet Pimpernel* (1937), *The Man Who Could Work Miracles* (1937), *Farewell Again* (1937), and *Knight Without Armour* (1937). When he required startling special effects for his production of *Things to Come* (1936) he brought over one of the great international cinephotographers, Eugen Schüffton, who had worked with Fritz Lang on another futuristic film, *Metropolis* (1927). Not only did he successfully negotiate a distribution arrangement with United Artists, he continuously sought an innovatory marketing edge, entering into an early contractual agreement with Technicolor, for example, and using the process to maximum effect in *The Four Feathers* (1939). For the first time numerous fledgling British technicians and directors were able to receive training from major cinematographers, editors and designers. Several of Korda's leading actors and actresses became stars: Laurence Olivier, Ralph Richardson, Vivien Leigh, Sabu, Merle Oberon, Robert Donat, Flora Robson and Charles Laughton all established their film acting careers at London Films.

On the back of Korda's success in America, 'hot' money, much of it from banks, was recklessly invested in the film business. Among the many beneficiaries was the producer Max Schach, who had been forced out of Emelka Studios, Munich, in December 1931 because of his lack of financial control. He came to Britain as a refugee in 1934 and soon established a string of film production companies, the Capitol Group, which included Trafalgar, Buckingham, and Cecil Films. According to the journalist Hans Feld, who as film editor of *Film Kurier* in Germany knew Schach, reputable figures such as the producer Erich Pommer steered well clear of him.[4] Rachael Low considers Schach's companies 'tramp' operations, travelling from studio to studio without homes of their own, but it should be emphasised that Denham was designed to be available to such tenant companies, and the money that the banks were only too ready to lend was not intended for studio infrastructure; it was speculative money riding on individual films. Korda's prosperity depended on a thriving non-studio-owning industry which hired space from him at Denham. Schach's and Korda's fortunes were, therefore, intertwined in a complex speculation in which the banks as much pursued film production companies as were sought out.

Where Korda was said to favour Hungarians, Schach's associates were generally Austrian: the singer Richard Tauber, the actor Fritz Kortner, the actress Elisabeth Bergner, the writer Rudolf Bernauer, the cinematographer Otto Kanturek, the designer Oscar Werndorff, and the director Karl Grune. His films, which include *Abdul the*

Austrian sophistication, Austrian extravagance. Karl Grune's The Marriage of Corbal *(1936).*

Damned (1935), *Land Without Music*, *The Marriage of Corbal*, and *Pagliacci* (all 1936), were failures, because Schach, duplicating his Emelka experience, was cavalier with budgets and failed to secure satisfactory distribution. Korda's films invariably exceeded their projected costs; *Things to Come* (1936), for example, finally cost £258,000, two and a half times as much as Schach's *Pagliacci*, but Schach's film lost all its money, whilst Korda's took £350,000 at the box office.[5]

Korda and Schach both possessed a major talent for charming money out of people. Monja Danischewsky, who was employed by Schach in the publicity department of Capitol, describes him as a man with 'immense charm and an irrepressible sense of humour'.[7] Tales abound of Korda's ability to calm the most irate of bankers and the most fragile of star temperaments. Rachael Low makes an unfavourable comparison between Schach and Korda. Schach, she feels, contributed nothing to the industry. Money went directly into people's pockets. Korda created stars, built Denham studios, provided opportunities for writers and directors, and encouraged the industry to find a significant place for itself in world markets.[8] But both, although one less deliberately, helped forge a national industry out of a combination of experienced mid-Europeans and eager but inexperienced British actors, directors, and technicians.

When Twickenham, a company that produced little of lasting interest, went under in 1937, there was a rash of bankruptcies. Schach's companies collapsed and Korda lost control of Denham to the Prudential and, ultimately, to Rank. Korda was blamed by City financiers for the failure of their own reckless speculation. The journalist Robert Bruce Lockhart, whose anti-Semitic views were well known, wrote in his diary:

Last night Bayliss-Smith, who is a leading chartered accountant and represents the creditors in some of the biggest cinema financial messes in this country, says the cinema industry here has cost the banks and insurance companies about £4,000,000. Most of this is lost by Jews – like Korda and Max Schacht [sic]. Latter already lost a packet for the German Government before Hitler. He has now done the same here. In Bayliss-Smith's opinion, and he would not say so lightly, Korda is a much worse man than Schacht. Schacht is just a slick Jew who sees financial moves ahead of the other fellow. Korda is a crook and, according to Bayliss-Smith, an evil man.[6]

The major writers, photographers, producers and even directors of feature films in Britain throughout most of the 1930s were not British, or at least were not British-born.[9] A glance at the 'Technical Section' of *Spotlight* for Winter 1935 reveals that no major British production company failed to have at least one European cinematographer under contract. Gaumont-British sported Mutz Greenbaum, London Films listed Georges Périnal and Hans Schneeberger. The small, under-financed company Criterion Film Productions, which had been created by Douglas Fairbanks Jnr with the Romanian producer Marcel Hellman, listed Günther Krampf. Even Basil Dean's Associated Talking Pictures, at its very English Ealing Studios, listed Jan Stallich as its studio photographer. The only significant company not to list a European cinematographer was Herbert Wilcox's British and Dominion.

Of the British-born cinematographers listed in this edition of *Spotlight* only three had notable careers: Freddie Young, Ronald Neame and Desmond Dickinson. Desmond Dickinson 'was so good', wrote Adrian Brunel, the director and writer, that 'it seemed incredible that he should have been relegated to shooting cheap films only, while foreign cameramen, infinitely less talented, were freely admitted into the country to shoot in our studios.'[10] Another British cinematographer, Erwin Hillier, was in fact born and educated in Berlin, and began a long film career in 1931, as assistant to Fritz Arno Wagner on Fritz Lang's *M*.

Most of the art directors who made creative interventions in the British film industry were Europeans. Leon Barsacq, in *Caligari's Cabinet and other Grand Illusions*, his book on film design, writes of 'the apathy and ignorance pervading British film studios' and of the encouragement Vincent Korda, a key figure at his brother's London Films, offered a generation of young, aspiring art directors.[11] The Hollywood art director Holmes Paul identified the transformation that was taking place in British studios when, in 1932, he wrote:

> A valuable advance in realism has been attained through the closer co-operation of the director and cameraman with the art director. This essential co-operation has been lacking in this country.... German producers, ever in the forefront where scenery is concerned, have always insisted on the closest attention to the building of sets which are intended to help the camera to secure the utmost realism.... The German studios have always realised that large sums of money and a great deal of time can be saved if the director, camera staff, and art director work in the closest harmony.[12]

As with photographers, each of the European art directors had an individual style, which was incorporated into a broad knowledge of film-making. Alfred Junge, Michael Powell observed, 'was head director at Balcon's Lime Grove ... he ran it like a machine ... Junge was a good organiser, a tremendous disciplinarian, and a very good trainer of young people ... besides being a very great designer himself.'[13] This view of Junge is confirmed by the cinematographer Christopher Challis:

Alfred was a martinet, he ran the art department like a hospital ... it was immacu-
late ... they literally wiped up your footprints as you went in ... Alfred was brilliant
with matte shots, hanging miniatures and all that sort of thing.... He would mark
on the set with a cross the position of the camera for the main shot and woe betide
anyone who tried to shift it.... He'd designed it from that position and that was it.
There was this cross and the size of the lens put on it.[14]

Europeans were less dominant in the areas of directing and editing, although here too
they were well represented. Paul Stein, Friedrich Feher, Hans Schwartz, Karl Grune,
Ludwig Berger, Berthold Viertel and the brothers Alexander and Zoltan Korda are
among those with major directorial credits. Feher's *The Robber Symphony*, for
example, which was designed by Ernö Metzner, is described by Elliot Stein as 'one of
the great and delightful eccentricities of European cinema in the thirties'.[15] It was said
to be the first 'composed' film, the first film shot to a prerecorded soundtrack. Michael
Powell claims that, although he never saw the film, he was 'haunted by it and longed
for a film subject where music was the master'.[16] It inspired him to create the atmos-
pheric end sequence of *Black Narcissus* (1947), the ballet in *The Red Shoes* (1949) and
the whole of *The Tales of Hoffmann* (1951).

In the spectrum of debate, Powell, who considered the collective truth of documentary no more valid or verifiable than his own personal one, was firmly at the European
end. He worked as second unit director on Korda's *The Thief of Bagdad* (1940) which,
until war and Korda's financial problems forced its evacuation to Hollywood, was directed by Ludwig Berger at Denham. *Kinematograph Weekly* noted that Berger, who 'is
also a great musician and has produced several operas on the Continent, has a revolutionary scheme for shooting the music first on *The Thief of Bagdad*.' It was to be 'the
first time that a full musical score would be played back and the sound "mixed" on the
set.'[17] 'In the end the only sequences shot to pre-composed music were those involving special effects – the gallop of the Flying Horse and the Silvermaid's Dance.'[18] But
the chaos associated with the experiment excited rather than dampened Powell's aesthetic enthusiasms.

The European film-maker in Britain during the 1930s was frequently better read
and better educated than his British counterpart. Powell felt that the European could
converse on a wide range of subjects. He was 'cultivated': Feher was a trained composer, Vincent Korda a reputable painter, Berthold Viertel a poet and Walter Goehr,
Allan Gray and Hanns Eisler students of Arnold Schoenberg. Powell was one of the few
British-born film-makers who was seduced, and not shamed, by this wealth of experience and erudition. He recognised that the particular combination of imagination and
technical skill which the European brought to the cinema could help create a less
parochial British cinema. Whenever he could, he associated with European artists. His
partnership with the Hungarian-born scriptwriter Emeric Pressburger began in 1938,
when Korda introduced them to each other at a script conference for *The Spy in Black*.
Thereafter Powell's designers were always European: Vincent Korda, Alfred Junge and
Hein Heckroth; and his main cinematographers were Georges Périnal and Erwin
Hillier until his collaboration with Jack Cardiff began with *A Matter of Life and Death*
(1946).[19] It could be argued that during the war, with Korda in America and British
cinema turning towards a form of British realism, they alone kept the Korda flag flying, using Korda stars and technicians whenever they could.

European actors and writers were also surprisingly important. Anton Walbrook,
Fritz Kortner, Conrad Veidt, Oscar Homolka, Frederick Valk and others all had to
battle with the English language. Dolly Haas was given parts which made her Russian

or Hungarian; on one occasion her accent was supposed to be Australian. Both Valk and Walbrook appeared successfully on the London stage in 1939, the latter in Noël Coward's *Design for Living*, but accent remained a determining factor in the parts they were offered. Conrad Veidt was compelled to speak his lines phonetically in his first British film. According to the actor Robert Morley, who worked with him briefly as dialogue director on *Under the Red Robe* (1937), he 'was a master at delivering lines. . . . He always spoke them very slowly when everyone else spoke rather fast, and softly when everyone else spoke loudly.'[20] He also knew about lighting and always carried a small pocket mirror in order to see how his face was lit, so that he could make suggestions to the cinematographer.[21] As was the case with other exiles, Veidt's roles were determined by his accent, which was one of the reasons Gaumont-British, to whom he was under contract, had problems finding him suitable parts. He became stereotyped as a German spy or a mysterious foreigner. Even when he moved to London Films, Korda found it difficult to find roles for him and, in the end, resorted to using him in much the same way.

In *The Spy in Black* (1939), Emeric Pressburger created a character which enabled Veidt to be located in an English film whilst retaining elements from his parts in German cinema. Powell put it this way: 'I knew all the German Expressionist films he had done and . . . [Veidt] said ". . . let him wear black overalls as the motorcyclist, make him a black figure" . . . . The way he comes out is just as much the myth of Veidt as the myth of the German spy.'[22] Pressburger makes use of the possibilities arising from a situation where one person speaks faltering English and the other speaks it perfectly. Valerie Hobson is a schoolteacher and a double agent, Veidt a U-boat commander who has just been landed on the coast. When they meet, they establish their credentials by exchanging a few words in German, but she loses no time in insisting on English and in correcting Veidt's pronunciation.[23]

In *The Life and Death of Colonel Blimp* (1943), Pressburger's most personal film script, he makes manifest the anxieties of a refugee from Nazi Germany. Anton Walbrook, as Blimp's friend, Theo Kretschmar-Schuldorff, is interrogated at an aliens tribunal by A. E. Matthews. The once patriotic, exuberant army officer of the First World War is now noticeably down-at-heel and depressed. In a statement transplanted from Pressburger's own experience and spoken without interruption, Theo explains why he has left Germany for Britain. He (unlike Pressburger himself) was not obliged to leave Germany, he had nothing to fear from Hitler. When Matthews observes that it took him some time to discover where he stood with regard to Hitler, Theo points out that the British, too, seem to have been in no great hurry. Matthews is taken aback and has to acknowledge the validity of Theo's remark. Pressburger's comment on this sequence in 1970 emphasises the intensity of his feelings:

> I wanted to express this feeling of mine that though my mother had died in a concentration camp and I was pre-conditioned about the whole thing, I always believed . . . that there are also good Germans . . . who didn't have to go away from Germany but chose to go away. . . . I had that kind of experience [in immigration control] obviously. England is a very, very difficult country for foreigners to come to. Of course, when I came my intention was to stay in England but you have to lie straight away . . . to the question, 'How long do you intend to stay here?' You mustn't say, 'I intend to stay forever' . . . so you answer, 'Six months', and then you extend the six months. . . . I believe that anyone that comes to the country under the same circumstances cannot love the Immigration Officers.[24]

The difficulties of adjustment to Britain and its language were never entirely solved by Pressburger himself, and this theme reappears throughout his career. *A Canterbury Tale* (1944) and *I Know Where I'm Going* are conventionally seen as examples of Powell's neo-romantic sensibility, but they also disclose Pressburger's sensitivity to being a stranger, confronted by an alien language and culture. In *A Canterbury Tale*, the stranger is an American G.I., Bob Johnson, played by a real one, Sgt John Sweet. Pressburger here displaces the problems of the refugee in Britain on to two characters: an English-speaking but foreign soldier and Alison (Sheila Sim), a Londoner, but now a land girl. Officially, the G.I. was a welcome guest in Britain, but the number of films that were made to help him adjust to its alien conventions suggests that difficulties were not easily overcome. Pressburger modulates the G.I.'s problems with trains, telephones and tea-drinking with a more deeply rooted cultural difference embodied by two English characters – Peter (Dennis Price), a cinema organist, and Alison, who works in a department store – urban aliens in a rural environment that the American, a country boy from Oregon, is more attuned to. In one of the most effective sequences in the film, Alison and Bob meet again at a wheelwright's yard. Alison is teased by the blacksmith for her ignorance of country matters, but an immediate rapport is reached between the wheelwright and the American soldier because of their shared knowledge and understanding of wood. As Bob and Alison ride off in the mended cart, Bob explains his acceptance (he has been invited to share the wheelwright's midday dinner) by telling her, 'We speak the same language.' To which she responds, 'I'm English and I don't speak their language.'

In *I Know Where I'm Going*, which was made towards the end of 1944, a prissy

A stranger confronted by an alien language and culture. Wendy Hiller on Mull. I Know Where I'm Going *(Michael Powell and Emeric Pressburger, 1946).*

English girl (Wendy Hiller) travels to Scotland to marry a rich industrialist. She finds herself in a country where she is bemused by the language and bewildered by the people she meets. She is transported to Scotland in a montage sequence which suggests Powell's fascination with *The Wizard of Oz*, but which, for Pressburger, is a further attempt to exorcise the painful experience of his forced flight to Britain. The film is a supreme example of the ways in which an émigré writer and an English director are able to harmonise their concerns and obsessions. The brilliant, almost show-off sequence of the journey from London to the Isle of Mull gives way to a journey of discovery for the protagonist once she arrives. Gaelic may substitute for English as the incomprehensible language of *I Know Where I'm Going*, but there is the same sense of bewilderment and difficulty that Pressburger's other 'alien' characters experience. Underneath the stand-offish character played by Wendy Hiller lies a yearning to understand and belong.

The Second World War did not kill off the 'international' film, but a British interpretation of realism gradually asserted itself. Basil Wright and others believed that the documentary film contributed significantly to the development and maturity of British feature films during the war. The producer Michael Balcon thought it 'the greatest single influence in British film production [which] more than anything helped establish a national style'.[25] Sir Arthur Elton, too, felt that the 'old school' was effectively left behind: 'Korda, who was a wonderful man, didn't finally come into the battle, which was between the old and the new. The attack was to get the Ministry of Information to base its policies on realism rather than 1914 romance.'[26] But matters were less simple than this. Cavalcanti, the Brazilian who headed the GPO Film Unit at the outbreak of the war, took a number of figures from documentary into feature film-making when he joined Balcon at Ealing. But Ealing and the Crown Film Unit were responsible for only a fraction of wartime feature films and many of the wartime realist classics – Powell and Pressburger's *One of Our Aircraft is Missing*, Sidney Gilliat's *Waterloo Road* and David Lean and Noël Coward's *In Which We Serve* – owed little to the documentary film movement.

Although there was frequently a nostalgia for Germany, European émigrés associated themselves with the Allied cause during the war. Their experience and knowledge of Hitler's Germany reinforced their feelings for Britain, and despite the indignity and unfairness of internment many of them embraced British values and contributed what they could to the war effort. Some of them undertook official responsibilities: Rudolf Bernauer, the co-writer of the screenplay for *Hatter's Castle* (Lance Comfort, 1941), was involved with 'black' propaganda broadcasts to Germany from Woburn Abbey; the composer Mischa Spoliansky and the actors Lucie Mannheim, Herbert Lom, Gerard Heinz and Walter Rilla worked for the BBC on 'white' propaganda broadcasts such as *Aus der freien Welt*. Korda, who was in the USA during the early part of the war, acted as a courier and gathered Intelligence information for the British government.[27]

By 1946 Korda had managed to re-establish London Films and he gradually attracted back the talented film-makers: Powell and Pressburger, Launder and Gilliat, Carol Reed, David Lean; who had made films for the Rank Organisation during the war. Rank-backed films such as Korda's *Blanche Fury* (1948), *Saraband for Dead Lovers* (1948), Ealing's *Hue and Cry* and *It Always Rains on Sunday* (1947), both produced by Henry (Heinz) Cornelius, and *Genevieve* (1953) which he directed, are frequently cited as exemplars of British cinema. They reveal only some of the ways in which British cinema evolved as a combination of European style and British subject material.[28] *The Third Man* (1949) and *Gone to Earth* (1950) show a flowering of sophisticated European-influenced British cinema. But by the end of the decade, as financial crisis stalked the industry, horizons contracted and smaller-budgeted, cosier, more parochial films became the norm. If the European exile can be said to have established the British Cinema in the 1930s, *The Tales of Hoffmann* (1951), Powell and Pressburger's homage to Friedrich Feher's *The Robber Symphony*, might be seen as the last gasp of that ambitious, expansive cinema which they brought to Britain. The 1950s was the decade of Ealing and Pinewood, whose very names betoken little England.

Notes

1. Graham Greene, *Spectator*, 5 June 1936, reprinted in *The Pleasure Dome* (London: Secker and Warburg, 1972), pp. 78–9.
2. The facts are quite opposite. The Cinematographic Act of 1927 defines a British film, for the purpose of the Act, as one that has 'been made by a … British subject', where 'the studio scenes must have been photographed in a studio in the British Empire', where the 'author of the scenario must have been a British subject' and where 'not less than seventy-five per cent of the salaries, wages and payments for labour and services in the making of the film (exclusive of payments in respect of copyright and of the salary or payments to one foreign actor or actress or producer, but inclusive of the payments to the author of the scenario) has been paid to British subjects or persons domiciled in the British Empire.' The review is quite clearly anti-Semitic.
3. Basil Wright, *The Long View* (London: Secker and Warburg, 1974), p. 109.
4. Interview with author, 12 July 1986.
5. Paul Tabori, *Alexander Korda* (London: Oldbourne, 1959), p. 178. The producers' revenue was, therefore, much smaller (£137,500), so the film still made a considerable loss.
6. Sir Robert Bruce Lockhart, *The Diaries* (London: Macmillan, 1973), p. 105. Bayliss-Smith was on the board of some of Schach's companies. Bruce Lockhart's attitudes towards Jews did not prevent him exploring the possibilities of working with Korda after the war. He eventually decided against becoming an adviser to Korda at £12,000 a year. 'Films are unclean and having anything to do with them is moral and physical degradation,' he wrote to his son on 8 January 1948. See *The Diaries: Volume Two, 1939–65* (London: Macmillan, 1980), p. 646.
7. Monja Danischewsky, *White Russian, Red Face* (London: Gollancz, 1966), p. 105.
8. Rachael Low, *Film Making in 1930s Britain* (London: George Allen and Unwin, 1985), pp. 218–29.
9. Korda, who arrived in Britain in 1931, became a British citizen on 28 October 1936, having been in Britain for the required minimum of five years; others, like the director Paul Czinner and the actors Elisabeth Bergner and Conrad Veidt, followed suit.
10. Adrian Brunel, *Nice Work* (London: Forbes Robertson, 1949), p. 180. Brunel, like others, found himself with divided loyalties for on another assignment, *The Return of the Scarlet Pimpernel* much of its effectiveness was due to Lazare Meerson, 'that genius amongst art-directors, as well as to the photography of "Mutz" Green (sic)', ibid., p. 181.
11. Léon Barsacq, *Caligari's Cabinet and other Grand Illusions: A History of Film Design* (New York: Little Brown, 1976), p. 220.
12. *Kinematograph Weekly*, 11 February 1932.
13. Michael Powell, interviews with author, 22 September 1970 and 30 August 1973, in Kevin Gough-Yates, *Michael Powell in Collaboration with Emeric Pressburger* (London: British Film Institute, 1971); Kevin Gough-Yates, *Michael Powell* (Brussels: Filmmuseum/Palais des Beaux-Arts, 1973).
14. Christopher Challis, interview with Rex Stapleton, 7 January 1984, in Stapleton, *A Matter of Powell and Pressburger: Group Dynamics and Notions of Authorship* (MA thesis, Polytechnic of Central London, 1984), p. 17.
15. Ibid., p. 228.
16. Michael Powell, *A Life in Movies* (London: Heinemann, 1986), p. 582. Privately, to the author, 20 July 1987, Powell admitted to having seen it at the Palace Theatre.
17. *Kinematograph Weekly*, 8 July 1939.
18. Miklós Rózsa, *Double Life* (Tunbridge Wells: Baton Press, 1986), p. 84.
19. Hillier was actually British, as his father had become naturalised. He first worked as a camera assistant on Fritz Lang's *M* (1931).
20. Robert Morley and Sewell Stokes, *Responsible Gentleman* (London: Heinemann, 1966), p. 89f.
21. Hillier, interview with author, 16 April 1987.
22. Powell, interview with author, in Gough-Yates, *Michael Powell in Collaboration*.
23. Cf. Richard Tauber taking English lessons from Paul Graetz in *Heart's Desire* (Paul Stein, 1936), Anton Walbrook and Walter Rilla practising their English in *Victoria the Great* (Herbert Wilcox, 1937).
24. Pressburger, interview with author, in Gough-Yates, *Michael Powell in Collaboration*.

25. Michael Balcon, *Michael Balcon presents ... A Lifetime of Films* (London: Hutchinson, 1969), p. 130. Balcon adds that he turned towards the documentary school of film-makers only because Ealing was 'denuded' of 'so many of our people', ie in the forces or in internment.
26. Elizabeth Sussex, *The Rise and Fall of British Documentary: The Story of the Film Movement Founded by John Grierson* (Berkeley: University of California Press, 1975), p. 120.
27. For 'black' propaganda from Woburn Abbey, see especially Denis Sefton Delmer, *Black Boomerang: An Autobiography, Vol. Two* (London: Secker and Warburg, 1962), and Lawrence C. Soley, *Radio Warfare, OSS and CIA Subversive Propaganda* (New York: Praeger, 1989), pp. 123–55.
28. Henry Cornelius was born in Berlin, not as commonly thought, in South Africa, and studied under Max Reinhardt. He trained as an editor at Korda's London Films and his own work shows the influence of René Clair, for whom he worked on *The Ghost Goes West* (1935). *Hue and Cry* is a British variation on the famous Erich Kästner Berlin story, *Emil and the Detectives*, and *It Always Rains on Sunday* is firmly in the Carné-Prévert tradition of the 1930s.

Bibliography

Barsacq, Leon, *Caligari's Cabinet and other Grand Illusions: A History of Film Design* (New York: Little, Brown, 1976).

Brunel, Adrian, *Nice Work* (London: Forbes Robertson, 1949).

Gough-Yates, Kevin, *Michael Powell in Collaboration with Emeric Pressburger* (London: British Film Institute, 1971).

Low, Rachael, *The History of British Film 1929–1939: Film Making in 1930s Britain* (London: George Allen and Unwin, 1997; reprinted, Routledge, 1997).

Macdonald, Kevin, *Emeric Pressburger: The Life and Death of a Screenwriter* (London: Faber and Faber, 1994).

Powell, Michael, *A Life in Movies* (London: Heinemann, 1986).

Tabori, Paul, *Alexander Korda* (London: Oldbourne, 1959).

Wright, Basil, *The Long View* (London: Secker and Warburg, 1974).

This essay derives from an earlier article that appeared in Günter Berghaus (ed.), *Theatre and Film in Exile: German Artists in Britain 1933–45* (Berg Publishers, 1989).

11
A Song and Dance at the Local: Thoughts on Ealing

Tim Pulleine

The production history of Ealing Studios under Michael Balcon spanned two decades, from 1938 to 1959. Yet four decades after the company's shutdown Ealing remains, with the possible exception of Rank, the likeliest response in any word-association game to the phrase 'British cinema'. Or more precisely, the response might be Ealing Comedy; and whilst of the nearly one hundred films made by Ealing, fewer than thirty are comedies, the fact is that in the handful of 'essential' Ealing movies comedies figure strongly.

In British film production itself, the Ealing legacy is frequently foregrounded. Among high-profile British pictures of the recent past, *A Fish Called Wanda* (1988) is the work of an ex-Ealing director, Charles Crichton, and reworks elements of its Ealing comedy predecessors, adding in the sex and violence which they excluded. *Chariots of Fire* (1980), which dramatises a true story of moral endeavour very much in an Ealing mould, bears a dedication to the memory of Sir Michael Balcon.

When Balcon took up the post of head of production at Ealing in 1938, he was already an established presence in British cinema, having filled the same position at both Gainsborough and Gaumont British.[1] In the interim, he had briefly and unhappily been involved in inaugurating the British production arm of Metro-Goldwyn-Mayer, with *A Yank at Oxford* (1938). Balcon's personal dissatisfaction with this phase of his career assumed a wider symptomatic value with his tenure at Ealing. A continuing refrain in British film history has been the question of whether to seek to challenge Hollywood on its own ground, or to play the 'national' card by embodying qualities of 'Britishness'. Balcon was in no doubt about endorsing the latter course, although his method of doing so – creating a team of personnel and concentrating on self-sufficiency and a policy of in-house promotion – was one which echoed the tactics of Hollywood companies such as MGM.

The first film of the new Ealing era, *The Gaunt Stranger* (Walter Forde, 1938), was a version of Edgar Wallace's previously filmed novel and play *The Ringer*, a conventional comedy thriller of the sort that might have been made at any other British studio. Pen Tennyson's *There Ain't No Justice* (1939), about the trials and tribulations of a small-time boxer, was more significant. Though recognisably made in the studio, the film depicts its Cockney working-class community with detailed affection, and the story ends with the protagonist turning his back on the fight game in favour of an 'ordinary' life.

The moral scheme (community life good/commercial machinations bad) may presage Ealing films to come, but a clearer indicator of Ealing's future is to be found in Walter Forde's *Cheer Boys Cheer* (1939), a comedy in which the family brewing firm of Greenleaf becomes a takeover target for the heavyweight Ironside company. It is with the foiling of this scheme that the plot is concerned. Greenleaf's product is advertised as 'the beer of Old England'; the Ironside owner is glimpsed reading *Mein Kampf*: given that the film appeared only weeks before the outbreak of war, the wider implications are inescapable. Charles Barr points up the correspondence between Greenleaf and Ealing itself: deliberately small, characterised by family atmosphere and a 'benevolent paternalism'.[2]

Forde also made *Saloon Bar* (1940), set in the precincts of a pub in a working-class area of London. A formula picture with an artificial comedy-thriller plot about clearing an innocent man's name, *Saloon Bar* has considerable incidental vitality. In particular, it draws an unpatronising picture of the *ad hoc* community of regulars, who rally round in a good cause, complete with running jokes and bits of character business. Short shrift is given to a group of rather unlikely toffs, who become the target of caustic mockery as soon as they have departed. And the coda is significant: the local bobby turns up to point out it is after closing time, only to discover that the landlord has become a father again and to be invited in for celebratory drinks. The policeman's response is a cheerful assent, and as the door closes on him the end title appears: we are left with the sense of a small, cosy clan that may know its place but is not going to stand for being messed about.

Most of Ealing's thirty or so wartime films are concerned with the war itself, though several are vehicles for such performers as George Formby and Will Hay as they take on spies, saboteurs and fifth columnists. In the sphere of war films proper, Ealing got off to an unsatisfactory start. Tennyson's *Convoy* (1940) made use of material shot in the North Sea, but married it uneasily to a romantic triangle plot amid the officer class, which the casting of Clive Brook and John Clements only renders the more theatrical. Much worse, though, is *Ships with Wings* (Sergei Nolbandov, 1941), a purported account of the Fleet Air Arm in peace and war which paints it as the sole preserve of what a later generation would term upper-class twits.

Balcon's recruitment of talented documentary film-makers like Alberto Cavalcanti and Harry Watt brought an influx of realism into Ealing's wartime films, and it is startling to compare *Convoy* and *Ships with Wings* with *Nine Men* (1943), the first fictional work to be directed by Watt. A film which deserves a wider reputation, it has been described by Laurence Kardish as 'the leanest, simplest and most paradigmatic of Ealing's wartime narratives'.[3] Running only sixty-eight minutes, *Nine Men* constitutes a flashback, narrated by a veteran sergeant (Jack Lambert) to men in training, describing the survival of a small patrol cut off in the Libyan desert. This is conspicuously an other ranks' war (the sole officer dies early on), with a spread of authentic-sounding regional accents, and while the language is necessarily expurgated, it achieves a vernacular, sometimes surprisingly near-the-knuckle, pastiche of soldiers' talk. The functional style mirrors the lack of rhetoric in the script; war is presented as a grimly unromantic job of work.

Coming between *Ships with Wings* and *Nine Men*, however, are a group of films released in 1942 – *The Foreman Went to France* (Charles Frend), *Next of Kin* (Thorold Dickinson) and *Went the Day Well?* (Cavalcanti) – which negotiate a transition in attitudes. The concept which in different ways they promote is that of a people's war, of democracy in action in its own defence. In *The Foreman Went to France* a Welsh engineer crosses the Channel at the time of the fall of France in a bid to retrieve machinery his firm has installed and keep it out of German hands. This is by its nature an amateur initiative, but that very fact is used to stress the need for a hard-headed, professional approach. The protagonist is aided by an American woman and by two British soldiers, a Cockney and a Scot, but when a British officer appears he is revealed to be a German spy. Unfortunately the film suffers from a not very French atmosphere, and the conclusion, in which the democratic theme is illustrated by a vote-taking among passengers on an escape vessel over whether to sacrifice their belongings in order to accommodate the machinery, seems hollow and schematic.

Next of Kin was initially commissioned by the War Office as a training film, and then expanded into a commercial feature. The narrative, showing how a German spy ring contrives to obtain details of a 'secret' British raid on the French coast, is tense and convincing in itself, but also acts as a critique of the easygoing British amateur spirit: at the final fade-out, the unapprehended chief spy is still at large and going about his business. *Went the Day Well?* is equally grim. It is set in a 'typically English' Hertfordshire village, where it transpires that the squire (played by four-square Leslie Banks) is a Nazi plant, waiting to do his bit for the Fatherland, when an invasion force of German commandos infiltrates the community in the guise of British soldiers on an exercise. Understated realism of behaviour and surroundings give the film the conviction which *The Foreman Went to France* ultimately lacks, and underscores its endorsement of the need to meet ruthlessness with ruthlessness. Fittingly, it is an old poacher (Edward Rigby), rather than any of the upper-class figures, who is most responsible for thwarting the German plan.

When Ealing returned to the war at sea with *San Demetrio-London* (Charles Frend, 1943), the democratic impulse is evident. The *San Demetrio* is a merchant ship, bringing oil from the US in 1940, abandoned after being holed in a German attack. Subsequently, survivors among the crew rediscover the ship still afloat, board her and contrive to sail her home. The men function as a unified team, with decisions taken by vote, and any division between officers and the rest becomes one of function. The effort and sacrifice involved are rendered the more affecting for the ostensible matter-of-factness of the narrative.

Ealing's wartime oeuvre, seen as a whole, cannot be described as documentary in the formal sense of utilising actual locales and non-professional actors. What it does evince, though, is a distinctive form of realism, a capacity for projecting a view of British character in convincingly direct terms.

How could this impetus be harnessed to the post-war situation? Balcon himself seemed uncertain: 'Because we felt we were at the beginning of a new era ... we were inclined to try out our talents on different sorts of films.'[4] The British cinema in the period immediately after the war was possessed of a spirit of confidence, evidenced in particular by the work of David Lean, Carol Reed, and Michael Powell and Emeric Pressburger. To a degree, Ealing sought to follow the path of prestige, via such films as *Scott of the Antarctic* (Charles Frend, 1948) and *Saraband for Dead Lovers* (Basil Dearden, 1948). *Scott of the Antarctic*, a popular success at the time, is in its latter stages impressively mounted, with locations in Norway, as a reconstruction of the ill-fated expedition to the South Pole, but it remains dramatically inert. *Saraband for Dead Lovers*, which was a commercial failure, is revealing in a complementary way. Again an elaborately mounted colour production, the film is a costume melodrama, recreating a doomed romance against the background of the eighteenth-century Hanoverian court. The self-consciously academic style stands in opposition to that of the Gainsborough pictures, and to the supposed vulgarity of Hollywood costume epics; the very title has an anti-popular ring to it; and the film itself unfortunately jettisons not only melodrama but drama itself. Both these films convey a striving for 're-spectable' status, and a concomitant sense of inhibition.

The film from Ealing's early post-war period that with hindsight becomes most in-dicative is a modest comedy, *Hue and Cry* (Charles Crichton, 1947). The representa-tive image of the film is its climax, a free-for-all amid the London bomb sites in which numerous boys, devotees of a blood-and-thunder weekly magazine, get the better of a gang of crooks who have been using a serial in its pages to disseminate information among themselves. The extensive use of locations, for all that they remain subordinate to a studio-based style, communicates a topicality patently not to be found in prestige literary pictures. *Hue and Cry* is, though, an exercise in fantasy, something which the down-to-earth surroundings serve to throw into relief; in fact, one of the most engag-ing sequences, in which two of the boys gain an audience with the eccentric author (Alastair Sim) of the serial in question, makes its effect through exaggeratedly mock-sinister lighting and composition. But the fantasy acts for the characters – and ar-guably for the audience as well – as a safety valve; at the end, they return to the quotidian round of school and work in the fantasy-free zone of austerity Britain.

Here is the genesis of Ealing comedy. Balcon commented in his autobiography: 'The bloodless revolution of 1945 had taken place, but I think our first desire was to get rid of as many wartime restrictions as possible and get going ... there was a mild anarchy in the air.'[5] The success of *Hue and Cry* led to *Passport to Pimlico* (Henry Cornelius, 1949) and *Whisky Galore!* (Alexander Mackendrick, 1949), films whose stock in trade is mild anarchy.

Passport to Pimlico turns on the comic conceit of an ancient document which reveals that the London borough of the title belongs to the kingdom of Burgundy and is thus

Small cosy clans. Walter Forde's Cheer Boys Cheer *(1939).*

Walter Forde's Saloon Bar *(1940).*

independent of British rule. The film's construction is artful, with a rapid exposition and a compression in the subsequent action which gives the impression of a hectic series of events being contained within a few days, when in mundane reality they would drag on for months. Early on, the idealistic shopkeeper (Stanley Holloway), who wants to set up a children's playground, is told at a council meeting, 'This borough is in no position to finance daydreams'; but the ensuing discovery of Burgundian treasure trove permits exactly this. The trouble is that the daydream is rapidly undercut by external events: the pubs stay open all day, but an army of spivs moves into the locality. The film turns, in a fashion that its surface speed serves partly to obscure, on a kind of double bluff: a supposed celebration of the jettisoning of wartime restrictions becomes a nostalgic evocation of the wartime spirit of solidarity. The rituals of evacuation and bundles for Britain are run through in a spirit of play. Finally, Pimlico returns to Britain, as the heatwave gives way to a downpour, a declension of mood which seems to presage a sense of relief. A contemporary comment by Richard Winnington is to the point: 'The apex of Burgundian emancipation is a song and dance in the local after hours.'[6] It is an allusion that reflects not only back to the jocular ending of *Saloon Bar* but also forward to the very last Ealing comedy, *Barnacle Bill* (Charles Frend, 1957), which concludes with a party of revellers being precipitately ejected from a drinking session under the eye of a policeman.

Drink is central also to *Whisky Galore!* 'It's a well-known medical fact that some men are born two drinks under par,' says the doctor (James Robertson Justice) who is 'fuelling' the repressed teacher (Gordon Jackson) for a confrontation with his domineering mother. Whisky, in this story of a Hebridean island community whose stock of it has run out until a ship carrying the stuff is wrecked offshore, is seen as a liberating force. The start of the film, once past a whimsical passage of mock-documentary narration, is dark and fog-bound, and it is only the unscheduled arrival of the cargo of spirits which brings music and an acceleration of tempo. The film, deriving via Compton Mackenzie's novel from an actual incident, is set in 1943, and can be seen as 'exploiting the dramatic conventions of a war film – or to be exact, a resistance movie'.[7] The resistance is, though, against the authorities on the British mainland (the posse of revenue men in black macintoshes imports overtones of the Gestapo), and specifically against the English commanding officer of the local Home Guard detachment, Captain Waggett (Basil Radford), who views the plunder as contraband. Through an understated, almost elliptical style, the film illustrates the series of ruthless stratagems by which the islanders undercut Waggett's position until he is finally rejected even by his wife and is condemned in the eyes of his superiors. The misanthropy of this, allied to the fact that the island community is not cosily united (the publican, put at a pecuniary disadvantage, informs on the conspirators), contrives to give the movie a genuine, albeit mild, edge of anarchy.

The third Ealing comedy of 1949, *Kind Hearts and Coronets* (Robert Hamer), is a very different matter. This is black comedy in an Edwardian period setting, the tale of an aristocrat in reduced circumstances who murders his way through the relatives standing between him and a dukedom (with Alec Guinness playing all the victims). Literary in tone, it is a work of structural intricacy, including at one stage a flashback within a flashback. The extensive use for ironic effect of a first-person narration, together with the periodic use of Mozart on the soundtrack, make it seem like a stylistic precursor of the French New Wave. Crucially, however, this is a film that centres on that most English, but generally un-Ealing, preoccupation of class distinction (the French release title was *Noblesse Oblige*), and although the plot is motivated by revenge for class-based snobbery, the impulse that sustains it is far from a democratic one. Moreover, it is defiantly amoral: despite the sop to censorship of a trick ending which suggests that the murderer may have delivered himself to subsequent justice, the tenor of the conclusion is that the claimant to the coronet has won the day.

The two melodramas which Hamer previously directed for Ealing – *Pink String and Sealing Wax* (1945), which shares the Edwardian setting of *Kind Hearts*, and *It Always Rains on Sunday* (1947), set in the contemporary East End – have in common with their successor a strongly marked formal configuration and a thematic concern with the clash between natural instinct and institutional restraint. In some respects Hamer's work invokes correspondences with that of Fritz Lang, and there is a specific association of Langian fatalism in the shot in *It Always Rains on Sunday* of the slowly spinning wheel of the bicycle discarded by the fleeing jailbreaker. Hamer refracts the studio's themes of community and togetherness through the prism of a socially agnostic sensibility, achieving a creative tension rare in British cinema. His distance from the Ealing ethos becomes apparent if one compares *It Always Rains on Sunday* with *The Blue Lamp* (Basil Dearden, 1950), which embodies with particular directness an ideal set of Ealing values: a good-humoured, stratified community in action in the defence both of itself and of wider society.

What becomes apparent in the concluding decade of Ealing production is not so much the absence of auteurist projects like Hamer's, an absence characteristic of British cinema in the wider scheme, but rather the manner in which the changing circumstances of British life – the social diversification and rising consumer affluence in the 'new Elizabethan' age – were increasingly at variance with the Ealing ethos.

In the comedy sphere, *The Lavender Hill Mob* (Charles Crichton, 1951) is indicative of an encroaching parochialism. By fitting paradox, the framing sequences take place in Latin America, where millionaire-in-exile Alec Guinness is recounting the saga behind his ill-gotten fortune. But the closing scene reveals that his confidant is a Scotland Yard man, to whom he is handcuffed in readiness for the journey home to retribution. This undercuts the screenplay's contention that 'the saddest words in the world are "it might have been"', reducing the action to a game in which the powers-that-be have an inbuilt right to win.

A divorcement from reality is heightened in *The Titfield Thunderbolt* (Charles Crichton, 1953), where the very fantasticality of the stratagems involved in saving 'the oldest branch railway in the world' tends to throw into relief the odd precepts on which the story rests. In what a contemporary reviewer called a 'Toytown village' it seems to be perpetual summer, where all and sundry appear to have limitless time and energy to devote to what is in effect a philanthropic enterprise, and where a trade union official's intervention is laughed off as a truculent irrelevance.[8]

The capital and labour issue is touched on to more pointed effect in two comedies by Mackendrick, *The Man in the White Suit* (1951) and *The Maggie* (1954). But while the first film may look in its early stages as if it will anticipate the 'white heat of technology' theme which the following decade's Labour administration would seek to promote, the story ends in whimsical retreat, and the light in which both sides of industry are depicted is sour enough to make some of the humorous business of chases and explosions assume an imposed air. *The Maggie* has something of the ruthlessness of *Whisky Galore!* in the humbling of its American tycoon protagonist, but the literally backwater nature of the setting conspires to lend this film, too, a feeling of whimsicality.

However, in Mackendrick's last Ealing comedy, *The Ladykillers* (1955), one does sense a critical engagement with the project's potential for whimsy. The opening scene includes the words 'It was all a dream', and the ensuing plot rests emblematically upon an elaborate sham. Within this scheme, the film proffers a caricatural cross-section of Britain both 'old' (the camel-coated bogus major, played by Cecil Parker) and 'new' (Teddy Boy-garbed Peter Sellers), while design and colour styling contrive to combine the higgledy-piggledy Toytown aspects of the milieu with intimations of the gothic world of the Hammer horror movies which would shortly make their entrance into British cinema. *The Ladykillers*, with its *reductio ad absurdum* narrative, functions as, in the older sense of the word, a cartoon; and with hindsight its implicit irony is redoubled by the knowledge that the then cosy King's Cross vicinity of London, where the story takes place, would subsequently become notorious as a red-light district.

When it comes to dramatic subjects, 50s Ealing tends to be typified by half-hearted stage adaptations such as Dearden's *The Gentle Gunman* (1952) and *The Square Ring* (1953), or, more worthily but not much more rewardingly, by Crichton's *The Divided Heart* (1954), a tug-of-love story set in post-war Germany which uneasily straddles emotional melodrama and documentary. A counter-example, however, is *The Ship that Died of Shame* (Basil Dearden, 1955), in which a trio of friends reunite some years after their wartime naval service, using their old motor gunboat for black-market smuggling. The loss of a wartime sense of purpose and the rise of a 'get rich quick' ethos (brilliantly embodied in Richard Attenborough's playing of a superior spiv) are pointedly dramatised. The semi-supernatural ending, with the vessel apparently wrecking itself, bespeaks the film-makers' lack of any sense of a positive way ahead.

The police procedural thriller *The Long Arm* (Charles Frend, 1956) climaxes in the thwarting of a scheme to rob the Royal Festival Hall, emblem of the 1951 Festival of Britain which had once symbolised post-war optimism. Five years on, such idealism had been displaced, and *The Long Arm*, whose storyline visits various parts of the country almost as if to offer a cross-section of British life, is low-key and ironic in tone. The film is efficiently mounted, but there is something dogged about its professionalism, perhaps symptomatic of Ealing's own position.

It is interesting to contrast *The Long Arm* with one of the last Ealing movies, *Nowhere to Go* (1958), the directorial debut of Seth Holt, who had for many years been an Ealing editor. Here again is a fragmented society, but in this case it is an underworld with little time for the tenet of 'honour among thieves', and the central figure is not a policeman but a plausible Canadian conman (George Nader), a loner anti-hero who represents a denial of any team spirit. While the film is in its latter stages over-reliant on a quota quickie plot, its stylistic accoutrements – jazz score, luminous camerawork – link it with the French New Wave movies and another kind of cinema altogether. The disparity heightens the feeling that, over and above the economic practicalities, Ealing itself had been left with nowhere very much to go.

It would be possible to see in Nader's lonely death an analogy with the fate of the fugitive in *It Always Rains on Sunday* a decade earlier; the crucial difference is that in the later film there is no alternative community to which the other characters, and the audience's allegiance, can be returned, and no further prospect of a song and dance at the local, after hours or not. And yet, down all the intervening years, the melody of such vanished celluloid get-togethers has proved obstinately inclined to linger on.

Notes

1. Film production at Ealing had begun in 1931, when the studio became the base of ATP, the company headed by Basil Dean. Dean left in 1938, and after Balcon's arrival the company's name was changed to Ealing.
2. Charles Barr, *Ealing Studios* (London: Cameron and Tayleur/David & Charles, 1977, revised ed. 1993), pp. 5, 6.
3. Laurence Kardish, 'Michael Balcon and the Idea of a National Cinema', in *Michael Balcon: The Pursuit of British Cinema* (New York: Museum of Modern Art, 1984), p. 57.
4. Michael Balcon, *Michael Balcon Presents ... A Lifetime of Films* (London: Hutchinson, 1969), p. 157.
5. Ibid, p. 159.
6. *News Chronicle*, 30 April 1949.
7. Philip Kemp, *Lethal Innocence – The Cinema of Alexander Mackendrick* (London: Methuen, 1991), p. 32.
8. Penelope Houston, *Sight and Sound*, vol. 22, no. 4, April–June 1953.

Bibliography

Balcon, Michael, *Michael Balcon Presents ... A Lifetime of Films* (London: Hutchinson, 1969).
Barr, Charles, *Ealing Studios* (London: Cameron and Tayleur/David & Charles, 1977, revised ed. 1993).
Cook, Jim, 'The Ship That Died of Shame', in Charles Barr (ed.), *All Our Yesterdays* (London: British Film Institute, 1986).
Danischewsky, Monja (ed.), *Michael Balcon's 25 Years in Films* (London: World Film Publications, 1947).
Houston, Penelope, *Went the Day Well?* (London: British Film Institute, 1992).
Kemp, Philip, *Lethal Innocence – The Cinema of Alexander Mackendrick* (London: Methuen, 1991).
Perry, George, *Forever Ealing* (London: Pavilion/Michael Joseph, 1981).
Michael Balcon: The Pursuit of British Cinema (New York: Museum of Modern Art, 1984).

12
Methodism versus the Market-place:
The Rank Organisation and British Cinema

Vincent Porter

The activities of J. Arthur Rank during the 1940s and 1950s lie at the very heart of British cinema history, for during that period he was both Britain's chief cinema owner and its principal film producer. He had to resolve the tensions between cinema exhibition and film production; and between domestic and international distribution. But Rank was also a devout Methodist. He felt his films should promote family values at home and the British way of life overseas.

Building an empire

Rank first became involved with the film industry in 1934 when he set up British National. The company's first film, *Turn of the Tide* (Norman Walker, 1935), was a melodrama about Yorkshire fishing folk with a moral message. Although it won third prize at the Venice Film Festival, it was denied a proper release and Rank decided to use some of his financial muscle to improve matters. In partnership with Sheffield builder Henry Boot, he built Pinewood Studios and backed C. M. Woolf, the leading film distributor, to develop his own company, General Film Distributors. But it was not until the end of 1941 that Rank emerged into the limelight. In October he bought the Gaumont British Picture Corporation with its chain of cinemas and the Gainsborough production unit at Shepherd's Bush studios. In December, Oscar Deutsch, chairman of Odeon Cinema Holdings, which Rank already half-owned, died suddenly, and Rank became chairman. He was now the most powerful figure in the British film industry.

Rank had acted on his religious principles when he set up GHW Productions in 1937. Run by the editor of the *Methodist Times*, the Reverend Benjamin Gregory, and Norman Walker, the director of *Turn of the Tide*, GHW Productions made several feature films with a religious message, all directed by Walker. They included *The Man at the Gate* (1941), *Hard Steel* (1942), *The Great Mr Handel* (1942), a Technicolor production in which the composer is restored to royal favour after writing *The Messiah* and *They Knew Mr Knight* (1945). Fascinating though they now seem, none of these films was successful at the box office and Rank's commercial instincts were better served by Independent Producers, which he established in 1942 to provide production finance and management facilities to a number of independent production companies. The principal beneficiaries were The Archers (Michael Powell and Emeric Pressburger), Cineguild (David Lean, Anthony Havelock-Allan and Ronald Neame), Individual Pictures (Frank Launder and Sidney Gilliat) and Wessex Productions (Ian Dalrymple). Two years later Rank acquired Two Cities Films, headed by the Italian producer Filippo Del Giudice, who was producing his films at Denham Studios, and signed a co-financing and distribution contract with Michael Balcon's Ealing Studios. Initially, Rank gave his producers a free hand, but when profits failed to materialise changes were made. At Two Cities, Del Giudice was replaced by Josef Somlo and Earl St. John; and at Gainsborough, Maurice Ostrer had to make way for Sydney Box.

In 1947, the government's attempt to tax imported films led to a boycott by Hollywood and thus a shortage of films. Rank increased production, but to do so he had to restructure his empire. He used his control of Odeon Theatres to buy the issued share capital of his production and distribution vehicle, the General Cinema Finance Corporation (GCF), which in turn owned Gainsborough, Two Cities and Independent Producers. His minority shareholders, notably the United Artists Corporation, were aghast. Suddenly their investments in the comparatively safe trade of cinema exhibition were being switched into the far more risky business of film production and distribution. By the time Rank's films were ready for release, the American boycott had ended and he had to compete with the best that Hollywood could offer. In October 1948, Odeon Theatres had a £13.6 million overdraft; the following year it rose to £16.3 million.

Rank's financial restructuring also affected his production policy. In order to increase his film output but to keep costs down, he tried to introduce new rules about budgets and the submission of scripts, progressively alienating the prestigious producer/director teams which worked under the Independent Producers' umbrella. Powell and Pressburger followed Carol Reed to British Lion, after disputes with Rank and his company secretary John Davis over the budget and the distribution plans for *The Red Shoes* (1948).[1] Launder and Gilliat soon followed, because of Rank's inflexibility over the distribution arrangements for *The Blue Lagoon* (1948).[2] Cineguild split up, as first Anthony Havelock-Allan and then David Lean moved from Pinewood to Shepperton. So did the Wessex team (Ian Dalrymple and Jack Lee), who went on to make their most successful film, *The Wooden Horse* (1950), for British Lion.

The differences between Rank and his most successful film-makers lay in the tension between quality and quantity. Rank and Davis wanted a steady supply of British films to fill the screens of their Odeon and Gaumont cinemas. When the financial crisis came, they were in a dilemma. What type of production should they cut back? To businessmen like Rank and Davis, the choices were contradictory. The most profitable, and most prestigious, films were those which did only moderately well at home but could be immensely profitable abroad.

The films released by Rank between January 1947 and June 1949 cost between £113,600 (*My Brother's Keeper*, 1948) and £572,500 (*Hamlet*, 1948), but the two most expensive, *Hamlet* and *The Red Shoes*, made the most profit – about £780,000 each.[3] Both did extremely well overseas, especially in the USA, and the company estimated that their foreign earnings would ultimately exceed £1 million each. But only eight of thirty cheaper films, which Rank and Davis considered more typical, were expected to make a profit. Worse, three of these films, *Great Expectations*, *Oliver Twist* and *The Blue Lagoon*, all made through Independent Producers, cost more than £300,000 each and none of them covered their costs in the UK. Only two (*Portrait from Life* and *Easy Money*) cost less than £150,000.

Rank and Davis had to choose between a few high-budget, high-risk and potentially highly profitable pictures and a greater number of lower-budget pictures. But they also had to supply Rank cinemas with British films. To meet their quota requirements, the Gaumont and the Odeon circuits each had to show sixteen British films a year. Rank also needed to keep his two film studios at Pinewood and Denham turning over. His business empire was like an overloaded bicycle: if it slowed down, it would fall to the ground. A quick glance at the group's financial results during the 1950s makes the company's structural problem clear (see Table). Its main income was from domestic exhibition, which produced approximately £3 million a year. Film production and distribution could as easily make a loss as a profit. As Rank told his shareholders in 1952, 'Each film produced is in effect a new enterprise and a prototype and although much care is taken before production starts, it is impossible to know whether a successful film will be made until the film is available for showing.'[4] The first task for Rank and Davis was to secure their principal revenue base – film exhibition. They had to opt for quantity. They therefore imposed an upper limit of £150,000 on each production. Even this figure was on the high side, for only four of their recent films had recouped this sum from their UK release, although each had cost far more to produce.[5]

Rank Group trading results 1950–1960

Year	1950	1951	1952	1953	1954	1955	1956	1957	1958	1959	1960
					[£ Millions]						
UK Exhibition	2.8	3.5	3.3	2.9	3.3	3.6	2.7	2.7	2.2	2.4	2.2
Overseas Exhibition	0.3	0.3	0.6	0.6	0.6	0.3	0.2	0.4	0.3	0.4	0.5
Production and Distribution	−2.1	−1.3	−0.1	+0.3	+0.8	+0.7	+0.9	+0.7	−1.3	−0.9	+0.2
Manufacturing	0.3	0.8	1.1	1.3	1.3	2.2	2.0	1.5	1.1	1.4	1.5
Studio/Labs	0.3	0.2	0.2	0.2	0.2	0.3	0.4	0.3	0.4	0.4	0.4
Miscellaneous activities	0.2	0.2	0.3	0.3	0.2	0.3	0.1	0.1	0.1	0.2	0.3
Total*	1.8	3.7	5.4	5.7	6.3	7.4	6.4	5.8	3.0	4.0	5.1

Source: Annual Reports and Accounts

* There are minor discrepancies in the totals because individual figures have been rounded up or down to the nearest hundred thousand pounds. After 1952, dividends received on trade investments have been apportioned over the various activities of the group. Tax figures, and dividends payable to shareholders, have been omitted.

Restructuring cinema exhibition

One way in which Rank and Davis sought to improve their revenue was to increase receipts from overseas exhibition. By 1956, in addition to his UK cinemas, Rank owned cinemas in Canada, the Republic of Ireland, Jamaica and Portugal; he also had partnership arrangements with cinemas in Australia, South Africa, New Zealand, Malaya, Ceylon and the Netherlands.[6] Overseas receipts doubled in five years, but cinema exhibition was not a cash cow which could be milked at will. The habit audience, on which the lazy exhibitor had come to rely, was already starting to stay at home; and as the decade progressed the struggle to maintain revenues became ever more difficult.

For Rank, a strict Methodist, his cinemas were not merely a source of profit. They also had a social role to fulfil. He told his shareholders:

> The motion picture theatre is in many ways a local and communal institution and its success is dependent on the standing of its Manager and his staff in the local

community. Our personnel are loyal, keen and enthusiastic men, who have taken a leading part in the social and economic problems of the communities in which they operate.[7]

His philosophy was to 'offer through the medium of cinema theatres, *healthy entertainment* under ideal conditions *for all members of the family*'.[8] He also promoted healthy entertainment for children with his Saturday morning film matinees. On Good Friday 1953, he even offered the Campaign for Methodist Advance the facilities for five-minute religious talks in more than 400 of his cinemas, while in a further twenty-four cinemas they were given permission to hold a full-scale service including a showing of the film *Which Will You Have?* But altruism was also the handmaiden of commerce. *Which Will You Have?*, a 36-minute film about the arrest and release of Barabbas the robber, had been produced in 1949 by one of Rank's own subsidiaries, GB Instructional.[9]

Rank's cinemas had access to the most popular American films through his ties with Columbia, Disney, 20th Century-Fox, United Artists and Universal. Indeed, during the 1950s American films regularly accounted for 70 per cent of Rank's circuit releases. The one significant constraint was the Government's requirement for a 30 per cent quota of British films, which Rank sought to fulfil as scrupulously as possible. The only quota year in which he seriously defaulted was 1949–50, when his bookers rejected eleven films they considered so poor that they could not be played as first features without incurring additional losses.[10] Rank's only subsequent quota failures, after the national shortage of British feature films in 1950–51, were with the 25 per cent quota for the supporting programme, but the Board of Trade did not consider this worth pursuing.[11]

With the decline in cinema audiences in the 1950s, Rank began to exploit its dominant position in order to increase its share of the market. In 1952, it owned 12 per cent of UK screens, but by 1965, although it only had 330 cinemas, they accounted for 16 per cent of screens.[12] Disgruntled independent cinema owners claimed that Rank was acting uncompetitively because he prevented them from obtaining access to the best films until he had fully exploited them in his own theatres. Rank cinemas often included barring clauses in the licensing agreement signed with a film's distributor, which ensured that no other cinema within a fifteen-mile radius could simultaneously show the film, thus eliminating all local competition. For 70mm films which were given longer runs in selected cinemas the radius was often increased to twenty-five miles. In addition to distance bars, there were also time bars – seven days for most films and fourteen days for 70mm films.[13] The distributors were usually happy to comply with these restrictions because they reduced the number of prints for which they had to pay.

Even so, Rank had to close many cinemas. Between 1954 and 1963 the corporation disposed of 189 cinemas because they were making a loss and a further 25 because of programming difficulties. In 1958, John Davis decided to merge the Odeon and Gaumont circuits into a single circuit. He also tried to establish a third circuit from some of his less successful cinemas and the remaining independents; but the other exhibitors declined to co-operate.[14] By 1960 there were only two cinema circuits in the UK, Odeon and ABC.

Production in the 1950s

The National Film Finance Corporation (NFFC) was established in 1949 to provide finance for independent film production, but it immediately had to loan £3 million of its funds to bail out British Lion. In order to provide continuity of production for the rest of the industry, the NFFC set up three new consortia. The Rank/NFFC consortium, British Film Makers (BFM), consisted of a group of producers who would theoretically retain their creative independence but who would also work together to ensure a properly planned and continuous production programme. The producer-director teams were advanced money to prepare a script and a budget. Rank and the NFFC then financed the films, and any profits went into a pool. BFM films received 70 per cent of their production finance from the National Provincial Bank against Rank's distribution guarantees. The remaining 30 per cent, £707,000 in all, came from the NFFC. Completion guarantees were jointly provided by the NFFC and General Film Distributors, Rank's distribution company.[15] Rank had to guarantee the distribution of BFM's films, but the only capital he had at risk was that shared with the NFFC for completion guarantees. In return, BFM provided Rank with a supply of British films for his cinemas at comparatively little cost.

Unfortunately, this semi-co-operative arrangement was torn by internal dissent. After eighteen months it had financed fourteen films – six produced by BFM alone, the other eight co-productions with independent producers. None of the BFM films was listed as a box-office winner, although *Appointment with Venus* (Ralph Thomas) was a 'notable attraction' in 1951; and *The Card* (Ronald Neame), *Hunted* (Charles Crichton), and *The Importance of Being Earnest* (Anthony Asquith) were 'notable attractions' in 1952. Rank's biggest box-office successes were two Ealing films, *Where No Vultures Fly* (Harry Watt, 1951) and *Mandy* (Alexander Mackendrick, 1952), and *The Planter's Wife* (Ken Annakin, 1952).[16]

Rank decided to establish a new production order by which he could maintain control over the subject of each film, and in late 1952 he ended his agreement with the NFFC and wound up BFM.

This was a critical period for Rank, for when his elder brother James died he also had to run the family flour business. He became less involved in the day-to-day problems of his film business, but tried to retain control over the films the company made by 'buying the brains that do know about films'.[17] He chose John Davis and Earl St. John, the head of production at Pinewood, for the task. From then on they effectively managed Rank's film business. The only subsequent occasion on which Rank rejected their advice was when he allowed Philip Leacock to make *The Kidnappers*, on condition that he would bring in 'the name of the Good Lord'.[18] Rank wanted films which would be representative of Great Britain and assist in upholding its prestige abroad. But they were also to have high entertainment value acceptable to world audiences. John Davis dutifully echoed his master's vision. 'The aim is to make films of high entertainment value, of good technical standards, in good taste, and with sound moral standards'.[19]

Not surprisingly, the Rank films produced during this period all reinforced family values in one way or another. Most of them were contemporary comedies, adventure pictures, or dramas. In Rank crime pictures the dramatic focus of the film was often not the crime itself but the morals and motives of those who were caught up in solving it.[20] 'Adult' subjects, like John Osborne's play *Look Back in Anger* or Alan Sillitoe's novel *Saturday Night and Sunday Morning*, were rejected. There were no science-fiction films and virtually no musicals. Historical subjects, if treated at all, were normally about British heroism or adventures in the Second World War, and those that were set in an earlier period, such as *A Tale of Two Cities* (Ralph Thomas, 1958) or *North West Frontier* (J. Lee Thompson, 1959), often had a central hero who

Bringing in the name of the Good Lord. Philip Leacock's The Kidnappers *(1953).*

unquestioningly fought off the enemy in order to defend British values or British interests.

Rank's principal production organisation, Group Film Producers, was based at Pinewood. The aim was to maintain a production programme of some fifteen films a year and to co-finance around six films from Ealing. After 1955, Rank ceased to support Ealing and production at Pinewood was increased to twenty films a year. In John Davis's view there were extremely few 'independent producers', as they did not either provide their own production finance or accept the financial risks involved. He therefore established an elaborate system of financial and organisational controls which shaped and limited the production of all Rank films. In return for their production finance, all producers who worked for Rank had to accept curbs on their creative freedom. Each project had to be approved by the board in two stages. The first was to agree the general treatment of a particular subject, such as a novel or a play, and to finance pre-production development. The second was to approve a detailed package of the final script, the principal players, the director, the production schedule and budget. For most films it could take almost a year to develop an idea or a story into a fully planned production.[21] Sometimes a film project, such as *Lawrence of Arabia*, which was to have been produced by Anatole de Grunwald and directed by Anthony Asquith, would fall at the second hurdle.[22] A Rank producer was also expected to use some of the stages at Pinewood, even though most film-makers preferred to shoot on location. In addition, a producer often had to cast some of Rank's contract artists.

During the 1950s the company maintained about forty contract artists, some of whom, such as Diana Dors, Jill Ireland and Anthony Steel, had been through the Rank Charm School. They were employed on long-term contracts, usually for seven years, although Rank retained the freedom to terminate the contract if the artist's behaviour was unsatisfactory. When the artist worked outside Rank, the contract was automatically extended to make up for any leave of absence. If a contract artist was assigned to a Rank film, the production company had to pay half the artist's annual salary. Thus assignment to two films would cover an artist's annual salary; any more, and a profit was made.[23] John Davis would frequently require a production to use Rank contract artists before he would give it the financial go-ahead. He forced Anthony Asquith to cast Dirk Bogarde, Jean Kent and Susan Shaw in *The Woman in Question* (1950) and he insisted that Powell and Pressburger use Dirk Bogarde in *Ill Met by Moonlight* (1957). Davis also insisted that contract artists be used for the leads in *Robbery Under Arms* (Jack Lee, 1957), and that Virginia McKenna star in *Carve Her Name with Pride* (Lewis Gilbert, 1958).[24] Theoretically, each contract artist was entitled to accept or reject any scripts offered by the Contract Artists Department, but if the artist rejected more than two scripts, there was trouble. Even Kay Kendall, one of Rank's biggest stars, was suspended after she had turned down scripts which she and her agent felt were unsuitable for her.[25]

John Davis and Earl St. John were unimaginative and conservative in their attitude to films and they appear to have had little feel for public taste. Davis was an accountant who often sought to exert control by fear; Earl St. John was an old-fashioned exhibitor who drank too much. Neither understood the changes in public taste that were taking place during the 1950s.[26] They often seemed intent in imposing their conservative views upon the public, although they could also perform a rapid volte-face in order to repeat unexpected commercial successes.

Earl St. John was only persuaded to support *Genevieve* (Henry Cornelius, 1952), one of Rank's most popular films, because the NFFC had agreed to participate.[27] He and Davis were extremely chary about financing both *Doctor in the House* (Ralph Thomas, 1953) and Norman Wisdom's first film, *Trouble in Store* (John Paddy Carstairs, 1953). At the preview of *Trouble in Store* at the Odeon, Camden Town, Davis and St. John gave Wisdom the brush-off, but once they saw how funny the audience found the film they changed their tune.[28] Similarly, on the first day of shooting on *Doctor in the House*, Earl St. John told producer Betty Box that the Rank board did not like hospital films, or films with the word 'Doctor' in the title. They wanted the title changed and the budget reduced.[29] Even when the film was completed, they insisted that all the stars should wear sports jackets, not white coats, in the publicity photographs.

If a film was successful, Davis insisted that the formula should be repeated. But many film-makers felt trapped by the limitations imposed on their creativity. Ted Willis found Pinewood creatively suffocating because it had him firmly tagged as a gag man.[30] Norman Wisdom was condemned always to play 'the gump' and denied his wish to play Hamlet or the Hunchback of Notre Dame.[31] Betty Box and Ralph Thomas were more astute, using their success with the *Doctor* films to their own advantage: they only agreed to make other *Doctor* films if they could be interspersed with films of their own choosing.[32]

During the mid-1950s Davis's managerial methods paid dividends, unpopular though they were with film-makers and contract artists. Between 1953 and 1957 the organisation's production and distribution activities made a small, if unspectacular, profit. In 1955, *Doctor at Sea*, *One Good Turn*, *Man of the Moment* and *Above Us the Waves* all did well at the box office.[33] The following year, the top box-office attraction was *Reach for the Sky* (Lewis Gilbert), starring Kenneth More as Douglas Bader. Two more Rank films about the Second World War also did well: *A Town Like Alice* (Jack

Sexual and political intrigue in a Rank X film. No Love for Johnnie. *(Ralph Thomas, 1961).*

Lee, 1956) and *The Battle of the River Plate* (1956), written, produced and directed by Michael Powell and Emeric Pressburger after seven years away from Rank.[34]

Rank and the international market

Only the most popular low-budget Rank films could recover their production costs in the UK. The differences between profit and loss depended on overseas revenues. The largest overseas market was the USA, but Rank's attempts at US distribution in the late 1940s had been a failure.[35] Outside the USA, however, results were much better. In 1953, when production and distribution activities made a £353,000 profit, half the company's film revenues came from overseas. Demand for British films had increased and Rank's colour film of the Coronation, *A Queen is Crowned*, was successful every-where except in the USA.[36] The following year, profits rose to £837,000. Remittances from Canada were the largest ever and demand in the Eastern hemisphere remained high.[37] In 1955 profits fell, but the following year, boosted by the sale of some older films to US television, profits from production and distribution rose to an all-time high of £925,000.[38]

In 1956, Rank announced a policy of only producing films 'which had international entertainment appeal' and which would be 'vigorously sold in foreign markets'.[39] The following year he and Davis established Rank Film Distributors of America (RFDA) to penetrate the US market and bypass the major American distributors. By March it had set up ten offices and leased cinemas in key cities to play Rank films. By mid-1958, RFDA had more than a dozen offices in the USA, but industry rumours insisted that it was absorbing great losses. In March 1959, eighteen months after it had opened for business, RFDA was closed down. At the Rank AGM in September, Davis told the shareholders: 'Our attempts to open up this market for British films through our own distribution organisation have thus failed, but I feel that at the time we commenced the venture we were justified in our efforts. Unfortunately, the trend of the industry has been against us'.[40] Davis seemed not to have learnt the lesson from the US successes of *Hamlet, The Red Shoes* and several Ealing films – that it was indigenous British subjects which were most successful in US markets. International subjects like *Manuela* (Guy Hamilton, 1957), *Campbell's Kingdom* (Ralph Thomas, 1957) and *Ferry to Hong Kong* (Lewis Gilbert, 1959) had little box-office appeal to either British or American audiences.

The decline of the Rank empire

Davis, like Rank, saw films as moral tracts and refused to show any 'X' certificate films in Rank cinemas. He set his face against any portrayal of extramarital sex, despite his own colourful private life.[41] Even so, intellectual guerrillas like Henry Cornelius and Jill Craigie managed to smuggle subversive behaviour into the films on which they worked. Cornelius cheerfully implied extramarital sex in *Genevieve*, and Jill Craigie sneaked progressive economic and political views into *The Million Pound Note* (Ronald Neame, 1954) and *Windom's Way* (Ronald Neame, 1957). It was not until 1961 that Davis recognised that times had changed and the cinema audience had more adult attitudes. *No Love for Johnnie* (Ralph Thomas) was the first Rank film to get an 'X' certificate, although Betty Box surmised that it was the left-wing politics of the film's adulterous MP which made it acceptable to Davis.[42]

The moral attitudes of British cinema audiences were changing fast. The new generation of teenagers and young single adults which dominated the cinema audiences of the late 1950s was ready to challenge the moral values and the cultural subservience of their parents. On the ABC circuit, a new and more irreverent type of comedy had already appeared. In 1958, Anglo-Amalgamated pulled off what *Kinematograph Weekly* termed 'a staggering long-shot', with *Carry On Sergeant* (Gerald Thomas); and in the following year the same team capped their success with *Carry On Nurse*, the biggest box-office attraction for 1959.[43] The new cinemagoing public was clearly ready for bawdier and more satirical films than Davis was prepared to produce.

Rank lost £1.3 million on film production and distribution in 1958 and £0.9 million in 1959, although it did make small profits between 1960 and 1962. By 1963, Davis had had enough. He regretfully concluded that 'film production in isolation is not possible'.[44] His strategy for saving the Rank Organisation was to diversify out of film. In 1956, he had signed a joint development agreement with the Halord Company in America for the non-US rights of the Xerox process. In 1963, Rank-Xerox became a subsidiary of the Rank Organisation and its profits were incorporated into the Rank accounts. In that year, the company earned more than half its profits from non-film activities.[45] Unlike film distribution and exhibition, Xerox was a system of photographic reproduction which could make money without the need to pay for the production of an expensive original copy. Rank's methodism had lost out to the economics of the market place.

Notes

1. Michael Powell, *A Life in Movies* (London: Methuen ed., 1987), pp. 647–62. The film went on to become a huge box-office success.
2. Geoff Brown (ed.), *Launder and Gilliat* (London: British Film Institute, 1977), p. 124.

3. Public Records Office: BT 64/4490. Overhead costs and earnings of British films, Schedule VI. *The Red Shoes* cost £505,600 and the producer's share of the ultimate film hire was estimated to be £1,291,300. The profit would therefore be £785,700. *Hamlet* cost £572,500 to produce and was estimated to earn the producer £1,352,200, a profit of £779,700.

4. Odeon Theatres, Annual Report to 28 June 1952, p. 5.

5. PRO: BT 64/4490, Schedule VI. The films were *Oliver Twist*, £244,500; *Great Expectations*, £222,600; *The Red Shoes*, £156,500; and *The Upturned Glass*, £156,000.

6. Odeon Theatres, Annual Report to 23 June 1956, Appendix. In 1956, Rank owned 584 cinemas in the UK, 124 in Canada, 19 in Ireland, 12 in Jamaica and one in Portugal. He had access to 135 cinemas in Australia, 123 in South Africa, 117 in New Zealand, 40 in Malaya, 22 in Ceylon and 18 in the Netherlands.

7. Odeon Theatres, Annual Report to 23 June 1951, p. 6.

8. Ibid. (the emphases are mine).

9. *The Times*, 27 March 1953.

10. PRO: BT 64/4483, R. H. Dewes (Licensing and Personnel Controller, Circuits Management Association) to R. G. Somervell (Films Branch, Board of Trade), 15 December 1950. The rejected films were *Torment, Bless 'em All, What a Carry On, School for Randle, Up for the Cup, Gorbals Story, High Jinks in Society, Skimpy in the Navy, Over the Garden Wall, Shadow of the Past*, and *Dark Secret*.

11. Ibid. Circuits Management Association to Board of Trade, 3 November 1952; and exchange of memoranda between SS and the President, 4 and 8 December 1952. In the quota year 1951–52, only four Rank cinemas failed to meet their supporting quota. These were the Empire, Darlington, and the Odeons at Bloxwich, Dunstall and Spalding, which were all small theatres in intensely competitive situations.

12. Great Britain: Monopolies Commission, *Films: A Report on the Supply of Films for Exhibition in Cinemas* (206) (HMSO, 1966), para. 93.

13. Ibid., para. 58.

14. John Davis, 'Re-organisation of Booking Methods of Odeon and Gaumont Circuits', *CEA Newsletter* no. 15 (Cinematograph Exhibitors Association, 17 October 1958), pp. 1–11.

15. Odeon Theatres, Annual Report to 23 June 1951, p. 5.

16. *Kinematograph Weekly*, 20 December 1951, p. 9; and 18 December 1952, p. 10. The failure of some of those films which were made in 1952 resulted in a considerable loss for the NFFC. As late as 31 March 1956, it had still not recouped £181,000, over a quarter of its original investment, although the National Provincial Bank, which put up the front money on each film, almost certainly made a profit on its loans.

17. Donald Sinden, *A Touch of the Memoirs* (London: Hodder and Stoughton, 1982), p. 190.

18. Brian McFarlane (ed.), *Sixty Voices* (London: British Film Institute, 1992), p. 156.

19. John Davis, 'Intermission – the British Film Industry', *National Provincial Bank Review*, August 1958, pp. 1–12, at p. 5. He gave a similar – but different – paper to the annual conference of the Chartered Institute of Secretaries, in Llandudno in May the same year.

20. For instance, although *The Spanish Gardener* (1956) is nominally a crime film, the real centre of the film is the struggle of a stern British consul, Harrington Brande (Michael Hordern), to retain his only son's affection and to prevent him coming under the influence of his charming Spanish gardener, José Santero (Dirk Bogarde), whom Brande distrusts and who has been falsely accused of theft by Brande's chauffeur (Cyril Cusack).

21. John Davis, 'The British Film Industry', Chartered Institute of Secretaries, Annual Conference, May 1958, p. 3.

22. The reasons are unclear, but it was probably because the budget was about £700,000. Bogarde, *Snakes and Ladders* (Harmondsworth: Penguin, 1979), pp. 170–2, and R. J. Minney, *Puffin Asquith* (London: Leslie Frewin, 1973), pp. 172–6.

23. Sinden, *A Touch of the Memoirs*, pp. 190–1.

24. Dirk Bogarde in McFarlane (ed.), *Sixty Voices*, p. 26; Michael Powell, *Million Dollar Movie* (London: Mandarin ed., 1993), p. 360. Vincent Ball and Lewis Gilbert, in McFarlane (ed.), *Sixty Voices*, pp. 24 and 98.

25. Donald Sinden, in McFarlane (ed.), *Sixty Voices*, p. 203. Dinah Sheridan turned down roles in a B-feature, *Grand National Night* (Talisman, d. Bob McNaught, 1953) and *Street Corner* (London Independent, d. Muriel Box, 1953) before accepting her role in *Genevieve* (see Dinah Sheridan, ibid., p. 200). Davis could also hire out a contract artist to another film company, normally for a sum equivalent to the artiste's annual salary. *The Times*, 22 December 1954, for Kay Kendall.

26. See for example, Sue Harper and Vincent Porter, 'Moved to Tears: Weeping and the Cinema in Post-War Britain', *Screen*, p. 37, no. 2 (Summer 1996), pp. 38–53.

27. Michael Balcon, *Michael Balcon Presents … A Lifetime of Films* (London: Hutchinson, 1969), p. 168.

28. Geoffrey McNab, *J. Arthur Rank and the British Film Industry* (London: Routledge, 1993), pp. 222–3.
29. Betty Box in McFarlane (ed.), *Sixty Voices*, p. 39. See also McNab, *J. Arthur Rank and the British Film Industry*, pp. 223–4.
30. Ted Willis, *Evening All . . . Fifty Years Over a Hot Typewriter* (London: Macmillan, 1991), p. 113.
31. Hugh Stewart, cited in McNab, *J. Arthur Rank*, p. 223.
32. Betty Box, in McFarlane (ed.) *Sixty Voices*, p. 38.
33. *Kinematograph Weekly*, 15 December 1955, p. 4.
34. *Kinematograph Weekly*, 13 December 1956, p. 6.
35. Annual Report to 24 June 1949; see also Robert Murphy, 'Rank's Attempt on the American Market', in James Curran and Vincent Porter (eds.), *British Cinema History* (London: Weidenfeld and Nicolson, 1983).
36. Odeon Theatres, Annual Report to 27 June 1953, pp. 4, 6.
37. Odeon Theatres, Annual Report to 26 June 1954, p. 7.
38. Odeon Theatres, Annual Report to 23 June 1956, p. 9.
39. Ibid., p. 73.
40. Thomas Guback, *The International Film Industry* (Indiana University Press, 1969), pp. 75, 76.
41. Like King Henry VIII, John Davis had six wives. He metaphorically beheaded two of them by omitting them from his entry in *Who's Who*.
42. Betty Box, in McFarlane (ed.), *Sixty Voices*, p. 39.
43. *Kinematograph Weekly*, 18 December 1958, p. 6; and 17 December 1959, p. 6.
44. Odeon Theatres, Annual Report to 19 June 1963, p. 21.
45. Ibid., p. 11.

Bibliography

Brown, Geoff, *Launder and Gilliat* (London: British Film Institute, 1977).
Davis, John H., 'Intermission in the British Film Industry', *National Westminster Bank Review*, August 1958, pp. 1–12.
Falk, Quentin, *The Golden Gong: Fifty Years of the Rank Organisation, Its Films and Its Stars* (London: Columbus Books, 1987).
Great Britain: Monopolies Commission, *A Report on the Supply of Films for Exhibition in Cinemas* (London: HMSO, 1966).
McFarlane, Brian (ed.), *Sixty Voices: Celebrities Recall the Golden Age of British Cinema* (London: British Film Institute, 1992).
McNab, Geoffrey, *J. Arthur Rank and the British Film Industry* (London: Routledge, 1993).
MacQuitty, William, *A Life to Remember* (London: Quartet, 1991).
Mullally, Frederic, *Films – An Alternative to Rank: An Analysis of Power and Policy in the British Film Industry* (Socialist Book Centre, 1946).
Murphy, Robert, 'Rank's Attempt on the American Market, 1944–49', in James Curran and Vincent Porter (eds.), *British Cinema History* (London: Weidenfeld and Nicolson, 1983), pp. 164–78.
Murphy, Robert, *Realism and Tinsel* (London: Routledge, 1989).
Perry, George, *Movies from the Mansion: A History of Pinewood Studios* (London: Elm Tree Books, 1982).
Powell, Michael, *A Life in Movies* (London: Heinemann, 1986).
Powell, Michael, *Million Dollar Movie* (London: Heinemann, 1992).
Sellar, Maurice, *et al.*, *Best of British: A Celebration of Rank Film Classics* (London: Sphere, 1987).
Sinden, Donald, *A Touch of the Memoirs* (London: Hodder and Stoughton, 1982).
Wood, Alan, *Mr. Rank: A Study of J. Arthur Rank and British Films* (London: Hodder and Stoughton, 1952).

13
Bonnie Prince Charlie Revisited: British Costume Film in the 1950s

Sue Harper

Although they both reinforce the act of social remembering, costume dramas and historical films are different from each other. Historical films deal with real people or events: Henry VIII, the Battle of Waterloo, Lady Hamilton. Costume film uses the mythic and symbolic aspects of the past as a means of providing pleasure, rather than instruction. It is a far more flexible form than historical film, and this flexibility makes it acutely unstable. It can splinter into further sub-genres, such as the imaginary biopic or the historical horror film. Moreover, it can alter radically over short periods of time, and constantly reform its definitions of national identity.

My book, *Picturing the Past: the Rise and Fall of the British Costume Film*, shows how in the 1930s and 1940s history was raided for political purposes by film-makers from the right and left of the political spectrum.[1] In the 1930s, groups such as the Historical Association and the British Film Institute struggled for control over the content and style of historical films, and they bewailed the popularity of such 'disrespectful' films as *The Private Life of Henry VIII* and *The Scarlet Pimpernel*, which audiences flocked to see. During the Second World War, the Ministry of Information was initially enthusiastic about the usefulness of history as a propaganda tool, and it favoured films which used the past to encourage and educate the public about the nation's war aims. Later in the war, another form of historical film emerged: the costume extravaganza. In films such as *The Wicked Lady* heroines wearing sumptuous frocks committed hubris, and caused mayhem among the unsuspecting populace.

Three conclusions can be drawn about British costume film from this earlier period. First, the entertainment afforded by costume films was frequently excoriated by the critical or social establishment. Costume films had especially low status because they appealed primarily to female audiences. Secondly, the historical and costume films which were most successful (both artistically and financially) were those made by the larger production companies such as Gainsborough or London Films. Thirdly, popular costume films expressed a coherent position on class, but this was always combined with a strong statement about gender stereotyping and sexual pleasure. The class which was made to work hardest in the costume texts was almost always the aristocracy, which was presented as a high point of style and confidence to which all other groups might aspire.

The costume genre altered radically during the 1950s. It was always expensive to produce, and was therefore more vulnerable to market fluctuations. Throughout the decade the British film industry was riven by economic difficulties and a decline in overall confidence. Changes in government policy and adjustments in the international film market brought problems in their wake. The relationship of British films to international audiences had always been volatile, and this was particularly so for the costume genre, predicated as it was on definitions of national identity: these were compelling enough to sell at home but prone to slippage and incoherence when exported abroad. In the intensively competitive and insecure market of the 1950s homegrown costume films were at a considerable disadvantage.

Another important determinant on British costume films was that, in the mid-1940s, the British Film Producers' Association (BFPA) brought its policy on fiction in the public domain into line with that of the Motion Picture Association of America (MPAA). All the major Hollywood companies worked on a system of registration of those novels whose authors had been dead for more than fifty years. Once a studio had registered an interest in filming such a novel, other studios were legally bound not to compete. This had profound effects on patterns of British production. It was only with the greatest difficulty, for example, that Cineguild was able to make *Great Expectations* and *Oliver Twist* in the 1940s.[2] Conversely, George Minter of Renown was not a member of the BFPA and so, although he was free to make his Dickens films in the 1950s, he stood no chance of gaining American (or even major British) distribution.[3] And the only reason Rank could make *A Tale of Two Cities* in 1958 was that Hollywood had made a successful version in the 1930s and did not wish to repeat it so soon.[4]

After the MPAA registration system took hold, costume film-makers in Britain no longer had first call on their own classic novelists. In effect, the most 'cinematic' novels of Scott, Dickens and Robert Louis Stevenson were the property of MGM and Disney, and the British were prevented from making films of them. Hence British producers' fondness for modern novelists who wrote historical fiction. One alternative was to choose a dead writer still in copyright and then negotiate with his heirs; that was how Arnold Bennett's *The Card* came to the screen in 1952. Another alternative was to commission purpose-made scripts, which was always a more risky procedure.

Besides the marketing, legal and industrial difficulties which assailed the costume genre, there were also profound changes in audience composition. The commercial success of the 1940s costume films depended largely on the fact that more women went to the cinema, and the genre came to be seen as a female prerogative which offered visual pleasures when other consumer pleasures were at a premium. All this changed in the 1950s, when British cinema audiences declined catastrophically. In 1950, 30 million people went to 4,500 cinemas every week; by 1960, only 10 million people went each week to 3,000 cinemas. More importantly teenagers, particularly unmarried male teenagers, were replacing female and family viewers.[5] The baby boom, commercial television and leisure activities such as Do-It-Yourself meant that families stayed at home, and it was the young people who increasingly sought leisure outside.[6] The following remarks by two middle-class women are typical:

> It's different when you're single, you've nothing else to do once you've had your supper and you're itching to go somewhere. Now with the baby I'd rather sit by the fire and listen to the wireless. You either get into the habit of going regularly, or you grow away from it as I have done.

> I haven't been since we had the television fixed. We just switch on the television and relax. Often there's a good play on. Besides so many of the films these days are so unsuitable for children.[7]

The tastes and desires of the audience were qualitatively different from those of the 1940s. There were more males (particularly young males) in the regular audiences, the female audience which had traditionally patronised costume films now tending to stay at home; and middle-class audiences, who had been the mainstay of the more respectable historical films, were increasingly alienated from the cinema.[8]

So the costume genre was in flux and crisis throughout the decade. The National Film Finance Corporation only supported it in an erratic and inconsistent manner.[9] However, there was a remarkable shift in critical opinion. Throughout the 1930s and 1940s, costume film had attracted the wrath of critics, who felt that its sensationalism impugned the historical heritage. But in the 1950s history in film was rehabilitated by journalists in the quality press. *The Times* film correspondent defended American representations of Helen of Troy, Diane de Poitiers and Catherine de Medici thus:

> The look of her dark little head set imperiously on a long slender neck will, for those that saw them, always accompany the thought of Catherine in the mind, and the possession of so bright an image is surely an enticement rather than a snare and a delusion ... it must give people who normally never think about the past at all the conviction that at least it once existed.[10]

And Peter John Dyer produced a taxonomy of the genre in *Films and Filming*, in an attempt to improve its status.[11]

What kind of costume films were produced in Britain in the 1950s? The decade opened with Gainsborough's last history film, *So Long at the Fair*. This was a far cry from the studio's early bodice-rippers, which had celebrated female energy. *So Long at the Fair* was set at the turn of the century, and dealt with a heroine whose brother contracts the plague. This is concealed from her, and the film is structured around the themes of female vulnerability and social duplicity. This pattern was repeated in such films as *Madeleine* (1950) and *Svengali* (1954). Other historical films were based on well-known literary texts, such as *Scrooge* (1951), *The Pickwick Papers* (1952), *Romeo and Juliet* (1954) and *Richard III* (1955).

Some films made in the early part of the decade tried to recapture the élan of earlier costume extravaganzas. Alexander Korda owned the rights to Baroness Orczy's *The Scarlet Pimpernel*, which he had released in 1935. He remade it as *The Elusive Pimpernel* in 1950, when it was scripted and directed by Powell and Pressburger. The film's narrative was rather incoherent, betraying the fact that its makers were 'all pulling in different directions'.[12] The aristocratic symbolism, which had been so subtly deployed in the 1930s film, was crude and inconsistent. Herbert Wilcox, too, tried to repeat the successes of his 1930s historical films with *Lilacs in the Spring* (1954), but failed dismally. Another producer, Anthony Havelock-Allan, had tried the same technique with *The Shadow of the Eagle* (1950), which borrowed themes and settings from 1930s British films such as *Catherine the Great* and *The Dictator*. However, the film's lavish decor was no substitute for good sense. Other film-makers tried to recreate and reassess key aspects of the Victorian period in a more sober way. Unfortunately *Tom Brown's Schooldays* (1951), *The Lady with the Lamp* (1951) and *The Story of Gilbert and Sullivan* (1953) were all worthy but dull.

From 1950 to 1958 British-financed historical films tended to concentrate on periods which were politically quiescent but economically turbulent; in doing so, they avoided the spectacular aspects of the past. American producers did exactly the opposite. After 1950, American film-makers took full advantage of the Eady Levy to make prestigious costume films using British actors and technicians.[13] Their films featured heroic individuals quite different from those in the home-grown costume films. The Americans preferred the medieval period and the eighteenth century, and they had an interest in Scottish settings. Disney made *Treasure Island* (1950), *The Story of Robin Hood and His Merrie Men* (1952), *The Sword and the Rose* (1953), *Rob Roy, the Highland Rogue* (1953) and *Kidnapped* (1960). Warners made *Captain Horatio Hornblower R.N.* (1951) and *The Master of Ballantrae* (1953). MGM made *Ivanhoe* (1952), *Beau Brummel* (1954) and *The Adventures of Quentin Durward* (1956).[14] Despite considerable commercial success, after 1957 the Americans gradually withdrew from making historical films in Britain and shifted to contemporary settings and stories.

In general, war films and comedies tended to dominate the British box office in the 1950s, but some costume films were successful. Hammer's costume frighteners did well at the British box office, though they did better business abroad.[15] *The Lady with the Lamp* earned an honourable mention in the *Kinematograph Weekly* listings of box-office winners, as did *The Card* (1952); *Scrooge* and *The Pickwick Papers* did fairly well, despite their distribution problems. *The Moonraker* (1958) made a reasonable showing, as did *A Tale of Two Cities* (1958) and *North West Frontier* (1959). But none of these were smash-hits; it was the American-financed historical films which made the real impact at the British box office. *Captain Horatio Hornblower R.N.* and *Ivanhoe* were major box-office hits. *The Black Rose, The Master of Ballantrae* and *The Crimson Pirate* made large profits. So did *Knights of the Round Table, Rob Roy, the Highland Rogue, Footsteps in the Fog* and *Kidnapped.*[16]

Clearly, both British and American backers recognised the need to nuance their product so as to take account of shifts in audience composition. Audiences were getting younger and proportionately more masculine, and the producer of costume films ignored this at his peril. But British producers failed to capitalise on the pattern of class relationships which had characterised the costume film in the 1930s and 1940s. In profitable films such as *The Scarlet Pimpernel* and *The Man in Grey*, the key alliances were between the aristocracy and the working class; on a symbolic level, this alliance circumvented the power of the middle class, and the aristocracy functioned as the powerful site of hidden and repressed pleasures. Aristocratic style (careless, flamboyant and inventive) was, in 1930s and 1940s films, a key resource, and a disguise in which to utter insights about the nature of social and sexual power.

But in British costume films of the early 1950s, the key classes were the middle and lower-middle, and British producers used the men of those classes to engage in covert homilies about entrepreneurial skills. *The Card*, for example, directed by Ronald Neame for Rank, centres on a hero (Alec Guinness) who tackles the lack of status attending small-scale investment. History was used as a lesson about the flexibility necessary to gain and maintain financial (and subsequently social) power. In a key scene, the hero profits from his investment in a small boat. The camera moves up and down, and pans across the busy lives of those working his will. An old sea-dog, bringing the latest haul to the sedentary hero, remarks that 'It's a mighty lot of money for doing nothing.' Here the camera halts on the poised face of the entrepreneur, who ripostes, 'But you see, I did do something. I thought of it.'

The Magic Box, made by the Boultings for British Lion in 1952, was part of the Festival of Britain celebrations, and was the biography of the cinematograph pioneer Friese-Greene. Duller and less popular than *The Card*, it too used the past as a lesson about the market-place's need for grit. The lower middle-class hero was inventive enough but fatally lacked entrepreneurial skills and energy. The Dickens adaptations in the early 1950s followed the same pattern. Renown's *Scrooge* and *The Pickwick*

136

Covert homilies about entrepreneurial skills. Alec Guinness and Glynis Johns in The Card *(Ronald Neame, 1952).*

Papers were both skewed, in their narrative construction and style of acting, towards the middle class and its provenance. They avoid the picturesque and sensational aspects of the past which were so evident in earlier British adaptations of Dickens, such as the 1934 *Old Curiosity Shop*. This was because their directors (Brian Desmond Hurst and Noel Langley, respectively) were sufficiently persuasive, combative and unconventional to impose their views on producer George Minter, who had hitherto specialised in low-budget and low-status enterprises such as the Old Mother Riley films.[17]

British producers used history for slightly different purposes in the later 1950s. Several films investigated male grace under pressure, and they often presented muscular strength as sufficient for any challenge. In *North West Frontier*, the hero (Kenneth More) vanquishes Indian opposition to British Imperial power by sheer derring-do; his energy obviates the need to think. In *A Tale of Two Cities*, the protagonist Dirk Bogarde has the strength of mind to sacrifice himself for love, but the film prevaricates about the resources on which he draws. It is the same with *The Moonraker*, which deals with the English Civil War. The pro-Cavalier hero (George Baker) displays a physical vitality which is unsullied by self-awareness. Tidy horsemanship has replaced intellectual prowess. It is instructive to compare *The Moonraker* with Hammer's *The Scarlet Blade* (1963), which has a very similar plot. In the Hammer film, the Cavaliers take refuge with a band of gypsies, and the combination of these two 'forbidden' groups gives them enormous symbolic weight. *The Moonraker* is far more conservative in its use of marginal groups, and far more mainstream in its interpretation of social power and personal motivation.

The Moonraker, like many other costume films of its period, contains a hero whose cultural resources are slim and unstable. Such a hero is unable to avail himself of the aristocratic manner which was so confidently deployed in previous costume films. This is acutely at issue in Rank's *The Gypsy and the Gentleman*, directed by Joseph Losey and released in 1958. It should have worked well, since it contained a number of traditional British costume themes: the wild gypsy, the imprisoned virgin, the dissolute aristocrat, the faithful black servant. But these themes were now too residual and fossilised for the cultural job in hand. *The Gypsy and the Gentleman* was a farrago which began unpromisingly with overhead shots of the hero wrestling with a greased sow. The aristocrat (Keith Michell) behaves like a petulant *ejaculator praecox*, and the gypsy (Melina Mercouri) elevates nostril-flaring into an art form. However, the film's artistic failure should not be laid solely at Losey's door, even though he had the temerity to claim it as realistic.[18] Rather, the cinematic times were out of joint for such an enterprise, at least for a British company.

American producers were also preoccupied by masculinity in their 1950s history films, but they tackled it differently. Many of their British costume films were set in the medieval period, where lords, vassals and thanes could not be easily translated into the ruling/working/middle-class divide. Instead, films like *Ivanhoe*, *The Knights of the Round Table* and *The Adventures of Quentin Durward* evoked a colourful world in which the heroes are limited only by fate or political intrigue. The medieval period has habitually been used in British literary culture (by Keats, Carlyle and Morris, for example) as a symbol of courtly love and craftsmanship. It was very rarely deployed by British film producers; whereas the Americans recuperated the period as a celebration of an energetic and classless masculinity.

The American producers also used Scottish landscape and history. Walt Disney suggested that the Scottish clans ignored the class system and permitted the expression of an aggressive male style. He said that in Scotland 'it took courage and a fierce love of freedom to conquer that rugged land', just like the American frontier of old: geography and history were coterminous.[19] American producers' attentions were centred on the 1745 period, with *The Master of Ballantrae*, *Rob Roy, the Highland Rogue* and *Kidnapped*. They used the Stuart rebellion against the Hanoverian dynasty for their own ends. The struggle had always been a tender issue in British national consciousness. British film producers had either avoided it entirely or failed dismally with it, as Korda did with *Bonnie Prince Charlie* in 1948. Korda had used the 1745 rebellion as a symbol of failure, and his misjudgments resulted in a disaster. American producers, on the other hand, used Bonnie Prince Charlie and the 'Glorious '45' for a double purpose. Firstly, they deployed the romantic Scottish rebellion against British rationality as a sort of 'prequel' of the American War of Independence, and were thus able to incorporate the rebellion into a debate about individualism versus legitimacy. Secondly, the fights and kilts afforded endless opportunities for masculine display. But the red beard and muscular calves of Rob Roy (Richard Todd) were not dished up solely for the pleasure of female viewers. This was a different kind of male beauty from that presented in, say, the Gainsborough bodice-rippers. There, the languid and often feminised heroes constituted a spectacle for females. In the Scottish epics, it was male *energy* which was celebrated. The heroes are better at running up a burn than they are at making love. These were costume films for men.

So the Scottish films are a rich concoction of political and gender issues, in which the heroes are granted mastery over women and over geographical space. The American producers also chose to revisit historical periods which had hitherto been a British speciality. The Tudor period had been represented in the first successful British

138

The heroes are better at running up a burn than they are at making love. Glynis Johns and Richard Todd in Rob Roy, the Highland Rogue *(Harold French, 1953).*

costume film, Korda's *The Private Life of Henry VIII* (1933), in which the eponymous hero displayed human frailty and the pitfalls of political power. Disney's *The Sword and the Rose* reinterpreted Henry (played by James Robertson Justice) as a loud and virile Machiavelli. The other period which had figured largely in British costume culture was that of the Regency and the Napoleonic wars. In films such as Korda's *The Scarlet Pimpernel* (1935) and Gainsborough's *The Man in Grey* (1943) the Regency had been represented as a period in which the aristocracy displayed a marvellous adroitness in its social dealings. MGM's *Beau Brummell*, made at enormous expense at Borehamwood, and chosen as the Royal Command Performance film of 1954, nuanced its account in a different way.

Through the work of designers who had been innovatory in previous British costume or 'fantastic' films, the American producers were able to reorient former film images of the Regency. Alfred Junge, the production designer on *Beau Brummell*, had played a key role in some of Powell and Pressburger's films. Junge's sets for *Beau Brummell* contain an unparalleled range of visual textures, in which mirrored doors, drapes, columns and *objets d'art* interpret the Regency as a period of symmetry and cultural confidence. Elizabeth Haffenden, who had constructed such skilful 'costume narratives' in the Gainsborough bodice-rippers, designed the costumes for *Beau Brummell*. The colour coding and symbolic resonance of Haffenden's costumes are a major source of visual pleasure in the film. Her varieties of white, cream, silver and grey encourage the eye to make subtle aesthetic distinctions.[20] The male was here in sole possession of stylishness and flexibility. The historical Brummell was outrageously finicky, and reputedly effeminate; but the MGM film presents him (via Stewart Granger) as a virile adventurer whose sole flaw is to put his faith in princes.

The same period was reassessed in Warner's *Captain Horatio Hornblower R.N.* Here, the hero is lonely and riven by self-doubt, and holds himself aloof from the aristocratic powers which he challenges and vanquishes. As played by Gregory Peck, Hornblower seems to have provided a powerful role model for British males in the audience, right up to the 1960s.[21]

American 'British' films, then, were qualitatively different from the home product in the way they used history. The scripts of American costume films contained much archaic language (many 'Sires' and 'forsooths'), while the British films attempted an awkward modernisation in their conversational style. American-financed costume films were based on classical novels (especially those of Scott and Stevenson), whereas the British films often had to commission custom-made scripts. American costume films were edited differently, too. They were assembled and cut on the movement of the hero, thus giving an impression of vitality and readiness. The British-financed histories tended to cut on the direction of the look, which impeded the fast flow of the narrative.

There was one British company which replicated the American disposition of gender elements, and considerably to its profit. Hammer Films shifted its policy from futuristic horror (*The Quatermass Experiment*, 1955) to historical horror, with the production in 1957 of *The Curse of Frankenstein*. From that time until the early 1970s, half Hammer's output had historical settings. The historical context permitted the studio to allude to hidden or forgotten elements in British popular culture; but it also opened up a space in which notions of national identity could be examined in a new way. Significantly, the critical rehabilitation of the costume genre did not extend to Hammer's films, which were frequently attacked for their supposed immorality, so much so that the studio ceased to give press showings.[22]

Hammer Films was organised in a rigorous way, and the producers ensured that the script was the dominant discourse. This tight control over the scripts profoundly affected the way in which history was deployed. The historical periods evoked by Hammer were extensive (myth, prehistory, ancient Egypt, mid and late nineteenth-century Europe). Absences were important too; there were no Roman films (doubtless because the Americans had captured that market) and no treatments of the rational and elegant eighteenth century. All Hammer's costume films contain an arrogant upper class and a sullen, oppressed underclass. Social relations between these two groups are never presented as contradictory in a fruitful sense: Hammer histories evoke a world in which social contradictions are absent.[23] Instead, archetypal contradictions are presented, such as those between male and female, human and animal, the quick and the dead. This shift from social to archetypal contradiction was perhaps a way of displacing and defusing the anxieties the audience may have had about social class.

Sexual anxieties are similarly displaced. Hammer's costume films do not celebrate sexual desire. They display a nervous preoccupation with the body: its orifices, its blood, its organs, its unfamiliar changes, its unratified penetration. Films such as the Frankenstein and Dracula cycles interrogate such anxieties, by broaching and breaking social taboos to do with the body. These taboos are usually dealt with by a ritual, and the films teach the audience how to distinguish between a ritual that pollutes and a ritual that ensures freedom from defilement.

Hammer costume films express intense anxiety about the female body. Some costume plots (*Blood from the Mummy's Tomb, The Plague of the Zombies, Countess Dracula*) are structured around the oozings of female blood. And others deal with manifestations of the monstrous-feminine (*The Reptile, The Gorgon, Frankenstein Created Woman, She*), in which the transgressive heroines are rigorously returned to the patriarchal order. The intensity of regard which Hammer costume films accord to the female body as the site of unspeakable excess suggests that the films were carefully targeted at male audiences.[24]

Hammer costume films can be said to use myth and history as a means of social as well as sexual *disavowal*. That is to say, they shift the audience's attention away from class difference and sexual difference, and neutralise the anxieties attending them. The manner of delivery of the films is ironic. This irony resides in the scripts, which encourage the audience to repudiate the importance of what they have seen or heard. This process of disavowal converts the potential dangers of the spectacle into something safe.

Hammer revived the motifs of popular history from previous decades, but it nuanced them differently. In Gainsborough melodramas, those on the periphery of society generated energy because they were ambiguously poised between the sacred and the profane. But in Hammer historical films such groups are profoundly disruptive. Aristocrats, wicked ladies, gypsies and pirates are like loose cannon: fun to watch but dangerous for those who get in the way.

Here we can draw important similarities between Hammer's and other costume films. British film culture of the 1950s used the historical context as a disguise in which to express disquiet about social change. The increasingly meritocratic world of the 1950s, with its radically new patterns of consumption and class allegiance, met with a conservative response from the costume genre. British costume films argued that a reformed middle class (and particularly the male of the species) was perfectly competent for the social job in hand. For them, aristocratic symbolism was a source of titillation, but nothing more. American producers working in Britain had an entirely different approach. They stripped history bare of its class resonance, and made it the threnody of an unambiguous and energetic masculinity.

Notes

1. Sue Harper, *Picturing the Past: the Rise and Fall of the British Costume Film* (London: British Film Institute, 1994).
2. Ronald Neame, 'Choosing a Film Story', in F. Maurice Speed, *Film Review* (London: MacDonald, 1949).
3. See, for example, PRO BT 64/4521, memo from R. Somervell to S. Golt, 1 September 1956. Here Somervell describes Minter's failure to persuade John Davis that his films should be given first feature bookings in Rank cinemas. Somervell, expressing the official Board of Trade view, suggests that Minter's films were too expensive to be second features and qualitatively too 'indifferent' to be first features.
4. For an account of the scripting problems on *A Tale of Two Cities*, see T. E. B. Clarke, 'Every Word in Its Place', *Films and Filming*, February 1958. For information on the way the 1952 version of *The Pickwick Papers* was used in schools, see H. Rawlinson, 'The Pickwick Papers on Film and Filmstrip', *Journal of Photography*, 16 January 1953.
5. *The Hulton Readership Survey 1950–1955*, *The Spending Habits of Cinemagoers* (London: Pearl and Dean, 1956), *The IPA National Readership Survey 1956–1957*, and *1959–1960*, and *The Cinema Audience: A National Survey* (London: Screen Advertising Association, 1961).
6. Clancy Sigal, 'Down at the Teenage Club: Voices in the Darkness', *Observer*, 7 December 1958.
7. Mass-Observation Report, *Why Do They Go to the Pictures?* (1950). These remarks are from women of 23 and 30 respectively; they are in unsorted material in Box 15. See also *Daily Film Renter*, 10 July 1950.
8. Sue Harper and Vincent Porter, 'Moved to Tears: Weeping in the Cinema in Post-war Britain', *Screen*, Summer 1996.
9. According to the Annual Reports of the National Film Finance Corporation, the proportion of costume dramas selected was very small and seemingly randomly selected. The 1950 report indicates that the costume films supported were *Angel with the Trumpet*, *The Elusive Pimpernel* and *Gone to Earth*. In 1951, they were *Tom Brown's Schooldays* and *The Magic Box*; in 1952, *The Card* and *The Importance of Being Earnest*; in 1953 *Gilbert and Sullivan*; in 1954, *Hobson's Choice* and

Svengali; in 1957, *The Curse of Frankenstein*; in 1958, *Dracula* and *The Revenge of Frankenstein*; in 1959, *The Man Who Could Cheat Death*, *The Hound of the Baskervilles*, *The Mummy* and *The Stranglers*; in 1960, *Sword of Sherwood Forest*, *Two Faces of Dr Jekyll* and *The Flesh and the Fiends*; in 1961, *The Hellfire Club*.

10. *The Times*, 21 February 1956. There are many similar pieces in *The Times* throughout the decade, not all by the same critic.

11. Peter John Dyer, 'From Boadicea to Bette Davis', *Films and Filming*, January 1959, and 'The Rebels in Jackboots', *Films and Filming*, March 1959. See also James Morgan, 'Coronatiana USA', *Sight and Sound*, July–September 1953.

12. Michael Powell, *Million Dollar Movie* (London: Heinemann, 1992), p. 26. Powell had originally wanted to make it as a musical: see Powell, *A Life in Movies* (London: Heinemann, 1986), p. 669.

13. In order to be classified as British, films had to be made by a British company (which could be set up by Americans or anyone else); 75 per cent of the labour costs (excluding one person) had to be paid to British workers, and the film had to be made in Britain or the Commonwealth. The venture was attractive to US producers because British labour costs were substantially cheaper. Costume films were a significant proportion of American output until 1957. In 1950, 3 out of 9 American-financed quota vehicles were historical. In 1951, the figures were 3 out of 4; in 1952, 5 out of 6; in 1953, 5 out of 13; in 1954, 3 out of 6; in 1955, 2 out of 6; in 1956, 3 out of 17; in 1957, 3 out of 27; in 1958, 2 out of 26 (figures compiled from Dennis Gifford, *The British Film Catalogue 1895–1985*, Newton Abbot and London: David and Charles, 1986).

14. This is by no means a complete list. For example, Columbia made *The Black Knight* in 1954 and *Footsteps in the Fog* in 1955. There was a rash of swashbuckling pirate films as well: Disney's *Treasure Island* (1950), Warner Bros' *The Crimson Pirate* (1952), RKO's *The Sea-Devils* (1953). Pirates were to American producers what gypsies had been to the British.

15. Hammer gained a third of its profits from Britain, a third from America and the rest from overseas. See Sue Harper, 'The Scent of Distant Blood: Hammer Films and History', in Tony Barta (ed.), *Screening the Past: Film and the Representation of History* (New York: Praeger, forthcoming).

16. *Kinematograph Weekly*, 14 December 1950, 20 December 1951, 18 December 1952, 17 December 1953, 16 December 1954, 15 December 1955, 13 December 1956, 12 December 1957, 18 December 1958, 17 December 1959 and 15 December 1960. See also *Motion Picture Herald*'s and *Picturegoer*'s annual surveys throughout the decade. *Films and Filming* also produced its version of box-office trends every year from 1958.

17. Langley had written some remarkable novels and had extensive scriptwriting experience. See his interview with the *Evening Standard*, 28 February 1955, on leaving for Hollywood: 'I seemed to be assessed as an alien influence ... and this has robbed me of my confidence.' See Hurst, *The Lady Vanishes*, *Sight and Sound*, August 1950, and unpublished autobiography in British Film Institute Library.

18. *Films and Filming*, January 1958.

19. Interview given by Walt Disney as a trailer for *Rob Roy, the Highland Rogue* on the Disney Home Video of the film. For Disney's views on another of his British-made films, see 'Why I filmed *Treasure Island*', *Daily Graphic*, 20 June 1950.

20. Interestingly, it was through her work with MGM-British, and particularly with this film, that Haffenden was invited to Hollywood. There, she won an Oscar for her costume work on *Ben-Hur*.

21. See Graham Dawson, 'Playing at War: an Autobiographical Approach to Boyhood Fantasy and Masculinity', *Oral History*, Spring 1990. The popularity of the film may have had something to do with the fact that the star (Gregory Peck) was then at the peak of his career. By contrast, Errol Flynn in *The Master of Ballantrae* was at the fag-end of his. He was exhausted, and it showed.

22. A typically negative review is in *Tribune*, 10 May 1957. See also Walter Lassally, 'The Cynical Audience', *Sight and Sound*, Summer 1956, Derek Hill, 'The Face of Horror', *Sight and Sound*, Winter 1958–9.

23. There is one exception, the extraordinary *Plague of the Zombies* (1965), in which the squire has learned the arts of voodoo while abroad. He uses his powers over the undead to create a compliant workforce for his tin-mines.

24. Hammer's publicity campaigns are an index of its gender orientation. The captions for posters (in British Film Institute Library) are significant. One urges the audience to see Dracula as 'The Terrifying Lover Who Died – Yet Lived', clearly making subliminal reference to fears of *le petit mort*. Another advertises a Dracula film with 'You Can't Keep a Good Man Down', implicitly linking Dracula's revival with his tumescence, via blood, of course.

Bibliography

Barta, Tony (ed.), *Screening the Past: Film and the Representation of History* (New York: Praeger, forthcoming).

Harper, Sue, *Picturing the Past* (London: British Film Institute, 1994).

Hutchings, Peter, *Hammer and Beyond: the British Horror Film* (Manchester: Manchester University Press, 1993).

Macnab, Geoffrey, *J. Arthur Rank and the British Film Industry* (London: Routledge, 1993).

Pirie, Dave, *A Heritage of Horror: the English Gothic Cinema 1946–1972* (London: Gordon Fraser, 1978).

Spraos, John, *The Decline of the Cinema* (London: Allen and Unwin, 1962).

14
Male Stars, Masculinity and British Cinema, 1945–1960

Andrew Spicer

In the early post-war period a survey showed that stars were the main reason for cinemagoers' choice of film.[1] British producers and studio heads were well aware of their importance and attempted to create British stars on Hollywood lines. Both the vertically integrated combines, Rank and ABPC, kept a roster of contract players who were assigned particular roles by producers or studio executives to help create a stable image which stayed broadly the same in order to allow audience recognition. A star's image was also carefully built up and managed through active promotion, including a specific fan club for each major star, fan magazines and personal appearances at circuit cinemas in chauffeur-driven Rolls Royces.[2] Rank trained and groomed potential stars through the 'Company of Youth' – the 'Charm School' as it was dubbed in the press.[3]

Their lack of institutional power led some stars, like Robert Donat in 1948, to renounce films and pursue careers in the theatre as actor-managers, where they had far greater artistic control; but this was exceptional. Most British actors opted for the security and wealth provided by a long-term studio contract, with occasional forays into live theatre. The most successful and clearly typecast male stars, Rex Harrison, James Mason, Stewart Granger and Michael Wilding, all left Britain to pursue careers in Hollywood, where the rewards were far greater.

Star images also circulated in widely selling journals like the fortnightly *Picture Show* and the weekly *Picturegoer*, which constructed a discourse about cinema that was largely oriented around stars. The popular press constantly commented on their lives, loves and careers, while their images also recurred in product endorsements. Though much of the attention was given to Hollywood stars, there was often a lively concern about British stars: were they getting enough promotion, recognition, the right roles?

The popularity of stars cannot be explained simply in terms of charismatic personalities or astute marketing. As Richard Dyer has argued, the most significant reason for stars' popularity is their typicality.[4] Male stars represent easily recognised types of masculinity which have been socially, culturally and historically constructed, embodying important beliefs about power, authority, nationality and class. Paradoxically, they embody the type in a way which is uniquely their own. This combination of typicality and uniqueness encourages audience identification, admiration and desire.

Because of their representativeness, images of male stars may give important clues as to the changing construction of masculinity in this period, but in a general survey I can only discuss the most popular stars. The *Motion Picture Herald* published an annual ranking of the box-office performance of the top ten British stars of either sex, based on exhibitors' returns. These returns were compiled by cinema managers who 'watch their audiences closely, studying them to see which star is making them laugh or cry. From that, they decide which of two stars in the same picture is the greater attraction.'[5] Despite this dubious basis, the *Motion Picture Herald*'s listings were highly influential, frequently quoted as authoritative evidence. *Picturegoer*'s annual 'Gold Medal' award also ranked the top ten male or female stars according to a readers' poll, but combined British and American stars. *Picturegoer*'s readers voted for a star's performance in a particular film, affording an insight into which were the key roles. There are many correlations and some interesting differences between the two lists which, taken together and supplemented where possible from *Kinematograph Weekly*'s intermittent listings (for which no criteria are given), provide a reasonable basis for discussion.[6]

The most popular male star from 1944 to 1947 was James Mason, who had a fan mail of 5,000 letters per week. Mason's popularity was based on the sex appeal generated by his performances in Gainsborough's costume dramas, which were specifically targeted at the predominantly female cinemagoing audience. As Lord Rohan in *The Man in Grey* (1943), Mason converted the traditional villain of stage melodrama – dark, menacing, deep-voiced – into a Byronic figure, often cruel and vindictive but also thrilling, fascinating and highly erotic. An article in *Picturegoer*, entitled 'Does this man make villainy too attractive?', suggested how Mason's individuality had animated a type so decisively different from conventional male leads.

> The Marquis of Rohan could not be played by the average British screen hero. It is a part needing more strength than a typical hero's role.... He has the strength; and his mobile face needs no make-up to transform it from its habitual pleasing good looks to a mask of ferocity and evil which suits the part. The thick eyebrows, the curved sensuous lips and the dark, compelling eyes, the wide nostrils and patrician nose are the foundations necessary for such a part as the proud, cruel Marquis.[7]

The writer also stressed that Mason cleverly underplayed, with slow movements and *sotto voce* delivery. Mason's haunting voice was a cinematic rather than a theatrical instrument, and his performance was astutely keyed to the greater intimacy of the film medium.

Mason worked a series of variations on his Man in Grey, beginning with the sadistic Lord Manderstoke in *Fanny by Gaslight* (1944). In *The Seventh Veil*, the top-grossing film of 1945, the image was adroitly updated in a contemporary melodrama about a brooding, cruel guardian and his hapless niece. They are eventually united after he has shown signs of compassion but above all a need to be loved, which softened the image and was much more popular than his bullying husband role in *They Were Sisters*, released earlier that year. Mason was back in period costume as a romantic outlaw in *The Wicked Lady*, the highest-grossing film of 1946. The dashing highwayman Captain Jerry Jackson has some moral scruples but offers an unbridled sexuality.[8]

The use of costume melodrama allowed Gainsborough the licence to construct flamboyant, erotic male figures as objects of female desire, their costumes displaying the male form in tight trousers and unbuttoned shirts. As Mason's opposite in several of these films, Stewart Granger, the second most popular male star, was the conventional romantic hero: honourable, dashing and brave. Granger possessed the necessary physical attributes, being tall, handsome and muscular. But there was an arrogant sensuality to Granger's performance and an irony in his delivery which lightened the tone and slightly distanced performer from role. In those films where he was the main protagonist rather than playing against Mason, Granger's roles became more openly glamorous and erotic. *Madonna of the Seven Moons* (1944), *The Magic Bow* and *Caravan* (both 1946) all use Mediterranean settings to licence an exotic, unEnglish transgressive masculinity. This is perhaps most apparent in *Caravan*, where Granger plays Richard Darrell whose prolonged amnesia makes him forget his love for an English lady, Oriana, and his aspirations towards gentility. He is refashioned as the dependent lover of the Granadian gypsy Rosal. The poster for *Caravan* displayed the gypsified Granger with long, dark, curled hair, earrings, even lipstick, and bearing a startling likeness to Valentino, the archetype of the erotic Latin lover.[9]

The popularity of Mason and Granger seems to indicate a female desire for fantasies about handsome but dangerous men. The appeal of Michael Wilding, also immensely popular at this time, was rather more conventional. Wilding came to prominence in Herbert Wilcox's highly successful 'London' series (1945–50), built round his wife Anna Neagle. Rex Harrison starred in the first, *I Live in Grosvenor Square* (1945), but was replaced in the remaining four by Wilding, whose image was a reworking of the debonair gentleman: idealistic, gentle, soft-spoken and 'genially amateur'.[10] Wilding was admired by one critic as possessing 'the looks and bearing of Lord Mountbatten' and the 'charm of Leslie Howard', indicating that his image could be read as acceptably masculine.[11] Less raffish than Harrison and less dreamy than Howard, Wilding produced a well-bred, well-spoken charm which was not so obviously upper-class, in keeping with a more egalitarian society. Wilding suffers nobly in a tragic wartime romance (*Piccadilly Incident*, 1946), and dons a series of becoming uniforms in a historical pageant (*The Courtneys of Curzon Street*, 1947), but he is at his most charming in the musical comedies *Spring in Park Lane* (1949) and *Maytime in Mayfair* (1950), where he is as elegant and urbane as Cary Grant, able to glide through the plot contrivances as effortlessly as he dances with Neagle in the set pieces.

However, *Maytime in Mayfair* was significantly less successful than its predecessor, indicating that the debonair gentleman was becoming a residual type, its appeal less relevant to audience needs.[12] Wilcox declared that his renovations of *noblesse oblige* were 'happy, unclouded pictures. We do not want sadism, abnormality and psychoanalysis.'[13] What he was referring to was a loose group of psychological melodramas (usually crime thrillers) which could be classified as British film noir.[14] The central type in these films was the misfit, often a fugitive, usually innocent and falsely accused, but always tormented, desperate, unable to find a safe haven or a secure identity. In some films these protagonists begin to doubt their own sanity, and the result is breakdown or uncontrolled violence. The emergence of this type suggests a profound social dislocation and a crisis of masculine identity.

Most of the major British male stars of the 40s appeared in these films: James Mason in *Odd Man Out* (1947) and *The Upturned Glass* (1947); John Mills in *The October Man* (1947); Rex Harrison in *Escape* (1948); Richard Todd in *For Them That Trespass* (1948) and *The Interrupted Journey* (1949); Trevor Howard in *They Made Me a Fugitive* (1947); Robert Newton in *Temptation Harbour* (1947), *Obsession* (1949) and *Waterfront* (1950); and David Farrar in *Frieda* (1947), *The Small Back Room* (1948), *Cage of Gold* (1950) and *Night Without Stars* (1951). But the actor who most often embodied this type was Eric Portman.

Portman, who had come to prominence through his performance as a fanatical Nazi in *49th Parallel*, the top-grossing film of 1941, starred in *Great Day* (1945), *Wanted for*

Murder (1946), *Dear Murderer* (1947), *The Mark of Cain* (1948), *Corridor of Mirrors* (1948), *Daybreak* (1948) and *The Spider and the Fly* (1949). In all these films he played tormented, sexually insecure failures. *Great Day* explicitly shows this as an inability to adjust. Captain Ellis (Portman), a First World War veteran used to excitement, male comradeship and command, cannot cope with the different demands of civilian life. In the climactic scene he breaks down, admitting he was 'frightened in peace', conscious of the dependency of his wife and daughter, of his failure to live up to what he understands to be a man's role: 'He's the lover, the protector, the strong man. Or he wants to be. In my case no fresh supplies came in.'

Although the appeal of these films is essentially to male spectators who could identify with these anxieties even if they could not admit to them, Leonard Wallace noted that Portman had a large female following:

> It's the strength being harried and tested by circumstances that really gets the girls suffering for him. . . . No-one is better than Portman at expressing with a haunted, tortured expression of the eyes in a face otherwise taut and immobile, the inner bitterness in a strong man's soul.[15]

Picturegoer readers, presumably from both sexes, voted him into fourth place in the 1947 poll for his performance as the tormented serial killer in *Wanted for Murder*.

The misfit, as a failed hero, was different from the other oppositional type of the late 40s, the spiv. A product of war and post-war rationing, the spiv became, in part, a kind of anti-austerity folk hero, represented as colourfully dressed, charismatic and enter-

The inner bitterness in a strong man's soul. Eric Portman watches Edana Romney in Corridor of Mirrors *(Terence Young, 1948).*

prising in affectionate caricatures by comedians, cartoonists and columnists.[16] Stewart Granger's performance as Ted Purvis in *Waterloo Road* (1945) helped fix the type, a portrait clearly based on popular stereotypes of the flashy, Americanised, work-shy, petty criminal wide-boy. Griffith Jones played a much more sinister variant in *They Made Me a Fugitive* (1947) and *Good Time Girl* (1948), indicating that the spiv's image was becoming more threatening.

It was these criminal traits which were transferred to the representation of the young delinquent. Several young actors played the type, including Richard Attenborough in *Brighton Rock* (1948), but it was Dirk Bogarde's engrossing performance as Tom Riley in *The Blue Lamp*, the top-grossing film of 1950, which had the most impact. Riley is neurotic, unstable and sexually threatening, his presence explicitly linked to wartime dislocation and the break-up of the family. Bogarde, despite playing such an obviously unacceptable character, gained seventh place for his performance in the *Picturegoer* poll, suggesting that the taste for the thrilling sadist had migrated to this type.[17]

The prominence of these oppositional types in the immediate post-war period was partly due to the difficulty British cinema experienced in producing heroic roles, a problem only resolved when war films came back into favour after 1950. But the heroes of these 50s war films were different from charismatic leaders like Laurence Olivier in *Henry V* or debonair gentlemen in uniform like Noël Coward in *In Which We Serve*: they were professional officers. As Harold Perkin argues, the interventionism of the Welfare State promoted the growth and status of a meritocratic professionalism which cut across traditional elites and class boundaries.[18]

The first star who embodied this emergent type was John Mills, always noted for his sincerity and believability rather than for romantic qualities. He topped the *Picturegoer* poll in 1947 for his performance as Pip, the personable everyman of *Great Expectations*. This ordinary decency was elevated in *Scott of the Antarctic* (1948) to the status of national hero. In place of the debonair gentleman's dash and charm, Mills embodies a boyish enthusiasm which is deepened by testing into a gritty determination to continue whatever the cost. In *Scott* it is the nobility of sacrifice for others which turns physical suffering and defeat into a spiritual triumph; a victory for the team rather than for charismatic individualism. Mills was also much admired in *Morning Departure* (1950) as a similarly inspirational leader, this time a submarine captain who has to encourage three of his crew, trapped with him in their stricken craft, to face death calmly. Despite his versatility as an actor, Mills continued to achieve his greatest success in similar roles: as Commander Fraser in *Above Us the Waves* (1955), and as Pat Reid, the head of the escape committee, in *The Colditz Story* (1955).

A similar typecasting moulded the mid-50s career of Richard Todd, who had starred in three exuberant Disney swashbucklers made in Britain: *The Story of Robin Hood and His Merrie Men* (1952), *The Sword and the Rose* (1953) and *Rob Roy, the Highland Rogue* (1953). Despite his wholesome athleticism and brio in these films, Todd's defining role was as another national hero, Wing Commander Guy Gibson in *The Dam Busters* (1955). The essence of Todd's performance is to downplay Gibson's personal charm in favour of a professionally disciplined dedication to the task in hand. Gibson succeeds through efficient organisation and teamwork.

The most successful representative of meritocratic professionalism was Jack Hawkins, the most popular male star in 1953 and 1954. Hawkins's massive physique, coupled with the deliberate, hesitating delivery of his gravelly voice, were expressive of the immense effort that war required: an unending tight-lipped vigilance, resulting in occasional hard-won victories. Though two years younger than Mills, Hawkins lacked the latter's boyishness and was cast in roles which made him a plausible father figure to the young officers who were on their first mission – a rite of passage into full manhood – in such films as *Angels One Five* (1952), *The Cruel Sea* (1953) and *The Malta Story* (1953). Denied any kind of love interest in these films, the emotionalism of the Hawkins character is channelled through male comradeship. As Commander Ericson in *The Cruel Sea*, the top-grossing film of 1953, Hawkins's scarcely mobile face sheds silent tears at the loss of the drifting British crewmen, blown up by his decision to depth-charge a suspected submarine. Shortly after, having drunk himself into insensitivity, Ericson is discovered slumped in his cabin by his 'son' Lockhart (Donald Sinden), who puts him tenderly to bed.[19] Later the two toast, with pink gins, their decision to see out the war together, a decision which Lockhart cannot explain to his girlfriend. The bonds of comradeship here, as elsewhere in the war films, offer a deeper and more sustaining relationship than that of heterosexual romance.

The appeal of war films is very much to males. By the mid-50s they outnumbered females in cinema audiences and critics were offering the qualities of these male stars for their admiration and emulation. Robert Otway celebrated Hawkins's 'rocky frame [which] has become a national institution, a kind of male Britannia', an appropriately regendered national icon.[20] Otway went on to contrast Hawkins's image with Mason's wicked gentlemen, while Jympson Harmon saw him as representing 'loyalty, courage, leadership, unselfishness, compassion and all those things that used to make this such a pleasant land to live and work in'.[21] Clearly the war heroes embodied an idealised golden age, and a patriotic noble Britishness, as well as meritocratic professionalism.

The dominance of the war films at the box-office in the mid-50s was interrupted by the success of *Doctor in the House*, the highest-grossing film of 1954. Josh Billings commented that the film had 'uprooted all records at the Odeon, Leicester Square.... What does this fantastic success signify? I suggest that a large part of the result is due to the buoyant youthfulness of the film. Here is freshness. Here is vitality'.[22] *Doctor in the House* gently debunked the do-gooding welfare state professional, reconstructing the rather untouchable and piously noble image of the doctor into something lovable. The professional could also be fun.

The role of Simon Sparrow allowed Dirk Bogarde to break with his earlier typecasting as a delinquent and to rework the unstable juvenile into a vulnerable and sensitive romantic lead. Although he faints in the operating theatre, hears the sea in his stethoscope and engages in a series of naively unsuccessful attempts at sexual initiation, he is also capable of delivering a baby and passing his exams. The film is another rite of passage for the young male who ends equipped to become a doctor and a husband, ready to take up a practice and to settle down. His wife-to-be is a sensible nurse and their relationship a representation of the post-war ideal of the companionate marriage. *Films and Filming* regretted that the 'good looks which have made out of the spiv, the deserter and the petty thug creatures of mystery and fascination' should have been neutered by the 'wide-eyed diffidence' of Bogarde's role as Simon Sparrow, confirming the trend of his films towards 'niceness'.[23] But most critics celebrated Bogarde's release from shabby macintosh roles.

The other star of *Doctor in the House* was Kenneth More as Grimsdyke, whose upper middle-class bohemian lifestyle is eccentric rather than rakish. Although he wears a succession of lurid waistcoats and lives on an allowance, he is reliable and caring both towards the younger males and towards his Austrian fiancée, whom he treats as an equal partner. Derek Granger congratulated More on transforming the 30s stereotype of the raffish young man, which he had employed so effectively in *Genevieve* (1953), into a rounded and convincing characterisation.[24] This suggests that More's perform-

Pugnacious, determined, redolent of robust good health and exuding self-confidence. Kenneth More as Douglas Bader in Reach for the Sky *(Lewis Gilbert, 1956).*

ance must be understood as a modernisation of the debonair gentleman, a combination of tradition and the contemporary. *Films and Filming* felt that More had 'all the virtues and none of the vices' of the upper-middle class, combining eccentricity and humour with sincerity and honesty.[25] In a general comment on the film, Dilys Powell enthused about these 'well-spoken' young men after all the representations of spivs and 'young workers with regional accents'.[26]

Because of their ability to embody, in very different ways, a youthful and ostensibly classless masculinity, Bogarde and More displaced Hawkins as the most popular male star and dominated the box-office until the end of the decade. Their star power was exploited by being deployed in a wide range of roles in which the consistency of their image was often more important than the demands of characterisation.

Bogarde was rushed into another domestic comedy, *For Better, For Worse* (1954), and Rank made him repeat the Simon Sparrow role in *Doctor at Sea* (1955) and *Doctor at Large* (1957), which were both huge successes. He also played romantic leads in action adventure (*Campbell's Kingdom*, 1957), war romance (*The Wind Cannot Read*, 1958) and historical drama (*A Tale of Two Cities*, 1959), all of which were highly popular with *Picturegoer* readers. With the partial exception of *Campbell's Kingdom*, these films exploit Bogarde's star image of the passive and sensitive male – a soft, expressive masculinity. A reviewer of *The Wind Cannot Read* commented that Bogarde with 'spaniel pathos in the eyes ... [was] prowling the screen demanding mother love from his millions of female fans'.[27]

More's appeal was rather different, since he was not a conventional romantic lead. In an interview he commented that his female fans were 'under fifteen and over thirty ... the others all go for a handsome bloke like Bogarde'.[28] A letter from a female admirer, unfortunately without the age given, praised his 'mature good looks' which were enough to send 'all thoughts of ... beautiful beefcakes out of my head'.[29] His pleasant, strong face was attractive rather than strikingly handsome, and his muscular, stocky physique not graceful or dashing but pugnacious, determined, redolent of robust good health and exuding self-confidence. The domestic comedy *Raising a Riot* (1955) characteristically shows him as the harassed officer father of three rather than as a newly wed. He is the attractive, often charming, mature man who captures the heart of a seventeen-year-old neighbour, but he rebuffs her with avuncular tact.

This maturity and strength meant that More was able to perform effectively as the officer professional, as well as in comedies. More's key part, like that of Mills as Scott and Todd as Gibson, was as an actual national hero: Douglas Bader in *Reach for the Sky*, (1956). More brought to this role his image as the ebullient hearty together with the introspection of his highly successful stage and film role as the maladjusted former fighter pilot Freddie Page in *The Deep Blue Sea* (1955). His depiction of Bader, more nuanced and emotional than is usually recognised, is vital to the success of a film which shows the literal smashing of the pre-war debonair gentleman and his re-creation as the robust, tenacious professional officer with an indomitable will to win. As with Scott, with whom Bader was frequently compared, this story was understood as another 'victory of the human spirit'.

By the end of 1957 Josh Billings thought that More was 'unquestionably a big draw' who could 'turn an ordinary film into a box-office success mainly on the strength of his name'.[30] This allowed him to be cast in a diverse range of films: J. M. Barrie's Edwardian castaway fantasy *The Admirable Crichton* (1957); an action drama about the sinking of the Titanic, *A Night to Remember* (1958); a John Buchan adventure, *The 39 Steps* (1959); a 1905 imperial epic, *North West Frontier* (1959); a comedy Western, *The Sheriff of Fractured Jaw* (1959); and a late naval war epic, *Sink the Bismarck!* (1960). The consistency is provided by More himself, who remains largely the same, displaying a resolute, chivalrous integrity, a 'rugged spiritual health', which is tested but never found wanting.[31]

But even More's presence cannot disguise the increasingly backward-looking nature of these films, and his career faltered in the early 60s along with those of other 50s stars.[32] They were replaced by pop stars like Cliff Richard, by Christopher Lee's subversively sexual Count Dracula, and above all by working-class heroes. Working-class masculinity had been conspicuously absent from British screens in the 50s. Parts which had demanded the ordinary bloke as action man had been played by fading or second-drawer American stars such as Forrest Tucker. However, towards the end of the decade such roles were played by Stanley Baker, who overtook Bogarde in the *Motion Picture Herald* ratings in 1959.

Baker – Welsh, strongly built and with a thin mouth, prominent jaw and 'falcon eyes' – was a new male type. In the early 50s he had been typecast as the villain, including the oafish bully Bennett in *The Cruel Sea*, until association with McCarthyite exiles Cy Endfield and Joseph Losey led to a series of more interesting and sympathetic roles. *Films and Filming* commented that he played 'hard, tough characters neither particularly sympathetic nor particularly villainous, [which proved that] ordinary men, doing everyday jobs, can be exciting and often are.'[33] As Tom Yately in *Hell Drivers* (1957) he is a resourceful ex-convict whose time inside has made him able to survive in a harsh, brutal and exploitative world. This 'hero with a sadistic streak ... showed an enormous increase in his fan mail from girls between the ages of 17 and 20', an indication that Baker had become identified with thrilling, sexually desirable and subversive masculinity.[34]

His policemen in *Violent Playground* (1957), *Blind Date* (1959) and *Hell is a City* (1960), in contrast to those of Jack Hawkins in *The Long Arm* (1956) or *Gideon's Day* (1958), are confused men, strangely drawn to the criminals they hunt and with unformed or unstable family lives. As Johnny Bannion in *The Criminal* (1960), his old-fashioned individual villainy is at odds with the new world of organised crime, making him again an ambivalent figure. Baker's tough, aggressive characters, confused about their social role, lead directly to the anti-heroes of the 'New Wave' films such as Albert Finney's Arthur Seaton in *Saturday Night and Sunday Morning* (1961).[35]

Michael Roper and John Tosh argue that 'masculinity has a history ... it is subject to change and varied in its forms.'[36] The images of the popular male stars which I have sketched illustrate this process, exhibiting a variety which changed in relation to the complex social and historical forces that shaped the needs and desires of cinema audiences. The immediate post-war period in British cinema needs to be understood as a transitional phase in which subversive representations of masculinity come to prominence, before a – very male – consensus re-emerges in the 50s. This consensus was represented by a caring and heroic professionalism which passed itself off as universal, effectively marginalising alternative forms of masculinity until the end of the decade, when that social formation began to break up.

Notes

1. *Kinematograph Weekly*, 20 December 1945, p. 71.
2. Several stars have written informatively about studio promotion in their autobiographies, especially Dirk Bogarde, *Snakes and Ladders* (London: Chatto and Windus, 1978); Stewart Granger, *Sparks Fly Upward* (London: Granada, 1981); Jack Hawkins, *Anything for a Quiet Life* (London: Elm Tree Books, 1973); James Mason, *Before I Forget* (London: Hamish Hamilton, 1981); John Mills, *Up in the Clouds, Gentlemen Please* (London: Weidenfeld and Nicolson, 1980); Kenneth More, *More or Less* (London: Hodder and Stoughton, 1978); Richard Todd, *Caught in the Act* (London: Hutchinson, 1986) and *In Camera* (London: Hutchinson, 1989).
3. For 'Charm School' details see Geoffrey Macnab, *J. Arthur Rank and the British Film Industry* (London: Routledge, 1993), pp. 141–6.
4. Richard Dyer, *Stars* (London: British Film Institute, 1979), pp. 53–68.
5. Peter Burnup, the *Motion Picture Herald*'s London editor, quoted in an article in the *Daily Express*, 13 December 1956.
6. I have also used the *Daily Mail*'s annual listings, again based on readers' choices, which ran from 1945–9.
7. *Picturegoer*, 4 December 1943.
8. Mason's success attracted Hollywood offers, and he left for America in 1947.
9. Granger also played romantic leads for other production companies, notably Apollodorus in *Caesar and Cleopatra* (Pascal/Rank, 1946) and Count Koenigsmark in Ealing's *Saraband for Dead Lovers* (1948). Granger left for Hollywood in 1949, occasionally appearing in British costume films such as *Beau Brummell* (1954) or in action adventures like *Harry Black* (1958).
10. Jeffrey Richards, *The Age of the Dream Palace* (London: Routledge, 1986), p. 167. Richards argues that the debonair gentleman was the dominant British male type of the 30s.
11. Ewart Hodgson, *Sunday Times*, 23 August 1946.
12. Wilding also pursued a career in Hollywood after 1950, rather unsuccessfully. He was less adaptable than Granger and less distinctive than Mason.
13. *Kinematograph Weekly*, 18 December 1947, p. 18.
14. Robert Murphy discusses these films in *Realism and Tinsel* (London: Routledge, 1989), pp. 168–90.
15. *Picturegoer*, 17 December 1949.
16. David Hughes, 'The Spivs', in Michael Sissons and Philip French (eds.), *Age of Austerity, 1945–1951* (London: Hodder and Stoughton, 1963; reprinted, Oxford University Press, 1986), pp. 71–88.
17. See Andy Medhurst, 'Dirk Bogarde', in Charles Barr (ed.), *All Our Yesterdays* (London: British Film Institute, 1986), pp. 346–54. Medhurst rightly argues that Bogarde's performance displaces the film's nominal hero, PC Andy Mitchell (Jimmy Hanley), unbalancing the film.
18. Harold Perkin, *The Rise of Professional Society* (London: Routledge, 1989), especially pp. 355–61. See also Harry Hopkins, *The New Look* (London: Secker and Warburg, 1963), pp. 158–61.

19. Sinden is one of Raymond Durgnat's keen cadets: 'grown-up boys, trusting, vulnerable, decently worried and ready aye ready'. *A Mirror for England* (London: Faber and Faber, 1970), p. 142.
20. *Sunday Graphic*, 10 January 1953.
21. *Evening News*, 15 October 1953.
22. *Kinematograph Weekly*, 22 April 1954, p. 5.
23. *Films and Filming*, August 1955, p. 3.
24. *Financial Times*, 19 March 1954.
25. *Films and Filming*, April 1955, p. 3.
26. *Sunday Times*, 21 March 1954.
27. Derek Monsey, *Sunday Express*, 7 August 1958.
28. *Sunday Graphic*, 3 November 1957.
29. *Photoplay*, December 1955, p. 4.
30. *Kinematograph Weekly*, 12 December 1957.
31. Quotation from the review of *The 39 Steps*, *Observer*, 11 December 1959.
32. More, Todd and Hawkins went into character roles or television leads. Bogarde effectively re-defined his 'idol of the Odeons' image by appearing in less populist films by Losey and Visconti.
33. *Films and Filming*, November 1959, p. 5.
34. Ibid.
35. For a detailed discussion see Christine Gledhill's essay, 'Albert Finney – a Working-class Hero', in Pat Kirkham and Janet Thumim (eds.), *Me Jane* (London: Lawrence and Wishart, 1995), pp. 66–72.
36. Michael Roper and John Tosh (eds.), *Manful Assertions: Masculinities in Britain since 1800* (London: Routledge, 1991), p. 1.

Bibliography

Though star autobiographies abound, academic studies of British male stars are rare. The most useful examination of stars from an earlier era is Jeffrey Richards's work on Leslie Howard and Robert Donat in *The Age of the Dream Palace* (London: Routledge, 1986). Julian Petley deals with the stars of the 'new British cinema' in '*Reaching for the Stars*', in Martyn Auty and Nick Roddick (eds.), *British Cinema Now* (London: British Film Institute, 1985).

Docherty, David, Morrison, David and Tracey, Richard, *The Last Picture Show? Britain's Changing Film Audiences* (London: British Film Institute, 1987).
Durgnat, Raymond, *A Mirror for England* (London: Faber and Faber, 1970).
Dyer, Richard, *Stars* (London: British Film Institute, 1979).
Dyer, Richard, *Heavenly Bodies* (London: British Film Institute, 1987).
Geraghty, Christine, 'Masculinity', in Geoff Hurd (ed.), *National Fictions: World War Two in British Film and Television* (London: British Film Institute, 1984), pp. 63–7.
Gledhill, Christine (ed.), *Stardom: Industry of Desire* (London: Routledge, 1991).
Hill, John, *Sex, Class and Realism: British Cinema 1956–1963* (London: British Film Institute, 1986).
King, Barry, 'Stardom as an occupation', in Paul Kerr (ed.), *The Hollywood Film Industry* (London: Routledge/British Film Institute, 1986), pp. 154–84.
Macnab, Geoffrey, *J. Arthur Rank and the British Film Industry* (London: Routledge, 1993).
McFarlane, Brian (ed.), *Sixty Voices* (London: British Film Institute, 1992).
Medhurst, Andy, 'Can Chaps Be Pin-Ups? The British Male Film Star in the 1950s', in *Ten-8*, no. 17, February 1985, pp. 3–8.
Medhurst, Andy, 'Dirk Bogarde', in Charles Barr (ed.), *All Our Yesterdays* (London: British Film Institute, 1986), pp. 346–54.
Morin, Edgar, *The Stars* (London: Grove Press, 1960).
Murphy, Robert, *Realism and Tinsel* (London: Routledge, 1989).
Richards, Jeffrey, 'Jack Hawkins: an officer and a gentleman', *The Movie*, no. 45, 1980, pp. 896–7.
Walker, Alexander, 'Random thoughts on the Englishness (or otherwise) of English film actors', in '*It's Only a Movie, Ingrid*' (London: Headline, 1988), pp. 207–81.

15
Women and Sixties British Cinema: The Development of the 'Darling' Girl

Christine Geraghty

Adolescents are the litmus paper of our society.
The Albermarle Report on the Youth Service, 1960.[1]

This essay is concerned with the changing position of women in 60s British cinema and in particular focuses on three films whose heroines I take to be emblematic of the changes that I am discussing – *A Taste of Honey*, *Darling* and *Here We Go Round the Mulberry Bush*. But I want to place questions of narrative and representation in these films in the specific social context of British society during this period and, in particular, to look at the way in which the discourses around the sexuality of young women which were constructed and reworked in the cinema can be placed within the context of educational and moral arguments about youth and sexual behaviour that are associated with the 60s.

The problems posed by youth in the post-war period can be traced in the official reports which sought to provide social and legal ways of examining what was needed and providing a remedy.[2] Those working with young people began to claim a professional expertise – teachers, youth workers, probation officers, social workers, psychologists, psychiatrists, magistrates – which placed emphasis on supporting and protecting young people in their engagement with the modern world.[3] In the literature which served these professionals and, in particular, in the paperback sociology books which were aimed at them and at the interested lay reader, we can see discourses developing in which youth could be explained and understood as a species marked off by surveys and services as being different from the adult world. Much of this work in the 50s focused on working-class young men and what was seen as their antisocial and sometimes violent behaviour. In so far as young women entered the picture, it was as adjuncts who attached themselves to such youths; and while there was concern about their sexuality, there was also the feeling that young women could, through their desire for home and family, be part of the process of settling their boyfriends down. In his study of delinquents, *The Insecure Offenders*, T. R. Fyvel reported that the Teddy girl retained 'the basic feminine ideal of a normal home life', and commented that 'even the wildest Teddy boy … arrives at the point where traditional morality reasserts itself usually at the point of a shotgun.'[4]

In the late 50s/early 60s, however, the debate shifted from delinquency to premarital sex and the figure of the young woman came into greater prominence.[5]

Sociologists such as Michael Schofield began to argue for a greater sympathy for young people's position; pre-marital sexual activity, he suggested in his 1965 study, *The Sexual Behaviour of Young People*, was not 'a minority problem confined to a few deviates. It is an activity common enough to be seen as one manifestation of teenage conformity.'[6] Schofield found that girls were more likely to associate sex with romance and love and to accept that, given the double standards applied by the boys, they had to be more circumspect than boys. Nevertheless, the survey also suggests some rather less conventional attitudes to sexual activity among the girls. Although sexual activity had traditionally been associated with working-class deviancy, Schofield reports a higher level of sexual activity among middle-class girls who 'were prepared to allow more sexual intimacies as long as these stop short of sexual intercourse'.[7] While such findings reflect the lack of access to contraception, which Schofield also reports, they may also reveal young women taking a degree of control over sexual behaviour which chimes with Schofield's comments that sexually experienced girls were strongly associated with 'a desire for freedom and independence'.[8]

It is not surprising that debates about youth can be found in films of the period since the cinema as an industry had much at stake in youth and its pleasures. Changing leisure patterns, including the arrival of television, meant that increasingly distributors and exhibitors relied on young people for their audiences. One of the attractions of cinemagoing for young people was its connection with dating and sexual behaviour. Fyvel, accompanying Teddy boys to the pictures, commented that 'the cinema is sex-dominated, the sanctioned place to take one's girl to, with sex on the screen and a good deal of it in the auditorium too.'[9] More generally, Schofield reported that 51 per cent of his sample went to the cinema on their first date and found that the cinema provided 'one of the few semi-private places a boy and a girl can go to make love'.[10] Thus filmgoing had a particular role in young people's social lives and, while the films of the 60s shared and indeed helped to shape the concepts of youth which are characteristic of the social and political discourses of the time, cinema's specificity in relation to young people's leisure activities means that the films could take a different attitude to the youth phenomenon from that of either sociological and educational treatises or the tabloid press. In addition, cinema's role in dating and sexual activity suggests a more distracted mode of viewing than that proposed by theories of 'the gaze' which have dominated much textual analysis in film study; this interrupted, 'back-row' viewing might be expected to privilege the impact of image and star rather than the logic of narrative in creating meaning.

The three films I have chosen to discuss allow us to trace some of the shifts in the representation of women in 60s films and to see how the social and moral issues which clustered round young women were reworked in the cinema. In each case I will look at the way in which certain thematic issues – the family, sexual behaviour, generational differences – are handled and suggest that in these films narrative and image may work against each other at crucial points to provide a contradictory account in which pleasures can be found in the image which the narratives try to deny.

A Taste of Honey (Tony Richardson, 1961) belongs to the 'new wave' of British film-making which characteristically drew on northern settings, working-class mores and young aggressive heroes. Films like *Saturday Night and Sunday Morning* (Karel Reisz, 1960) and *A Kind of Loving* (John Schlesinger, 1962) seem to mark a shift in attitude to young people compared with earlier films such as *The Blue Lamp* (Basil Dearden, 1949) or *The Scamp* (Wolf Rilla, 1957). While they could be critical of their youthful protagonists, the 'new wave' films suggested that problems with their behaviour lay with society rather than in the innate delinquency of youth or the failure of their individual families. *A Taste of Honey* differed, however, by centring its narrative on a young woman, Jo, played by Rita Tushingham, a change which skews some of the characteristic themes of the 'new wave' – consumerism, sexual energy, generational differences – and gives them a somewhat different purchase.

The narrative of *A Taste of Honey* deals with Jo's dissatisfaction with the family life created by her mother, Helen, and her unsuccessful struggle to escape from it. From the beginning, the film emphasises her mother's inadequacies as the pair do a moonlight flit to escape unpaid rent and set up a new home in impoverished and run-down rooms. Helen's fecklessness extends to her sexual activities, and her choice of Peter as a husband – based on sexual need rather than his suitableness for a paternal role within the family – is used to underline her careless attitude to Jo. Helen, as Terry Lovell has pointed out, exists 'on the margins of working-class culture and community', but her pleasure in sex is firmly linked to working-class culture and Jo is excluded from both.[11] A trip to Blackpool ends with Jo being sent home alone and Helen's vivacious excitement in the pub and the dance-hall is contrasted with Jo's haunting of the wastelands and canals. The effect of this elision is to associate Jo's dissatisfaction with her family with a rejection of working-class culture and the film thus links her efforts to move out of the family with an attempt to make for herself a kind of 'youth culture' in which she can literally feel at home. *A Taste of Honey* marks an early attempt at the creation of a proto-family in which support is given, often by members of the same generation, in a less restrictive but more careful way than that given by the family. Jo meets Jeff, whose youth credentials are established by an interest in art and style, and the two set up home together. Their attempt to decorate the loft/flat which they share is markedly different from Helen's careless muddle: it indicates the way in which Jo and Jeff strive to create a space in which a different form of family can emerge, one which provides emotional support but is a move away from the messy clutter of Helen's attempts at domestic comfort.

Jo's move away from home is precipitated by her sexual encounter with the black sailor, Jimmy but this occurs after she is rejected by Helen on the Blackpool trip and returns to Manchester, lonely and angry. Thus Jo's entry into sexuality is associated not with a move into adult desires but with a childlike need for help; the association with innocence and loss is underlined by the children's songs which accompany Jo and Jimmy as they walk along together and the long leave-taking scene in which Jo watches the deserted boat depart through the empty industrial landscape of the canal. Later in the film, Jo's pregnancy and Jeff's homosexuality serve narratively to prevent Jo's sexuality from being further explored and the contrast between this chasteness and her mother's lack of sexual control is a motif throughout the film.[12]

This childlike quality is reflected in Tushingham's appearance, a marked contrast to the mature women stars of 50s films such as Diana Dors and Virginia McKenna. Tushingham's Jo is a schoolgirl at the beginning of the film and never loses her childish features – thin body, big eyes, wide cheekbones, gawky stance. Jo is presented as being unconventional and quirky; she tells the truth at awkward moments, acts on impulse and is quick to express her feelings even when this might hurt others. Thus youth is associated with a transparency of purpose, a refusal to compromise or pretend. These traits which mark Jo as a character are consonant with the image of Rita Tushingham as a new kind of female star; interviewers commented approvingly on her 'wide-eyed appeal' and the natural way in which she pulls 'the sort of apprehensive face a schoolgirl might if she were caught doing something bad'.[13]

A Taste of Honey ends with Helen reclaiming Jo, the break-up of the 'youth family' and the denial of Jo's possibilities for freedom. This punishing closure suggests that Jo has lost, is trapped in 'a resigned acknowledgment of things as they are'.[14] But to place too much emphasis on their endings is to miss what these films offered young audiences. For while the end of *A Taste of Honey* returns Jo to the situation she has fled, the combination of character and star has suggested other routes. The 'problem' of the teenage pregnancy is dealt with by the narrative, but codes of characterisation and stardom suggest other possibilities for a young audience. The emphasis throughout the film on Jo/Tushingham's unconventionality, her truthfulness and her desire for different kinds of relationship survives the film's ending. With *A Taste of Honey*, we can begin to see the emergence of a specific discourse around young women which was highly significant for 60s British cinema.

As debates on the sexual behaviour of young people took centre-stage in discussion of youth, the role of young women became critical. What begins to emerge from studies such as Schofield's is the figure of the middle-class, educated teenage girl who has a measure of control over her own pleasure and behaviour. Schofield's research suggested that 'it does appear that the higher up a girl is on the social scale, the more sexual experience she is likely to have'.[15] Whether this was actually the case is less important for our purposes than the change in image. The delinquent girl who can be led astray (a common figure in 50s films – for example, *Cosh Boy* [Lewis Gilbert, 1953] and *I Believe in You* [Basil Dearden, 1952]) becomes in these studies someone who calculates how far she can or wants to go and is more sexually active than many of the working-class boys who had formed the vanguard of youth culture up to this point.

The early 60s thus sees the creation of a set of sociological discourses which suggest that young women might be more powerful and more confident than before. Two further factors are important. Firstly, like the working-class youth of the 50s, the 60s girl was placed firmly within the context of consumption. She was a figure around whom the wheels of marketing were spinning and liberal commentators worried about how far a desire to conform lay behind her purchases, making her prey to the designs of big business and the media. Nevertheless, in some senses the attempts of advertising, magazines and television to appeal to the young woman reinforced the impression that she was exercising choices which she could wilfully withdraw. The second factor was the Profumo affair, which had at its heart the capacity of a young woman of dubious morals to bring down a government minister. The Denning Report of 1963, which was widely read and publicised in the popular press, painted a picture of Christine Keeler's demi-monde in which she swam naked in the swimming pools of aristocrats, casually picked up a Cabinet minister and was fought over by 'coloured' lovers. The Profumo affair associated young women with sexual power, exemplified in the ability of a girl to destroy a man's career and the insouciance of Mandy Rice-Davies's casual put-down when confronted with denial: 'Well, he would say that, wouldn't he?'

The characterisation of the young woman in *Darling* (John Schlesinger, 1965) takes on some of this flavour as it pushes much further representations which *A Taste of Honey* only suggests. In *Darling*, the shift from the North to London, from the working class to the middle class, means that different possibilities come into play. The family, which had been such a key point of rebellion for the 'new wave', hardly features for the film's protagonist, Diana; a middle-class convent childhood is sketched in, as is her relationship with her sister, but since the film treats Diana as an enigma her family cannot be pinned down as the source of the problem she poses. Nevertheless, Diana cannot ignore the family, and much of the film's narrative traces her failure to establish her own family. She cannot build a successful relationship with Robert or Miles and her abortion destroys the possibility of a 'normal' family life. Her proto-family relationship with the gay Malcolm (like that of Jo and Jeff in *A Taste of Honey*) has

Sometimes it's hard to be a woman. Julie Christie in Darling *(John Schlesinger, 1964).*

possibilities of friendship, fun and style, free of heterosexual complications, but the fantasy of living together in Capri is destroyed by Diana's jealousy. The family she adopts through her marriage to the Italian prince is dominated by conventions and rules to which she cannot conform. Thus a narrative pattern like that of *A Taste of Honey* is set up in which a search for a different form of family is an important mainspring of the plot but one which is doomed to fail.

Darling, however, differs markedly from the earlier film in its representation and organisation of female sexuality. Here, sexuality is associated with power rather than innocence and Diana is presented as using her desirability as a means of control. The film inextricably links female sexual desire with the desire for power and thus makes it impossible to untangle the two, to judge, for instance, whether Diana is pursuing her own sexual interests when she seduces Miles or furthering her career. There are strong links to the Profumo case in the notion that male desire for young women is linked to the dubious and worn-out politics of the Establishment figures whom Diana meets on her way to the top. Diana (like Keeler) mixes in the crossover world between politics, business and showbiz; the orgies, masks and sexual games which Diana is drawn into by Miles have the seedy flavour of the 'rumours' investigated in the Denning Report.[16] Rather more prosaically, Diana's sexual confidence in the first part of the film recalls Schofield's findings about middle-class girls who were sexually experienced but who seemed to control the stages of sexual activity which they were prepared to participate in. Described in male terms, Diana is both powerful and a tease, a combination which, as both Carrie Tarr and John Hill indicate, is punished by the ending when, rejected and abused by Robert, Diana is dispatched back to Italy.[17] From a female viewpoint, though, the presentation of Diana's sexuality may suggest that pleasure on one's own terms is imaginable if not narratively possible.

158

The question of where this female viewpoint might or might not be found is central to Tarr's discussion of the film. Certainly it is hard to find in Diana's voice-over, which is consistently undermined by the images and serves to present her as hypocritical and self-pitying. In addition, as Tarr indicates, the identification of Diana with the media world to which she aspires means that the film's critique of that world turns into a critique of its heroine. The critical attitude of the film to its heroine was echoed by the contemporary quality press critics, allowing little space for pleasure to be taken in the representation of the young woman. Yet the impact of Julie Christie in the role was enormous. Sarah Maitland, looking back on the 60s, speaks for many, I suspect, when she refers to Julie Christie as 'the symbol of all my yearning adolescent hopes'.[18] Christie herself, musing on the character she played, recalls that 'She was extraordinary ... Here was a woman who didn't want to get married, didn't want to have children like those other kitchen-sink heroines; no, *Darling* wanted to have *everything*.'[19]

As with *A Taste of Honey*, the possibilities for interpretations which work against rather than with the ending are to be found in the characterisation and star image rather than the working out of the plot. Two key factors are important here – the use of fashion and the establishment of Christie's star persona outside the film. The narrative of *Darling* makes much of Diana being trapped in the artificial world of modelling but the way in which Diana/Christie is dressed speaks of a self-confidence based on but not limited to a new approach to fashion and style. Her clothes mix the mod (tartan skirt, knee-length socks, hairbands) with the traditional (her evening dress at the charity function). Both styles are worn with an individual flourish, and the emphasis in her dress is not so much on following a 60s style but creating it, controlling fashion rather than conforming to it. This sense of creativity and control potentially has the effect of assuring young women that, while sociologists might be worried about a tendency to conformity among the young, fashion can be remade to express your own personality. Christie's clothes, while marked as those of a star, would also have been available through boutiques and dressmaking patterns to young women in the audience and the emphasis on accessories – headscarves, velvet bows, handbags – made it easy to adapt styles to the individual. This emphasis on individuality and personal freedom is reinforced by Christie's star image, which built on her appearance in *Billy Liar* (John Schlesinger, 1963) and emphasised her impulsiveness, her lack of calculation, her overwhelming desire for freedom. Like Tushingham, Christie is approachable, 'friendly but honest', and she has 'real friends' who are not in show business; her middle-class origins (she was born in India) are disguised by her then 'rather nomadic' existence – 'I just dossed down in the flats of my friends.'[20]

Some of these traits can be found in Diana – the car ride round Trafalgar Square or the impulsive trip to Fortnum's – but in the main it is precisely the clash between Christie's star image and the characterisation of Diana as manipulative and cold which is significant. Kenneth Tynan remarked that Christie was 'temperamentally miscast. . . . Her niceness is blazingly evident.'[21] In this disjunction, femininity itself becomes a performance, something which is ironically played on. While Diana's voice-over reveals her to be self-pitying and deluded and the narrative tells us that she is confused and greedy, we actually see something rather different. Take, for example, the scene in which Diana and Miles enter his empty office: the changes in the register of her voice as she teases Miles, the transformation of the board table into a catwalk, the *faux-naïf* admiration of the 'Glass millions' refer us to the character's ambition but the star's naturalness and integrity transform this into a display of femininity which she controls even in the seat of big business. Thus, Christie's image and performance call the

159

narrative into question by suggesting that feminine discourses of beauty and fashion are not the property of the Establishment but a way of claiming a feminine identity which can be used as a mode of self-expression, particularly around sexuality.

Christie thus added sexual power and confidence to the honesty and unpredictability of Tushingham and created a figure which was to be carried through in British cinema into the late 60s. But the difficulty in maintaining the possibilities of identification for young women can be seen in the rapidity with which it turned into a stereotype of what Robert Murphy identified as the late-60s figure of 'a spontaneous, vulnerable, sexually willing young woman.'[22] When the gap between star and narrative, voice-over and image is removed there is less space for a female viewpoint and it was difficult for this figure to avoid becoming a male fantasy of sexual availability rather than a female fantasy of control. An examination of a later film, *Here We Go Round the Mulberry Bush*, may show how this happened.

Here We Go Round the Mulberry Bush (Clive Donner, 1967) gives the narrative voice to a teenage boy, Jamie, whose viewpoint and voice-over underpin the film. The story is a picaresque tale of pursuit which follows Jamie's clumsy efforts to lose his virginity. Thus, unlike *A Taste of Honey* and *Darling*, the film lacks a female narrative viewpoint and the story is reminiscent of the 'new wave' narratives of male desire, although its tone and new town setting are markedly different. The tone is now humorous and the girls wield power not by their conformity to the traditionally feminine aspirations of marriage and a home, but by their control over sexual behaviour. In addition, *Here We Go Round the Mulberry Bush* has none of the artistic or aesthetic aspirations which mark the other two films and instead generically attempts to combine the traditional humour of a British sex comedy with the psychedelic trendiness of a 'youth' film. Here, the youth audience is being appealed to directly without the explanatory tone for an adult audience found in the earlier films.

Mary, the key female figure in *Here We Go Round the Mulberry Bush*, shares many of the qualities of Diana. Her family (whom we never see) is comfortably middle-class; she lives on a better part of the estate, a Jag is casually tucked into the garage, and she is comfortable in the social world of the well-to-do at the sailing club. But her manners and behaviour are classless in that, while she mixes with the crowd, she has her own unpredictable criteria for action and openly pursues her own pleasures without thought for conventional morality. Like Diana, however, she is narratively punished by being rejected by Jamie and condemned, through failing her A-levels, not to go to university. Like Diana, also, she uses fashion and style as a means of attraction and control, and the film's lighting and close-ups emphasise the similarities between Julie Christie and Judy Geeson with their blonde tousled hair, wide cheekbones and disarming smiles. This similarity means, however, that Geeson's star image cannot be authentic; she apes Christie and by doing so calls attention to her lack of the very naturalness on which Christie's star image is based.

The central joke of *Here We Go Round the Mulberry Bush* is the reversal of conventional gender expectations of earlier films, the contrast between Jamie's innocence and the sexual experience of the girls who surround him. 'What are young girls coming to these days?' he muses as Mary strips off in front of him for an impromptu swim in the lake. While Jamie is bemused, Audrey, Caroline and even the church-going Paula treat sexual activity in an entirely practical fashion, something to be seized as the opportunity presents itself but not to get worked up about. It is Jamie who learns the narrative lesson of the film, that promiscuity is 'a drag' and that marriage may have something going for it after all.

The film's attitude to sexuality is split between a matter-of-fact acceptance of teenage behaviour and the lessons to be drawn from the moral journey made by its young hero. The relentlessly male viewpoint means that, while the audience is offered a position which is, in certain respects, critical of Jamie, no access can be given to the internal life of the girls he tries to get into bed. The importance of this is seen in the treatment of Mary at the end. Geeson's lack of a star image means that she can be defined through narrative in a way that Christie could not and the ending can thus dispatch her more effectively. Jamie's problem with Mary is not so much her behaviour as her frankness, the way she speaks; she makes dates with other men in front of him and refuses to be conventionally romantic about their love-making: 'I can do what I like and you can do what you like. Remember we made a bargain. . . . You can go with someone else and I wouldn't mind.' Jamie is shocked – 'That's the worst thing I've ever heard you say' – and he finishes the relationship. This rejection of Mary's frank speech is reinforced by the images with which the film ends. Jamie watches, but does not overhear, Mary talking to her friend Claire. Claire walks away in long shot so that, with Jamie, we can assess her legs, but turns to exchange glances in a close-up of her speechless, smiling face as he ponders, 'That's the kind of girl I'd like to marry.'

Despite this ending, it was the figure of Mary – like that of Jo and Diana earlier – which dominated 60s British cinema. This representation of an unpredictable, spontaneous, emotionally honest, sexually active young woman shows how cinema worked within the broader social context in its attempt to reflect contemporary attitudes to what was seen as a 60s phenomenon. But the figure of the young woman was particularly important to British cinema in this period because it fed two specifically cinematic purposes. Firstly, it continued the trend set by 'new wave' films such as *Saturday*

'That's the kind of girl I'd like to marry.' Barry Evans ogles Judy Geeson and Diane Keen in Here We Go Round the Mulberry Bush *(Clive Donner, 1967).*

161

Night and Sunday Morning which established British cinema as being both contemporary and shocking; this was a cinema 'for adults' in which the sexual promise of the 'X' certificate could be justified by the social examination of the young woman as a contemporary phenomenon. Secondly, the figure of the young woman allowed British cinema to appeal to one of its key audiences – the youth market – by offering an entertainment which, like music and fashion, marked young people as a different species. It was common for sociologists in the late 50s and 60s to see the cinema as one of the sites where a commercial 'youth subculture' was being created which had an undue influence on teenage behaviour. But it seems more likely that the influence was not all one-way and that discourses of female sexuality in 60s film need to be understood in the context of changing behaviour and attitudes to which British cinema, with its commercial need for young audiences, had to speak. Thus while the films' narratives, as we have seen, typically punish sexual activity, the codes of stardom developed in the 60s associated female sexuality with honesty, independence and freedom and could suggest, to young audiences at least, that young women were not 'the problem' but offered possibilities for a solution.

Notes

1. *Report of the Committee on the Youth Services in England and Wales* (HMSO, 1960), quoted in Michael Schofield, *The Sexual Behaviour of Young People* (Harmondsworth: Penguin, 1968), p. 25.
2. Examples include: in 1959, the *Report on the Central Advisory Council for Education in England* (the Crowther report), which looked at the educational provision (or the lack of it) for 15- to 18-year-olds; in 1960, the *Report of the Committee on the Youth Services in England and Wales* (the Albermarle report) and *the Report of the Committee on Children and Young Persons* (the Ingleby report); and in 1963, *Half Our Future* (the Newsom report), looking at the education of 13- to 16-year-olds of average or less than average ability.
3. T. R. Fyvel, for instance, called for 'educational reform ... to keep the country's adolescents right out of the racket of the commercial youth market' (*The Insecure Offenders*, London: Chatto and Windus, 1961, p. 318), and the National Union of Teachers saw the need for educators to encourage young people and those involved with them 'to recognise the need for discrimination in accepting the offerings of the mass media'. Denys Thompson (ed.), *Discrimination and Popular Culture* (Harmondsworth: Penguin, 1964), p. 7.
4. Fyvel, *The Insecure Offenders*, pp. 136–7.
5. Jeffrey Weeks in *Sex, Politics and Society* (London: Longman, 1989) comments that by the end of the 50s 'pre-marital sex was *the* subject of anxious debate' (p. 238), and that 'sexuality of youth ... provoked the fiercest debates in the 60s and 70s' (p. 254).
6. Schofield, *The Sexual Behaviour of Young People*, p. 224.
7. Ibid., p. 55.
8. Ibid., p. 233.
9. Fyvel, *The Insecure Offenders*, p. 107.
10. Schofield, *The Sexual Behaviour of Young People*, p. 57; p. 143.
11. Terry Lovell, 'Landscapes and stories in 1960s British Realism', *Screen*, vol. 31, no. 4, Winter 1990, p. 374.
12. Lovell (ibid.) gives a detailed account of the film in the context of the British 'new wave' and emphasises, in her reading, the relationship between Jo and her mother.
13. *Daily Express*, 7 September 1961; *News of the World*, 7 October 1962.
14. John Hill, *Sex, Class and Realism: British Cinema 1956–63* (London: British Film Institute,1986), p. 167.
15. Schofield, *The Sexual Behaviour of Young People*, p. 117.
16. Lord Denning's 1963 Report (London: HMSO) includes a chapter on 'Rumours arising out of the Profumo Affair' and sub-sections on 'The "Darling" Letter' and ' "The Man in the Mask" ' who was one of the attractions at 'parties in private of a perverted nature' (p. 108).
17. Carrie Tarr, '*Sapphire*, *Darling* and the boundaries of permitted pleasure', *Screen*, vol. 26, no. 1, 1985; Hill, *Sex, Class and Realism*.
18. ' "I believe in yesterday" – an introduction', in *Very Heaven: Looking back at the 1960s* (London: Virago, 1988), p. 4.
19. 'Everybody's Darling: An interview with Julie Christie', in Maitland, *Very Heaven*, p. 171.

20. *Daily Mail*, 15 September 1965; *Sunday Express*, 18 July 1965.
21. *Observer*, 19 September 1965.
22. Robert Murphy, *Sixties British Cinema* (London: British Film Institute, 1992), p. 154.

Bibliography

Fyvel, T. R., *The Insecure Offenders* (London: Chatto & Windus, 1961).

HM Government, *Report on the Central Advisory Council for Education in England* (the Crowther report) (London: HMSO, 1959).

— *Report of the Committee on the Youth Services in England and Wales* (the Albemarle report) (London: HMSO, 1960).

— *Report of the Committee on Children and Young Persons* (the Ingleby report) (London: HMSO, 1960).

— *Lord Denning's Report* (London: HMSO, 1963).

— *Half Our Future* (the Newsom report) (London: HMSO, 1963).

Hill, John, *Sex, Class and Realism: British Cinema 1956–63* (London: British Film Institute, 1986).

Lovell, Terry, 'Landscapes and stories in 1960s British Realism', *Screen*, vol. 31, no. 4, Winter 1990.

Maitland, Sarah, *Very Heaven: Looking back at the 1960s* (London: Virago, 1988).

Murphy, Robert, *Sixties British Cinema* (London: British Film Institute, 1992).

Schofield, Michael, *The Sexual Behaviour of Young People* (Harmondsworth: Penguin, 1968).

Tarr, Carrie, '*Sapphire, Darling* and the boundaries of permitted pleasure', *Screen*, vol. 26, no. 1, 1985.

Thompson, Denys (ed.), *Discrimination and Popular Culture* (Harmondsworth: Penguin, 1964).

Weeks, Jeffrey, *Sex, Politics and Society* (London: Longman, 1989).

PART TWO

16
British Film Censorship

Jeffrey Richards

It is impossible to understand the development and nature of the British cinema without a full appreciation of the work and influence of the censors. They provided the framework within which cinema operated. They dictated the limits of what was permissible on the screen.

When cinema first appeared in Britain, it was totally unregulated. But from the outset society's moralists were expressing concern about the influence of films. The charge that cinemagoing among the young led directly to juvenile delinquency was made early and has continued to be made ever since. Teachers, clergymen, magistrates, public morality bodies and influential middle-class organisations like the Mothers' Union demanded control of the new art form, which had from its first appearance derived its greatest support from the working classes and the young.

It was concern about fire hazards which prompted the 1909 Cinematograph Act. This act gave local authorities the right to license cinemas but its wording also allowed them to act as censors of film content. Local councils began banning and censoring films. The London County Council (LCC) was the first, in 1910 banning a film of the recently staged fight for the heavyweight championship of the world in which a black man, Jack Johnson, had beaten a white man, James J. Jeffries.

The prospect of 688 local authorities all taking different views on whether individual films could be shown so terrified the film industry that in 1912 they voluntarily set up the British Board of Film Censors (BBFC). The Board was financed by fees paid by the producers to the censors for viewing the films. Its decisions were to be final and the industry committed itself to abide by those decisions. The Board took its lead from the Lord Chamberlain's office, which censored stage plays. Indeed, it appointed as its first president George A. Redford, a play reader in the Lord Chamberlain's office. He was given four assistants, all anonymous, and they classified films as 'U' (suitable for universal viewing) and 'A' (for adults only, i.e. those over sixteen). In its first year the Board banned twenty-two films.

On the Home Office's recommendation, most local authorities accepted the Board's rulings. But they retained and indeed still retain the right to censor, and this has led to periodic episodes when that right has been systematically exercised. In 1932, for instance, Beckenham Council briefly set up its own film censorship board and began cutting, banning and reclassifying films already certificated by the BBFC, until forced to abandon its operations by mounting opposition both from the picture houses which saw audiences falling drastically and from the audiences, forced to travel to neighbouring boroughs to see the current popular films.

Although Redford was president of the Board from 1912 until his death in 1916, he was in ill health for much of his tenure and the key figure in the day-to-day running of the Board from its inception in 1912 until his retirement in 1948 was Joseph Brooke Wilkinson. A former Fleet Street journalist and then secretary of the Kinematograph Manufacturers' Association, Wilkinson became arguably the most influential figure in the British film industry during his thirty-six years of office. A man of Victorian principle and stern moral rectitude, he established for more than three decades the moral tone of British films. In its obituary of him, *Kinematograph Weekly* characterised him as 'highly respected for his personal charm, integrity of character and unfailing tact'.[1] Veteran documentarist John Grierson was rather more caustic:

> Poor dear censor Wilkinson, with his Blake's poetry and his beloved Pre-Raphaelites, has, in the jungle of Wardour St., the strength of ten. Great figure he is, for on his charming old shoulders, he carries the burden of our servility and our shame. Created by the trade as an image of gratuitous fright, it is not surprising that his slogan of *No Controversy* is abjectly obeyed.[2]

The control exercised over the content of films was far tighter than that exercised over stage productions by the Lord Chamberlain, precisely because the cinema was *the* mass medium, regularly patronised by the working classes, and the working classes were deemed to be all too easily influenced. The pamphlet *Censorship in Britain*, issued by the BBFC to explain its policies, confirms that this idea was central to its thinking. It was guided, it said, by

> the broad general principle that nothing will be passed which is calculated to demoralize the public ... Consideration has to be given to the impression made on the average audience which includes a not inconsiderable proportion of people of immature judgement.[3]

It is evident that moral censorship was the Board's primary aim. T. P. O'Connor, the Board's second president, said in 1919 that the Board was concerned to ensure that nothing was passed 'that can teach methods of or extenuate crime, that can undermine the teachings of morality, that tends to bring the institution of marriage in contempt or lower the sacredness of family ties'.[4] His successor, Edward Shortt, put it more succinctly when he said in 1934: 'My job is to prevent our morals being made worse than they already are.'[5] Initially the Board had only two rules – no nudity and no depictions of the figure of Christ. But these were rapidly expanded and were outlined by O'Connor in his evidence to the 1917 National Council of Public Morals inquiry into cinema. They became known as 'O'Connor's 43'.[6] Thirty-three of these rules concerned matters that may properly be called moral: banning the depiction of prostitution, premarital and extramarital sex, sexual perversion, incest, seduction, nudity, venereal disease, orgies, swearing, abortion, brothels, white slavery and so on.

The other area of concern for the censors was essentially to maintain the political status quo. So no criticism was permitted of the monarchy, government, church, police, judiciary or friendly foreign countries. There should also be no depiction of current controversial issues (strikes, pacifism, the rise of Fascism, for instance). 'No controversy' was the rule, and 'harmless' was the censors' favourite term of approval for film projects. From its inception to the early 1970s the Board banned some 500 films completely for breaching its rules.[7] Many more were subjected to cuts.

It was extremely convenient for the Home Office that the BBFC should be independent. For whenever film censorship was debated in parliament, the Home Secretary could declare that the Board operated by its own rules free of government interference. But this was being economical with the truth. The presidents of the Board were always appointed after consultation with the Home Secretary, and after the death of the first president, Redford, they were always prominent political figures and experts in the moulding of public opinion. T. P. O'Connor, president from 1916 until his death in 1929, was a veteran Liberal MP, journalist, author and editor, and Father of the House of Commons in the 1920s. His successor, Edward Shortt, president from 1929 until his death in 1935, had been a Liberal MP and served both as Chief Secretary for Ireland and Home Secretary, in which posts he had achieved considerable success in countering Sinn Fein and Communist agitation. He was succeeded by Lord Tyrrell of Avon, president from 1935 until his death in 1947, and formerly head of the news department of the Foreign Office, chairman of the British Council and ambassador to Paris. All three were privy councillors.[8] Shortt certainly made no bones about his desire to use the cinema to shape public opinion: 'There is in our hands as citizens, an instrument to mould the minds of the young, to mould the mind of the adolescent and create great and good and noble citizens for the future.'[9] Not only were the BBFC presidents senior public figures but all controversial subjects were regularly referred to the appropriate government department for comment. So in 1938 the BBFC banned production of *The Relief of Lucknow*, a film about the Indian Mutiny, because the India Office felt that it was inexpedient to remind the Indian population of past conflict when they were attempting to find a peaceful constitutional settlement to current Indian unrest.[10]

So satisfied with the operation of film censorship was the government that there was only one serious attempt to take it over, and that was in the very early days. A plan was published by Home Secretary Sir Herbert Samuel to set up a state censorship board on 1 January 1917. But before it could be put into effect there was a change of government and the new Home Secretary abandoned the plan. Criticism of the existing system was further deflected by publication in 1917 of the report of the National Council of Public Morals' inquiry into the state of the cinema, which, although it recommended the institution of state censorship, admitted that the BBFC was doing its work well. The appointment of the respected O'Connor to succeed Redford as chief censor clinched the Board's survival. Thereafter the attitude of the government towards the BBFC was summed up by the Labour Home Secretary, J. R. Clynes, when he told the Commons in 1930 that he had 'no reason to believe that any alternative system so far proposed would produce better results or command general support, or that the standard of censorship in this country was not at least as high as that in any other'.[11]

The successful co-operation between the BBFC, government departments and the government's press censorship apparatus during the First World War further convinced the Home Office that the Board could be relied upon. Initially the government banned film of military operations at the front and the BBFC faithfully implemented its wishes. But later the Ministry of Information became a convert to film propaganda, and towards the end of the war documentary films of the conflict were permitted.

Although by 1918 the system was well and truly entrenched, there were throughout the interwar years successive controversies and disputes about individual films. Immediately after the war there was censorial concern about social problem films, which were both controversial and in breach of the Board's morality bans. A succession of such films were banned: the anti-abortion film *Where are My Children?* (1916);

the white slavery exposé *White Slave Traffic* (1919); a film on the effects of venereal disease, *Damaged Goods* (1919); and the anti-drugs film *Human Wreckage* (1923). But Dr Marie Stopes fought hard to get a film version of her birth control book *Married Love* made and passed. It emerged in 1923 as *Maisie's Marriage*, a romantic drama with an underlying birth control message, which O'Connor wanted to ban but the LCC were willing to pass. In the end there was a compromise: the film was released but only after cuts.[12]

In the early 1930s the vogue for horror films caused the censors great unease. The president said of them in the Board's 1935 Annual Report: 'I cannot believe that such films are wholesome, pandering as they do to the love of the morbid and the horrible.'[13] So Rouben Mamoulian's *Dr Jekyll and Mr Hyde* (1931) was heavily cut, and both Tod Browning's *Freaks* (featuring real-life circus freaks) and Erle C. Kenton's *Island of Lost Souls* (1932, from H. G. Wells' *Island of Doctor Moreau*), which included vivisection, were banned. But horror films were popular with audiences and continued to be produced by Hollywood. A compromise was reached in 1933 which led to the introduction of the 'H' (for horrific) certificate, which remained in force until 1951 when it was replaced by the 'X' certificate. Thirty-one films between 1933 and 1939 received an 'H' certificate. *Island of Lost Souls* remained banned until 1958 and *Freaks* until 1963.[14]

Individual *causes célèbres* included Cecil B. DeMille's epic film version of the life of Christ, *King of Kings* (1927). This was not shown to the BBFC because it offended against the prime directive banning depictions of the materialised figure of Christ. But it was shown to churchmen, gained their approval and was subsequently licensed by local authorities and widely shown. The Foreign Office pressured the BBFC to ban Herbert Wilcox's *Dawn* (1928), about the life and death of Nurse Edith Cavell, because it would offend the Germans. But Wilcox mounted a major publicity campaign, whipped up patriotic outrage against the authorities for seeking to denigrate a British heroine, and got the film widely licensed by local councils.[15]

The primary duty of the censors was to examine all films and classify them for exhibition. But the censors' control over the production of films tightened in the 1930s with the introduction of the practice of script-vetting to eliminate unacceptable material before shooting began. The process was voluntary but was regularly encouraged in the Board's annual reports. It was pointed out that producers would save money by submitting scripts for vetting because they would then not run the risk of having to reshoot offending scenes. The evidence suggests that about a third of all films produced in Britain in the 30s were approved at script stage, including all the prospective productions of Gaumont British.[16] A study of the scenario reports reveals an overwhelming desire to preserve propriety and decorum.[17] So there are endless requests for the toning down of language and systematic deletions of such words as 'nuts', 'bum', 'lousy', 'gigolo', 'belly', 'bawdy', 'nappy', 'prostitute' and 'nymphomaniac'. There were many requests to tone down or eliminate undressing scenes. 'O'Connor's 43' were rigidly enforced. A proposal to film D. H. Lawrence's *Lady Chatterley's Lover* was summarily rejected, for instance. A film based on Walter Greenwood's influential novel *Love on the Dole* was rejected because it contained swearing, sexual immorality and scenes of the police charging unarmed hunger marchers. A filmed life of the notorious seventeenth-century 'Hanging Judge', Lord Jeffreys, was rejected as likely to bring the legal system into disrepute.

But there was clearly a double standard when it came to crime films. British films critical of prisons and police were regularly rejected, but the American crime drama *Each Dawn I Die* (1939) was passed with a foreword stating: 'Prison conditions revealed here could never exist in Great Britain but they are tragically true of many penal establishments where corruption defeats justice and the voices of men who fight for justice are lost in the solitary cells.' This suggests that at bottom the censors were more concerned with the political effects of films attacking the prison system in Britain than the moral effects of prison dramas *per se*.[18]

Politics in films was frowned upon. In 1936 Lord Tyrrell, who had become President of the Board the previous year, told a conference of exhibitors: 'Nothing would be more calculated to arouse the passion of the British public than the introduction on the screen of subjects dealing with religious or political controversy.' He added, 'So far we have had no film dealing with current burning political questions.'[19] The kind of film the censors liked was *The Last Barricade* (1938), set during the Spanish Civil War, of whose script the censor wrote: 'Quite harmless love story. The setting though purporting to be Spain might just as well be Ruritania for all the political significance it possesses.'[20]

It tended to be left-wing politics that produced bans. A three-minute pacifist film, *The Peace of Britain*, was banned in 1936, causing an outcry in the press and the rescinding of the ban. The Russian classics *Battleship Potemkin*, *Mother* and *Storm Over Asia* were banned as likely to provoke revolutionary outbursts. But when in 1933 anti-war activists demonstrated at showings of a patriotic naval film, *Our Fighting Navy*, the censors took no action against the film.

The censors followed a policy of appeasement when it came to overseas governments. Scripts which involved 'friendly foreign countries' were regularly referred to the relevant embassies. Thus Alexander Korda's long-cherished plans for an epic film on the life of Lawrence of Arabia never came to fruition because of objections from the Turks at being portrayed as the villains and pressure on Korda from the Foreign Office.[21] In 1933 a number of proposals for films denouncing Nazi persecution of the Jews were all rejected, with comments like those on the proposed *The Mad Dogs of Europe*: 'This is pure anti-Hitler propaganda and as such I think unsuitable for production as a film.' The film-makers sought to get round the censors' prohibitions by using a fictitious or a historical setting. In *The Lady Vanishes* (1938) and *The Four Just Men* (1939), the enemy is the Gestapo but it is never named as such. A drama about anti-Jewish persecution in eighteenth-century Württemberg, *Jew Süss* (1933), contains the line '1730, 1830, 1930 – they will always persecute us'.[22] Nevertheless script-vetting and strict censorial enforcement of the rules led to the tightening of studio control over film production. In 1933 the BBFC banned twenty-one films; by 1936 they found it necessary to ban only six.

Opposition to the activities of the BBFC came from two directions. The liberal and left-wing intelligentsia, described by *The Film in National Life* (1932) as 'numerically negligible but culturally important', were concerned about political censorship and campaigned for greater freedom for film-makers to tackle the subjects they wanted to.[23] But there was even more pressure coming from religious groups, teachers' unions, morality councils and middle-class pressure groups for tighter censorship. The complaint was that films were teaching sex, criminality and bad values to the youth of Britain.[24] The BBFC, steering a course between the two currents, aimed to maintain the status quo politically, socially and morally – and did so successfully. The practical effect was to limit film producers to a diet of 'harmless' comedies, musicals and thrillers; but judging by surveys such as that undertaken by Mass-Observation, this is what people wanted.[25]

During the Second World War, the BBFC continued to function but its scope was restricted because much censorship activity was transferred to the Ministry of

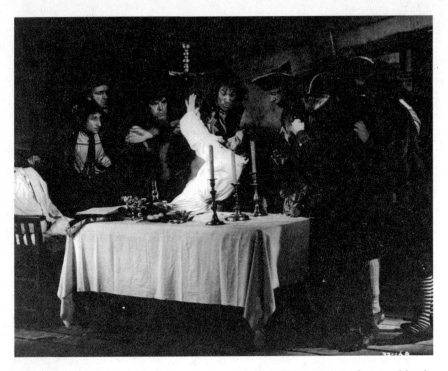

'1730, 1830, 1930 they will always persecute us.' Anti-Hitler propaganda missed by the BBFC. Jew Süss *(Lothar Mendes, 1934).*

Information and the armed services, each of which had its own censor. The BBFC was now chiefly concerned with moral matters. Four minor American horror films were banned during the war. But the pre-war ban on criticism of Germany and Japan was lifted and the Boulting brothers' *Pastor Hall*, a grim drama based on the persecution of Pastor Niemöller by the Nazis, rejected in July 1939 by the censors, was rushed into production as soon as war broke out and became a valuable tool of British film propaganda.[26]

The Ministry of Information co-ordinated the use of film propaganda, took over censorship of newsreels, and controlled the allocation of raw film stock and the licensing of club showings of non-certificated films. In the circumstances of war, a certain relaxation was allowed by the censors. The hitherto banned words 'bloody' and 'bastard' were permitted in wartime films like *In Which We Serve* (1942) and *Western Approaches* (1944) as long as they were applied to the Germans. The sensitive subject of labour relations was allowed to be treated in films like *The Stars Look Down* (1940) and *The Proud Valley* (1940). *Love on the Dole*, banned throughout the 1930s, was filmed and released in 1941 as an illustration of the kind of world Britain was not going back to after the war. 'What a difference a war makes', commented the *Sunday Pictorial*.[27] Winston Churchill, a great film fan, sought to interfere in censorship, usually unsuccessfully. The most celebrated case was his attempt to ban *The Life and Death of Colonel Blimp* (1943), which criticised the mindset of the old-style officer and gentleman. His bid failed, merely serving to give publicity to the film, which was billed as 'the film they tried to ban'.[28]

At the end of the war, the old guard which had been in charge of film censorship for two decades or more stood down. Colonel J. C. Hanna, deputy chief censor since 1930, retired in 1946. Lord Tyrrell died in 1947, aged 83. J. Brooke Wilkinson retired in 1948. A new generation of censors prepared to face new problems. Sir Sidney Harris, the new president, and Arthur Watkins, the new secretary, were both former civil servants from the Children's Department of the Home Office. They had to deal with an upsurge of violence and sexuality in British films, which can be traced directly to the social dislocation of the war. The Gainsborough costume melodramas and a cycle of British spiv and gangster films cleaned up at the box office but outraged those critics who were committed to documentary realism, literary respectability and moral uplift as dominant values. They excoriated the new film genres with a venom which did nothing to dent their box-office popularity. The storm finally broke in 1948 over a British imitation of American gangster films, *No Orchids for Miss Blandish*, which to the film critics symbolised the unacceptable level of sex and violence in post-war British cinema. Although much toned down from James Hadley Chase's lurid original novel, and vetted by the censors through several different scripts before the finished film received a certificate, it was denounced by parliamentarians, film critics and the press in general as nauseating and disgusting, and London County Council demanded further cuts.[29] Sir Sidney Harris apologised for 'failing to protect the public'. But as memories of the war receded, so the vogue for sex and violence for the moment passed and audiences settled for blander film fare.

A new subtlety entered the censors' considerations during Watkins's regime. Artistic considerations became more important than they had been under Wilkinson. The quality of the film and the intentions of the director began to count for something, and on these grounds films such as *Rashomon* and *La Ronde*, which otherwise transgressed the Board's moral rules, were allowed to pass. The 'X' certificate was intro-

Nauseating and disgusting. Jack La Rue, Linden Travers, Walter Crisham in No Orchids for Miss Blandish. *(St John L. Clowes, 1948).*

duced in 1951 to allow the licensing of films for viewing by adults. This applied in the main to foreign films which contained more sex and violence than was permitted in British films.

The principal social concern of the early 1950s was juvenile delinquency. It was the theme of films such as *The Blue Lamp* (1949) and *Cosh Boy* (1953). But concern about British youth imitating the exploits of American juvenile delinquents led to six minutes of cuts in *The Blackboard Jungle* (1955) and the complete banning in 1954 of *The Wild One*, in which a gang of bikers led by Marlon Brando terrify a Californian town. It was only finally certificated in 1967, by which time it looked distinctly tame.

Despite the relaxation in attitudes towards foreign films, Watkins still believed that the Board was 'performing a service both to the public and to the film industry if it removed offensive and distasteful material which cannot be regarded as entertainment and which if not excluded would in the long run do harm to the kinema's claim to that universal patronage on which its economy rests'.[30]

In 1956 Arthur Watkins resigned and was replaced by John Nichols, who had a fondness for both Japanese films and the works of Ingmar Bergman, which he passed uncut. Watkins's concept of artistic criteria was still being pursued in regard to foreign films. Elsewhere the usual strict rules applied. Director J. Lee Thompson was so outraged at the demand for ninety cuts in the script of his Second World War drama *Ice Cold in Alex* that he organised a meeting between the British Film Producers' Association and the BBFC to discuss the possibility of 'a more enlightened and adult approach to censorship'.

In 1958 Nichols resigned and was replaced as secretary by John Trevelyan, a former teacher and educational administrator who was to preside over what Anthony Aldgate has called 'the slow, complex and fraught process of liberalisation'.[31] Trevelyan was the guiding spirit of the BBFC during the 1960s, a time of rapid and far-reaching social and cultural change. He had to endeavour to keep up with changing public taste while fighting lengthy battles with writers and directors who resented having to make any changes in their films, and at the same time deflecting criticism from vocal forces in society bitterly opposed to any relaxation of censorship.

Trevelyan began the process by allowing adult films to deal with adult themes in a responsible fashion. He wrote in his autobiography:

> In my time at the Board we worked on a general policy of treating with as much tolerance and generosity as possible any film that seemed to us to have both quality and integrity, and of being much less tolerant of films which appeared to us to have neither of these qualifications.[32]

The landmark film in this process was Jack Clayton's adaptation of John Braine's controversial best-seller *Room at the Top* (1958). Although advertised as 'a savage story of lust and ambition', it was in fact a serious-minded, non-exploitative social realist film. Trevelyan judged that the public was ready for a film which discussed issues of sex and class seriously, and the popular reaction persuaded him to grant an 'X' certificate to responsible films on serious adult subjects.

In retrospect, the changes in the censorship system appear startling and speedy. Nudity had been banned from films until 1951. Thereafter some discreet nudity was allowed in the naturist films which began to appear in the 1950s. But the first full-frontal female nude was allowed in the Swedish film *Hugs and Kisses* (1968). Full-frontal male nudity was specifically forbidden in the 1963 film *This Sporting Life* but allowed for the first time in *Women in Love* (1969). Homosexuals were shown sympathetically in *Victim* (1960) and *A Taste of Honey* (1963). The depiction of an abortion was banned in *Saturday Night and Sunday Morning* (1960) but allowed in *Up the Junction* (1967). Drug-taking was banned in *The Trip* (1967) but permitted in *Easy Rider* (1969). The prohibition on swearing was steadily relaxed, with 'bloody' heard regularly from 1963, 'bugger' from 1967 and 'fuck' from 1970. By 1970 the old moral prohibitions of the BBFC had been almost totally abandoned.

However, sensationalism in dealing with sex, violence, drugs and madness still elicited bans for films, and the Hollywood productions *Lady in a Cage*, *The Naked Kiss*, *Shock Corridor*, *The Wild Angels* and *The Trip* were all banned in the 1960s. With public opinion changing rapidly, Trevelyan abandoned the explicitly moralistic stance the Board had adopted since its inception and redefined its role:

> The British Board of Film Censors cannot assume responsibility for the guardianship of morality. It cannot refuse for exhibition to adults, films that show behaviour which contravenes the accepted moral code, and it does not demand that 'the wicked' should always be punished. It cannot legitimately refuse to pass films which criticise 'the Establishment' and films which express minority opinions.[33]

Henceforth the censors were to see their work as limiting excessive displays of sex, violence and anti-social behaviour.

As censorship relaxed, films became more and more explicit in the areas of sex and violence. The 1960s saw the development of private cinema clubs showing uncertificated pornographic films. In the mainstream commercial cinema, the censors showed an increasingly relaxed attitude towards sex and violence. In the early 1970s, they certificated *The Devils* (1970), *A Clockwork Orange* (1971), *Straw Dogs* (1971), *Deliverance* (1972) and *Last Tango in Paris* (1973). This provoked a backlash amongst critics and moralists. Moral campaigners like Mary Whitehouse, politicians and the popular press now combined to blame the cinema for moral decline and the measurable increase in violence in society. Stephen Murphy, who had succeeded Trevelyan in 1971, fought a losing battle to defend his position. In 1975 he resigned, and was replaced by James Ferman.

Ferman was an American-born documentary film-maker whose expertise in the medium enabled him personally to supervise the cutting of offensive material from films in such a way as not to disrupt the narrative flow or visual coherence. He was a master of public relations. He persuaded the Labour government in 1977 to bring films within the scope of the Obscene Publications Act, which would allow them, like books, to be defended in court on grounds of public interest, educational value or artistic validity. It looked like a bid to strengthen censorship but, as Tom Dewe Mathews points out, no certificated film has ever been successfully prosecuted, so the law acted as a bulwark for existing BBFC practice.[34]

Ferman had much better luck than his predecessor. There were moralists' *causes célèbres* during his term, particularly the outcries against *Monty Python's Life of Brian* (1979) and *The Last Temptation of Christ* (1988). But these created far less stir than the sex and violence films of the early 1970s because the objections hinged on blasphemy, much less resonant an offence in a country which had become one of the most secularised in the world.

In 1977 the Labour government set up a commission to investigate film censorship and obscenity. Headed by Professor Bernard Williams, it recommended the end of local authority censorship and the creation of a statutory authority to take over the censoring powers of both the local authorities and the BBFC. But it also argued that the ability of films to 'deprave and corrupt' remained unproven. After a change of government in 1979, the report was shelved.

In 1982 the old 'U', 'A', 'X' system of certificates was replaced by a new system: U (universal), PG (parental guidance), 15 and 18, with an R18 rating for licensed sex cinemas only. But the most significant development of the 1980s was the appearance of a new form – the video – and with it a flood of horror films onto the shelves of the video shops. Video became the focus for a changing climate of popular opinion which increasingly favoured tighter censorship.

A vogue for films featuring violence against women began in 1976. In that year fifty-eight films featuring rape were submitted to the BBFC. Nearly all of them were cut or banned, but the trend provoked a feminist backlash and the demand from influential women's groups for greater censorship.[35] Concern to protect children from video violence built up, spearheaded by veteran campaigners like Mrs Whitehouse, who coined the phrase 'video nasty' and enlisted the support of prominent parliamentarians and the tabloid press.

The Director of Public Prosecutions issued a list of titles that were potentially actionable under the Obscene Publications Act. Publicity focused initially on *The Evil Dead* (1982). It was eventually cleared of obscenity in the courts, but the case led directly to the Video Recordings Act (1984), which required all video recordings to be certificated. Greater stringency was demanded of the censors in view of the fact that the recordings were being sold for home-viewing. There was renewed controversy in 1993 when the murder of baby James Bulger was linked to the video *Child's Play III*, which had been given a certificate by the BBFC, and the Criminal Justice Act (1994) ordered the censors to pay particular attention to the way in which videos dealt with violence, criminality, horror and drugs.

The duty of video censorship devolved on the BBFC, now renamed the British Board of Film Classification with its secretary renamed director. Where four staff had censored about 400 films a year, there were now seventy-one staff processing some 4,000 films and videos each year. James Ferman maintains that the artistic criteria defined by Trevelyan still apply and he continues to endeavour, like his predecessors, to remain in tune with public opinion and to tread a line between the libertarians demanding total freedom and the moralists demanding stricter restriction.

The arguments for censorship (social control, moral concern, protection of the innocent) and against it (artistic liberty, freedom of expression, consumer choice) have remained the same since films first arrived in Britain. It is public concern that has risen and fallen in cycles during the century of cinema.

Notes

1. *Kinematograph Weekly*, 27 July 1948.
2. Quoted in Charles Davy (ed.), *Footnotes to the Film* (London: Lovat Dickson, 1938), p. 141.
3. Ibid., p. 267.
4. BBFC Annual Report for 1919, p. 3.
5. *Kinematograph Weekly*, 1 March 1934.
6. They are reprinted in Neville March Hunnings, *Film Censors and the Law* (London: Allen and Unwin, 1967), pp. 408–9.
7. James C. Robertson, *The Hidden Cinema: British Film Censorship in Action 1913–1972* (London: Routledge, 1989), p. 2.
8. Nicholas Pronay, 'The First Reality: film censorship in Liberal England', in K. R. M. Short (ed.), *Feature Films as History* (London: Croom Helm, 1981), p. 122.
9. Conference on 'The Influence of Cinema', 29 May 1933, BBFC, Verbatim Reports 1932–5, pp. 13–14.
10. Jeffrey Richards, *The Age of the Dream Palace* (London: Routledge, 1984), pp. 144–5.

11. House of Commons Debates, vol. 342, p. 127.
12. Annette Kuhn, *Cinema, Censorship and Sexuality 1909–1925* (London: Routledge, 1988).
13. BBFC Annual Report for 1935, p. 8.
14. James C. Robertson, *The British Board of Film Censors* (London: Croom Helm, 1985), pp. 56–9, 183–4.
15. James C. Robertson, '*Dawn* (1928): Edith Cavell and Anglo-German Relations', *Historical Journal of Film, Radio and Television*, no. 4 (1984), pp. 15–28.
16. Richards, *The Age of the Dream Palace*, p. 108.
17. BBFC Scenario Reports, 1930–47, are held in the British Film Institute Library.
18. Richards, *The Age of the Dream Palace*, pp. 112–20.
19. BBFC Annual Report for 1936, p. 6.
20. Richards, *The Age of the Dream Palace*, p. 122.
21. Jeffrey Richards and Jeffrey Hulbert, 'Censorship in action: the case of *Lawrence of Arabia*', *Journal of Contemporary History*, no. 19 (1984), pp. 153–70.
22. Richards, *The Age of the Dream Palace*, pp. 126–8.
23. Commission on Educational and Cultural Films, *The Film in National Life* (London, 1932), p. 34.
24. Richards, *The Age of the Dream Palace*, pp. 48–85.
25. Jeffrey Richards and Dorothy Sheridan (eds.), *Mass-Observation at the Movies* (London: Routledge, 1987).
26. James C. Robertson, 'British film censorship goes to war', *Historical Journal of Film, Radio and Television*, no. 2 (1982), pp. 49–64.
27. *Sunday Pictorial*, 1 June 1941.
28. James Chapman, '*The Life and Death of Colonel Blimp* (1943) Reconsidered', *Historical Journal of Film, Radio and Television*, no. 15 (1995), pp. 19–54.
29. Robert Murphy, *Realism and Tinsel: Cinema and Society in Britain 1939–48* (London: Routledge, 1989), pp. 187–90.
30. Tom Dewe Mathews, *Censored* (London: Chatto and Windus, 1994), p. 135.
31. Anthony Aldgate, *Censorship and the Permissive Society: British Cinema and Theatre 1955–1965* (Oxford: Clarendon Press, 1995), p. 152.
32. John Trevelyan, *What the Censor Saw* (London: Michael Joseph, 1973), pp. 66–7.
33. Mathews, *Censored*, p. 174.
34. Ibid., p. 222.
35. Ibid., p. 224.

Bibliography

Aldgate, Anthony, *Censorship and the Permissive Society: British Cinema and Theatre 1955–1965* (Oxford: Clarendon Press, 1995).
Hunnings, Neville March, *Film Censors and the Law* (London: Allen and Unwin, 1967).
Knowles, Dorothy, *The Censor, the Drama and the Film* (London: Allen and Unwin, 1934).
Kuhn, Annette, *Cinema, Censorship and Sexuality 1909–1925* (London: Routledge, 1988).
Mathews, Tom Dewe, *Censored* (London: Chatto and Windus, 1994).
Phelps, Guy, *Film Censorship* (London: Gollancz, 1975).
Pronay, Nicholas, 'The first reality: film censorship in Liberal England', in K. R. M. Short (ed.), *Feature Films as History* (London: Croom Helm, 1981), pp. 113–37.
Richards, Jeffrey, *The Age of the Dream Palace: cinema and society in Britain 1930–39* (London: Routledge, 1984).
Richards, Jeffrey and Hulbert, Jeffrey, 'Censorship in Action: the case of *Lawrence of Arabia*', *Journal of Contemporary History*, no. 19 (1984), pp. 153–70.
Robertson, James C., *The British Board of Film Censors: Film Censorship in Britain 1896–1950* (London: Croom Helm, 1985).
Robertson, James C., 'British film censorship goes to war', *Historical Journal of Film, Radio and Television*, no. 2 (1982), pp. 49–64.
Robertson, James C., '*Dawn* (1928): Edith Cavell and Anglo-German relations', *Historical Journal of Film, Radio and Television*, no. 4 (1984), pp. 15–28.
Robertson, James C., *The Hidden Cinema: British Film Censorship in Action 1913–1972* (London: Routledge, 1989).
Trevelyan, John, *What the Censor Saw* (London: Michael Joseph, 1973).

17
Lindsay Anderson and the Development of British Art Cinema

Erik Hedling

Very little scholarly work has been done on the British art cinema, on its aesthetics and its auteurs. Until recently British cinema as a whole has tended to be over-looked by film scholars, and the general critical bias inspired by the Althusserian–Lacanian paradigm of contemporary film theory of the late 70s and 80s has emphasised popular film genres or historical overviews of specific periods. In terms of British cinema history, the concept of art cinema has mostly been used in connection with the documentary-realist tradition, or as a term that describes how the intellectual film culture of the 40s understood British 'quality cinema' of the period.[1]

Art cinema as a specific, historically determined mode of narration in post-war European cinema has been clearly defined by David Bordwell, and it is in this sense that the term is used here. Bordwell writes:

> The art film is nonclassical in that it creates permanent narrational gaps and calls attention to processes of fabula construction. But these very deviations are placed within new extrinsic norms, resituated as realism or authorial commentary. Eventually, the art-film narration solicits not only denotative comprehension but connotative reading, a higher-level interpretation.[2]

Art cinema was mainly targeted at an educated, middle-class audience, and heavily in-fluenced by modernist literature. The art cinema tried to achieve higher levels of real-ism, objectively – as in the spatial and temporal verisimilitude of Italian neo-realist works like De Sica's *Bicycle Thieves* (1948) – and subjectively, for example in the highly symbolic uses of cinematic style in Ingmar Bergman's *Wild Strawberries* (1957). The works of art cinema were often 'open works', in Umberto Eco's sense, relying on narrative ambiguity: the beginning and the end of the story difficult to discern in traditional terms, the plot episodic, and often concerning some kind of individual psychological crisis.[3] The film could be highly self-conscious, and attention was drawn to the process of cinematic narration. Art cinema films were often marketed as per-sonal visions, with a strong emphasis on the director, the creative artist. In terms of thematic content, art cinema films tended towards a leftist bias. And as Steve Neale has pointed out, art cinema challenged the dominant norms of film-making, as well as sustaining itself financially by a tendency towards sexual explicitness.[4]

Britain did not have an internationally well-known art cinema in this sense until Peter Greenaway, Derek Jarman and other film-makers emerged in the 1980s. There were, nevertheless, critical and cinematic practices which connected British film culture to the development of the European art cinema in the post-war period, most clearly in the journal *Sequence*, published between 1947 and 1952, and the film movement which came out of it.

Although a small specialist magazine, edited by a few cinema enthusiasts from Oxford University, *Sequence* became a force behind a British art cinema aesthetic and an intellectual venture to be reckoned with.[5] Influenced by romanticism and the literary new criticism, the writers of *Sequence* spurned most contemporary British cinema, especially the documentary doctrines of John Grierson and his beliefs in the utilitarian aspects of film. Lindsay Anderson, one of the editors summed up his argument for a creative, non-industrially based cinema: 'What is required is a cinema in which people can make films with as much freedom as if they were writing poems, painting pictures or composing string quartets.'[6] Cinema, then, was an art, and not a Griersonian institution of public education. The key notions in the Andersonian discourse were 'poetry' and 'poet', metaphorically used to describe film art and the cinematic artist.

Anderson discussed at length the question of cinematic authorship, presenting a strong argument for the director in articles like 'Creative Elements' and 'The Director's Cinema?'[7] Although he expressed his deep admiration for European film-makers like the Italian neo-realists and the French surrealist Jean Vigo, his preferred auteur was John Ford. In his writings on Ford, Anderson stressed the aspects of Ford's film-making which could be connected to what were later identified as formal properties of the European art cinema. Accordingly, in a close reading of Ford's *They Were Expendable* (1945), Anderson found that the film deconstructed traditional narrative, and that it was also an expression of a deep personal vision.[8] Close-ups were spontaneous, silent pauses were inserted and the long takes were often allowed to transcend their narrative motivation, being there for their own sake or as a kind of pure 'artistic' matter. The cult of Ford among the writers of *Sequence* also had political implications, besides the struggle for a more personal kind of cinema. The films they championed – like *She Wore a Yellow Ribbon* (1949) – were the ones that celebrated specifically American values, thus representing a counter-cultural challenge to the class-ridden, chauvinistic and traditionalist British heritage.

The critical paradigm introduced by *Sequence* at the end of the 1940s – objective realism, cinema as an art, the harmonic relationship between form and substance, the director as author – became the general trend of British film criticism in the 50s, as interest grew in the European art cinema. In his writings in *Sight and Sound* – the flagship of British film culture – during the 50s, Anderson altered his critical approach, and began to incorporate some of the Griersonian doctrines that he had earlier rebelled against. These ideas were articulated in pieces on Elia Kazan's *On the Waterfront* (1954) and the critical manifesto 'Stand Up! Stand Up!' in 1956, where Anderson, now associated with the New Left, called for a more socially conscious and responsible British cinema as well as for personal vision.[9] Anderson's stress on personal style and leftist politics points forward to the development of a British art cinema based upon radicalism in form as well as in substance.

In 1956 Anderson and others organised a series of screenings at the National Film Theatre under the label 'Free Cinema', with documentary films by Anderson, Karel Reisz and Tony Richardson, and Lorenza Mazzetti; other Free Cinema programmes included films by Truffaut, Chabrol, Polanski, Tanner and Goretta. Anderson's first contribution was his twelve-minute documentary *O Dreamland* (1953), a film that can be regarded as paradigmatic for his later practice as an auteur.[10] In the spirit of Richard Hoggart, the film attacks the leisure habits of the masses at 'Dreamland', an amusement park at Margate. Anderson's world-view is expressed by constant manipulations of cinematic style, like the self-conscious and ironic juxtaposition of Frankie Lane's song 'I Believe' against images of vulgar popular pleasures.

As important for the development of art cinema as the influence of the 'poetic' realism of Free Cinema was the theatrically inspired stylisation which came out of the Royal Court Theatre in the late 50s and early 60s. Both Anderson and Tony Richardson directed at the Royal Court, where they utilised Brechtian devices which later became part of the standard repertoire of art cinema.[11] Anderson, Reisz and Richardson soon made the transition from low-budget documentaries to feature films, largely through Richardson's connection with the theatre. Richardson had directed the phenomenally successful stage production of John Osborne's *Look Back in Anger*, and Osborne was able to insist that he should direct the film as well. Richardson then invited Reisz to direct *Saturday Night and Sunday Morning* (1960), and Reisz, in his turn, invited Anderson to make *This Sporting Life* (1963).[12]

The Brechtian influence on the Free Cinema directors was not immediately apparent in their first feature films: Anderson's adaptation of David Storey's *This Sporting Life*, with its carefully constructed flashback pattern and naturalistic acting, conformed to a classical model in terms of narrative progression and *mise en scène*, in spite of its ambitious 'artiness'.

The art cinema aesthetic, in the sense elaborated by Bordwell, is much more obvious in later works, Anderson's rarely shown *The White Bus* (1966), for example. It was based on a short story by Shelagh Delaney and filmed as part of a cinematic triptych that was never completed. In this film, Anderson employs the ingredients that came to be typical of the European art cinema of the period: surrealist devices (in the shape of recurring instances of narration representing thought rather than spoken word), manipulations of time and space (continuous soundtrack over ellipses in the im-

This Sporting Life *(1963). Richard Harris and Lindsay Anderson.*

agery), unclear relation between plot and story (moments of stasis in the diegesis), arbitrary colour alterations (the image suddenly bursts into colour without codified meanings), recurring allusions and quotations (for instance the live replications of paintings by Manet, Fragonard and Goya), separation of elements (the sudden fore-grounding of weird diegetic sounds), anti-Establishment rhetoric (the sexual hypocrisy of the mayor, who condemns contemporary literature for its perversion but later tries to feel the heroine's leg in the bus), avant-garde music (Misha Donat's un-predictable synthesizer sounds), irony (the distance created between the mayor's brag-ging and the visual depiction of the drab life in Salford) and self-reflexivity (Anderson's allusions to Humphrey Jennings, whose 1939 film *Spare Time* clearly lingers in the background). Anderson also explicitly quotes Brecht by inserting a per-formance where Anthony Hopkins sings Brecht and Eisler's song 'Resolution' from *Die Tage der Commune*. In a typical art cinema strategy, the song operates metaphorically, commenting on the failure of liberalism to deal with oppression both in the days of the Paris Commune and in modern society.

If... (1968), Anderson's second feature, echoes some of the formal devices of *The White Bus* – arbitrary colour alterations, surrealism, allusions, authorial self-reflexivity, the open ending and the Brechtian device of chapter headings – but in a more commercial and recognisable genre, the public school film. The narrative refers back to Vigo's surrealist classic *Zéro de conduite* (1933), a film about boys revolting against their masters which Anderson had praised as a critic. There is a general strategy of quotation and allusion at work in *If...*, which deconstructs traditional narratives in a typical art cinema fashion: Kipling's poem 'If' in the title, the references to Byron, Wordsworth, Tennyson, Blake, Kleist and Plato, the cinematic allusions to Hitchcock, Lean, Ford, Jennings and even to Anthony Pelissier's *The History of Mr Polly* (1949), a film that Anderson, in spite of his otherwise general dismissal of 40s British cinema, had reviewed favourably in *Sequence*.[13] The allusions were conceived as a kind of Brechtian *Verfremdungseffekt*, constantly drawing attention to the artificial nature of narrative by crossing the fictional borders of the diegesis.

Writing in 1973, Thomas Elsaesser characterised the new European art films – by Herzog, Chabrol, Tanner – in terms of their irony: 'In almost all cases the stance is one of ironic "as-if".'[14] Elsaesser rejects *If...*, although it does fit very well his description of Brechtian art films during the period. The 'as-if' dimension can be seen in surreal moments, as for instance when the headmaster pulls out the chaplain from the locker in his office, a scene of stylised theatricalisation, staged within what is otherwise per-ceived as a 'real' scene. The device is shocking because it is so sudden and ostensibly out of style, but the film constantly challenges stable notions of fantasy and reality.[15]

If... received enthusiastic reviews in the British press, did well at the box office and even won the prestigious *Palme d'or* at the Cannes film festival in 1969, at a time when the European art cinema was at its height (its main competitors were Costa-Gavras' *Z* and Bo Widerberg's *Ådalen 31*). It also played a decisive role in crossing the 60s sex barrier with its scenes of full-frontal female nudity. Alan Lovell stresses Anderson's im-portance for the British cinema at the time, in particular his attempt 'to grapple with the problem of the British cinema's relationship with the American cinema and the art cinema by positively combining elements from both'.[16]

The art cinema aesthetic was by no means limited to the films of Lindsay Anderson, although his work is crucially important. In his book on 60s British cinema, Robert Murphy claims that at the end of the decade new dimensions had entered British films:

Fantasy sequences (in which everything becomes possible), slapstick (in which the world collapses into chaos), outrageous visual jokes, distancing devices such as the use of a narrator, inter-titles or direct address to camera spread across films as different as *The Bliss of Mrs Blossom* and *Poor Cow, Here We Go Round the Mulberry Bush* and *If...*[17]

Apart from the inspiration from *Sequence*, Free Cinema and the Brechtian practices at the Royal Court, the incorporation of art cinema practices into British cinema was also influenced by foreign directors at work in Britain during the 60s, such as Joseph Losey, Roman Polanski and Michelangelo Antonioni. In an essay on Nicolas Roeg and Donald Cammell's *Performance* (1969), a film which represents the ethos of 1968 and the British film industry's flirtations with a counter-culture, Peter Wollen claims that it is the 'British film which comes closest to a modernist art film in the New Wave mould', and that 'its direct predecessors were *The Servant* (1963), *Repulsion* (1965) and *Blow-Up* (1967), all London films made by foreigners – Losey, Polanski, Antonioni.'[18]

Many other examples of art cinema practices can be seen throughout the 60s: the Brechtian narrative of Richardson's *Tom Jones* (1963), the *kammerspiel* aesthetics of Jack Clayton's *The Pumpkin Eater* (1964), the bold deconstruction of classical narrative in Richard Lester's *A Hard Day's Night* (1964), the modernist montage of John Schlesinger's *Darling* (1965), the radical uses of style to present psychological crisis in Karel Reisz's *Morgan* (1966), the use of ironic cartoons in Richardson's *The Charge of the Light Brigade* (1968) and the sexually explicit imagery of Ken Russell's *Women in Love* (1969). The art cinema, then, had a considerable impact on British cinema during this period.

Because of the decline of British cinema in the 1970s, directors like Karel Reisz, Tony Richardson, John Schlesinger and Jack Clayton went to America. Anderson was marginalised after failing at the box office with his grand epic *O Lucky Man!* (1973), an explicitly Brechtian film which failed to sustain his reputation as a significant auteur. The rejection of the film for its reactionary aesthetics by *Screen* pointed to the generation gap between Anderson's 1950s New Left liberalism and the explicitly Marxist approach of much academic critical discourse of the 70s.[19]

O Lucky Man! was really an extension of the story and narrative strategy of *If...*, following the progress of Michael Travis (played by Malcolm McDowell) from heroic rebel to capitalist errand boy and finally to actor. The film is a road movie, with echoes of Preston Sturges's *Sullivan's Travels* (1941). It is also self-consciously constructed as a cinematic labyrinth in the style of Fellini's *8½* (1963). The film ends where it really started with Travis applying for the role in the movie *O Lucky Man!* (this scene, where McDowell is photographed with a gun and books, and with a cameo appearance by Anderson himself, was according to scriptwriter David Sherwin based on McDowell's audition for his role in *If...*).

One of the most radical aspects of the film was the use of rock musician Alan Price's songs, which were interweaved with the narrative, with brief glimpses of Price and his band in the studio ironically contrasting Travis's follies, much like the Street Singer in Brecht's *Threepenny Opera*.[20]

The actors, most of them belonging to Anderson's stock company, play multiple roles which often refer back to their parts in previous Anderson films. They are Brechtian 'social types', or 'humours' as Anderson himself preferred to call them.[21] The style is caricature rather than psychological realism. Peter Jeffrey's director and prison warden are clearly reminiscent of his headmaster in *If...*, and Mary McLeod's lovesick landlady is similarly based on the matron in that film. Geoffrey Chater as the priest and Anthony Nicholls as the general play the same parts in both films. Patricia Healy's

O Lucky Man *(1973). Alan Price, Lindsay Anderson and Miroslav Ondreicek.*

brief guest appearance brings *The White Bus* to mind, while Rachel Roberts once again portrays the poverty-stricken working-class widow from *This Sporting Life.* In contrast, McDowell's identity as Travis is constantly undermined by the difference from the character in *If...*, by references to his role as Alexander de Large in Kubrick's *A Clockwork Orange* (1971), and by the allusions to McDowell's well-publicised personal life. The film also contains the other art cinema devices which Anderson championed: intertextual allusions (Browning, Coleridge, Gorki, Eisenstein, John Ford, etc.), intertitles and authorial self-consciousness.

In Anderson's third story about Michael Travis, his last British feature film *Britannia Hospital* (1982), the hero, once again played by McDowell, dies at the hands of modern science gone berserk. This film is formally more traditional, but it conforms to the theatrical stylisation and Brechtian 'lessons' established in *If...* and *O Lucky Man!* A lively intertextuality informs the film, most famously at the end when Professor Millar (Graham Crowden, who was also Millar in *O Lucky Man!*) has his monstrous creation quote Hamlet's 'What a piece of work is man'. There are, surprisingly in view of Anderson's reputation as an auteur in the European art cinema tradition, several positively charged allusions to the 'low' genres of the 60s, particularly the hospital comedies (the hospital as metaphor for society), the *Carry On* series (literally when the nurse tells Travis, 'Your work will carry on') and the Hammer horror films (the professor as Frankenstein, Travis as the monster). Anderson mobilises the ironic potential of popular genres in order to create something of the carnivalesque, in Bakhtin's sense – a counter-cultural, self-conscious vulgarity used for a fiercely satirical attack on contemporary attitudes and policies.[22]

If..., *O Lucky Man!* and *Britannia Hospital* form a cinematic trilogy. This is another aspect that binds Anderson closer to the European art cinema, for as Thomas Elsaesser points out, 'A look at the filmographies of Godard, Antonioni, Truffaut, Wenders, Herzog, Kieślowski shows how important a prop the idea of the trilogy is for the self-identity of the European auteur'.[23]

Many writers have argued that the 1980s represented a renaissance in British cinema. James Park, for example, claimed in 1984 that the British cinema had finally learnt to 'dream' by incorporating new and more radical forms.[24] And Thomas Elsaesser writes of

> a relatively new and perhaps overdue phenomenon in British cinema (*pace* Nicolas Roeg), which has had the effect of opening out film narrative towards more adventurous forms of fiction. A heightened, emblematic or dream-like realism has appeared, for which the implements, objects, customs, the visual (and often musical) remnants of a bygone popular culture have become the icons of subjectivity.[25]

What had happened was that art cinema had finally established itself as a prominent and critically acknowledged mode in British cinema. Elsaesser's words are an apt description of the art cinema aesthetics of works like Peter Greenaway's *Drowning by Numbers* (1988), Terence Davies's *Distant Voices, Still Lives* (1988) or Dennis Potter's television work *The Singing Detective* (1986). They could also describe *If . . .* and *O Lucky Man!*, which, it could be claimed, prefigure the British art cinema of the 80s.

The connection between the art cinema of the 1960s and the new cinema of the 1980s is most evident in the films of Peter Greenaway and Derek Jarman. Greenaway's *The Draughtman's Contract* (1981) explores a similar theatrical stylisation to that in *If . . .* and *O Lucky Man!*, in the use of multiple symbolic layers, the acting within 'quotation marks', the self-conscious artificiality, the intertextuality and the labyrinthine storyline. Jarman's *Caravaggio* (1986) uses theatrical space, a complex pattern of allusion (like the reference to Waldo Lydecker typing in his bath in Otto Preminger's *Laura*), and art cinema devices such as the anachronistic appearance of a typewriter in a film set in the seventeenth century. Jarman explicitly quotes Anderson's *mise en scène* of riot police in *Britannia Hospital* in his bold adaptation of Marlowe's *Edward II* (1991).

In an article on the films of Greenaway and Jarman, Peter Wollen explores their common backgrounds as artists in the 60s, and describes their films in terms of a late cinematic modernism in Britain.[26] Wollen denies the 60s British 'new wave' the status of art cinema, because of the lack of auteurs in the established sense and because the films were based on literary material. He claims that these films fall into the category of traditional 'good realism' rather than art cinema. But he does admit that 'A good case can be made for Lindsay Anderson as a bilious but authentic "auteur"'.[27]

I have tried to make that case. In response to Wollen, one could claim that Lindsay Anderson was an auteur in the established European sense. Films like *If . . .*, *O Lucky Man!* and *Britannia Hospital* were not based on literary texts but were original scripts, written by Anderson's friend David Sherwin. Anderson himself never explained his films in terms of traditional notions of realism; indeed, he repeatedly challenged these notions in order to stress the 'poetic' aspects of film, which in his own words meant that 'you should operate suggestively on people so that you let their imagination run free'.[28] This is, of course, exactly the opposite of the traditional notion of realism.

Anderson's position within a tradition of British art cinema has been noted by the new auteurs themselves. Greenaway says that he found Anderson's *If . . .* 'painfully accurate', and Derek Jarman repeatedly expressed his admiration for Anderson, insisting that *Britannia Hospital* is one of the masterpieces of British cinema.[29]

The internationally acclaimed British art cinema of the 80s and early 90s could, then, be seen as having its roots in aspects of 60s film culture, which in turn could be referred back to the 40s and in particular to Powell and Pressburger and Humphrey

Jennings. Ironically as British commercial film production dwindles to an insignificant trickle, British directors – Jarman, Greenaway, Davies, Loach, Leigh – have at last been welcomed to the pantheon of European art cinema.

Notes

1. See Andrew Higson, *Waving the Flag: Constructing a National Cinema in Britain* (Oxford: Clarendon Press, 1995), pp. 262–71.
2. David Bordwell, *Narration in the Fiction Film* (London: Methuen, 1985), p. 212.
3. Umberto Eco, 'The Poetics of the Open Work', in *The Role of the Reader: Explorations in the Semiotics of Texts* (London: Hutchinson, 1979), p. 63.
4. Steve Neale, 'Art Cinema as Institution', *Screen*, vol. 22, no.1, 1981, pp. 11–39.
5. 'Across the intervening decades, one found tantalizing references to it in the writing about cinema, suggesting how influential it had been among those who took cinema seriously', writes Brian McFarlane in 'Sequence: Saying exactly what we liked', *Filmviews*, Autumn 1988, p. 31.
6. Lindsay Anderson, 'A Possible Solution', *Sequence*, no. 3, Spring 1948, p. 9.
7. Lindsay Anderson, 'Creative Elements', *Sequence*, no. 5, Autumn 1948, pp. 8–12, and 'The Director's Cinema', *Sequence*, no. 12, Autumn 1950, pp. 6–11, 37.
8. Lindsay Anderson, 'John Ford and *They Were Expendable*', *Sequence*, no. 11, Summer 1950, pp. 18–31.
9. Lindsay Anderson, 'The Last Sequence of *On the Waterfront*', *Sight and Sound*, January–March 1955, pp. 127–30, and 'Stand Up! Stand Up!', *Sight and Sound*, Autumn 1956, pp. 63–9.
10. For conflicting views of *O Dreamland* see John Hill, *Sex, Class and Realism: British Cinema 1956–63* (London: British Film Institute, 1986), p. 152; and Paul K. Cornelius, *Images of Social Dysfunction in Films of Lindsay Anderson* (Dissertation, University of Texas at Dallas, 1987), pp. 26–40.
11. Thus Anderson's productions of Harry Cookson's *The Lily White Boys* (1960) and Keith Waterhouse and Willis Hall's *Billy Liar* (1960) were noticed for their Brechtian aesthetics. See Peter Mathers, 'Brecht in Britain: From Theatre to Television', *Screen*, vol. 16, no. 4, Winter 1975–6, p. 81.
12. See the interview with Anderson in Eva Orbanz, *Journey to a Legend and Back: The British Realist Film* (Berlin: Volker Spiess, 1977), p. 48.
13. Lindsay Anderson, 'The History of Mr Polly', *Sequence*, no. 7, Spring 1949, pp. 41–2. The allusion occurs when Mick Travis looks towards the Archangel Michael, who is painted on the chapel window. The subjective image corresponds exactly to the similarly romantic and dreamy Mr Polly focusing on the church windows when entering what proves to be a disastrous marriage.
14. Thomas Elsaesser, 'The Cinema of Irony', *Monogram*, no. 5, 1973, p. 1.
15. Harold Pinter thought the device 'very out of style'. See Elizabeth Sussex, *Lindsay Anderson* (London: Studio Vista, 1969), p. 86.
16. Alan Lovell, 'The British Cinema: The Unknown Cinema', BFI Education Department Paper, 13 March 1969.
17. Robert Murphy, *Sixties British Cinema* (London: British Film Institute, 1992), p. 3.
18. Peter Wollen, 'Possession', *Sight and Sound*, September 1995, p. 23.
19. See Colin MacCabe, 'Realism and the Cinema: Notes on Some Brechtian Theses', *Screen*, vol. 15, no. 2, Summer 1974, p. 26, and Alan Lovell, 'Brecht in Britain – Lindsay Anderson' (on *If...* and *O Lucky Man!*), *Screen*, vol. 16, no. 4, Winter 1975–6, pp. 62–80.
20. 'The use of the chorus as an instructive device is particularly Brechtian, especially due to the fact that Alan Price's presence in the film is not hidden or masked or used in a conventional "musical film" sense', writes Carl David Ferraro in a study comparing the Brechtian aspects of the films by Anderson, Fassbinder and Buñuel. See *Toward a Brechtian Film Aesthetic, with an Investigation into the Films of Lindsay Anderson, Rainer Werner Fassbinder and Luis Buñuel* (Dissertation, Wayne State University, Detroit, 1988), p. 164.
21. See David Robinson, 'Stripping the Veils Away', *The Times*, 21 April 1973.
22. Many critics noticed the Frankenstein/*Carry On* connection, without making too much of it. A good description of the film was the heading of Michael Wood's review, 'Carry On Hamlet', in *New Society*, 3 June 1982, p. 392.
23. Thomas Elsaesser, 'Putting on a Show: The European Art Movie', *Sight and Sound*, April 1994, p. 26.
24. James Park, *Learning to Dream: The New British Cinema* (London: Faber and Faber, 1984), p. 13.
25. Thomas Elsaesser, 'Games of Love and Death, or an Englishman's Guide to the Galaxy', *Monthly Film Bulletin*, October 1988, p. 291.
26. Peter Wollen, 'The Last New Wave: Modernism in the British Films of the Thatcher Era', in Lester

Friedman (ed.), *British Cinema and Thatcherism: Fires Were Started* (London: UCL Press, 1993), pp. 35–51.
27. Ibid, p. 37.
28. Quoted from the interview in Joseph Gelmis, *The Film Director as Superstar* (Garden City, NY: Doubleday, 1970), p. 106.
29. Jonathan Hacker and David Price, *Take Ten: Contemporary British Film Directors* (Oxford: Clarendon Press, 1991), pp. 208 and 259.

Bibliography

Aldgate, Anthony, *Censorship and the Permissive Society: British Cinema and Theatre 1955-65* (Oxford: Clarendon Press, 1995).

Anderson, Lindsay, 'A Possible Solution', *Sequence*, no. 3, Spring 1948.

— 'Creative Elements', *Sequence*, no. 5, Autumn 1948.

— 'The History of Mr Polly', *Sequence*, no. 7, Spring 1949.

— 'Stand Up! Stand Up!', *Sight and Sound*, Autumn 1956.

Cornelius, Paul K., *Images of Social Dysfunction in Films of Lindsay Anderson* (Dissertation, University of Texas at Dallas, 1987).

Elsaesser, Thomas, 'Games of Love and Death, or an Englishman's Guide to the Galaxy', *Monthly Film Bulletin*, October 1988.

Ferraro, Carl David, *Toward a Brechtian Film Aesthetic with an Investigation into the Films of Lindsay Anderson, Rainer Werner Fassbinder and Luis Buñuel* (Dissertation, Wayne State University, Detroit, 1988).

Hacker, Jonathan and Price, David, *Take Ten: Contemporary British Film Directors* (Oxford: Clarendon Press, 1991).

Higson, Andrew, *Waving the Flag: Constructing a National Cinema in Britain* (Oxford: Clarendon Press, 1995).

Hill, John, *Sex, Class and Realism: British Cinema 1956–63* (London: British Film Institute, 1986).

Lovell, Alan, 'Brecht in Britain – Lindsay Anderson' (on *If...* and *O Lucky Man!*), *Screen*, vol. 16, no. 4, Winter, 1975–6.

Mathers, Peter, 'Brecht in Britain: From Theatre to Television', *Screen*, vol. 16, no. 4, Winter 1975–6.

McFarlane, Brian, 'Sequence: Saying exactly what we liked', *Filmviews*, Autumn 1988.

Murphy, Robert, *Sixties British Cinema* (London: British Film Institute, 1992).

Orbanz, Eva, *Journey to a Legend and Back: The British Realist Film* (Berlin: Volker Spiess, 1977).

Sussex, Elizabeth, *Lindsay Anderson* (London: Studio Vista, 1969).

Wollen, Peter, 'Possession', *Sight and Sound*, September 1995.

— 'The Last New Wave: Modernism in the British Films of the Thatcher Era', in Lester Friedman (ed.), *British Cinema and Thatcherism: Fires Were Started* (London: UCL Press, 1993).

18
Paradise Found and Lost: The Course of British Realism

Geoff Brown

The cinema, it seemed for a moment, was about to fulfil its natural destiny of discovering mankind. It had everything for the task. It could get about, it could view reality with a new intimacy; and what more natural than that the recording of the real world should become its principal inspiration?

John Grierson, 'The Course of Realism'

The particular moment John Grierson writes about in his famous essay about cinema realism was the earliest years of the twentieth century, when 'our local lady brought to our Scottish village the sensation of the first movies'. The first movies from France, Grierson recalls, were simple realist enterprises: Louis Lumière aimed his Cinématographe at workers leaving the Lumière factory in Lyon, at the train puffing into La Ciotat station, or his brother Auguste and his wife feeding their baby. In Grierson's eyes the moment of bliss and natural innocence did not last long. The Lumière workmen were scarcely out of the factory, he writes, than cinema 'was taking a trip to the moon and, only a year or two later, a trip in full colour to the devil. The scarlet women were in, and the high falsehood of trickwork and artifice was in, and reality and the first fine careless rapture were out.'[1]

Grierson writes about Georges Méliès and his films of fantasy almost as though Méliès were Satan himself, hurling a wrecking ball at the Garden of Eden. There is a reason for this. Grierson's childhood upbringing was among Presbyterians, who took the Calvinist view that play-acting was sinful. Imagine the shudder, then, when instead of documenting places, people and their workaday lives, cinema took off to visit the devil's lair itself.

In Britain, cinema began in the same way that Grierson reported in France. It observed the world. In 1895 Birt Acres used his camera to record actual sporting events – the Oxford and Cambridge Boat Race on 30 March, the Derby on 29 May – or natural spectacles like *Rough Sea at Dover*. Once again the devil's work – trick shots and fantasy – soon appeared. Robert Paul, who collaborated on the camera used in Acres' early films, proved particularly adept at exploring slow motion, superimpositions, and other simple ways of moving beyond what Grierson called 'the recording of the real world'.

Grierson's commitment to the realist cause did not blind him to other aesthetics:

187

this was the man who had a passion for marionettes, and supervised some film shorts in 1928 featuring puppet burlesques of Hollywood stars. But through word and deed he proselytised so hard for what he termed 'the documentary idea' that when serious film criticism developed in Britain (from the late 1920s onwards) realism quickly became accepted as British cinema's worthiest goal and greatest strength. The talents drawn into the Empire Marketing Board Film Unit, the GPO Film Unit and other documentary outfits of the 1930s were also the country's brightest critics: in articles and reviews for *Cinema Quarterly*, *World Film News* and other organs, Grierson himself, Paul Rotha, Basil Wright and Edgar Anstey proved passionate champions of realist films and skilled debunkers of whatever pap poured from Hollywood or Denham.

'The British film lacks honest conception,' Paul Rotha thundered in his seminal book *The Film Till Now*, first published in 1930. In Rotha's eyes it also lacked a British nationality: British film-makers were either aping American models or groping vaguely for the stylistic and psychological habits of the German school. The world beyond the studio doors was being ignored: 'Our railways, our industries, our towns, and our countryside,' he wrote, 'are waiting for incorporation into narrative films.'[2]

At the time, Rotha only had Grierson's own herring fleet film, *Drifters*, completed in 1929, to place on a pedestal as 'a suggestion of that which waits to be accomplished'. As the 1930s developed, there were occasional film documents for the realist propagandists to praise – Flaherty's *Man of Aran*, or Wright's *Song of Ceylon* – but they found slim pickings in a fictional cinema dominated by the extravaganzas of Korda or the vocal twirlings and high kicks of Jessie Matthews. The railways, the industries, the whole realist aesthetic, were waiting still. Only in the Second World War, when Britain's feature film-makers received new blood from the documentary field, did mainstream cinema begin to win critical favour for reflecting life beyond the studio gates.

The success of the British wartime product, from *Fires Were Started* (1943) to *Millions Like Us* (1943) and *The Way Ahead* (1944), further cemented the realist aesthetic as the critics' preferred mode for British films. Few later writers quite shared Grierson's religious zeal, but you can certainly feel an echo of the Calvinist distaste for fiction coursing through the influential pages of the *Penguin Film Review* in the 1940s. To Roger Manvell and the other earnest evangelicals of the *Review*, it was far better to stare soberly at fishermen's nets or bren guns than to gaze in delight at Betty Grable. From their perspective, the national ideal remained *In Which We Serve* (1942) or some other wartime epic of quiet heroism, shot in various shades of battleship grey. The national disgrace was the dingy sensationalism of *No Orchids for Miss Blandish* (1948), or *They Made Me a Fugitive* (1947) and its fellow spiv dramas.[3]

The British cinema revival of the late 1950s only strengthened the critical orthodoxy that enthroned the realist aesthetic. The British New Wave of Richardson, Anderson, Reisz and Schlesinger was greeted with fanfares because the films faced people's emotions head on and swept away what had grown to be regarded as dull studio artifice. Cameras went out and about, especially up north, far from the Rank Organisation's domain in Pinewood, where Dirk Bogarde preened in pretty pullovers, or the theatre's stronghold in Shaftesbury Avenue, which had stocked the cinema with so many actors and so much material. Characters were not cosy couples in Mayfair or the shires, but working-class people, tart and passionate. The same value was found in Ken Loach's focus on social problems and the under-privileged in *Poor Cow* (1967) and *Kes* (1969); though for some the suspicion was growing that in abandoning the drawing-room for the kitchen sink, British cinema had substituted one easy formula for another. Reviewing *Poor Cow* appreciatively in the *Sunday Times*, Dilys Powell still observed that 'the cinema, in fact, is as class-ridden as ever, and a new snobbery has been substituted for the old'.[4]

Only in the 1970s and 80s did the pendulum decisively swing the other way, against realism. Critical and popular appreciation grew for what you might almost term Satan's cinema: the adventurous work of Derek Jarman or Peter Greenaway, or, reclaimed from the past, the films of Powell and Pressburger, Hammer horrors, and Gainsborough melodramas. At the same time, in the magazine *Screen* and numerous academic havens the very mechanics of cinema were being investigated; films and their meaning were deconstructed into codes, signifiers and modes of representation. This put the entire notion of realism under threat in a different way: if what we saw on the screen was a mere chimera, an illusion manufactured through symbols and audience expectations, how could we ever believe again in Grierson's herrings, Humphrey Jennings's firemen, or the other touchstones of British realism?

The increasing technical sophistication of the films that audiences see has brought its own damage to the realist aesthetic. Our gaze now is not so trusting or innocent. But the history of British screen realism remains: a persistent, convoluted history stretching from the fishermen of *Drifters* and the down-and-outs of John Baxter's *Doss House* (1932) to the fliers, gunners and factory workers of the Second World War, the northern lads of *Room at the Top* (1958) and its New Wave successors, right up to the urban flotsam of Mike Leigh's *Naked* (1993) or Ken Loach's *Ladybird Ladybird* (1993). The history includes an iconography, too. Think British realism, and you think inevitably of kitchen sinks, factory chimneys, cobblestones, railway arches, bleak stretches of moor or beach, graffiti-lined council estates, people and landscapes placed in spare and striking juxtaposition. You also tend to think black-and-white: the perfect colour scheme for grey skies, smokestacks, and poetic melancholy.

The same history teaches us that one decade's notion of what constitutes realism rarely matches another's. Eyes that have become used to the raw dialogue exchanges and lurching camerawork of contemporary fly-on-the-wall TV will always find fault with most vintage films that carry the realist label. Looking now at Laurence Harvey's portrayal of Joe Lampton in *Room at the Top*, we tend to see Harvey the glamorous and pushy film star, strutting about with his porcupine brush of hair and carefully applied northern accent, rather than John Braine's original character of the vulgar opportunist desperate to escape the mean streets of his small Yorkshire town. In some ways Harvey's characterisation is not much of an advance on the Yorkshire fisherfolk depicted in J. Arthur Rank's first venture into feature film-making, *Turn of the Tide* (1935), an important realist milestone in its day but now rendered quaint by, among other things, the number of times that Irish-born actor Niall MacGinnis tries to prove his new nationality by saying 'Champion'. Similarly, in *San Demetrio London* (1943), one of Ealing's main contributions to realist cinema, admiration for the script's expression of homely heroics as the crew of a sunken tanker struggle home across the Atlantic is compromised, however slightly, by the knowledge that their life-and-death battle with the elements takes place in the studio tank.

Film history also demonstrates that realism in British cinema has marked class boundaries. The notion that realist films could embrace characters of the upper-middle class and beyond has rarely been considered. Realistic characters in British films wear cloth caps, not top hats, though most of the chief industry personnel would have been far more at home in the Mayfair nightclubs and hotels that haunt British films, of the 30s and 50s especially, than in any eel and pie shop. Should the accepted iconography of British realism be extended, then, to include the padded armchairs of gentlemen's clubs, complete with monocled twit slumbering over *The Times*, or a butler holding out cocktails on a silver tray, or the marbled halls that were home to Anna Neagle and Michael Wilding in escapist frolics like *Spring in Park Lane* (1948)? It is worth a thought.

Communist, zoologist and intermittent film-maker Ivor Montagu certainly realised the camera's ability to record the aristocracy, follies and all. Entrusted by Gaumont-British with filming linking sequences for *Wings Over Everest*, an account of a 1933 flying expedition financed by the flamboyantly patriotic Lady Houston and led in the air by the Marquess of Clydesdale, he found he had inadvertently made what he later described as 'the most perfect picture of the English governing class that has ever been seen'.[5] There is realism of a sort, too, in the parade of stilted officers who appear as themselves in propaganda shorts of the Second World War, answering phone calls from Whitehall, briefing pilots, pointing at targets on maps, sometimes venturing to speak words of uplift straight to the camera. Vowels, moustaches, body language: all now belong to a vanished world, preserved by the camera like a fly in amber.

During the 30s, boom years alike for British commercial production and the documentary movement, you can clearly see the tussle in films between the gospels of realism and artifice. It was not only Grierson, Rotha and their colleagues who proselytised for a greater reflection of real life in British films; film company executives, mindful of the prevailing critical mood, also emerged with ringing declarations of patriotic intent. Here is Michael Balcon, two years before he established himself at Ealing, writing in the London *Evening News* in October 1936:

> We see the dramatic entertainment in the life of the farmer on the fells of the North, of the industrial worker in the Midlands, of the factory girls of London's new industrial areas, of the quiet shepherds of Sussex. I believe that the sweep of the Sussex Downs against the sky makes as fine a background to a film as the hills of California; that Kentish and Worcestershire orchards and farms are as picturesque as the farmlands of Virginia; that the slow talk of labourers round an English village pub fire makes as good dialogue as the wise-cracks of 'City Slickers' in New York.[6]

Balcon, however, was writing after five years as head of production at the Gaumont-British studios of Shepherd's Bush, where you would more likely find Ruritanian royalty, American gangsters or music-hall Cockneys than slow-talking farm workers supping pints. Only once had Gaumont-British allowed something approaching the realism that Grierson favoured through its portals; and that was Flaherty's *Man of Aran*, a somewhat romantic account of the Aran islanders' daily battles with sea and seaweed, potatoes and sharks, off the Galway coast, for which Flaherty began preliminary investigations in 1931.

For Gaumont-British the project meant cultural prestige, and a way of fending off increasing criticism that British films, theirs included, neglected real life. With *Man of Aran* finally completed in 1934, every possible publicity angle was utilised to bring home the film's exotic appeal. Maggie Dirrane, the islander who played the wife of the nameless Aran man whose travails provided the slender story, was paraded in Selfridges by the *Daily Express* and asked for her opinion of silk stockings. A stuffed basking shark was put on display in the window of Gaumont-British's Wardour Street offices. Since the shark was too large for the available space, a chunk was removed from its middle, to Flaherty's fury: a choice symbol for the way market forces squeezed realism out of mainstream British cinema.[7]

Ballyhoo and the lure of Flaherty's images made the film a modest commercial success. But it scarcely paved the way for regular doses of realism, even of Flaherty's highly scented variety. Like *Man of Aran*, Rank's *Turn of the Tide*, directed by Norman Walker, won a prize for Britain at the Venice Film Festival, but no ballyhoo was whipped up by the distributors – Gaumont-British again – and lack of promotion ensured a quiet death at the box-office.

Until the months before the Second World War, when two adaptations of novels by A. J. Cronin, *The Citadel* (1938) and *The Stars Look Down* (1939), caught some aspects of working-class conditions, realism had led an almost subterranean life in British feature films. Efforts to reach down into society were relegated to low-budget second-feature ventures like John Baxter's *Doss House*, a brave excursion into the flotsam and jetsam gathered at a London hostel, an exercise repeated in later Baxter films like *Hearts of Humanity* (1936), *The Common Touch* (1941) and *Judgment Deferred* (1951). From today's perspective it is easy to smile at the sentimental colouring Baxter gives to his down-and-outs, and his naive belief that kindness alone will make the world a better place. Easy, too, to grate the teeth at the amount of cap-doffing and the acquiescent talk about 'people like us'. But Baxter still showed a keen eye and ear for the detail of working-class life. Even John Grierson recognised the value of Baxter's approach: his films, Grierson wrote, were 'sentimental to the point of embarrassment; but at least about real people's sentimentalities'.[8]

With the onset of war, Baxter contributed much simple, morale-boosting entertainment. He also made a film from Walter Greenwood's 1933 novel about a Lancashire family in the teeth of the Depression, *Love on the Dole*, a project that had only recently emerged from the British Board of Film Censors' ban on prospective film versions. The BBFC had objected to bad language, the conflict between unemployed workers and the police, and the fate of the heroine, Sally Hardcastle, who escapes from poverty only by becoming an entrepreneur's mistress. War changed the climate; and the film

The Common Touch *(John Baxter, 1941). A keen eye for the detail of working class life.*

duly arrived in 1941, hampered occasionally by studio artifice and the theatrical poise of Deborah Kerr (Sally) and Clifford Evans (her agitator fiancé), but carried through to victory by pungent dialogue and depth of feeling.

Not everyone was gratified. 'Why *Love on the Dole* now when *Love in a Shelter* would perhaps be more apt?', Paul Rotha commented in November 1940 when Baxter's film was in production.[9] In time British cinema got to grips with shelters, dug-outs, cock-pits, factory canteens and the other arenas of war on the home front and abroad. Only now did expectant talk about 'putting the real Britain on the screen' produce concrete results: after years of uncertainty and a good deal of trailing in America's shadow, the war finally gave British films a distinctive subject to pursue, and a moral reason for doing so. For their escapist entertainment, audiences would now turn mostly to America: aside from our comedies and thrillers, where some old habits persisted, British films began to be peopled by men in uniform, women at the workbench, girls in the ATS, or the old faithfuls in the Home Guard.

Wartime realism did not arrive overnight. When Balcon mounted *Convoy*, his first fictional war feature, in the spring of 1940, the extensive location material shot in the North Sea had to fight it out with Clive Brook festooned with gold braid viewing the war through binoculars, a dull romantic triangle, and a U-boat crew who talk about firing 'torpedo number Zwei'. Even though Balcon's ranks at Ealing were swelled with recruits from the documentary field, like Cavalcanti and Harry Watt, artifice ran ram-pant one year later through *Ships with Wings*, a drama about the Fleet Air Arm con-taining puppet characters and unusually bad model work. Asked for his opinion as he emerged from a private screening, Noël Coward could only utter one word, 'Gamages': the name of the London toy store.[10]

At the time Coward, helped by co-director David Lean, was preparing his own naval war drama, *In Which We Serve*, one of the films that helped establish the parameters for feature-film realism not just during the war but throughout the 50s, when British cinema fought the war all over again with Kenneth More or Jack Hawkins. In this drama inspired by the fortunes of Mountbatten's ship, HMS *Kelly*, the classes were clearly defined – working, middle and upper; the dialogue crisp, a touch theatrical, es-pecially when Coward himself (as the Mountbatten surrogate Captain Kinross) was talking. Once talk stopped, however, and action took over, sharply paced editing and sober, documentary-style photography lifted the film away from the theatre to present a convincing cinema reflection of the prevailing mood of all classes pulling together for Britain.

The success of *In Which We Serve* and others enthroned realism as the preferred national style. It 'set a new standard in the English cinema', Dilys Powell wrote in 1947.[11] Without the urgent necessity of war, however, British cinema began slipping from paradise. The post-war years saw the Technicolor follies of Powell and Pressburger, the Expressionist angles and dark shadows of *Odd Man Out* (1946) and *They Made Me a Fugitive* (1947). The realistic approach persisted but atrophied as the range of fresh material tackled by British movies shrank, and location material was wrapped around dim, anodyne family comedies or dramas.

Searching for moments of piercing realism or contemporary relevance in British films of the early and middle 50s is a doleful task. Surveying the scene from 1945 on-wards in his 1957 essay 'Get Out and Push!', Lindsay Anderson penned a litany echoing the lists of British cinema's missing ingredients drawn up by Rotha and others decades earlier:

The nationalisation of the coal fields; the Health Service; nationalised railways;

compulsory secondary education – events like these, which cry out to be interpreted in human terms, have produced no films. Nor have many of the problems which have bothered us in the last ten years: strikes; Teddy Boys; nuclear tests; the loyalties of scientists; the insolence of bureaucracy ...[12]

Though staring at British cinema in the 50s is like staring into a void, the realistic surface of the films never entirely disappears. A negative brand of realism exists in the *Scotland Yard* series of low-budget crime shorts hosted by Edgar Lustgarten, where inspectors sit in dingy offices surrounded by Eastlight box files and track down criminals at 30 mph in their Wolseley cars. Livelier examples bubble to the surface in a stage comedy on film like *Sailor Beware* (1956), directed by Gordon Parry, which taps into the humorous vernacular that sustained British music-hall, and demonstrates a sharp nose for lowly detail. In the home of Ma Hornett, the dragon whose daughter is getting married, the camera cuts to a teapot stain on a newly polished sideboard. Cigarette ash is tapped, perforce, into a cast-off shoe. A seedy church organist pedals away in his socks. Such details may not be what Grierson had in mind when he wrote about the cinema being able to 'view reality with a new intimacy', but they linger in the mind and their force should be not denied.

Ironically, it was the producers of *Sailor Beware*, Jack Clayton and the Romulus-Remus outfit, who proceeded to *Room at the Top*, one of the films that gave British cinema its much needed kick in the pants in the late 50s. Laurence Harvey's impersonation of a Northerner may have been a sop to the old star system, just as Simone Signoret's casting in a role conceived in John Braine's novel as a Yorkshirewoman reinforced the old-fashioned notion that loose, dangerous women were usually foreign and generally French. But future films called on the services of a new breed of actors, mostly from the North, trained in the theatre, whose faces, accents and rebellious spirit helped immeasurably to strengthen the new brand of realism. There was Albert Finney in *Saturday Night and Sunday Morning* (1960); Tom Courtenay in *The Loneliness of the Long Distance Runner* (1962) and *Billy Liar* (1963); Richard Harris (Irish-born) in *This Sporting Life* (1963); Rita Tushingham in *A Taste of Honey* (1961).

To many British audiences and film-makers, the industrial landscapes and bleak northern skies shown in these films had an almost exotic lure. 'Directors certainly were enchanted with the North,' Keith Waterhouse, the co-author of *Billy Liar*, recalled in 1993. 'At one time you couldn't walk around the slag heaps without tripping over a light cable.'[13] Slag heaps, smoking chimneys, canals: the black-and-white photography of Denys Coop or Walter Lassally revelled in them all.

However, the new urge to rush out on location and probe neglected areas of Britain did not derive directly from the realist tradition of Grierson. The impetus to look and think afresh came partly from the spate of new writing and theatre in the mid-50s: the era of the Angry Young Man, personified most memorably by John Osborne's creation Jimmy Porter, who sprawled among Sunday newspapers in a dingy Midlands flat in *Look Back in Anger*, spewing out vitriol. Encouragement also came from the films of the French *nouvelle vague*: those of Godard and Truffaut gloried especially in the hand-held camera's giddy freedom as it sped along streets catching passers-by unawares.

Any documentary allegiances claimed by the new breed of British directors were rather to the brief phenomenon of Free Cinema, a label originally attached to six programmes of shorts and documentaries presented at the National Film Theatre between 1956 and 1959, including Lindsay Anderson's portrait of the Covent Garden market, *Every Day Except Christmas* (1957), and Karel Reisz's *We Are the Lambeth Boys* (1959). Their accompanying publicity emphasised the importance of artistic freedom and a commitment to portraying contemporary society; the films' styles combined documentary reportage with the cinema tools of montage and the poetic image.

In the event the British New Wave proved more of a ripple. As the 60s advanced and naturalism's novelty waned, so did the cinema audience's taste for the bleaker side of life. Directors like Anderson, Richardson and Schlesinger shifted their ground, back to theatre or forwards to Hollywood. Anderson's *This Sporting Life*, the most uncompromising of all the New Wave features, fared badly at the box-office in 1963; *Billy Liar*, where realism and fantasy jostled in the hero's larkish mind, was more to the public taste. At the end of the film Billy was supposed to flee the parochial North and take a train to London. At the last minute he ducks the challenge, leaving his girlfriend (Julie Christie) to go alone. British cinema duly followed, discovering – indeed half-inventing – Swinging London. Realism was edged out; caricature and parody moved in.

By the mid-60s, images of direct social observation were far more likely to be found on television than in the cinema. No British cinema film of 1966 had a fraction of the force of *Cathy Come Home*, Jeremy Sandford's play about a homeless mother, filmed by Ken Loach for the *Wednesday Play* slot on BBC2. The camerawork was unadorned, the tone unrelenting, almost belligerent. *Wednesday Play* dramas ripped stories from headlines, and made television seem the natural place for the airing of social issues.

Thirty years later, for all the tension between broadcasters and government that developed during the Thatcher years, this is still largely so; and the continuing history of British cinema realism is inextricably linked to the box in the living-room corner. Film-makers will follow the funding: and for many with a naturalistic bent this has led them to the BBC and, since 1982, to Channel 4.

The continuing history of British realism is also inextricably linked to Ken Loach, who has shown remarkable steadfastness to socialist beliefs and a realistic aesthetic during years of upheaval among unsympathetic governments and the changing faces of film and television executives. All the concern Loach shows for Sandford's homeless mother in *Cathy Come Home* is lavished almost three decades later on the prickly heroine of *Ladybird Ladybird* (1993), a single mother with a violent streak who runs foul of the Social Services.

Not that Loach's brand of realism has been set in concrete. His first cinema feature, *Poor Cow* (1967), based on a novel by Nell Dunn, the author of *Up the Junction*, adopts a naturalistic mode for the acting but punctuates and cradles scenes with the devices made popular by the *nouvelle vague*, Godard particularly, and the newly influential stage practices of Brecht. Captions interrupt the action; the heroine's commentary comes and goes. The later Loach forgoes embellishments and stylistic disruption. He appreciates the telling image, like the rat caught in the opening shots of *Riff-Raff* (1991) scurrying by a crumpled NHS prescription form; but his message is mostly conveyed by an unfussy camera directed often at non-professional actors.

Any variations in tone between Loach's films stems rather from the writers. Bill Jesse, in *Riff-Raff*, provides salty comedy and always makes his building site crew of Geordies, Scots, blacks, whites, dreamers and activists people rather than political mouthpieces. Jim Allen, whose collaborations range from the four-part TV series *Days of Hope* (1976) to *Raining Stones* (1994) and *Land and Freedom* (1995), has a keen eye and ear for life at the bottom of society's ladder, but tends to mount his soapbox. Trevor Griffiths, meanwhile, rides literary hobby-horses, burdening *Fatherland* (1986) with symbols and allusions that Loach's camera finds hard to penetrate.

Sixties realism. Carol White in Poor Cow *(Ken Loach, 1967).*

Loach's realism is realism with a cause, and few other current directors share his passionate commitment. Mike Leigh, who has also alternated between television and film, works in an ostensibly realistic mode but often treats ordinary life as the subject for cruel satire, not compassion. He came into film through theatre, continuing his stage practice of hammering out characterisations and action with his cast through weeks of intense improvisation. *Bleak Moments* (1971), his first film, assembled a string of uncomfortable social encounters between London suburban types, twisting the silences and halting words into a painfully comic portrait of repressed, wasted lives. Subsequent work, largely for television or theatre until the late 80s, swiftly revealed that for all the use of group improvisation to ward off the cadences learned in acting schools, Leigh's brand of realism can come perilously close to caricature.

From *Bleak Moments* to *Abigail's Party* (1977), *Grown-Ups* (1980) and *Secrets & Lies* (1996), the class and character of Leigh's creations are constantly pinned down through verbal or physical tics: a tradition some might trace back to Ben Jonson's comedies of humours or even the *commedia dell' arte*. In *Bleak Moments* characters are defined through their nervous gasps of breath, the grimaces of their mouths, the way they finger a nose. Over twenty years later, in *Naked* (1993) – Leigh's most ambitious and mature work for cinema – the tactic still holds. Sophie the dopehead speaks through her teeth. Jeremy the yuppie landlord punctuates brutal remarks with a snorting laugh. Sandra, away in Zimbabwe for most of the turmoil that unfolds in her

London flat, arrives back unable to finish a sentence, chopping the air with her hands. And David Thewliss's Johnny, the Jimmy Porter of the 90s, lambasts and mocks all and sundry in a Manchester drawl.

Yet for all its patterned behaviour and pockets of stylised photography, in the British cinema of the 1990s a film like *Naked* still reverberates as a realist document, a guided tour round the London of the dispossessed. For these are hard times for the realist aesthetic, and they have been for some years. True, the arrival of Channel 4 generated an explosion of small-scale television films with a realist surface: there were tales of adolescent love, of illness and urban disillusionment. The impoverished London of Stephen Frears's *My Beautiful Laundrette* (1985), written by Hanif Kureishi, struck a chord, but too much of the product plumbed no depths and hurt no one.

Aside from realism in fictional form, however diluted, television in the 80s increasingly played host to fly-on-the-wall documentary series such as Roger Graef's *Police* (1982), where the cameras spied on a division of the Thames Valley police as they went about their daily business. Saturated at home with real-life dramas, whether authentic or feigned, audiences found less need to seek them out in the cinema; and film-makers, financiers and distributors felt less need to provide them. The late 70s had seen the rebirth of the Hollywood escapist spectacle, with *Star Wars*, *Jaws* and their successors. Such films pulled a new, younger audience into the cinemas, an audience keyed to American tastes. You went to the cinema to be amazed, showered with special effects and the unreal. If you really wanted two British people arguing round a kitchen sink, you stayed at home and watched your parents, or switched on the box.

Britain made its own contribution to Hollywood's new cinema of wonder: in many cases we supplied the studios and technicians. Our indigenous product followed the fashion, too, though at a distance. Aside from Loach, Mike Leigh, the Amber Collective's dramas of life in north-east England, or the intense and poetic biographical excavations of Terence Davies, British cinema in the 80s was weighted towards fantasy, the surreal, and period nostalgia. Peter Greenaway built a cult audience for the eccentric artifice of *The Draughtsman's Contract* (1982) and its successors. With films like *Caravaggio* (1986) and *The Garden* (1990), Derek Jarman achieved his own following for his exuberantly personal work, combining avant-garde stylistics with a strongly romantic sensibility.

Helped by the novels of E. M. Forster, the Merchant-Ivory production team consolidated their position as chief purveyors of 'heritage cinema', producing films that coalesce in the mind into a dream picture of Edwardian bliss, of country houses, parasols, ormolu clocks, pretty ladies and willowy young men. Films such as *Howards End* (1992), perhaps the most accomplished of the breed, offer an escape into an imaginary paradise. Like the BBC's adaptations of novels by Austen, George Eliot or lesser mortals, they are comfort blankets for a hostile age.

Out in British cinema's commercial sector, a hundred years after the medium's birth, Grierson's concern for 'recording ... the real world' finds scant reflection. Paul Anderson's *Shopping* (1994) and Danny Cannon's *The Young Americans* (1993) use joy-riding, ram-raiding, drug-taking and other youthful flings as a background for multiplex fodder, slam-bang action with an American beat. The black comedy thriller *Shallow Grave* (1994) and the comedy of heroin addiction, *Trainspotting* (1995), from the team of director Danny Boyle, producer Andrew Macdonald and writer John Hodge, have higher ambitions and pay careful attention to their urban settings (chiefly Edinburgh). But they share the same urge to connect with young audiences whose natural film language is American, not British, and whose God is Quentin Tarantino. Their kinetic force, use of stylised studio decor, subjective camerawork and driving pop music carry both films far from the dictates of social realism, which is seen by Britain's young film-makers as yesterday's cinema.

'We made a very early decision . . . that it wasn't realism and we didn't want to do it like that,' Andrew Macdonald recalled about *Trainspotting*. 'Real cinema,' he declared elsewhere, 'is about the imagination, about fantasy': sentiments which his grandfather, Powell's collaborator Emeric Pressburger, would have heartily approved.[14] With such people in the driving seat, the Griersonian paradise is not about to be immediately regained.

Notes

1. John Grierson, 'The Course of Realism', in Forsyth Hardy (ed.), *Grierson on Documentary* (London: Collins, 1946), p. 132; originally included in Charles Davy (ed.), *Footnotes to the Film* (London: Lovat Dickson, 1937).
2. Paul Rotha, *The Film Till Now*, revised and enlarged edition (London: Spring Books, 1967), p. 315.
3. For a wider discussion of the *Penguin Film Review* and its reflection of post-war attitudes, see Geoff Brown, 'Which Way to the Way Ahead? Britain's Years of Reconstruction', *Sight and Sound*, Autumn 1978, pp. 242–7.
4. Dilys Powell, *Sunday Times*, December 1967, collected in Christopher Cook (ed.), *The Dilys Powell Film Reader* (Manchester: Carcanet, 1991), pp. 26–7.
5. Geoff Brown, 'Table Tennis Over Everest', *Sight and Sound*, Spring 1984, p. 98.
6. Michael Balcon, 'Putting the *Real* Britain on Screen', London *Evening News*, 1 October 1936.
7. Details of *Man of Aran*'s promotion from Arthur Calder-Marshall, *The Innocent Eye: The Life of Robert J. Flaherty* (London: W. H. Allen, 1963), p. 164; and John Grierson, 'Summary and Survey: 1935', in *Grierson on Documentary*, p. 110.
8. John Grierson, 'The Course of Realism', in *Grierson on Documentary*, p. 143. For more on John Baxter see Geoff Brown and Anthony Aldgate, *The Common Touch: The Films of John Baxter* (London: British Film Institute, 1989).
9. Paul Rotha, 'The British Case (1)', in *Rotha on the Film* (London: Faber and Faber, 1958), p. 217.
10. Information from Sidney Gilliat.
11. Dilys Powell, *Films Since 1939* (London: Longmans Green, 1947), excerpted in *The Dilys Powell Film Reader*, p. 5.
12. Lindsay Anderson, 'Get Out and Push!', in Tom Maschler (ed.), *Declaration* (London: MacGibbon and Kee, 1957), p. 160.
13. Interview in 'Northern Lights', the first programme of *Hollywood UK*, produced by Charles Chabot and Rosemary Wilton, BBC Television, 1993.
14. 'The Boys Are Back in Town', *Sight and Sound*, February 1996, p.10; 'The Hit Squad', *The Times* (magazine section), 20 January 1996, p. 21.

19
Traditions of British Comedy

Richard Dacre

In the silent period the heritage of British comedy was largely ignored or wasted as raw material for the cinema. Film was used to record music-hall sketches, but it was not until the coming of sound that comedy began to come into its own. Sound meant that writers were encouraged to pen pages of witty repartee, and a whole army of clowns came into films between 1929 and 1939, recruited from music hall, variety, musical comedy and the radio. Most of those who came from the halls shared roots with and maintained the allegiance of their predominantly working-class following. Often their films were set in working-class communities, and the sense of solidarity between performer and audience enabled them to command first-feature status, at least on a regional basis, despite the fact that the films were made cheaply.

When Gracie Fields made her first appearance on film in *Sally in Our Alley*, she already possessed vast experience in music hall, concert party and revue. Her character had a Northern directness which, coupled with a fine singing voice and a natural exuberance, was well captured by the cinema.[1] Fields had been signed up by Basil Dean, the theatrical impresario who founded Ealing Studios. In 1934 he recruited George Formby and set about maximising his comic potential. Formby's basic stage persona of the northern simpleton with a boyish sexuality was retained but made acceptable to southern audiences by having him dress neatly and by setting the action outside his own stamping ground of industrial Lancashire. Though forever bewildered by the dizzying events into which he was pushed, Formby's screen character was a natural survivor who foiled the villains and won the girl at the end. Formby's popularity was enhanced by his songs, accompanied on his banjulele, which revealed an impish, sexually active alter ego, and he soon emerged as Britain's top comic with such films as *No Limit* (1935) and *I See Ice* (1938).

The South's chief rival to the Lancashire comics was Max Miller, 'The Cheeky Chappie', but he seemed an unlikely prospect for film comedy. On stage he hardly ever did sketches or revues, and he was seldom seen in pantomime. His act was brash, rapid-fire, front-cloth delivery, based on impeccable timing and audience manipulation. His trademarks were outrageousness in dress and in patter, which he would intersperse with a few songs and a laconic dance routine. He had a smash hit with *Educated Evans* (1936), sadly now lost, which, like the still extant *Hoots Mon!* (1939), let him do what he did best – tell jokes. His writers allowed him considerable freedom: 'I never paid much attention to the script. It was agreed that I put the speeches into the sort of words I could get across.'[2]

Though he is now forgotten and most of his films are lost, Kent-born Leslie Fuller was once popular enough to purchase his own studios at Elstree. Fuller's background was that of the seaside concert-party; with the coming of the talkies he took himself into a string of broad, homely comedies. His character, Bill, was known for his jovial rubber face and for being plunged into plots riddled with misunderstandings in films like *Doctor's Orders* (1934), *The Stoker* (1935) and *One Good Turn* (1936). In the words of one of his directors, he portrayed 'a character ... brimful of cheerful spirits ... loveable disposition ... intensely human in a simple, unintelligent way ... a "dumb-bell".'[3]

The idea for the Crazy Gang stemmed from the appearance of three double acts on the same bill at the London Palladium. In 1933 the first of seven Crazy Shows was mounted with the classic line-up of Flanagan & Allen, Nervo & Knox, Naughton & Gold, abetted by 'Monsewer' Eddie Gray. The double acts had different styles which made them a potent mix: Flanagan and Allen's sophisticated cross-talk and lilting songs; Nervo and Knox's knockabout physical slapstick and juggling; Naughton and Gold's juvenile buffoonery. In such films as *Okay for Sound* (1937), *The Frozen Limits* (1939) and *Gasbags* (1940) the Gang's surreal unpredictability led to comparisons with the Marx Brothers, but their cinema work never matched the inventive spontaneity of their stage work.

Will Hay came to the cinema in 1933, but it was only with his third starring role in *Boys Will Be Boys* (1935) that he used the schoolmaster character he had developed on the stage over many years. Though born in the North, he covered up his roots to portray a variety of bogus authority figures with a run-down seediness that became his hallmark. All of them aspire to a middle-class respectability beyond their reach and are never able to shake off the remnants of a mysteriously disreputable past: the headmaster in *Good Morning Boys* (1937), the station master in *Oh, Mr Porter!* (1937), the police sergeant in *Ask a Policeman* (1939). Depth of characterisation, strong plots, expert supporting players and Hay's extraordinary timing make his films satisfying viewing.[4] Hay always saw himself as a comic character actor, and he can be seen as the stepping stone between music-hall comedies and comedies populated by character actors playing comic roles. Hay took an interest in the mechanics of the cinema, eventually co-directing his later films, but his ability to make bits of business out of mundane props and his expert visual timing derived from his music-hall training.

The music-hall tradition embraced middle- and upper-class comics such as Claude Dampier, a twittering 'silly ass' or occasional country bumpkin; the bald old Etonian Ronald Frankau; and Oliver Wakefield, who told stories and gave lectures, missing out the crucial words and flowing off at a tangent. The most successful comics of this period, however, were the brothers Jack and Claude Hulbert, the only ones to have a series of films built around them. Jack Hulbert's background was revue and musical comedy, stemming from his university days as a member of the Cambridge Footlights, but he never eschewed slapstick. He was blessed with a suitably comic face, was capable of good comic delivery, could carry a tune and was a superb dancer. Unlike many artists whose first love was the theatre, Jack Hulbert brought the same care and creative imagination to his films as he had done to his stage work, eventually taking both dialogue and director credits. His big-chinned, goofy, happy-go-lucky character breezed his way through a series of films which included *Sunshine Susie* (1931), *Love on Wheels* (1932) and *Jack of All Trades* (1936). His wife, Cicely Courtneidge, was a musical comedy star in her own right, and they made a number of films together, including *Jack's the Boy* (1932) and *Falling for You* (1933).

Claude Hulbert, also a Footlights graduate, made several appearances with the Aldwych team early in his career. He managed to extend the range of the 'silly ass' character beyond the farces and made a big impact in a series of films for Warner Bros at their small British studio at Teddington. Serious consideration of his talents is constrained by the fact that most of these films have been lost, but his bumbling, eager-to-please character enhanced Will Hay's *The Ghost of St Michael's* (1941) and *My Learned Friend* (1943).

Literary and theatrical comedy flourished in the 1930s, but with their class-bound structures and formulaic plots – rich young gentleman impersonates member of the lower classes to court woman of his dreams; country mansion overrun with thieves and/or blackmailers; the hero mistaken for a thief – they have dated badly. The main exceptions are the Aldwych farces – *Rookery Nook* (1930), *Thark* (1932), *A Cuckoo in the Nest* (1933) and *Dirty Work* (1934) – scripted from his plays by Ben Travers and relying on a highly gifted team of performers – Tom Walls, Ralph Lynn, Mary Brough and Robertson Hare.

By the late 30s radio was producing innovative shows and stars which would have an impact on the big screen – notably *Band Waggon* (1938–9) with Arthur Askey, and *It's That Man Again* ('ITMA', as it was universally referred to; 1939–49), anchored by Tommy Handley. Askey made his starring debut in the film version of *Band Waggon* (1940), which successfully combined a putting-on-a-show format with a far-fetched yarn about spies. *ITMA* (1943) also used a show format, which helped preserve the radio series' anarchic mix of a multiplicity of characters, catchphrases and topical allusions. In their wartime radio shows both Askey and Handley achieved a national fame which transcended class barriers, but their films had to compete with vehicles for traditional working-class variety performers such as Arthur Lucan's cantankerous Irish washerwoman, Old Mother Riley, and the North's most popular comedy star, Frank Randle.

That Randle is not better remembered is partly a consequence of southern critical neglect, but it is also posthumous revenge on a man who waged a lifelong war against anything that reeked of respectability. Randle's background included a spell as a circus acrobat and clown and he perfected his command of the stage with a long apprenticeship in revue and music hall in a wonderfully crude act. He made his first film, *Somewhere in England*, in 1940 with the Manchester-based Mancunian Films. Randle's films were not as scandalously offensive as his much-prosecuted stage manifestations, but he nevertheless proved to be one of the most successful transfers of a music-hall comedian to the screen. The motto of Mancunian was to spend as little as possible, keep the camera steady and let the comic get on with it. This suited Randle, who brought to his films bits and pieces of the stage creations which had sustained him for most of his professional life. His act seems at least in part to be drunkenly improvised, the conversations with his stooges in broad Lancashire dialect meandering all over the place with hilarious disregard for the norms of comic development.

About two-thirds of the British film comedies made during the war were from the slapstick music-hall tradition, but peacetime brought a radical change. Though they produced no comedies between Will Hay's *My Learned Friend* in 1943 and *Hue and Cry* in 1947, Ealing Studios were at the centre of this change. In 1949 they released *Passport to Pimlico*, *Whisky Galore*, *Kind Hearts and Coronets* and *A Run for Your Money*, the first of which was scripted by T. E. B. Clarke, the architect of Ealing's cosy whimsicality. Most of Clarke's comedies – *Passport to Pimlico*, *The Lavender Hill Mob* (1951), *The Titfield Thunderbolt* (1953) – depict a Britain of shopkeepers, friendly spivs, jolly coppers, incompetent but honest bureaucrats, kind-hearted squires, contented old-age pensioners and a variety of eccentrics. If there are villains, they tend to be hard-nosed businessmen – most other sections of society are ignored or are minor

Frank Randle – waged a lifelong war against anything that reeked of respectability.
Somewhere in England (John E. Blakely, 1940).

irritants. The Clarke structure can be taken as a crystallisation of Ealing's values, and the comedies of Robert Hamer – *Kind Hearts and Coronets* – and Alexander Mackendrick – *Whisky Galore, The Man in the White Suit* (1951), *The Maggie* (1954), *The Ladykillers* (1955) – a dark commentary on those values.

Ealing comedy brought the literary comedy tradition to the fore, demanding actors with a gift for comedy who could flesh out the well-constructed scripts. The chief beneficiary was Alec Guinness, a master interpreter of comic scripts who could undertake a wide range of roles, as in finely delineated performances as a family of eight doomed aristocrats in *Kind Hearts and Coronets*. Subsequent comedies cast him as a timid bank robber (*The Lavender Hill Mob*); a naive scientist (*The Man in the White Suit*); a detective-priest (*Father Brown,* 1954)) and a psychopath (*The Ladykillers*).

The classic Ealing comedies were made over a very short period of time. With the exception of the two Mackendrick films *The Maggie* and *The Ladykillers,* the post-1951 Ealing comedies either work to a different set of commands (and are seldom revived or even remembered as Ealing comedies) or are tepid reworkings of Clarke's earlier successes.[5] But the influence of the studio on popular comedy films of the 50s is pervasive. As Ealing itself began to falter, the trend was taken up by others, and such films as *Brandy for the Parson* (1952), *Fast and Loose* (1954) and *Alive and Kicking* (1958) could easily be mistaken for Ealing product.

In 1953 the Rank Organisation released *Genevieve* with Kenneth More, John Gregson, Dinah Sheridan and Kay Kendall (a project turned down by Ealing), and its huge success accentuated the move towards middle-class comedy epitomised by *Doctor in the House* (1954) and its successors.

Another popular series emerged from the writer/producer/director team of Frank Launder and Sidney Gilliat, who had contributed to Gainsborough's stream of comedies in the late 30s before their directorial debut, *Millions Like Us* (1943). *The Happiest Days of Your Life* (1950), based on John Dighton's farce about a girls' school being accidentally billeted with a boys' school, starred two great eccentrics of British cinema, Margaret Rutherford and Alastair Sim, and was a huge success. The St. Trinian's films, based on the cartoons of Ronald Searle, worked to a similar pattern. In *The Belles of St. Trinian's* (1954) Alastair Sim appropriated Rutherford's role as the headmistress. A wonderful cast of supporting players, led by Joyce Grenfell, George Cole, Richard Wattis, Eric Barker and Terry-Thomas, was built up for two further films, *Blue Murder at St. Trinian's* (1957) and *The Pure Hell of St. Trinian's* (1960).[6] Though these films were developed directly for the cinema they are an extension of the farce tradition, skilfully utilising strong comic plots while showcasing the comic adroitness of the performers.

Similarly, a group of films from the producer/director team of John and Roy Boulting used a sparkling ensemble of actors led by Ian Carmichael, Peter Sellers, Richard Attenborough and Terry-Thomas. The scripts generally involved the contribution of one of the brothers in collaboration with Frank Harvey or Jeffrey Dell. The best were broadly played satires. *Private's Progress* (1956) dealt with the army; *Lucky Jim* (1957) with snobbery in universities; *I'm All Right, Jack* (1959) with bloody-mindedness in industry; *Carlton-Browne of the F.O.* (1959) with ineptitude in the diplomatic service; and *Heavens Above* (1963) with hypocrisy in the Church. Ironically, the Boultings faded as the satire boom heralded by television's *That Was the Week That Was* (1962–3) took off.

The great discovery of the Boultings was Ian Carmichael, whose well-meaning blunderer is best seen in *I'm All Right Jack*. Though more restricted in his range than Alec Guinness, he could be equally impressive. Another of the mainstays, Peter Sellers, played a far wider range of characters. His background was stage and radio (notably 'The Goon Show'), and fine performances in *The Smallest Show on Earth* (1957) as a drunken projectionist and in *The Naked Truth* (1957) as a murderous family entertainer confirmed his promise in the cinema. Sellers combined skilful interpretation with a clown's ability to work in 'pieces of business'. Where Guinness was a straight actor taking on comic roles, Sellers was an insecure clown submitting himself to the confines of a script. In 1963, when cast as the bumbling French detective Inspector Clouseau in *The Pink Panther*, he discovered a comic persona – one wholly within the music-hall tradition – strong enough to maintain a series.

The end of the war had marked a major change in the fortunes of the established stars of the music-hall tradition. Most of those who had made audiences laugh during the war made little or no further impact in the cinema. Will Hay made his last film in 1943, George Formby bowed out with *George in Civvy Street* in 1946 and the Crazy Gang came together only for a nostalgic reunion, *Life is a Circus*, in 1958. Only Arthur Lucan, Arthur Askey and Frank Randle struggled on into the 50s.

The coming of peace saw an influx of new talent hoping to make their names as comedians. People whose careers had been interrupted by the war rubbed shoulders with those who had gained a taste for entertaining in Army concert parties, with ENSA or with the Gang shows. They were lucky in having the remnants of a variety circuit in which to work, since perfecting routines through practical experience was and is indispensable for developing slapstick comedy, timing and audience control.

The most celebrated of the theatres which gave a chance to up-and-coming comics was the Windmill, where the comedians had the thankless task of filling in between the

Passport to Pimlico *(Henry Cornelius, 1949). Ealing's world of shopkeepers, friendly spivs, jolly coppers and assorted eccentrics.*

nudes. The roll-call of comics who trod those boards is a 'Who's Who' of post-war comedy. Some failed the audition, like Norman Wisdom, Benny Hill and Charlie Drake; many were sacked, most famously Morecambe & Wise; but some survived for a run, like Tommy Cooper, Richard Murdoch, Arthur English, Tony Hancock, Peter Sellers and Jimmy Edwards. To perform at the Windmill was a tremendous training opportunity. Jimmy Edwards recalled: 'I certainly learned a lot ... the frequency with which I had to do my act turned out to be a good thing, for it meant that I could modify my lines and my "business" from hour to hour, retaining the successful bits and throwing out the failures.'[7]

Radio provided another training ground. The rise to fame could be accelerated by appearances on such programmes as *Henry Hall's Guest Night, Workers' Playtime* and *Variety Bandbox.* The oddest was Peter Brough's *Educating Archie* (1950–60), centred as it was on a ventriloquist's dummy, a curious concept for the radio. Of all the series popular on radio at the time it was the most important in launching or establishing names: Hattie Jacques, Max Bygraves, Tony Hancock, Harry Secombe, Benny Hill, Ronald Shiner, Bruce Forsyth, Sid James, Alfred Marks, Beryl Reid, Dick Emery, Jerry Desmonde, Warren Mitchell, Bernard Bresslaw and Marty Feldman all played a part in giving the dummy an education.

Most of the early comedy shows on television were in the variety format, generally one-off specials, though series such as *Val Parnell's Sunday Night at the London Palladium* emerged later. Veteran Arthur Askey was joined by newcomers Norman Wisdom, Arthur Haynes, Tommy Cooper, Benny Hill, Frankie Howerd, Ken Dodd, Charlie Drake, Jimmy Edwards and Morecambe and Wise, most of whom were given their own series in the 50s and early 60s.

Most of these newcomers were destined to have little effect in the cinema. Ken Dodd made no films, Arthur Haynes played only cameos and Tommy Cooper was confined to supporting roles, except in Eric Sykes's semi-silent film *The Plank* (1967). Jimmy Edwards showed cinematic potential in *Treasure Hunt* (1952), as did Frankie Howerd in *Jumping for Joy* (1956), but their subsequent films were disappointing. Charlie Drake's cocky self-confident character was well served in his first three films – *Sands of the Desert* (1960), *Petticoat Pirates* (1961) and *The Cracksman* (1963) – which allowed him plenty of space to display his witty and inventive slapstick, but he was never able to match his small-screen success. Benny Hill made no real effort in the cinema after appearing in *Who Done It?* (1956) and *Light up the Sky* (1960). His cheery, unsentimental characterisation could have had a huge impact, but he preferred to work in television. Eric Morecambe and Ernie Wise remained a front-cloth, cross-talk act in the old tradition, even on television. A film series was envisaged, starting with *The Intelligence Men* (1965), but they were over-constrained by the plots and only two more were completed: *That Riviera Touch* (1966) and *The Magnificent Two* (1967). Similarly, a later television feature, *Night Train to Murder* (1984), failed to build on their strengths and proved only fitfully amusing.

The one exception to this cinematic misuse of talent was Norman Wisdom, who went on to become the most successful of all the post-war screen clowns. Wisdom entered the business after the war, working his way through an apprenticeship in variety and pantomime. He was on television by 1947 and rapidly became the small screen's top comedian. Film soon beckoned, and *Trouble in Store* (1953) made him a major cinema star and led to a string of successors such as *Up in the World* (1956), *There Was a Crooked Man* (1960) and *A Stitch in Time* (1963). Wisdom's success lay in incorporating acrobatic physical comedy within a plausible narrative framework. His character, known as the Gump, was remarkably consistent over the years – a little man who wants to fit in but whose childlike trust in people, coupled with his need for love and acceptance, make him easy prey for the less than honest, the unkind or the unthinking. Like Formby, Wisdom achieved worldwide popularity, except in America.[8]

By the mid-1950s television series with some sort of narrative framework began to emerge and, as with their radio predecessors, some – like Denis Norden and Frank Muir's *Whack-O!* (1956–60) and Sid Colin's *The Army Game* (1957–61) – led to feature films.[9] Television provided opportunities to comedians outside the variety format, and the chief beneficiary was Tony Hancock. Ray Galton and Alan Simpson created *Hancock's Half Hour* for radio in 1954, and the series was transferred to television in 1956 with Hancock visually perfect for his comic persona as the pretentious middle-class remnant of the new affluence. Galton and Simpson also scripted *The Rebel* (1961), which extended the familiar Hancock format into a feature-length film by casting him as an amateur painter who assumes the mantle of a genius. It is a fine film, with the script giving Hancock ample space to display his comic abilities within a coherent narrative. By the time he made *The Punch and Judy Man* (1962), Hancock had lost writers Galton and Simpson and was losing his own battle with alcohol. The film still works well, with Hancock superb as a down-trodden seaside entertainer, but an aura of melancholy finally overwhelms it.

Sid James, memorable as Hancock's crooked sidekick in *Hancock's Half Hour*, found even greater popularity as part of the *Carry On* team, though he did not actually join them until the fourth film, *Carry on Constable* (1960). Kenneth Williams, Charles Hawtrey and Kenneth Connor had been there from the beginning in *Carry On Sergeant* (1958); Joan Sims joined for *Carry On Nurse* (1959), and the final key member, Barbara Windsor, was recruited in 1964 for *Carry On Spying*. The early films, written by Norman Hudis, work to a basic formula in which a group of incompetents are let loose in a familiar institution – an army camp, a hospital, a school, with a subsidiary romance woven in to give the film a happy ending.

Once Hudis left, the scripting was taken over by Talbot Rothwell, and it is from his films that most people take their image of the series. Hudis's scripts had become increasingly ribald, but Rothwell eschewed all subtlety, broadening the basic concept and delighting in a peculiarly British bawdiness and use of *double entendre*. Running out of institutions to mock, he generally resorted to pastiche and parody, *Carry On Spying* (1964), *Carry On Cleo* (1964) and *Carry On . . . Don't Lose Your Head* (1967) being the best examples. After *Carry On Up the Khyber* (1968) the films allowed themselves more leeway in explicit nudity while still maintaining a basic innocence. Talbot Rothwell's scripts continued Hudis's exploitation of expert ensemble slapstick while emphasising the individual development of the performers into a set of distinct comic personas. This, coupled with strong dialogue but loose plotting, marked a straddling of the music-hall and literary traditions.

The loss of Talbot Rothwell in 1974 was a blow from which the *Carry On* films were never to recover, and Britain's most successful and long-lived comic series spluttered to an ignominious close. It is unlikely, though, that even Rothwell's skills could have sustained the series. Other companies put together more explicit sex-romp comedies, notably the 'Confessions' and 'Adventures' films, with which the ageing *Carry On* team could not hope to compete.[10]

By the mid-60s, British pop music and television were at their most inventive, London was in full swing and American finance encouraged British cinema to ride the surf of Britain's cultural centrality. Much British comedy output was unaffected by all this, but some producers did react to what was going on around them. *Please Turn Over* (1959) was a jaunty debunking of 'Angry Young Men'; *The Pot Carriers* (1962) and *Sparrows Can't Sing* (1963) carried the new realism into comedy; and *Billy Liar* (1963), *Smashing Time* (1967), *Alfie* (1966) and the Beatles' films *A Hard Day's Night* (1964) and *Help!* (1965) combined comedy with the ethos of the Swinging Sixties. It was a short-lived flirtation, however, and American finance was rapidly withdrawn. Since then the troubled industry has all but terminated the music-hall tradition, but a succession of writers – Bill Forsyth (*Gregory's Girl*, 1981), John Cleese (*A Fish Called Wanda*, 1988), Richard Curtis (*Four Weddings and a Funeral*, 1994), and Peter Chelsom and Peter Flannery (*Funny Bones*, 1995) – has kept alive the literary tradition of British comedy.[11]

In these days of the writer-comedian or the comedic actor, the presence of the clown on television and film is a rare event and even variety is being taken over by the stars of television sitcoms and soaps. Nevertheless, there are optimistic signs. The alternative cabaret clubs pioneered by London's Comedy Store and Comic Strip have provided a training ground for another generation of performers and writers who look capable of enriching British cinema comedy in all its traditions.

Notes

1. Fields' honest, brassy character often transcended her background and 'made good', a characteristic that brought her to the attention of Hollywood. She signed with 20th-Century Fox but insisted on shooting the films in Britain.
2. Quoted in John M. East, *The Cheeky Chappie* (London: W. H. Allen, 1977), p. 134.
3. Norman Lee, *Money for Film Stories* (London: Pitman, 1937), p. 53.
4. Hay's sidekicks in the classic 30s films were Moore Marriott and Graham Moffatt, who went on to support Arthur Askey, Ben Lyon and Bebe Daniels, and Tommy Handley.

5. The former include *Meet Mr Lucifer* (1953), *The Love Lottery* (1954), *Touch and Go* (1955) and *Who Done It?* (1956; ironically, scripted by Clarke); the latter include *The Titfield Thunderbolt*, (1952) and *Barnacle Bill* (1957).
6. The last two films of the series, *The Great St. Trinian's Train Robbery* (1966) and *The Wildcats of St. Trinian's* (1980), lacked most of the regulars and were dismal affairs.
7. Jimmy Edwards, *Take It from Me* (London: Werner Laurie, 1953), p. 149.
8. Wisdom did triumph on Broadway with his Tony-nominated performance in *Walking Happy* (1967), which led to his one American feature, *The Night They Raided Minsky's* (1968).
9. *Bottoms Up!* (1960) and *I Only Arsked!* (1958), respectively.
10. The 1992 revival, *Carry On Columbus*, made by the regular director/producer team of Gerald Thomas and Peter Rogers, tried to exploit a renewed interest in the series, but without any of the central acting team it was a critical and commercial flop.
11. The one comic with strong working-class roots to have snubbed the trend, ignoring television and succeeding on video, is Roy 'Chubby' Brown, though it is to be hoped that he will improve on his 1993 debut cinema feature, *UFO – the Movie*.

Bibliography

Brown, Geoff, *Launder and Gilliat* (London: British Film Institute, 1977).
Busby, Roy, *British Music Hall* (London: Paul Elek, 1976).
Clarke, T. E. B., *This is Where I Came in* (London: Michael Joseph, 1974).
Dacre, Richard, *Trouble in Store* (Dundee: T. C. Farries, 1991).
Dean, Basil, *Mind's Eye* (London: Hutchinson, 1973).
East, John, *The Cheeky Chappie* (London: W. H. Allen, 1977).
Edwards, Jimmy, *Take It from Me* (London: Werner Laurie, 1953).
Fisher, John, *Funny Way to be a Hero* (London: Frederick Muller, 1973).
Hulbert, Jack, *The Little Woman's Always Right* (London: W. H. Allen, 1975).
Kavanagh, Ted, *Tommy Handley* (London: Hodder and Stoughton, 1949).
Kendall, Henry, *I Remember Romano's* (London: Macdonald, 1960).
Lee, Norman, *Money for Film Stories* (London: Pitman, 1937).
Montgomery, John, *Comedy Films* (London: George Allen and Unwin, 1954).
Moules, Joan, *Our Gracie* (London: Robert Hale, 1983).
Nathan, David, *The Laughtermakers* (London: Peter Owen, 1971).
Nobbs, George, *The Wireless Stars* (Norwich: Wensum, 1972).
Quinlan, David, *Illustrated Directory of Film Comedy Stars* (London: Batsford, 1992).
Rix, Brian, *My Farce from My Elbow* (London: Secker & Warburg, 1975).
Seaton, Roy and Martin, Roy, *Good Morning, Boys* (London: Barrie & Jenkins, 1978).
Smith, Leslie, *Modern British Farce* (London: Macmillan, 1989).
Travers, Ben, *Vale of Laughter* (London: Geoffrey Bles, 1957).
Walker, Alexander, *The Mask Behind the Mask* (London: Weidenfeld and Nicolson, 1981).
Wilmut, Roger, *Artiste* (London: Eyre Methuen, 1978).

20
British Cinema and Black Representation

Jim Pines

The objective of colonial discourse is to construe the colonised as a population of degenerate types on the basis of racial origin, in order to justify conquest and to establish systems of administration and instruction.[1]

Black representation in British cinema is inextricably bound up in colonial and race relations discourses. Typically, narrative stress tends to be on ideological constructions of 'blacks' as either exotic or threatening 'Other'. This Eurocentric motif, moreover, is usually articulated with equally divisive constructions of 'whiteness' or 'Britishness' (the two identities are conflated in this context), in which Empire looms large as a kind of Manichean framing device.[2] The articulation of racial difference in terms of sharply differentiated and easily recognisable character (or racial) types and dramatic situations thus plays a crucial role in structuring colonial and race relations narratives. The racially motivated oppositions in colonial/race relations stories tend not to be satisfactorily resolved, however, either at the fundamental human level or in terms of social idealism.

The history of black representation in British cinema is marked by discontinuities, along with intermittent moments during which particular racial and/or colonial motifs might feature prominently. The first of these moments was the cycle of popular colonial adventure films made in the 1930s, which included *Sanders of the River* (1935), *King Solomon's Mines* (1937), *The Drum* (1938) and *The Four Feathers* (1939), and culminated in the propaganda classic *Men of Two Worlds* (1946). However, the core themes and images that define the genre are already evident in the silent film, *If Youth But Knew* (1926), which centres on an English doctor who goes to work as a regional medical officer in colonial Africa (Nigeria). The twin themes of personal sacrifice and character-building are much in evidence in this drama – as, for instance, in the doctor's decision to leave his fiancée behind with the promise that he will save enough money for them to marry and buy a house when he returns to England. An inter-title – 'The Dawn of the New Century – After four years hard work in the land of the white man's grave!' – reminds the audience that this is not a cosy romantic adventure. The personal danger which the English colonialist doctor faces and overcomes is central to the story, although this epitaph can also be read as an oblique pathologisation of the African setting. 'Empire ... provided one of the conditions under which men and women could be expected to use their mental and physical resources to the full.'[3] The notion that the Empire also provided a setting for certain

207

classes of Europeans to 'find themselves' not only defines the film's colonialist doctor 'hero', but also drives the narrative. Typical scenes show the doctor caring for the sick (during what appears to be an epidemic of some kind), and longing for his fiancée and England. But his personal sacrifice is underpinned by a clearly articulated sense of his moral superiority and political domination over the natives.

While the first half of *If Youth But Knew* centres round paternalistic colonialism, epitomised by the English doctor, the second half focuses on white colonial domination and the representation of natives as 'degenerate types'. This shift in narrative focus is signalled by the arrival (eighteen years later) of big-game hunters, which is quickly followed by a series of provocative vignettes involving witchcraft, native rebellion and the exercise of white authority. *If Youth But Knew* begins to take on a rather nasty tone at this point, reminiscent in some respects of Griffith's *The Birth of a Nation* (1915): we see the natives using American plantation idioms, such as referring to the white male authority figure as 'massa', being whipped, and so on.

Curiously, there is even a hint of miscegenation in the film – between an Englishman and an African woman (played by a white actress in blackface, of course) – but this subplot is largely framed in terms of the European's sense of Christian missionary duty. Despite her expressed devotion to 'massa', the 'African' woman is still denied the possibility of their relationship being consummated. Needless to say, the colonialist doctor hero emerges from all these experiences a new man, returning to England to resolve the failures of past relationships with all the stoicism and chivalry that befits the classic colonial hero.

One of the features of cinematic colonial narratives is that they are located in 'other' places, and invariably centre on white characters' predicaments. *If Youth But Knew* is a little unusual in this respect, in that England itself features as an important location, to which the doctor hero eventually returns. Otherwise, the film conforms to the generic conventions. The colonial setting provides the backdrop against which European adventures and melodramas can be played out. Questions of racial or cultural equality, or of the integration of the European into the social and political sphere of the 'Others', or vice versa, are not propositions that the genre ever seriously entertains.

British colonial film policy was concerned with promoting an acceptable image of Empire, largely through the Colonial Film Unit, set up by the Ministry of Information in 1939 'to make and distribute propaganda films designed to encourage the colonial war effort, chiefly in Africa'.[4] This strand of colonial representation existed alongside more popular – or more commercial – orientations, but it was different in two important respects. First, it was highly institutionalised within the official discourses of government colonial policy; second, it had strong undertones of paternalism with regard to images of the colonial subject. *Men of Two Worlds* (Thorold Dickinson, 1946), for example, was originally commissioned by the Colonial Office, and was intended not only to boost domestic morale, but also to represent colonial development as a humane policy.[5]

The film's story centres on an African concert pianist living in Britain who returns to his village on a humanitarian mission to assist colonial administrators in a mass resettlement operation, following an outbreak of sleeping sickness. He is immediately thrown into conflict with the local 'witch-doctor', who is leading local resistance. The battle of wills that ensues between these two Africans is mediated, or, more accurately, stage-managed by the British District Commissioner, a paternalist figure who is represented as working for the welfare of the villagers as a whole. The film's view of colonial power relations and authority turns on the relationship between these arche-

The Europeanised African. Robert Adams (with topee) in Men of Two Worlds *(Thorold Dickinson, 1946).*

typal figures – the Europeanised African, the local 'witch-doctor', and the colonial District Commissioner – but, more significantly, it is delineated in terms of colonial notions of cultural identity. The Europeanised African's cultural identity and allegiance are constantly called into question by the witch-doctor figure, who regards him as a European with black skin and therefore as an instrument of colonial rule. The dramatic tension between the two Africans serves to heighten the Europeanised African's cultural angst, his sense of dislocation. Colonial mediation enters into the equation in the form of the District Commissioner, who promotes the idea of the 'New Africa' in terms of a synthesis of 'the best of Africa' (its spirituality) and 'the best of Europe' (its rationalism).

This imposed definition of Africa is only partly personified by the film's Europeanised African 'hero'; but in any case the mediation is fundamentally Eurocentric, designed to work primarily in the interest of the European colonial power. Significantly, the District Commissioner figure never directly confronts the local power of the witch-doctor; instead, he is able to defeat this source of opposition through the control he exercises over his Europeanised African protégé. Colonial authority is thus maintained through a form of indirect rule.

Men of Two Worlds is an excellent example of the way in which a colonial narrative attempts to rework and 'liberalise' ideological constructions of the colonial 'Other', in order to reposition itself in relation to the new political (neo-colonial) circumstances which were beginning to emerge by the end of the Second World War. But like the earlier films in the genre, *Men of Two Worlds* does not question the basic premise of Empire, nor is it suggesting the possibility of (say) the cultural assimilation of colonised subjects. The film reaffirms notions of 'cultural difference', but in terms of its re-configuration of the interests of neo-colonialism. Despite its liberalism, the film is unable to articulate an alternative vision of the 'New Africa'.

The demise of Empire more or less coincided with the first major influx of immigrants from the Caribbean and the Indian subcontinent, with all the social and political implications that were to follow. Although many of the old colonial constructions persisted intact, small shifts had already started to appear in relation to cinematic black representation. *Pool of London* (1950), one of the earliest post-war British films to focus on the theme of racial intolerance in Britain, signalled this shift within the context of an otherwise non-racial storyline. It wasn't until the Notting Hill 'race riots' of 1958, however, that issues concerning race relations became central themes. The two landmark films from this period, *Sapphire* (Basil Dearden, 1959) and *Flame in the Streets* (Roy Baker, 1961), belong to the cycle of British 'social problem films' made between the late 1950s and the early 1960s.[6]

These two films are especially interesting for the way they dramatise early anxieties about the 'black presence' in post-war Britain; that is, before immigration became the dominant theme in race relations discourses. This is thematised partly in terms of white racial prejudice and partly in terms of blacks being represented either as 'victims' (*Flame in the Streets*) or as 'social problem' (*Sapphire*). Neither film is particularly concerned with notions of social justice, integration, or assimilation, although both can be read as liberal humanist pleas for racial tolerance. The thematic focus of the films centres on how the white characters are affected by, and come to terms with, the presence of 'race' in their lives. Black characters in the films tend to function primarily as catalysts for the expression of white characters' anxieties. These anxieties are not rooted in race or racial prejudice as such, but they are activated as a direct result of encounters with blacks.

Two aspects of this representation of British race relations should be noted here. First, the representation of blacks as 'victims' or 'social problem' limits the possibility of developing black characterisation beyond the narrow parameters of this dual stereotype; it also reinforces the broader notion of 'black communities' representing marginal, alien and potentially threatening positions on the fringe of civil society. This is a quite explicit undercurrent in both *Flame in the Streets* and *Sapphire*. Secondly, the theme of racial prejudice is constructed mainly in terms of individual psychopathology, the white working-class domestic setting becoming the primary site of racist angst and tension. The wider social context of racial interaction is suggested, but functions primarily as a backdrop against which the domestic melodramas unfold.

Both films end on a similar note: the traumatised white family facing the reality of 'race' in their lives. And, interestingly, both films identify a female member of the family as the primary source of familial and racial angst. The men at the centre of the drama are seen to possess the capacity for 'rationality' – ie they are able to reason their way out of difficult situations and overcome their prejudices. The 'irrationality' of prejudice is explicitly located in the realm of women's anxieties, triggered by the threat of direct inter-racial contact. In both films this threat appears in the form of an inter-racial sexual relationship between a member of the white family (not the traumatised woman) and a black person.

This imaginary threat to the stability of the family unit, which the inter-racial encounter triggers, provokes the films' troubled women characters to play out a series of familial and racial set-pieces with a near-neurotic intensity. But their racism is more than just a fear of blacks as such; it is rooted in a deeper sense of insecurity which these characters articulate within and about their family. It turns on their sense of unfulfilment both as mothers and as wives, which the racial element dramatically activates.

One of the effects of this representation of race relations is that it clearly emphasises the marginality, and the powerlessness, of the black subjects who get drawn into the drama. The notion of blacks as the 'Other', the personification of an alien and disruptive presence, goes unchallenged in both films, it is merely exploited for dramatic purposes. While it could be argued that black representation in *Flame in the Streets* and *Sapphire* is more sophisticated than hitherto in British cinema, it is still not developed to the extent where black characters themselves assume a more proactive role. Black characters are marginalised within the narrative, which is shaped by its focus on white characters' anxieties about their encounter with 'race'.

These examples of racial representation from the late 1950s and early 1960s illustrate the post-Second World War shift from colonial motifs situated in 'other' places to 'race relations' narratives located in Britain itself. However, there was little subsequent development in the next two decades. The proliferation of films and, especially, television documentaries dealing with race relations topics during the 1970s may suggest another major shift in racial representation in British media, but this was not the case. Like the colonised subjects in earlier colonial narratives, the metropolitan black subjects in contemporary British race relations drama remained fixed within the narrow parameters of the 'social problem' paradigm, with only rare instances of alternative approaches in either narrative fiction or documentary.[7]

By the 1970s television had become the dominant medium for representing British race relations, generally in the form of sociological documentaries examining various aspects of so-called immigrant life. These television programmes tended to pathologise black experiences, rather than offering new perspectives on the subject. During this period multiculturalism reached its height of influence, but although the representation of a multicultural Britain signalled a relatively progressive step forward, in the political sense, culturally it did not seriously challenge the traditional ethnocentricity of colonial and race relations discourses. Black representation, in other words, continued to be framed in terms of its relevance to the wider white public. The threat of the 'Other' might have been less accentuated than in the past, but it remained a force in the public imagination.

One of the characteristics of colonial and mainstream race relations discourses is the absence of the colonised subject as an active voice; that is to say, the colonised subject does not have access to the means of self-representation. This changed with the arrival of black film and cultural practitioners. Commenting on the uneasy relationship between black literature and critical practice, Henry Louis Gates, Jr. writes: 'For all sorts of complex historical reasons, the very act of writing has been a "political" act for the black author ... And because our life in the West has been one political struggle after another, our literature has been defined from without, and rather often from within, as primarily just one more polemic in those struggles.'[8]

The same observation can be made regarding black independent film-making in Britain and elsewhere, which faces a similar dilemma because it is perceived largely in terms of race relations and protest-oriented representation. Indeed, what Gates calls the received critical fallacies which frame standard readings of black literary texts also applies to problems which underlie the critical and institutional recognition of black film and cultural practices. This is evidenced partly in public perceptions of what a 'black' film is, and partly in an institutional funding policy which tends to be uncertain about the social and polemical scope of black cinematic practice. Consequently, films which attempt to break the sociological race relations mould, or which try to explore the issue of black representation through the deployment of alternative (non-realist) narrative strategies, tend to be less easily accommodated within conventional race relations paradigms.

In that respect, *Pressure* (1975), the first British feature film made by a black director (Horace Ové), can be read as a landmark transitional film. While it draws heavily on a number of familiar race relations motifs, it reworks them into the film's documentary-like fictional narrative with effects quite different from mainstream black representations. More importantly, the film sets out to 'depathologise' black British experience by examining the notion of 'Black Britishness' itself. It can thus be read as a critique of British multiculturalism and institutionalised race relations. The closing image of black political protest – an image which effectively reinstates an active black voice in black representation – is nonetheless deliberately pessimistic in tone, accurately reflecting the general sense of despair over the 'failure' of race relations politics that was felt within black communities by the mid-1970s.

Burning an Illusion (1981), the second British feature film made by a black director (Menelik Shabazz), marked another important shift in the representation of 'race'. As in *Pressure*, narrative stress is placed on the idea of black politicisation, but here there is little interest in commenting on the failure of multiculturalism, or exploring problems concerning black–white relations in the wider social context. *Burning an Illusion* focuses instead on relationships within black communities, especially those between men and women. Thus the notion of black identity is defined from within the context of a black community rather than being mediated by dominant race relations discourses, and the question of 'Britishness' has no special significance in terms of the film's representation of black experience. This can be seen in the film's portrayal of racial victimisation, for example. Despite the deployment of this archetypal motif (blacks as victims) during key moments in the plot, it plays a relatively minor part in the main thrust of the narrative, functioning instead as a plot device which helps to move the story on. By placing narrative stress on such intra-ethnic or intra-black community concerns, *Burning an Illusion* introduced a more culturally militant tone to black representation within British narrative fiction.[9]

The first British feature film made by a black director. Pressure *(Horace Ove, 1975).*

In the 1980s, with the emergence of a new generation of black British independent film-makers, another shift occurred, one that was part of a broader crisis in representation. Two important things had happened. First, essentialist notions of cultural identity began to be challenged, resulting in a radical reconceptualisation of cinematic black representation. Second, black independent film-makers in Britain institutionalised themselves, in response to the growing institutionalisation of film cultural policy and funding. These developments could only have happened in the context of post-multicultural Britain in the 1980s, when black film-makers abandoned traditional race relations discourses and gained access to the means of self-representation. This resulted in a series of major cultural shifts during the decade, not only in the area of black film imagery and representation, but also in the relationship between black film and cultural practitioners on the one hand, and dominant cultural institutions on the other.

This remapping of the black British film cultural terrain effectively helped to shift the cultural terms of reference away from the narrow scope of traditional race relations and multiculturalism and towards new ways of conceptualising the role and status of black representation. The notion of the black diaspora, for example, was mobilised in such a way as to reconfigure the geographical boundaries of 'black' film-making, giving it an entirely different political inflection. In addition, there was a tendency towards evolving a cinematic black historiography which would 'excavate' black people's own histories and re-present them through new forms of audiovisual practice.[10] Empire itself became the object of interrogation.

Three films in particular herald the arrival of this critical moment in black representation: *Territories* (Isaac Julien, 1985), *The Passion of Remembrance* (Maureen Blackwood and Isaac Julien, 1986), and *Handsworth Songs* (John Akomfrah, 1986). These films effectively changed the cultural agenda, by demonstrating that it was possible to engage in formal experimentation and to take cultural media intervention beyond the narrow bounds of race relations iconography. Initial reaction to the films centred on their alleged elitism, a response which derived from popular assumptions about what a 'black' film ought to be vis-à-vis notions of realism and accessibility. But as Kobena Mercer observed, the critical debates which the films provoked – the first public debates of their kind in Britain – highlighted 'the way image-making has become an important arena of cultural contestation – contestation over what it means to be British today; contestation over what Britishness itself means as a national or cultural identity; and contestation over the values that underpin the Britishness of British cinema as a national film culture.'[11]

The critical challenge to essentialist notions of 'blackness' provided the means by which black representation itself could be recast in new terms. This signalled a major shift, enabling black film and cultural practitioners to extricate themselves from traditional race relations paradigms. As Stuart Hall states:

> What is at issue here is the recognition of the extraordinary diversity of subjective positions, social experiences and cultural identities which compose the category 'black'; that is, the recognition that 'black' is essentially a politically and culturally constructed category, which cannot be grounded in a set of fixed trans-cultural or transcendental racial categories and which therefore has no guarantee in Nature. What this brings into play is the recognition of the immense diversity and differentiation of the historical and cultural experience of black subjects.[12]

The notion that cultural identities are based on a less fixed sense of 'race', and that they necessarily incorporate other identities such as class, gender and sexuality, became a primary motif in certain strands of black representation. *My Beautiful Laundrette* (Stephen Frears, 1985) and Isaac Julien's *Young Soul Rebels* (1991) both explore hitherto unspoken areas of black (gay) sexuality as one of the means of breaking the mould of social problem representation.

There is nevertheless a general sense in which the destabilising effect of what Hall calls 'the end of the innocent notion of the essential black'[13] has resulted in a kind of cultural eclecticism which denies the black subject any coherent sense of (ethnic) identity – that is, an identity which, in the last instance, I would suggest, is centred on the 'fact of blackness'. This is not intended to reduce the totality of black experience to 'race', or to celebrate some untenable concept of 'blackness' as such, but rather to give ethnicity far more significance than is allowed for in some contemporary radical cultural theory. Indeed, the sense of ethnicity as an underlying principle, a means by which people bring structure to their lives, is implicit in both *My Beautiful Laundrette* and *Young Soul Rebels*.

It has been suggested that the emergence of new, multifarious black identities since the 1970s is bound up in the historical process of fragmentation which currently afflicts the postmodern Western world. This conceptualisation has to be contested. Postmodern angst and fragmentation may well be part of the psychic experience of sections of the (black and white) creative intelligentsia, but there is little evidence to suggest that it is a common experience, or a prevalent attitude in everyday black life, or in (self-)representation, for that matter. One is therefore inclined to resist calls for assimilation through fragmentation.

This conclusion could be accused of cultural nationalism, and of aestheticising 'blackness' – a practice which results in unacceptably simplistic representation. Nothing substantive can be gained from conjuring up images of 'pre-colonial innocence and authenticity', to use Paul Willemen's words, or promulgating essentialised symbols of a cultural identity which simply mirror dominant practices.[14] On the other hand, the 1990s have seen the emergence of a completely new cultural and political agenda in Britain, which has temporarily halted any radically new interventions in the area of black representation. This does not bode well for the immediate future.

Notes

1. Homi K. Bhabha, 'The Other Question – the Stereotype and Colonial Discourse', *Screen*, vol. 24, no. 6, 1983.
2. Abdul R. JanMohamed, 'The Economy of Manichean Allegory: The Function of Racial Difference in Colonialist Literature', in Henry Louis Gates, Jr. (ed.), *'Race', Writing and Difference* (Chicago: University of Chicago Press, 1986), pp. 78–106.
3. David Trotter, 'Colonial subjects', in *Critical Quarterly*, vol. 32, no. 3, 1990, pp. 3–20.
4. Rosaleen Smyth, 'Movies and Mandarins: the Official Film and British Colonial Africa', in James Curran and Vincent Porter (eds.), *British Cinema History* (London: Weidenfeld and Nicolson, 1983), p. 132. See also Jeffrey Richards, ' "Patriotism with Profit": British Imperial Cinema in the 1930s', ibid.
5. Smyth, 'Movies and Mandarins', p. 135.
6. For an excellent study of this genre, see John Hill, *Sex, Class and Realism: British Cinema 1956–1963* (London: British Film Institute, 1986).
7. The best examples are *Blacks Britannica* (d. David Koff, 1978), an independent production made for WGBH-Boston, which critically examined Britain's colonial legacy; and Colin Prescod's series of documentary films, *Struggles for the Black Community*, produced by the Institute of Race Relations in 1983.
8. Henry Louis Gates, Jr., 'Criticism in the Jungle', in Gates *et al.* (eds.), *Black Literature and Literary Theory* (New York and London: Methuen, 1984), p. 5.
9. See Jim Pines, 'The Cultural Context of Black British Cinema', in Mbye B. Cham and Claire

Andrade-Watkins (eds.), *BlackFrames: Critical Perspectives on Black Independent Cinema* (Cambridge, Mass.: Celebration of Black Cinema, Inc. and MIT Press, 1988). Reprinted in Houston A. Baker, Jr., *et al.* (eds.), *Black British Cultural Studies – A Reader* (Chicago: University of Chicago Press, 1996), pp. 183–93.

10. For the role of critical theory in black film practice, see Robert Crusz, 'Black Cinemas, Film Theory and Dependent Knowledge', in *Screen*, vol. 26, nos. 3–4, 1985, reprinted in Baker, Jr., *et al.* (eds.), *Black British Cultural Studies – A Reader*; see also Kobena Mercer, 'Diaspora Culture and the Dialogic Imagination: The Aesthetics of Black Independent Film in Britain', in Cham and Andrade-Watkins (eds.), *BlackFrames*; *Screen*, vol. 29, no. 4, 1988, which carries the intentionally ironic title, 'The Last "Special Issue" on Race?'; and Reece Auguiste, 'Black Independents and Third Cinema', in Jim Pines and Paul Willemen (eds.), *Questions of Third Cinema* (London: British Film Institute, 1989).

11. Kobena Mercer, 'Recoding Narratives of Race and Nation', in Mercer (ed.), *Black Film, British Cinema* (London: Institute of Contemporary Arts/British Film Institute, 1988), p. 5.

12. Stuart Hall, 'New Ethnicities', in Mercer (ed.), *Black Film, British Cinema*; reprinted in Baker, Jr., *et al.* (eds.), *Black British Cultural Studies* (Chicago: University of Chicago Press, 1996).

13. Hall, 'New Ethnicities', p. 28. For an interesting development of this critical reformulation, see Stuart Hall, 'Cultural identity and cinematic representation', *Framework*, no. 36, 1989; reprinted in Baker, Jr., *et al.* (eds.), *Black British Cultural Studies*.

14. Paul Willemen, 'The Third Cinema Question: Notes and Reflections', *Framework*, no. 34, 1987, p. 26; reprinted in Pines and Willemen (eds.), *Questions of Third Cinema*.

Bibliography

Auguiste, *et al.*, Reece, 'Black Independents and Third Cinema: The British Context', in Jim Pines and Paul Willemen (eds.), *Questions of Third Cinema* (London: British Film Institute, 1989), pp. 212–17.

Bhabha, Homi K., 'The Other Question – the Stereotype and Colonial Discourse', *Screen* 24, no. 6, November–December 1983, pp. 18–36.

Crusz, Robert, 'Black Cinemas, Film Theory and Dependent Knowledge', *Screen* 26, nos. 3–4, May–August, 1985, pp. 152–6. Reprinted in Houston A. Baker, Jr., *et al.* (eds.), *Black British Cultural Studies – A Reader* (Chicago: University of Chicago Press, 1996), pp. 107–13.

Dyer, Richard, 'White', *Screen* 29, no. 4, Autumn 1988, pp. 44–64.

Gates, Jr., Henry Louis, 'Criticism in the jungle', in Henry Louis Gates, Jr. (ed.), *Black Literature and Literary Theory* (New York/London: Methuen, 1984), pp. 1–24.

Hall, Stuart, 'New Ethnicities', in Kobena Mercer (ed.) *Black Film, British Cinema* (London: Institute of Contemporary Arts Document 7/British Film Institute Production Special, 1988). Reprinted in Houston A. Baker, Jr., *et al.* (eds.), *Black British Cultural Studies – A Reader* (Chicago: University of Chicago Press, 1996), pp. 163–72.

Hall, Stuart, 'Cultural identity and cinematic representation', *Framework* 36, 1989. Reprinted in Houston A. Baker, Jr., *et al.* (eds.), *Black British Cultural Studies – A Reader* (Chicago: University of Chicago Press, 1996), pp. 210–22.

Hill, John, *Sex, Class and Realism: British Cinema 1956–1963* (London: British Film Institute, 1986).

JanMohamed, Abdul R., 'The Economy of Manichean Allegory: The Function of Racial Difference in Colonialist Literature', in Henry Louis Gates, Jr. (ed.), *'Race,' Writing and Difference* (Chicago: University of Chicago Press, 1986), pp. 78–106.

Mercer, Kobena, 'Diaspora Culture and the Dialogic Imagination: The Aesthetics of Black Independent Film in Britain', in Mbye B. Cham and Claire Andrade-Watkins (eds.), *BlackFrames: Critical Perspectives on Black Independent Cinema* (Cambridge, Mass.: Celebration of Black Cinema, Inc. and MIT Press, 1988), pp. 50–61. Reprinted in Kobena Mercer, *Welcome to the Jungle* (London: Routledge, 1994), pp. 53–66.

Mercer, Kobena, 'Recoding Narratives of Race and Nation', in Kobena Mercer (ed.), *Black Film, British Cinema* (London: Institute of Contemporary Arts Document 7/British Film Institute Production Special, 1988. Reprinted in Kobena Mercer, *Welcome to the Jungle*, London: Routledge, 1994), pp. 69–96.

Parry, Benita, 'Problems in Current Theories of Colonial Discourse', *The Oxford Literary Review*, vol. 9, nos. 1–2, 1987, pp. 27–58.

Pines, Jim, 'The Cultural Context of Black British Cinema', in Mbye B. Cham and Claire Andrade-Watkins (eds.), *BlackFrames: Critical Perspectives on Black Independent Cinema* (Cambridge, Mass.: Celebration of Black Cinema, Inc. and MIT Press, 1988), pp. 26–36. Reprinted in Houston A. Baker, Jr., *et al.* (eds.), *Black British Cultural Studies – A Reader* (Chicago: University of Chicago Press, 1996), pp. 183–93.

Richards, Jeffrey, ' "Patriotism with Profit": British Imperial Cinema in the 1930s', in James Curran and Vincent Porter (eds.), *British Cinema History* (London: Weidenfeld and Nicolson, 1983), pp. 245–56.

Ross, Karen, *Black and White Media: Black Images in Popular Film and Television* (Cambridge: Polity Press, 1996).

Shohat, Ella and Stam, Robert, *Unthinking Eurocentrism: Multiculturalism and the Media* (London: Routledge, 1994).

Smyth, Rosaleen, 'Movies and Mandarins: the Official Film and British Colonial Africa', in James Curran and Vincent Porter (eds.), *British Cinema History* (London: Weidenfeld and Nicolson, 1983), pp. 129–43.

Trotter, David, 'Colonial subjects', *Critical Quarterly*, vol 32, no. 3 , Autumn 1990, pp. 3–20.

Willemen, Paul, 'The Third Cinema Question: Notes and Reflections', in Jim Pines and Paul Willemen (eds.), *Questions of Third Cinema* (London: British Film Institute, 1989), pp. 1–29.

Young, Lola, *Fear of the Dark: 'Race', Gender and Sexuality in the Cinema* (London: Routledge, 1996).

21
Exhibition and the Cinemagoing Experience

Allen Eyles

Getting started

In cinema's early years, from 1896 to 1909, the exhibition of films took place in three contrasting types of venue. Music halls drew especially large audiences when newsreels of topical events were presented. Shops and spaces like railway arches were converted into cinemas with little more than brown paper over the windows and benches on the floor. Public halls and specially constructed fairground booths were used by travelling showmen, and sometimes had capacities of up to 1,000.

Licensing came into effect in 1910 to ensure that premises showing inflammable film were suitable for the purpose (with a separate projection box and more than one exit in case of fire). This encouraged the construction of purpose-built cinemas with seating on raked floors to give better sightlines. Many cinemas had separate entrances down a side passage for the cheaper seats nearest the screen: this avoided disturbance to the patrons seated further back, as well as saving them from the odours associated with the 'great unwashed' – 'a very real problem to the public entertainer', noted the 1912 book *How to Run a Picture Theatre*. Attendants used hand-sprays between and during performances to prevent disease and provide a sweet scent. The advent of feature-length films led to larger cinemas with better facilities, although major films were initially presented as special events and often shown in theatres with separate performances at high prices. The Italian epic *Quo Vadis* (1913) was presented at the Albert Hall, and seen by the King and Queen.

Rare examples of early purpose-built cinemas that have been restored and still show films are the Duke of York's, Brighton (1910), Brixton Pavilion (1911, now the Ritzy), and the Electric, Harwich (1911). These early cinemas were usually rectangular in form, with seating on a single floor beneath barrel-vault ceilings, payboxes open to the street and minimal foyer space. Pianists or small orchestras were employed to accompany the silent films, while many cinemas employed an effects artist to provide sound effects such as galloping horses, rolling waves on the seashore, or the shutting of a door. With much lower overheads than the music hall, cinemas were able to charge very low prices and attract whole families.

From 1908 numerous companies began building chains of cinemas, some dispersed over a wide area, others concentrated in particular towns or regions. The most significant of these companies was Provincial Cinematograph Theatres (PCT), formed in 1909 with capital of £100,000 to open fifteen cinemas in cities and towns outside

London with a population of at least a quarter of a million. PCT provided a standard of luxury and elegance – restaurants, cloakrooms, lounges for reading and writing – designed to attract affluent middle and upper-class patrons who would not have stooped to enter the average early picture house.

The outbreak of war in 1914 led to difficulties for most cinema operators. Feature films had made programmes longer and more costly to hire, while reducing the number of performances; war newsreels were very expensive to hire; box-office takings were down because servicemen paid only half price; and cinemas were less efficiently run because skilled management and staff were called up. In addition, a hastily conceived 'temporary' Entertainments Tax was introduced in May 1916, which most affected the cheaper prices of admission. Many cinemas closed for good.

The film business had its opponents, particularly the National Council of Public Morals. The most serious charges levelled against the cinema were an increase in juvenile crime and indecent conduct among the audience. It was suggested that children were influenced by crime on the screen to steal the money for admission, that they spread diseases like ringworm, and that they were at risk of being molested in the darkness. However, it was conceded in favour of the cinema that it countered the attraction of the public house.

There was considerable opposition to cinemas opening on Sundays, prompted mostly by the threat to church attendances. Cinemas were permitted to open in certain areas, sometimes with restrictions (in Hartlepool, only after the church services; in Southport, only admitting those over 16 years of age), but Sunday opening did not become universal until the 1950s.

In 1920, attendances surged to their highest level yet, and exhibitors regained their confidence. The first super-cinemas, inspired by American examples, arrived in 1921, including PCT's widely acclaimed Regent in Brighton, the Capitol in Cardiff and the Rivoli at Whitechapel in London. These were followed by such giants as the Piccadilly, Manchester, the Majestic, Leeds, and the Pavilion at Shepherd's Bush, West London.

Start of the combines

Until 1926, exhibition was essentially independent of production and distribution. But vertical integration of these branches of the industry had flourished in the United States and new combines soon appeared in Britain. In 1927, merchant banker Isidore Ostrer created the Gaumont-British Picture Corporation, and in 1928 GBPC succeeded in acquiring PCT and became the largest film combine in the country. It was rivalled by British International Pictures, which formed a subsidiary, Associated British Cinemas (ABC), combining three existing cinema circuits. This expanded rapidly by acquiring and building cinemas.

The 1930s was the great decade for the construction of new cinemas in Britain (whereas American movie palaces were largely built in the 20s). Cries of 'saturation', 'surfeit' and 'over-building' were commonplace as existing cinema owners attempted to block newcomers, almost always in vain. Comparatively few older cinemas were forced to close, but most of them had to accept an inferior position as newer, larger buildings opened up in direct opposition. Prices in the West End and provincial centres were much higher than in the suburbs and small towns. In 1934, audiences paid from one shilling-and-sixpence (7½p) to eight shillings and sixpence (42½p) at the premiere-run Tivoli in London's Strand, but would be asked for only sevenpence (2½p) to two shillings (10p) at a local super-cinema such as the Broadway at Stratford, East London, when films arrived there many weeks later. Lesser cinemas would have even lower prices. A cinemagoer always paid more to sit in the best seats, usually in the front circle and usually paying three or four times as much as those who sat in the front stalls. Queues formed for particular seat prices, and the cheapest seats usually sold out first.

A specialised form of programming suited to smaller existing cinemas or small new spaces was the newsreel theatre, showing approximately an hour of newsreel material and shorts. Originated in the United States in 1929, this policy was successfully introduced at some struggling cinemas in Britain and, later in the 30s, purpose-built newsreel cinemas appeared in most major cities. These newsreel cinemas were often placed in or near terminal stations to take advantage of the many people with time on their hands, waiting for trains to arrive or depart. Other uses for small cinemas were as art houses (beginning with the Academy in London's Oxford Street from the early 1930s) or as repertory cinemas (notably the Classic chain, which built a flagship cinema in London's Baker Street).

In the 30s, the Gaumont chain added fifty-one purpose-built cinemas, while the ABC circuit erected ninety-eight. Many smaller chains also competed: Granada built seventeen cinemas, including huge Gothic-style properties at Tooting and Woolwich in the London suburbs. The Union circuit was a particularly aggressive competitor until its financial collapse in 1937, after which it was taken over by the ABC chain. The Hollywood majors in general restricted themselves to operating West End flagships to launch their product: Metro-Goldwyn-Mayer had the Empire, Leicester Square; Warner Bros built the Warner a few doors away. Paramount was more aggressive: it had the Plaza and Carlton in the West End, acquired a suburban chain of four large Astorias at Brixton, Finsbury Park, Streatham and Old Kent Road, and built large city-centre cinemas in Birmingham, Glasgow, Leeds, Liverpool, Manchester and Newcastle.

The most striking newcomer of the 30s was the Odeon circuit, the brainchild of Birmingham businessman Oscar Deutsch, who had promoted some cinemas in the late 20s and opened one Odeon at Perry Barr in 1930. Deutsch drew up plans for a circuit in 1932 and began opening cinemas the following year. By the end of the decade, 136 Odeons had been inaugurated, including the flagship Odeon in Leicester Square. Deutsch gave his circuit a distinctive image, in particular through a stylised, straight-edged name sign that is used to this day. He also encouraged his architects (principally the Harry Weedon, George Coles and Andrew Mather practices) to create eye-catching streamlined exteriors with curved corners, slab towers and much use of yellow faience tiles (the Leicester Square cinema was faced in black to provide a deliberate contrast). Whereas the new cinemas of other chains often included variety acts, elaborate stage facilities, organs, vast restaurants and even dance halls, Deutsch wanted more economical buildings dedicated to showing films.

Deutsch built Odeon into a national circuit which rivalled Gaumont and ABC by the end of the 30s. In order to obtain quality British films and to meet quota obligations, he went into a partnership with United Artists, which distributed Alexander Korda's productions. Odeon's numerical strength was increased by a number of acquisitions, including the County chain and the Scottish Singleton circuit, and capped by the takeover (outside the West End) of the small but powerful Paramount circuit, which gave it large properties in the major city centres.

Deutsch had his eye set on taking over Gaumont-British, which was in an unhealthy financial state because of losses on production and distribution. However, the entrepreneur's own poor health took a turn for the worse after he was injured in a bomb blast during the Second World War, and he died in December 1941 at the age of forty-eight. By this time J. Arthur Rank had become closely involved in both Odeon and

Odeon, Kingstanding, Birmingham.

Gaumont and his companies took control of the two circuits, although the Board of Trade required them to be run as separate, competing entities.

The Second World War

When war was declared in September 1939, cinemas and other places of public enter-tainment were closed for a week as a safety precaution until it was realised that people needed them as a refuge – literally so, when bombs eventually rained from the sky. Although messages would be flashed on the screen warning of imminent air raids, most cinemagoers preferred to stay put, realising that they were safer in a massive, well-constructed building than out on the street or in their own homes. The Second World War put a freeze on cinema construction, and it was not until 1955 that build-ing restrictions were relaxed to enable cinemas only half-completed to be finished, and those severely damaged by bombing to be reconstructed and re-opened.

Helped by a shortage of alternative entertainments, picturegoing boomed in the war years, except when areas were subjected to intense bombing during the London Blitz. South-coast cinemas also suffered because of population decline through evacuation and restricted access to the area. In 1941, attendances rose by an amazing 30 per cent over the preceding year, and they continued to climb to an all-time peak of 1,635 million admissions in 1946. After this, attendances fell year by year, but it was not until 1957 that they reached pre-war levels of under 1,000 million.

In 1947, the Labour government, in an attempt to stem the flow of sterling across the Atlantic, imposed a 75 per cent ad valorem levy which resulted in the American companies refusing to import any new films. Their backlog of new titles already in Britain was eked out with reissues from the autumn of 1947 until May 1948, when the tax was suddenly withdrawn. British film production had been stepped up to fill the screen time, and suddenly a number of hastily conceived, cheaply made British productions were forced to compete with a huge influx of Hollywood pictures. The American product had, however, to fit in around a legal quota requirement that 45 per cent of main features and 25 per cent of supporting features should be British. This latter figure could include a number of reissues of older films, often abridged. Patrons were frequently hostile to new British 'B' features, and resented watching films they had seen before. But many British main features were successful, and the top attractions for the years 1947–49 were British: *The Courtneys of Curzon Street, Spring in Park Lane* and *The Third Man*. The main feature quota was eased to 40 per cent in 1949 and to 30 per cent from 1950.

By 1948, the ABC circuit totalled 442 cinemas, Odeon had 317, and Gaumont 304. Although the circuits controlled a minority of the 4,700 cinemas in Britain, they had a disproportionate power because they were virtually guaranteed the first showing of the best films. For a film to be widely exhibited it had to be given a circuit release by one of these majors (in places where a chain was unrepresented another cinema would step in to take its release).

Extended runs were confined to London's West End cinemas and, occasionally, other city-centre cinemas. Fixed well in advance, West End runs were often inflexible since a film's general release had already been scheduled and the next attraction fixed. There were one-week pre-release presentations at seaside resorts in the holiday season, concurrent with the West End showings. Films began their general release with the London suburbs. There had been a simple North London–South London split, but in order to reduce the number of prints in wartime the London suburbs were divided into three regions: North and West, North and East, and South. Films played from Monday for six days, with Sunday (when part of the takings went to charity) being devoted to revivals, Normally, there was no question of a film being held over for a second week: this would have dented the business of other cinemas waiting to play the film. The weekly change of programme was also favoured because many patrons went to the same cinema virtually every week, regardless of what was showing.

Normally, two feature-length films were shown with a newsreel and trailers. Occasionally long, spectacular productions played with a 'full supporting programme' of shorts and cartoons rather than a supporting feature. After touring London, films played the rest of the country, taking as long as six months on their first run. Many older, smaller cinemas, and some newer independent ones that did not have the booking power of the major circuits, survived by showing films that had not obtained a circuit release, either because they were comparatively unappealing or because they were handled by a minor distributor; these cinemas also revived the most attractive films that had played the major circuits.

The Big Decline

In the United States, movie attendances slumped dramatically after 1947, and in the early 50s Hollywood attempted to combat television by making more films in colour, 3-D and CinemaScope.

In Britain, the slow decline in attendances almost halted in 1954, the year in which CinemaScope and stereophonic sound were introduced. The process was owned by 20th Century-Fox, which fell out with Rank's Odeon and Gaumont circuits over their refusal to give extended playing time to Fox pictures and install full stereophonic sound. Consequently, Fox created a new circuit to show its films, consisting mainly of Essoldo and Granada theatres, and the Odeon and Gaumont circuits lost the often popular Fox product.

Between 1956 and 1960 British cinema attendances more than halved, from 1,101 million to 501 million. During this period over 1,000 cinemas shut down. Apart from reducing admissions, since not all patrons switched to other cinemas, these closures also made cinemagoing seem unfashionable – they prompted newspaper headlines and the unwanted buildings often became derelict eyesores. The broad reason for the cinema's decline was, as in the United States a few years earlier, rising standards of living. Whereas some patrons in the 1930s had never stepped on carpet until they went into a super-cinema, in the post-war period comfort in the home often outstripped that of cinemas.

In the late 1930s British cinemas had experimented with the new medium of television, offering large-screen presentations of live events such as the 1938 Derby. Television closed down during the war, but the BBC resumed transmissions in 1945 and gained a huge boost from the 1953 Coronation of Queen Elizabeth II. But it was the coming of ITV that particularly hurt cinemas as the regional commercial TV companies aimed to appeal to a mass audience; they also acquired libraries of still attractive old Hollywood films, some of which they showed on Saturday evenings.

Another significant problem faced by cinemas was the decline in the number of new major Hollywood features. Cinemas were struggling to find enough attractive features to maintain the four-circuit system – many reissues and second-rate programmes went out just to fill the screens. The circuits even played some subtitled foreign-language films, including *Le Salaire de la peur* (*The Wages of Fear*, 1954) and *Rififi* (1955), which had been major hits in the West End. Rank initially resisted showing X-certificate films on the Odeon and Gaumont circuits because they prevented families from attending, but they gradually relented. Independent cinemas without access to one of the circuit releases had even fewer films to choose from, and the survivors turned increasingly to exploitation material: cheap horror and science-fiction pictures, nudist features, and 'sexy' Continental titles.

Audiences were losing the habit of attending cinemas regularly, only going in large numbers to a few hit films each year. Ancillary sales (ice-creams, soft drinks) became increasingly important, as did the revenue from screen advertising. Larger cinemas also developed evenings of live shows with pop stars.

In 1958, the problem of product shortage was finally addressed. Fox began to wind down its separate release programme and Rank regrouped its best Odeon and Gaumont cinemas into a new weekly Rank release. Redundant cinemas were converted to dance halls, bowling alleys and bingo clubs or pulled down to make way for supermarkets and office blocks.

In the 1960s, major mainstream films were released to either the ABC or Rank (Odeon) circuits. For a while, Rank was tied to a disproportionate number of Hollywood majors, dating from the time when it operated two circuits, but first Paramount and then Universal switched from Rank to ABC, which retained its connection with MGM and Warner Bros. Besides its own and other British productions, Rank was left with Disney, Columbia, United Artists and 20th Century-Fox pictures.

In the 1960s it became apparent that most cinemas were too large: it was uneconomic to maintain them, and depressing for audiences to be scattered in handfuls around a vast auditorium. Initially, many buildings were split horizontally into two halves. Sometimes, the downstairs half became a dance hall or bingo club; sometimes both halves functioned as cinemas, often making redundant a cinema elsewhere. The first mini-cinema opened in former restaurant space at the Odeon, Preston in 1970 with 105 seats, the old auditorium having already been divided into a ground-floor dance hall and upstairs cinema. However, the fall in cinema attendances continued, annual admissions dropping from 501 million in 1960 to 193 million in 1970. The number of cinemas fell from 3,034 to 1,529.

In the 1970s most profitable Odeons and ABCs were converted into three-screen film centres. New equipment had been devised, requiring only one projector that could basically run itself, with the programme on large reels on a tower or horizontally placed on a platter. ABC favoured closing sites for several months to create two cinemas in the former stalls and one in the circle, each with new screens and curtains, and attempted to relaunch these film centres as a new creation. Rank preferred to spend less money with 'drop-wall' conversions whereby the space beneath a balcony was closed off and divided down the middle to create two mini-cinemas while the circle functioned as the largest cinema, using the existing screen, and stayed open for all or most of the conversion period to maintain some income and keep the cinemagoing habit alive.

Picturegoers found themselves with a greater choice of films since in many suburbs and towns there were competing ABCs and Odeons, each with three screens. Hit films like *Percy* and *Women in Love* were now being given standard two-week runs, but in three-screen centres they could stay even longer on a smaller screen. A smash hit, like *Jaws*, played at some local cinemas for as long as six months.

Cinemagoers became increasingly selective, partly because admission prices were no longer cheap. Only the main feature mattered now, so double bills, shorts and supporting features vanished: a single feature, and advertising, was shown with separate performances replacing the time-honoured continuous show. Regular children's Saturday shows declined in the face of television's alternative appeal, then ceased altogether.

Competition between the three major circuits in 1952.

Apart from a sharp rise in 1978, fuelled by a raft of box-office successes led by *Star Wars*, attendances continued to decline, and the relative cheapness and flexibility of video seemed to pose a real threat to cinemagoing. The future of cinemas had never looked bleaker. More cinemas closed, even some of those converted to three screens. Press and display advertising was cut back. Small-print advertisements for cinemas in local papers created a poor impression, as did the fronts of some cinemas, which now permanently displayed a large sign – 'You can't beat a good film' – rather than naming the actual picture showing. By 1984, annual attendances were down to 58 million, Odeon had only 75 cinemas with 194 screens, while ABC (now part of the Thorn-EMI conglomerate) had 107 sites and 287 screens.

Return of the audience

In 1985, attendances went up to 71 million, and recovery was sustained by the arrival of the multiplex. British exhibitors and leisure operators were well aware that the multiplex cinema had revitalised film exhibition in North America, but doubted if the idea would work in Britain because of the high cost of land. However, Bass Leisure, in developing the Point leisure complex at Milton Keynes, wanted a multiplex and linked up with a leading US chain, American Multi-Cinema (AMC), to obtain one. AMC decided to import its operating practices wholesale rather than adapt to local conventions. It was rewarded when the ten-screen cinema at the Point, opened in October 1985, achieved one million admissions within its first year of operation.

Even before the opening of the Point, the ABC circuit had laid plans for multiplexes, but the parent company decided to dispose of the circuit to an American company, Cannon, which applied its name to the cinemas, including Britain's second multiplex, the eight-screen Cannon at Salford Quays, Manchester, opened at the end of 1986. (Cannon renamed its multiplexes and some older properties MGM Cinemas after acquiring the MGM studio.)

AMC led the way by opening seven more multiplexes before it was taken over by another American operator, CIC, soon becoming the UCI chain. Other American concerns burst onto the British exhibition scene, National Amusements opening Showcase cinemas with as many as fourteen screens. Warner Bros spread beyond its long-standing Leicester Square launch-pad to open multiplexes, beginning with a twelve-screen cinema at Bury in Lancashire that seated 3,996 (just short of the biggest single-screen cinemas of the past) and cost £9 million. Multiplexes, with their soft drinks and popcorn, out of town sites and computerised box-offices, have succeeded by attracting an audience of affluent, car-owning young people.

Many old-fashioned cinemas, including some in nearby town centres, have been forced to close by multiplex competition. Others, however, have benefited from the general resurgence of interest in the cinema brought about by multiplexes. Odeon, the one chain that has survived throughout in its original British ownership, belatedly joined the multiplex revolution and also made most of its older cinemas more competitive by introducing extra screens. In 1994, the Cannon/MGM chain was acquired by Virgin, which has been developing new design and branding concepts for future multiplex development.

Most British multiplexes were built in the Midlands and North, where land was cheaper and more sites were available, but the South now has many new cinemas. Although the opening of multiplexes slowed down in the early 90s, it gathered pace in 1995 and the current rate of growth and climate of aggressive competition suggest that there will be an overabundance of multiplexes in certain areas. A measure of the inroads made by multiplexes is that, in 1994, they occupied 10 per cent of cinema sites, had almost exactly one third of the nation's screens and achieved a 46 per cent share of admissions.

The revival has not been entirely confined to major operators and mainstream cinemas. Some areas such as Greenwich and Brixton, in South London, have regained cinemas through government funding or grants, the Brixton Ritzy being one example of expansion in the art-house sector.

Admissions climbed steadily between 1985 (71 million) and 1994 (124 million). Although they fell back in 1995 (to 115 million), this has been widely regarded as a temporary setback attributable to an exceptionally weak year for films, an unusually hot summer, and the bunching together of the most popular releases.

The spread of the American-style filmgoing experience of the multiplex has been accompanied by an increased enthusiasm for watching American films. British-made films have not revived to the point of providing top box-office attractions, with the exceptions in 1994 of *Four Weddings and a Funeral* (which was largely foreign-financed), in 1995/96 of *GoldenEye* (American-financed and distributed) and in 1996 *Trainspotting*. British films, including co-productions with American and European companies, gained only 13 per cent of the home box-office in 1994. British films have generally been low-budget and restricted in appeal, but the revival in attendances may yet encourage more ambitious domestic production.

Bibliography

BFI Film and Television Handbook (London: British Film Institute, 1983 to date). Statistics of cinemas, screens, admissions.

The Cinema: Its Present Position and Future Possibilities, Being the Report of and Chief Evidence taken by the Cinema Commission of Inquiry Instituted by the National Council of Public Morals (London: Williams and Norgate, 1917).

How to Run a Picture Theatre (London: E. T. Heron, 1912).

Kinematograph Year Book, 1914 to 1959; *Kinematograph and Television Year Book,* 1961 to 1969 (London: various publishers). Listings of cinemas, circuits, etc.

Picture House (Cinema Theatre Association). Magazine started in 1982 containing articles and interviews about cinema design and operation, circuit histories, programming, etc.

Atwell, David, *Cathedrals of the Movies* (London: Architectural Press, 1980).

Docherty, David, Morrison, David, and Tracey, Michael, *The Last Picture Show? Britain's Changing Film Audience* (London: BFI Publishing, 1987).

Eyles, Allen, *ABC, The First Name in Entertainment* (Burgess Hill, West Sussex: Cinema Theatre Association/London: BFI Publishing, 1993).

Eyles, Allen, *Gaumont British Cinemas* (Burgess Hill, West Sussex: Cinema Theatre Association/ London: BFI Publishing, 1996).

Eyles, Allen, 'Oscar and the Odeons', *Focus on Film,* no. 22, Autumn 1975.

Eyles, Allen, and Skone, Keith, *London's West End Cinemas* (Sutton, Surrey: Keytone Publications, 1991).

Halliwell, Leslie, *Seats in All Parts* (London: Granada, 1985). Reminiscences of Bolton's cinemas.

Kelly, Terence, with Norton, Graham, and Perry, George, *A Competitive Cinema* (London: Institute of Economic Affairs, 1966).

McBain, Janet, *Pictures Past: Recollections of Scottish cinemas and cinema-going* (Edinburgh: Moorfoot, 1985).

Manders, Frank, *Cinemas of Newcastle* (Newcastle upon Tyne: City Libraries & Arts, 1991).

O'Brien, Margaret, and Eyles, Allen (eds.), *Enter the Dream-House* (London: Museum of the Moving Image/BFI Publishing, 1993). Interviews about going to the cinema and working in the cinema.

22
Traditions of the British Horror Film

Ian Conrich

In *A Heritage of Horror* (1973), David Pirie wrote that the British horror film is 'the only staple cinematic myth which Britain can properly claim as its own'.[1] He charted an area which until then had been part of a 'lost continent' of British cinema, but subsequent writings on British horror have done little to explore beyond the Hammer films which were the focus for Pirie's study.[2]

Trick films, transformations and true crime

As early as 1898 elements of horror were being presented in G. A. Smith's series of trick films. These comic shorts employed double exposure, which enabled the creation of transparent images to represent spirits or ghosts. Labelled the 'spectral effect', it was demonstrated in Smith's 1898 films *The Corsican Brothers*, *Photographing a Ghost* and *Faust and Mephistopheles*.[3] More sophisticated effects enabled film-makers to present detached heads and limbs, for example in James Williamson's *The Clown Barber* (1899) in which a man who has been accidentally decapitated is seen being shaved. 'Transformation narratives' such as *The Vampire* (1913) and *Heba the Snake Woman* (1915) showed women metamorphosing into snakes, while *The Fakir's Spell* (1914) had a man turning into a gorilla.

Society's concern with recidivism was one factor behind the large number of silent film productions based on true crimes. Early examples of the exploitation film, these productions foregrounded violence and employed 'whodunnit' narratives developed in the popular detective dramas. The murder of Maria Marten in 1827 was a source for three early films (in 1908, 1913 and 1923), and *In the Grip of Iron*, based on the Paris Strangler, was filmed in 1913 and 1920.

Horror films and horror film censorship, 1930–1950

Tod Slaughter is one of the key figures of British horror film before 1950. A theatre actor, he specialised in stage productions of familiar horror and crime dramas, which were known as 'Strong Meat' melodramas. Film versions, most of them directed by George King, were made of a number of his most successful productions: *Maria Marten* (1935), *Sweeney Todd, the Demon Barber of Fleet Street* (1935), *The Face at the Window* (1939) and *The Curse of the Wraydons* (1946).

Slaughter's films seemed immune to censorship. *The Crimes of Stephen Hawke*

(1936), for instance, features a notorious murderer known as 'The Spine Breaker', who at the beginning of the film bends the back of an inquisitive boy over his knee and breaks his spine. The only one of Slaughter's films that appears to have been censored was *The Greed of William Hart* (1948), where the grave-robbers Burke and Hare had to be fictionalised as Moore and Hart.[4]

Deriving from the popular forms of Victorian theatre, the films were marked by sensationalism, a heightened theatricality, and Slaughter's larger-than-life villains. By mixing elements of sadism and Grand Guignol with pantomime, the films gave 'a none-too-subtle leering wink at the audience, letting the viewer in on the fact that no one concerned considered this anything but good fun'.[5]

The British Board of Film Censors (BBFC) was more critical of the influx of American horror films that began in 1931 with Universal's *Dracula* and *Frankenstein*. In January 1933 it added an 'H' classification to the 'U' and 'A' certificates. Purely advisory and not yet a form of film certification, the 'H' stood for 'horrific', and covered non-horror films such as Abel Gance's 1938 anti-war film *J'Accuse* and the 1945 *United Nations War Crimes Film* as well as the American horror film.

The first British film to receive an 'H' rating was *The Ghoul* (1933), starring Boris Karloff; *The Tell-Tale Heart* (1934) and *The Man Who Changed His Mind* (1936, also starring Karloff) were similarly rated. An 'H' rating created immediate difficulties for a film: some cinemas and local councils refused to exhibit any film with this rating. *The Ghoul*'s distributors took care to reassure exhibitors about its content, declaring in the publicity booklet that 'while perhaps, it is not exactly the type of film which a very sensitive person should see, it most decidedly is not on the horrific plane of other mystery thrillers.'

The first film to receive an H rating. The Ghoul *(T. Hayes Hunter, 1933).*

227

An official BBFC 'H' certificate (the first official 'adults only' film certificate) was introduced in June 1937. The 1939 film *The Dark Eyes of London*, with Bela Lugosi, was the first British film to receive the certificate, but in 1940 horror films came under renewed criticism. It was argued that 'there was enough horrifying action in the world today without having to pay to see it at the cinema'.[6] The BBFC banned all 'H'-certificate films in 1942, and over the next three years twenty-three films were denied certificates. In January 1951 the 'H' certificate was subsumed into the newly created 'X' certificate.

Even before the war, problems with censorship meant that film-makers tended to import horror into comedies and thrillers rather than attempting to make outright horror films. In comedian horror films an actor such as Will Hay, Arthur Askey, Arthur Lucan or Herbert Mundin, would find themselves at a train station, an old house, a lighthouse or an inn, which would then be revealed to be haunted by real or fake ghosts. By the film's conclusion the comedian would have solved a mystery and uncovered a group of criminals who had been using the haunting as a cover for their fiendish activities. These films – *What a Night!* (1931), *Immediate Possession* (1931), *Forging Ahead* (1933), *Ask a Policeman* (1939) and *Old Mother Riley's Ghosts* (1941) – are similar to the American films *The Cat and the Canary* (1939), *The Ghost Breakers* (1940), *Ghosts on the Loose* (1943) and *The Ghost Catchers* (1944), though the American films are recognised as horror films, while their British equivalents are regarded as comedies.

Psychopaths and murderers featured in a number of gruesome thrillers, such as *Condemned to Death* (1932), *The Frightened Lady* (1932 and 1940) and *Sabotage* (1936). The production of these films increased during and just after the war, with films such as *Gaslight* (1940), *Tower of Terror* (1941), *Wanted for Murder* (1946), *Daughter of Darkness* (1947) and *Obsession* (1948) reflecting a British fascination with morbidity at a time of social and economic instability. A possible comparison can be made between these films and the brooding films noirs that were being simultaneously produced by Hollywood. *The Night Has Eyes* (1942) is a notable example of this type of film. It featured murders on the Yorkshire moors, death by quicksand and James Mason as a reclusive composer who could be a killer. The film's British pressbook declared, 'Death strikes at full moon as the mad killer seeks his victims in the lone house on the moors.'

Another kind of horror can be seen in films built around seances and the role of clairvoyants. The contacting of spirits was presented in a number of films, including *At the Villa Rose* (1930 and 1939), *The Barton Mystery* (1930), *The Clairvoyant* (1935) and *Latin Quarter* (1945). *Spellbound* (1941) and *Things Happen at Night* (1948) both featured evil spirits and possession. The former film was temporarily banned by the BBFC and was only passed once a foreword had been provided by the Spiritualist Church. The period between 1944 and 1946 saw the production of two of the most famous British pre-Hammer horror films *Halfway House* (1944) and, in particular, *Dead of Night* (1945). As Robert Murphy has written, with death part of everyday life during the Second World War, 'it is not surprising that there should have been an up-surge of interest in spiritualism and the supernatural'.[7]

Hammer horrors

In 1935, Enrique Carreras and Will Hinds (stage name, Will Hammer) formed the dis-tribution company Exclusive Films. Their sons, James Carreras and Anthony Hinds, joined later and in 1947, Hammer, a small independent production company, was formed.[8] The company's identity was strengthened by their decision to buy a country house to act as their own studio. The building and its surrounding land served to provide a multitude of sets and consequently reduced production costs.

Many of the early productions were adaptations of radio plays such as *Dick Barton Special Agent* (1948), *Celia* (1949) and *Meet Simon Cherry* (1950) or genre films patterned on Hollywood successes. In 1951, Hammer moved to a large gothic house at Bray. It was from here that their most famous horror films were produced.

The success of two of their science-fiction films, *The Quatermass Experiment* (1955) and *X – The Unknown* (1956), led Hammer to produce the first of their horror films. *The Curse of Frankenstein* (1957) was even more profitable; made for approximately £65,000, it grossed around £300,000 in Britain, £500,000 in Japan and £1 million in America.[9] Previous British horror films had relied on shadows, mysteries, suspense, passion, spectral figures and the viewer's imagination. Hammer's films, generally made in colour, used excess, explicitness, sensuality and violence. Derek Hill's attack on the new British horror films, in 1958, was primarily aimed at this switch to a more visceral approach: 'instead of attempting mood, tension or shock, the new Frankenstein productions rely almost entirely on a percentage of shots of repugnant clinical detail. There is little to frighten ... but plenty to disgust.'[10] Further attacks on the early Hammer horrors included a call for an 'SO', 'Sadists Only' certificate.[11]

In the 30s, Hollywood had adapted Mary Shelley's *Frankenstein*, Bram Stoker's *Dracula* and Robert Louis Stevenson's *The Strange Case of Dr Jekyll and Mr Hyde*. But the success of *The Curse of Frankenstein* led to Hammer acquiring from Universal the rights to their gothic horror films. As Pirie writes, 'even Universal had realised by this time that England was reclaiming its own myths'.[12] *Dracula* was Hammer's second horror production, released in 1958; *The Mummy* (1959), *The Curse of the Werewolf* (1960) and *The Two Faces of Dr Jekyll* (1960) followed. Hammer was to produce a further six Frankenstein films, six Dracula and nine vampire films, three mummy films and one more Dr Jekyll and Mr Hyde film.

Most of Hammer's gothic horrors operated within strong moral frameworks depicting the struggle between the forces of good and evil, the spirit and the flesh, science and superstition and the familiar and the unknown. Carnal desire is presented as dangerous; characters, in particular women, susceptible to its power and therefore requiring to be contained. It is only with the destruction of monstrous or deviant sexuality that social order and normality can be reinstated.

Hammer was also responsible for a series of psychological thrillers. These 'invisible' Hammer horrors are either trampled in the stampede to examine the gothic horror films, or, as in Denis Gifford's *The British Film Catalogue*, listed as crime and not horror films. The first such film, *Taste of Fear* (1960), scripted by Jimmy Sangster, was inspired by the recently released *Psycho* (1960). Of the ten films which followed, eight – *Maniac* (1962), *Paranoiac* (1962), *Nightmare* (1963), *Hysteria* (1965), *The Nanny* (1965), *The Anniversary* (1967), *Crescendo* (1970) and *Fear in the Night* (1972) – were scripted by Sangster; *Fanatic* (1964), was scripted by Richard Matheson and *Straight on Till Morning* (1972) by Michael Peacock.

In these films an individual, generally female, is trapped in a large, isolated house. Here she is tormented and scared by scheming relatives or associates, who require her to be punished, destroyed or made to appear deranged. The narrative is structured upon a systematic series of persecutions and night-time disturbances and occasionally broken by an hallucination or nightmare sequence. Plot twists, a choice of suspects and false moments of terror, are closer to the 'whodunnit' narratives of the early British horror films than to the explicitness of Hammer's gothic horrors.

The proliferation of the horror film

The success of *The Curse of Frankenstein* inspired many other British production companies to produce horror films.[13] Amicus, managed by the Americans Milton Subotsky and Max Rosenberg, employed an omnibus format similar to that of *Dead of Night* in such films as *Dr Terror's House of Horrors* (1970), *Torture Garden* (1967), *The House That Dripped Blood* (1970), *Asylum* (1972), *Tales from the Crypt* (1972), *The Vault of Horror* (1973), *From Beyond the Grave* (1974) and *The Monster Club* (1980). In these films a group of individuals find themselves gathered in a single space (catacombs, a railway carriage, a fairground sideshow or a basement room), where during their time together they hear or recount unusual stories. Alternatively, this specific space (a house, club or antique shop) is entered into by characters who in turn enable an episode to commence. The films resemble the style of the American EC comics (from which *Tales from the Crypt* and *The Vault of Horror* took their names) and the episodes frequently conclude with a twist, irony or deliberately gory or shocking image.

The episodic structure can also be observed in the Vincent Price 'revenge-with-a-theme' horror films of the early 70s. American International's *The Abominable Dr Phibes* (1971) and *Dr Phibes Rises Again* (1972) and Cineman's *Theatre of Blood* (1973) are films which both establish a link with the past and anticipate the future horror film. Price's theatrical performances, the sardonic humour and the interest in macabre methods of death are reminiscent of Tod Slaughter's horror films of the 30s and 40s.

Anglo-Amalgamated is most famous for its 'Sadian' trilogy – *Horrors of the Black Museum* and *Circus of Horrors*, both produced by Herman Cohen in 1959, and Michael Powell's *Peeping Tom* (1960). Their treatment as a trilogy has, however, led to the exclusion of Anglo-Amalgamated's *Cat Girl* (1957) and *Konga* (1960) and the Herman Cohen productions *Berserk!* (1967), *Trog* (1970) and *Craze* (1974). British reaction to *Peeping Tom* was hostile: Derek Hill wrote at the time that 'the only really satisfactory way to dispose of *Peeping Tom* would be to shovel it up and flush it swiftly down the nearest sewer'.[14] Michael Powell's film career, unfortunately, was never to recover.

Circus of Horrors was part of a larger group of British horror films that featured operations, surgery and biological experimentation. Derek Hill described the films as being part of a 'clinical cult', though the term 'surgical horrors' is preferable.[15] *Circus of Horrors* borrowed both Anton Diffring and his role as a crazed surgeon from Hammer's *The Man Who Could Cheat Death*, made the previous year. It told the story of a sadistic plastic surgeon who assembles around him in his circus disfigured and ugly women upon whom he operates. Dramatic deaths are arranged for those women who exhaust his interest. The idea of a circus psychopath and spectacular deaths as part of the performances was re-used by Herman Cohen for *Berserk!*

Another surgical horror film, *Corridors of Blood* (1958), made by Producers Associates, is even more sadistic than *Circus of Horrors*. A surgeon, played by Boris Karloff, who works quickly and without anaesthetic, only succeeds in horribly mutilating his patients. Filmed back-to-back with another Karloff film, *Grip of the Strangler*, the gory and, for some, unpalatable proceedings were an indication of the future form of exploitation. Titan's *Corruption* (1967) added elements of Jack the Ripper, with the plastic surgeon, played by Peter Cushing, displaying a compulsion to mutilate and decapitate women. Containing gratuitous violence, graphic surgery and nudity, it is absent from most discussions of the genre. Yet it is important. The filmmakers had previously made the more restrained costume horror *The Black Torment* (1964), but director Robert Hartford-Davis and screenwriters Derek and Donald Ford had acquired their experience making British sexploitation films.

Flesh films and the dark decades

Between 1967 and 1974, the relaxation of censorship and the import of more explicit foreign films led to an increasing reliance on nudity and graphic violence in British horror productions.[16] Individuals who had previously worked on sexploitation films, such as Pete Walker, Norman J. Warren and Antony Balch – switched to horror and brought with them a willingness to foreground sensational elements.

The film producer and distributor Tony Tenser represents the way elements of the British sex film permeated British horror. His first company, Compton-Cameo, was formed with Michael Klinger, who later produced the series of Robin Askwith 'Confessions of' sex comedies. Compton-Cameo distributed early sexploitation films and produced their own examples such as *Saturday Night Out* and *The Yellow Teddybears*, both in 1963. Their first horror film, *The Black Torment*, generated a sufficient financial return for Compton to invest in Roman Polanski's *Repulsion* (1965) and *Cul-de-Sac* (1966). In 1967, Klinger and Tenser parted and Tenser formed a new company, Tigon.

Tigon's biggest critical success was *Witchfinder General* (1968), directed by the 24-year-old Michael Reeves, who died of a sleeping pill overdose soon after finishing the film. The company attempted to exploit its rustic horror theme with the more macabre and gruesome *Blood on Satan's Claw* (1970). But Tigon seemed torn between the market demand for lurid pornographic films and its desire to make costume horrors such as *The Blood Beast Terror* (1967) and *The Creeping Flesh* (1972). In 1972 Tenser sold Tigon, 'tiring of the explicit violence he was having to inject into his films'.[17]

Reeves's first film for Tigon, *The Sorcerers* (1967), had shown two old people attempting to control, manipulate and experience the vibrant sensations of youth. Similar themes are explored in Pete Walker's nihilistic horrors in which youth's hedonism is repressed. Individuals are seized, punished and destroyed by ascetic elders apparently jealous of the sensation-based experiences of a counter-culture. Institutions such as law and order (*House of Whipcord*), the church (*House of Mortal Sin*) and the family (*Frightmare*, 1974) are exposed as corrupt, and David Sanjek points out that similar 'antiestablishment paranoid narratives' can be observed in *Scream and Scream Again* (1969) and *The Wicker Man* (1973).[18]

Hammer itself had moved from Bray to the confines of Elstree Studios in 1966. By 1968, when the company received the Queen's Award for Industry, it had already begun to decline. Required to transgress further in order to compete, Hammer produced three lesbian-vampire films, *The Vampire Lovers* (1970), *Lust for a Vampire* (1970) and *Twins of Evil* (1971), which presented scenes of soft-core pornography. Other elements were introduced, such as vampirism merging with martial arts in *The Legend of the 7 Golden Vampires* (1973) to exploit the success of recent Bruce Lee films. *Captain Kronos – Vampire Hunter* (1972) mixed vampirism with elements of the adventure film and the Western. Dracula, meanwhile, was injected with new blood to increase his commercial viability. Fresh methods by which he could be destroyed were introduced, such as lightning and hawthorn bushes, and the stories were modernised – *Dracula AD 1972* (1972), originally titled *Dracula Chelsea '72*, placed him among youth in swinging London.

The success of the American trio of demon films, *Rosemary's Baby* (1968), *The Exorcist* (1973) and *The Omen* (1976), led to a spate of films featuring satanism, demonic children and the occult. Most British imitations, such as *I Don't Want to be Born* (1975), *Satan's Slave* (1976) and *The Godsend* (1980), were small independent productions. Hammer's *To the Devil a Daughter* (1976) was a European co-production,

Individuals are seized, punished and destroyed by ascetic elders. House of Whipcord
(Pete Walker, 1974).

employing a large budget and American stars. It was poorly received and Hammer,
sharing in the general decline of the British film industry, collapsed.

The new wave of American horror films, which emerged between the late 70s and
mid-80s, overshadowed British horrors. The advances made in special effects created
a largely American sub-genre of horror films fascinated with exploding, bleeding and
mutating bodies. British attempts to imitate these films failed both commercially and
critically. *Dream Demon* (1988), *Beyond Bedlam* (1993) and *Funny Man* (1994), which
patterned themselves on the *Nightmare on Elm Street* series, appeared clumsy and
derivative.

Americanised British horror films such as *Hellraiser* (1987) and *Hardware* (1990)
foregrounded spectacles and action sequences. They reduced the narrative to a secondary role and consciously opposed the theatrical and literary tradition of British
cinema. A number of adaptations of English gothic literature have appeared but these
mainstream, big-budget films – *Dracula* (1979), *The Awakening* (1980), *The Bride*
(1985), *The Monk* (1991) and *Mary Shelley's Frankenstein* (1993) – have failed at the
box-office. *The Company of Wolves* (1984) and *Shallow Grave* (1994) were more interesting and successful. Neither film required a large budget and both drew strongly on
British culture rather than imitating the style of the American horrors.

Closure

British horror film production did not cease after the mid-70s, but many of these 'Lost
Continent' films are submerged at a depth at which critics have assumed that nothing
can exist. Andrew Higson, for instance, sees a termination of production after 1980:

232

'This was the end of the low-budget British genre film, one of those cinematic forms that proved to be no longer commercially viable.'[19] On the contrary, the dramatic growth in the home video market since the early 80s has helped support the production of a number of small-budget, exploitation, British horror films. *Screamtime* (1983), *Don't Open Till Christmas* (1984), *Rawhead Rex* (1986), *Bloody New Year* (1987), *Goodnight, God Bless* (1987), *Hand of Death Part 25* (1988), *I Bought a Vampire Motorcycle* (1989), *Living Doll* (1989), *Edge of Sanity* (1989), *Cold Light of Day* (1990), *Revenge of Billy the Kid* (1991) and *Funny Man* (1994) may have experienced limited theatrical exhibition, but it is now arguably a film's sale to a video distributor that is its main source of income.

Most of these films are part of a counter-cinema which is actively transgressive, challenging standards of cultural acceptability and definitions of good taste. Jeffrey Sconce writes that paracinema is 'a most elastic textual category' which would include 'Japanese monster movies, beach-party musicals, and just about every other historical manifestation of exploitation cinema from juvenile delinquency documentaries to soft-core pornography'.[20]

The more aggressive and excessive forms of British exploitation, in particular those films that emerged in the early 70s, have been deemed as lacking in value and consequently banished from the critical agenda. In comparison to the popularisation of Hammer, whose horror films have gradually been reclassified as worthy and acceptable, sensational films such as *The Beast is in the Cellar* (1970), *Death Line* (1972), *Horror Hospital* (1973), *The Mutations* (1973), *Scream and Die* (1973), *Vampyres* (1974), *Symptoms* (1974), *Frightmare* (1974), *The Beast Must Die* (1974), *House of Whipcord* (1974), *Expose* (1975) and *Killer's Moon* (1978) still await serious examination.

Notes

1. David Pirie, *A Heritage of Horror: The English Gothic Cinema 1946–1972* (London: Gordon Fraser, 1973), p. 9.
2. See Julian Petley, 'The Lost Continent', in Charles Barr (ed.), *All Our Yesterdays: 90 Years of British Cinema* (London: British Film Institute, 1986), pp. 98–119.
3. Rachael Low and Roger Manvell, *The History of the British Film 1896–1906* (London: Allen & Unwin, 1948), p. 44–5.
4. Denis Gifford, *A Pictorial History of Horror Movies* (London: Hamlyn, 1974), p. 204.
5. Ken Hanke, 'Tod Slaughter', *Films in Review*, vol. 8, no. 4, April 1987, p. 207.
6. *Today's Cinema*, 29 May 1940, p. 16.
7. See Robert Murphy, *Realism and Tinsel: Cinema and Society in Britain 1939–49* (London: Routledge, 1992), pp. 168–9.
8. A film production company, Hammer Productions Ltd, had been registered in November 1934. Its chairman was Will Hinds and it produced four films, *The Public Life of Henry the Ninth* (1935), *The Mystery of the Marie Celeste* (1936), *The Song of Freedom* (1936) and *Sporting Love* (1937).
9. Robert Murphy, *Sixties British Cinema* (London: British Film Institute, 1992), p. 162.
10. Derek Hill, 'The Face of Horror', *Sight and Sound*, vol. 28, no. 1, Winter 1958–59, p. 9.
11. Pirie, *A Heritage of Horror*, p. 99.
12. Ibid., p. 43.
13. Tyburn, an important British company, produced *Persecution* (1974), *The Ghoul* (1974) and *Legend of the Werewolf* (1975); the team of Robert S. Baker and Monty Berman produced *Blood of the Vampire* (1958), *Jack the Ripper* (1958) and *The Flesh and the Fiends* (1959).
14. Derek Hill, *Tribune*, 29 April 1960. Quoted by Ian Christie, 'Criticism: The Scandal of *Peeping Tom*', in Ian Christie (ed.), *Powell, Pressburger and Others* (London: British Film Institute, 1978), p. 54.
15. Hill, 'The Face of Horror', p. 9.
16. One useful text that has attempted an examination of this period is David Sanjek, 'Twilight of the Monsters: The English Horror Film 1968–1975', in Wheeler Winston Dixon (ed.), *Re-Viewing British Cinema, 1900–1992: Essays and Interviews* (New York: State University of New York Press, 1994), pp. 195–209.

17. Mike Wathen, 'For Adults Only! Home Grown British Crud, 1954–1972', in Stefan Jaworzyn (ed.), *Shock Xpress 2* (London: Titan, 1994), p. 102. See also David McGillivray, *Doing Rude Things: The History of the British Sex Film 1957–1981* (London: Sun Tavern Fields, 1992), p. 130.
18. Sanjek, 'Twilight of the Monsters', p. 197. For a discussion of Pete Walker see McGillivray, *Doing Rude Things*, pp. 58–65; and Alan Jones, 'House of the Long Shadows – The Terror Film Career of Pete Walker', *Starburst*, no. 57, May 1983, pp. 16–20.
19. Andrew Higson, 'A Diversity of Film Practices: Renewing British Cinema in the 1970s', in Bart Moore-Gilbert (ed.), *The Arts in the 1970s: Cultural Closure* (London: Routledge, 1994), p. 224.
20. Jeffrey Sconce, ' "Trashing" the Academy: Taste, Excess, and an Emerging Politics of Cinematic Style', *Screen*, vol. 39, no. 4, Winter 1995, p. 372.

Bibliography

Brown, Paul J., *All You Need is Blood: The Films of Norman J. Warren* (Upton, Cambridgeshire: Midnight Media, 1995).

Eyles, Allen, Adkinson, Robert, and Fry, Nicholas (eds.), *The House of Horror: The Complete Story of Hammer Films* (London: Lorrimer, 1984).

Gifford, Denis, *A Pictorial History of Horror Movies* (London: Hamlyn, 1974), pp. 192–210.

Gifford, Denis, *The British Film Catalogue 1895–1985* (Newton Abbot/London: David & Charles, 1986).

Hanke, Ken, 'Tod Slaughter', *Films in Review*, vol. 8, no. 4, April 1987, pp. 206–17.

Hutchings, Peter, *Hammer and Beyond: The British Horror Film* (Manchester: Manchester University Press, 1993).

Landy, Marcia, *British Genres: Cinema and Society, 1930–1960* (Princeton: Princeton University Press, 1991), pp. 388–431.

Murphy, Robert, *Sixties British Cinema* (London: British Film Institute, 1992), pp. 161–200.

Petley, Julian, 'The Lost Continent', in Charles Barr (ed.), *All Our Yesterdays: 90 Years of British Cinema* (London: British Film Institute, 1986), pp. 98–119.

Pirie, David, *A Heritage of Horror: The English Gothic Cinema 1946–1972* (London: Gordon Fraser, 1973).

Sanjek, David, 'Twilight of the Monsters: The English Horror Film 1968–1975', in Wheeler Winston Dixon (ed.), *Re-Viewing British Cinema, 1900–1992: Essays and Interviews* (New York: State University of New York Press, 1994), pp. 195–209.

23
The British Cinema: The known Cinema?

Alan Lovell

The great French film-maker, François Truffaut, once famously said that there was a certain incompatibility between the words British and Cinema. Well, bollocks to Truffaut.

Stephen Frears

In the late 1960s I presented a paper, 'The British Cinema: The Unknown Cinema', to a British Film Institute seminar group. Its starting point was a suggestion that scholarly neglect of the British cinema was so great that it was effectively an unknown cinema. A lot has changed since then. Today, British film scholars can hardly be accused of neglecting their national cinema. In the space of twenty-five years we have moved from scarcity to abundance. There are now available solid histories of the British cinema; detailed explorations of British genre film-making; analyses of important historical 'moments'; critical examinations of influential film-makers; wide-ranging anthologies; informed discussions of the economic and cultural context of current British film-making; informative accounts of Welsh and Scottish film-making.

Inevitably, there are still gaps. My priorities for further investigation would be: the contribution of cameramen, editors, sound recordists, set and costume designers, special effects – and of their union, ACT (later ACTT, now BECTU); British film acting, especially the rich late 1940s and early 50s tradition of female acting represented by Kathleen Byron, Googie Withers, Joan Greenwood, Pamela Brown, Jean Simmons and Deborah Kerr; and the historical development of British film audiences, including a detailed acount of film exhibition.[1]

Despite these gaps, increasing critical interest has meant that the British cinema now exists as an object for study. Its contours, at least, are visible. Undoubtedly this is a substantial achievement. But what are the consequences of this work? How is the British cinema now perceived?

It is certainly perceived more positively. If you engage in a substantial act of critical recovery/discovery, you need some belief in the value of what you are doing. When I wrote my paper, British film criticism showed strong signs of that built-in antipathy to 'things British' which George Orwell complained of[2] The basic perspective was Marxist, with modern capitalism portrayed as being heavily dependent on the effects of ideology for maintaining its dominance. Cinema was seen as a major ideological institution and realism the form through which it sought to 'naturalise' capitalism.

But as Raymond Williams points out in *Keywords,* realism has a variety of meanings, some of which are contradictory.[3] It's a particularly difficult term to pin down in the context of the British cinema because definitions tend to be casual and operational rather than sustained and reflective. To encourage a more sympathetic and detailed interest in realism, I'll offer a sketch of its historical development.

In what sense were the documentary film-makers of the 1930s realists? They were realists because they believed it was the purpose of art to provide a true understanding of the world. Art had therefore to be socially responsible, it had to have a *serious* relationship with society. This general belief was given a more specific character by a belief in the 'heroism of modern life', a heroism which was principally located in the activities of working people.[4] Art could best provide a 'true understanding' if it focused on those activities. Artistically, this second belief is important because it pushes artists towards naturalism, which I take to be a commitment to the importance of describing surface appearances.

The belief in social responsibility has been enormously influential on the British cinema. It is most often articulated in terms of the cinema having a serious relationship with society. As such its acceptance runs pretty much without challenge through the history of the British cinema from the 1930s to the 1990s. Its power can be seen in its acceptance by the film-makers and critics of the *Screen* generation, despite their claim to be 'anti-realists'.

The belief that cinema ought to have a serious relationship with society was one of the clearest motivations for strengthening the presence of realism in feature film-making in the early 1940s. The commitment to describing the heroism of everyday life was made easy by the war, but revealing the underlying forces of social change hardly seemed relevant when what mattered was winning the war.

In pre-war documentaries like *Coal Face* (1935), heroism was expressed through a formalist concern with visual composition and the use of sound. Increasingly, the documentarists came to think that this formalism was inappropriate. They felt it made the films remote, cutting them off from desired audiences. A preference for naturalistic description began to shape films. *Night Mail* (1936), with its awkward mixture of naturalism and formalism, marks this change very well.

A successful naturalistic representation depends heavily on the ability to convince audiences that what is being represented has been accurately observed. Because of the demands of manual work and the nature of the cinema, the documentarists found it easy to represent manual work convincingly. They didn't find it so easy to represent informal, personal relationships. *Night Mail* is again a good example. The representation is convincing when the men are deftly sorting the letters because they are sufficiently absorbed to ignore the film-makers. But when they are chatting and joking, they are clearly aware of the presence of the film-makers and their banter is awkwardly self-conscious.

Realist feature films faced similar problems. *In Which We Serve* (1942) is impressively convincing when it represents the ordinary seamen in action. When it represents their personal life, the conviction disappears. The problems are most evident in the dialogue, which is constructed around ungrammatical forms and catchphrases giving the characters a 'quaint' quality. The actors add to the problems. In speaking the dialogue, they make frequent shifts between working-class and middle-class articulations. The overall effect is to patronise characters and/or make them comic.

Whatever the problems, realism clearly was a creative force in wartime feature film-making. In particular, *In Which We Serve* and *Fires Were Started* (1943) seem to me to be films any national cinema could be proud of. But the creative impact of realism was closely tied to the war. In the post-war British cinema, its creative impact diminished.

The belief that films should have a serious relationship with society was increasingly reduced to the exploration of topical subjects from within a conventional moral/social perspective. Naturalistic description became limited to scripts based on the lives of 'ordinary' people plus location shooting.

As a strong, creative presence, realism was not revived until the second half of the 1950s, when the Free Cinema writers and film-makers (Lindsay Anderson, Karel Reisz, Tony Richardson) reaffirmed realist beliefs. In his essay 'Get Out and Push!' Anderson incisively criticised liberal critics and artists for their irresponsibility and frivolity. He also argued for the urgency and importance of providing convincing representations of working-class life.[5]

Anderson's arguments were influential and played an important part in re-energising British film-making. His work was supported by the emergence of new scriptwriters (Alan Sillitoe, David Storey, Shelagh Delaney) and new actors (Rachel Roberts, Albert Finney, Richard Harris, Rita Tushingham) who, for a variety of reasons, were better able to cope with the demands of representing working-class life.[6]

For all its energy, this 'kitchen sink' realism was a short-lived and limited phenomenon. If we date its beginning with *Room at the Top* in 1958, it was pretty much over by 1965. In fact, the dominance of realism was even more attenuated than this suggests. After *Saturday Night and Sunday Morning* (1960), Karel Reisz directed *Night Must Fall* (1964), an adaptation of a 1930s stage thriller/melodrama. He followed this with an adaptation of David Mercer's surrealistic fantasy, *Morgan, A Suitable Case for Treatment* (1965). Lindsay Anderson's first feature, *This Sporting Life* (1963), has obvious expressionist elements. Tony Richardson's first three films, *Look Back in Anger* (1959), *The Entertainer* (1960) and *A Taste of Honey* (1961), showed realist impulses, particularly through location shooting, but all three were based on successful stage plays.

However, realism was not abandoned. Rather, it changed its form. In the late 1950s Brecht's work increasingly had an impact on British artistic culture. Crucially Brecht was a realist without being a naturalist – he believed that it was art's job to provide a 'true understanding' but he didn't believe this could be achieved through a description of the surfaces of life. The encouragement his work gave to a move from naturalism was supported by the influence of Surrealism which was also prevalent at that time.[7]

Lindsay Anderson's work clearly reveals both these forces at work – Surrealism in *If . . .* (1968), Brecht in *O, Lucky Man!* (1973). The same processes can be seen at work in television drama. Dennis Potter's *Nigel Barton* plays (1965) are strongly marked by the influence of Brecht. David Mercer moved from the naturalistic drama of the *Where the Difference Begins* trilogy (1961–63) to the surrealist-influenced *A Suitable Case for Treatment* (1962).

It can be argued that realism with a strong naturalistic dimension survived in series and serial television forms, from *Z Cars* and *Coronation Street* to *Between the Lines* and *Brookside*. In terms of the British cinema, however, only one film-maker has maintained a commitment to a naturalistic realism. Ken Loach has been an isolated figure precisely because of this commitment.[8] Loach's struggle to maintain realism as a viable artistic form has been a heroic one. His project has been its modernisation. To achieve this, he used the advances in camerawork and sound made possible by the *cinéma-vérité* movement. He also addressed the problems posed by acting for naturalistic realism in a radical way, using little-known or non-professional actors and only giving them pages of the script on a day-by-day basis in order to keep them fresh. But perhaps his greatest commitment has been the reaffirmation of the critical dimension of realism by giving it a Marxist perspective.[9]

The strongest positive thrust from the new scholarship has been an attempt to validate 'anti-realist' film-making. Contemporary scholars have explored areas of film-making represented by Hammer horror films, Gainsborough melodramas and the *Carry On* comedies. Julian Petley outlines this position very clearly in his essay 'The Lost Continent':

> Of course, the vaunting and valorising of certain British films on account of their 'realism' entails as its corollary, as the other side of the coin, the dismissal and denigration of those films deemed un- or non-realist . . . These form another, repressed side of British cinema, a dark, disdained thread weaving the length and breadth of that cinema, crossing authorial and generic boundaries, sometimes almost entirely invisible, sometimes erupting explosively, always received critically with fear and disapproval.[10]

The work which has been done in this area has been invaluable in calling attention to films and film-makers which have languished for too long without proper critical attention. If the claims made for them were persuasive, then a new and interesting account of the British cinema would have been constructed. Unfortunately the case for the anti-realist genres has been much weakened by its dependence for its sense of value on a 'dilute surrealism'. Effectively, surrealism has operated as a form of easy genre valueing, privileging the 'excess' of horror films, melodrama, and low comedy as against the oppressiveness of realism.

Dilute surrealism? Dawn Archibald as the witch woman in Neil Jordan's The Company of Wolves *(1984).*

The treatment of melodrama first alerted me to the weakness of the case. I remember preparing for a course on British cinema by reading the plot summaries of all the films made in 1946–47. What appeared to be a melodramatic current stood out. Many films seemed to be marked by extravagant plotting and characterisation. The dramatic forces which shaped the dramas were emotional and large-scale, the fictional worlds marked by erotic cruelty, violence and perverse relationships. I thought I had uncovered an extraordinary and disturbing area of British cinema.

Seeing the films proved a huge disappointment. I quickly become aware of how the elements which had interested me were downplayed and made safe by the writing, camerawork, acting and direction. I shouldn't have been surprised. As contemporary scholars are fond of pointing out, British cinema has been heavily marked by qualities like good taste, restraint, reticence. Why should melodramas (or horror films or comedies) be free of these characteristics? Gavin Lambert sensibly remarked that he found it difficult to take *The Wicked Lady* (1945) seriously because its notion of wickedness was so suburban!

I think contemporary scholarship has fallen into a trap by posing excess and restraint against each other. British cinema is often most exciting when restraint and excess interact with each other. *Brief Encounter* (1945) provides a classic example of what can be achieved when the interaction takes place, and of the problems created when one dominates the other. The film is structured around Laura's monologue, which dramatically explores a struggle to use language to contain powerful, disruptive emotion. That may seem a simple operation, so it is easy to miss the art involved in making it work. Coward's language appears simple, almost banal. But, through the use of varying sentence rhythms, it supports and encourages a performer to capture both restraint and excess. Similarly the railway station evokes both the 'ordinariness' of a branch line station and the 'adventure' of train journeys.

In other parts of the film, the film-makers aren't able to create a successful interaction between restraint and excess. Alec, the other central character, is weak because his emotional situation is poorly defined. Little information is given about his relationship with his wife and he doesn't have the resources of interior monologue to express his feelings. As far as locations are concerned, David Lean and Robert Krasker are unable to generate images of either the countryside or small-town life which have the dramatic power of the railway station.

The creative interaction between excess and restraint can often be seen in films directed by Michael Powell. In *The Small Back Room* (1949) the hero, Sammy Rice, has an artificial leg that gives him great pain which he tries to ignore. As he sits in an underground train with his girlfriend Susan, the pain is so great that he stands up to be more comfortable. Standing in a crowded train, Susan and Sammy are forced to become more physically intimate. Responding to his pain, she embraces him. The scene now gains an extra charge as the experience of pain produces a physical expression of sympathy with an erotic undertone. This charged feeling is carried over by a dissolve to the entrance to Sammy's flat, where the couple's physical intimacy is heightened by big close-ups of their faces in soft light with deep shadows as they embrace and kiss. The erotic feeling heightens as Susan takes off her coat and they embrace on the sofa. The erotic intensity which has been slowly built up is dispersed by a phone call asking Sammy to investigate a bomb explosion.

I have deliberately introduced Michael Powell into my discussion because he has been a key figure in the critical attempt to construct a British anti-realist cinema. Undoubtedly the renewed interest in Powell has revealed a substantial film-maker. However, I believe his work has been treated in an uncritical way which hasn't helped

British cinema is often most exciting when restraint and excess interact. Kathleen Byron and David Farrar, The Small Back Room *(Michael Powell and Emeric Pressburger, 1949).*

the anti-realist case. For example, film criticism which has been otherwise alert to questions of national identity has been indulgent of the complacent and reactionary version of English identity dramatised in *The Life and Death of Colonel Blimp* (1943) and *A Matter of Life and Death* (1946). Film criticism which has been alert to questions of class and gender has been indulgent of the snobbery and misogyny present in *Peeping Tom*. The Powell/Pressburger partnership has never been critically scrutinised. The scripts of their films often have obvious weaknesses. Narrative development is uncertain, central characters thinly drawn, the comedy insubstantial and the whimsy irritating. Can we blame Emeric Pressburger for these faults or is the responsibility a collective one?

One of the most interesting areas of new scholarship has been the attempt to construct a case against a Thatcherite free-market approach to film production. It draws heavily on the way British films are thought to have constructed national identity, and has been put most sympathetically and intelligently by John Hill. Recognising the difficult economics of British film production, Hill argues that the case for government support has to be based on cultural grounds. It is necessary to establish that films play a valuable role in British society. For Hill, that value can be established through attention to the way films construct national identity. He points out that most of the scholarship which has explored this issue has been unsympathetic to the way films have done this. It has seen the identity they have produced as 'narrowly nationalist or else in hock to a restricted homogenising view . . .'[11] He goes on to argue that this doesn't have to be so; a positive case for the British cinema can be made on its potential for constructing national identity:

> . . . it is quite possible to conceive of a national cinema, in the sense of one which works with or addresses nationally specific materials, which is none the less critical of inherited notions of national identity, which does not assume the existence of a unique, unchanging 'national culture', and which is capable of dealing with social divisions and differences.[12]

Hill's support for this possibility depends on a rather guarded affirmation of recent independent cinema, as represented by films like *My Beautiful Laundrette* and *Passion of Remembrance*. He suggests that films like these provide a more acceptable construction of national identity. Why they should be able to do this isn't explained. I suspect that beneath a sophisticated surface, a simple critical position is evident – good films are ideologically sympathetic, bad films are ideologically unsympathetic. Since good (ideologically sympathetic) films can't be made within a market framework, there needs to be government intervention. I don't think this is a strong case either intellectually or politically.

The problems generated by this kind of discussion and possible ways out of them have been illuminated by a critical exchange in *Sight and Sound*. In a review of *Braveheart*, Colin McArthur attacked the film for its reactionary account of Scottish national identity. The attack was based on an intelligently detailed account of the way 'regressive discourses' shaped the film. For McArthur these discourses are of an ideological kind – he talks about the film's 'ideological project' and in a reply to critics says that *Braveheart* has to deliver 'an ideological framework conducive to a mass audience'. He doesn't try to explain *Braveheart*'s success with audiences.

McArthur's critics, Sheldon Hall and Martin Price, both point out that a proper understanding of the relationship between *Braveheart* and its audiences can be better achieved through a discussion of artistic issues like genre and identification rather than political ones of national identity.[13] I am sympathetic to their position because I think they open up ways of dealing with a film's popularity with audiences.

Colin McArthur's and John Hill's position is fundamentally a realist one. Films should be judged by the way they provide 'true understanding' – for Hill, an expanded version of Britishness through a sensitivity to social difference; for McArthur, a historically accurate account of Scottish history. I don't think a satisfactory account of how films interact with their audiences can be developed from such an assumption. It's much too limiting and blocks off a proper discussion of entertainment in the cinema.[14]

This persistent linking of British film production with the question of national identity is odd. It has run through discussion of the British cinema for much of its history. That such a link exists is, at one level, a truism – any activity engaged in by British citizens can be seen as a way of constructing national identity. In discussions of British cinema it is taken for granted both that the link exists and that it is a politically important one – it often seems as if the cinema is the *key* tool for the construction of British national identity. At present, the belief in the importance of the link seems to depend heavily on the unacknowledged acceptance of the old view of the cinema as having magical powers of expression.

A few years ago, a teaching experience encouraged me to reflect on my attitudes to the British cinema. I saw *Saturday Night and Sunday Morning* along with *Rebel without a Cause* (1955) and *Breathless* (1959) as part of a day school for students. Most of those students hadn't been born when any of the films were made and knew little about them. *Saturday Night and Sunday Morning* was the one they most enjoyed. It had a simplicity and directness which was very attractive. In comparison *Rebel without a Cause* seemed sentimental and overwrought and *Breathless* clever-clever.

The students' response made me think how much British cinema had been underrated. My view was strengthened by Stephen Frears' robust affirmation of British cinema in his television documentary 'Typically British'.[15]

Frears' enthusiasm is surely justified. At the very least, a cinema which can produce films as varied as *The 39 Steps, Fires were Started, Black Narcissus, Henry V, The Ladykillers, Saturday Night and Sunday Morning, If . . ., Kes, Withnail and I, Distant Voices, Still Lives* and *Butterfly Kiss* deserves celebration. Arguments can be made that comparable cinemas like the French or Italian have, over their whole history, been superior to the British cinema but the differences are only relative ones. British cinema isn't a special case. There isn't some fundamental British cinematic deficiency which needs to be accounted for. Bollocks to Truffaut indeed!

Notes

1. A start has been made with Duncan Petrie's *The British Cinematographer* (London: British Film Institute, 1995) and the BECTU Oral History Project.
2. See, for example, Victor Perkins 'The British Cinema', *Movie*, no. 1, 1962; Tom Nairn, 'Deceased at the Paramount Cinema Piccadilly – The British Cinema', *Cinema* 3, June 1969; Thomas Elsaesser, 'Between Style and Ideology', *Monogram* 3, 1972.
3. Raymond Williams, *Keywords* (London: Flamingo, 1976), pp. 257–62. See also Eric Auerbach's *Mimesis* (Princeton, 1953).
4. The phrase is Baudelaire's but I've taken it from Linda Nochlin's book *Realism* (Harmondsworth: Penguin, 1971).
5. 'Get Out and Push!' was published in the Angry Young Man anthology *Declaration*, (ed.) Tom Maschler (London: Macgibbon & Kee, 1957).
6. A comparison between Googie Withers in *It Always Rains on Sunday* and Rachel Roberts in *This Sporting Life* is instructive. Both actresses give their characters a hard edge by limiting their expressiveness. The combination of the characters' hardness and the actresses's erotic physical presence makes the characters vivid and distinctive. In contrast to Rachel Roberts, Googie Withers' performance is partially undermined by her delivery of dialogue, which consistently has middle-class articulations.
7. Surrealism influenced British pop music of the period, especially in the work of the Beatles. Its principal conduit was the art schools. David Mercer was originally an art student.
8. Karl Francis, although he has worked primarily in the context of Welsh television, has shown similar ambitions.
9. It is a mark of the political limitations of much contemporary film scholarship that a book about the contemporary British cinema – *British Cinema and Thatcherism: Fires Were Started* (UCL Press, 1993) – has substantial discussions of Peter Greenaway's work and none of Ken Loach's.
10. Julian Petley, 'The Lost Continent', in Charles Barr (ed.), *All Our Yesterdays* (London: British Film Institute, 1986).
11. John Hill, 'The Issue of National Cinema and British Film Production', in Duncan Petrie (ed.) *New Questions of British Cinema* (London: British Film Institute, 1992) p. 15.
12. ibid., p. 16.
13. Colin McArthur's review of *Braveheart* is in *Sight and Sound*, September 1995. Sheldon Hall's letter is in *Sight and Sound*, October 1995. Martin Price's letter with Colin McArthur's reply to both critics is in *Sight and Sound*, February 1996.
14. Film criticism has relied for too long on Richard Dyer's discussion of the issue in 'Entertainment

and Utopia', in Bill Nichols (ed.), *Movies and Methods* (California, 1985). This was a brave attempt but its flaws are now obvious, particularly its failure to confront the art/entertainment distinction.

15. 'Typically British' (BFI TV) was first broadcast on Channel 4 on 2 September 1995. Frears could not have made his case without the benefit of our new knowledge of the British cinema. It is no accident that one of the writers of the programme was Charles Barr, who has probably done most to develop the new study of British cinema.

Bibliography

Armes, Roy, *A Critical History of the British Cinema* (London: Secker and Warburg, 1978).

Barr, Charles, *Ealing Studios* (London: David & Charles, 1977).

Barr, Charles (ed.), *All Our Yesterdays* (London: British Film Institute, 1986).

Berry, David, *Wales and Cinema* (Cardiff: University of Wales, 1994).

Christie, Ian, *Arrows of Desire: The Films of Michael Powell and Emeric Pressburger* (London: Waterstone, 1985).

Curran, James, and Porter, Vincent (eds.), *British Cinema History* (London: Weidenfeld and Nicholson, 1983).

Harper, Sue, *Picturing the Past* (London: British Film Institute, 1994).

Higson, Andrew, *Waving the Flag* (Oxford: Clarendon Press, 1995).

Hill, John, *Sex, Class and Realism* (London: British Film Institute, 1986).

Kemp, Philip, *Alexander Mackendrick* (London: Methuen, 1991).

Landy, Marcia, *British Genres: Cinema and Society 1930–1960* (New Jersey: Princeton University Press, 1991).

McArthur, Colin (ed.), *Scotch Reels: Scotland in Cinema and Television* (London: British Film Institute, 1982).

Murphy, Robert, *Realism and Tinsel: Cinema and Society in Britain 1939–49* (London: Routledge, 1989).

Petrie, Duncan (ed.), *New Questions of British Cinema* (London: British Film Institute, 1992).

Richards, Jeffrey, *The Age of the Dream Palace: Cinema and Society in Britain 1930–39* (London: Routledge, 1984).

Ryall, Tom, *Alfred Hitchcock and the British Cinema* (London: Croom Helm, 1986).

24
British Cinema as National Cinema: Production, Audience and Representation

John Hill

Following the Oscar-winning success of *Chariots of Fire* (1981) on 23 March 1982, the film was re-released and showed successfully across Britain in the weeks which followed. On 2 April, the Argentinians invaded the Falklands/Malvinas and, three days later, the Thatcher government despatched a naval task force from Portsmouth which successfully retook the islands in June. In a sense, the coincidence of Oscar-winning success in Los Angeles and subsequent military victory in the Falklands seemed to link the two events, and the idea of a national resurgence in both cinema ('the British are coming') and national life became intertwined. Indeed, Hugo Young reports that David Puttnam, the producer of *Chariots of Fire*, was a subsequent guest of the Prime Minister's at Chequers and that there was 'much talk in the Thatcher circle about the desirability of something similar being put on to celluloid to celebrate the Falklands victory'.[1]

There are, however, two factors which complicate this story. Despite its reputation, *Chariots of Fire* is a more complex work than is commonly suggested. Indeed, a film which is reputedly so nationalist is surprisingly conscious of the complexities of national allegiance, focusing as it does on the running careers of two 'outsiders': Harold Abrahams, a Jew of Lithuanian background, and Eric Liddell, a Scotsman born in China. If *Chariots of Fire* did become identified with renascent national sentiment, then this was probably not so much the result of the ideological outlook which the film itself manifests as of the moment at which its success was achieved. The other complicating factor is that when the film was re-released it was as a part of a double bill with *Gregory's Girl* (1980). While this double bill was undoubtedly intended to showcase the range of new British cinema, there is also something a touch subversive in the way these films were coupled. For while both are British, they also represent rather different kinds of British cinema.

Chariots of Fire, at a cost of £3 million, was a comparatively expensive film for British cinema in 1980. And although it was strongly identified with 'Britishness' it was actually funded from foreign sources, including Hollywood. *Gregory's Girl*, by contrast, cost only about £200,000 and was financed from domestic sources, including the National Film Finance Corporation and Scottish Television. A clear contrast in formal approach is also apparent. Despite some play with temporal relations, *Chariots of Fire* employs a relatively straightforward narrative structure, organised around goal-oriented action and positive heroes. *Gregory's Girl* opts for a much looser, more episodic form in which surface realism, comedy and domesticated surrealism are combined in a way which successfully fuses British comic traditions with a modernist sensibility. These differences also extend to content. While *Chariots of Fire* is focused on the past, *Gregory's Girl* is resolutely of the present. The version of the past which *Chariots of Fire* constructs, moreover, is strongly identified with the English upper classes and male achievement, while *Gregory's Girl* is set amongst the suburban middle and working classes and gently subverts conventional stereotypes of male and female roles. And if both films are 'British', *Chariots* is very much an 'English' film whereas *Gregory's Girl* is clearly 'Scottish'.

While both films are, at least partly, set in Scotland, there is a significant difference between the representations of Scotland which they provide. *Chariots of Fire* tends to look at Scotland from the outside (or rather from the metropolitan English centre), associating it with the 'natural' and the 'primitive'. *Gregory's Girl*, on the other hand, uses the 'new town' of Cumbernauld to avoid the conventional signifiers of 'Scottishness' and, in doing so, suggest an altogether more complex sense of contemporary Scottish identity. This, in turn, has links to what might be characterised as the films' different modes of cultural address. *Chariots*, with its enthusiasm for the past and links with conventional notions of English 'national heritage', offers an image of Britain which generally conforms to the expectations of an international, and especially American, audience. *Gregory's Girl* is a much more obviously local and idiomatic film. It too has an international appeal, but for an audience more likely to be European than American. And while *Chariots of Fire* is conventionally taken to be the landmark in the revival of British cinema, it may in fact be *Gregory's Girl* which

Chariots of Fire (Hugh Hudson, 1981). Focused on the past and strongly identified with the English upper classes.

provided the more reliable indicator of the way in which British film-making was developing.

Production

In the 1980s British cinema returned to the position in which it found itself in the 1920s when the government first introduced a quota for British films. In 1925 some 10 per cent of films exhibited in British cinemas were British; by 1926 this had dropped to 5 per cent.[2] The bulk of films shown were, of course, from the US. Following the abolition of the quota in 1983, the percentage of British films on British screens dwindled to similar proportions. Thus in 1992 the US had a 92.5 per cent share of the British exhibition market while British films accounted for only 4 per cent.[3]

The responses to US domination which have been available to the production sector of the British film industry in the 1980s and 1990s are, however, different from those of the 1920s. In his essay on the conceptualisation of national cinemas, Stephen Crofts identifies a number of strategies available to national cinema production. For the British cinema the most important are what he describes as the imitation of Hollywood, competition with Hollywood in domestic markets, and differentiation from Hollywood.[4] The imitation of Hollywood involves the attempt to beat Hollywood at its own game, a strategy which has been tried at various junctures in the history of British cinema: by Alexander Korda in the 1930s, by Rank in the 1940s, by EMI in the 1970s, and by Goldcrest in the 1980s. Given the competitive advantage which Hollywood enjoys over other national industries by virtue of its scale of production, size of domestic market and international distribution and exhibition network (amongst other factors), this has proved an economically unviable strategy and, despite some success with individual films, all such attempts have resulted in financial disaster. It is therefore the second, competitive strategy which has constituted the mainstay of British cinema.

As a result of the quota (and, later, some additional forms of state support), the existence of a commercial British cinema which did not compete with Hollywood internationally but only in the domestic market proved possible from the 1930s to – just about – the 1970s. The basis of this cinema, however, was a size of audience sufficient to sustain a domestic film industry. As cinema audiences began to decline, especially from the 1950s, the commercial viability of a cinema aimed primarily at British audiences came under threat. As a result, regular British film production (characteristically popular genre film-making) aimed at the domestic market came to a virtual halt after the 1970s when Hammer horror, the *Carry Ons* and the *Confession* films all ceased to be produced. While it had previously been possible for British films to recoup their costs on the home market, this became an exception from the 1970s onwards. Only a minority of British films achieved a domestic gross of over £1 million during the 1980s, and even an apparently popular success such as *Buster*, which grossed £3.7 million in 1988, failed to recover its production cost of £3.2 million from British box-office revenues (given that only a fraction of these actually returns to the producer).

In consequence, the place of British cinema within the international film economy has had to change. Writing in 1969, Alan Lovell argued that, unlike its European counterparts, the British cinema had failed to develop an art cinema (or at any rate that the documentary film had served in its place).[5] During the 1980s, however, it was art cinema which was to become the predominant model of British film-making. The category of 'art cinema' is not, of course, a precise one and it is used here in a relatively generous sense. David Bordwell, for example, has attempted to define 'art cinema' as a distinctive 'mode of film practice' characterised by realism, authorial expressivity and ambiguity.[6] His definition, however, is too tied to the 1960s and fails to do justice to the range of textual strategies employed by art cinema in the 1980s and 1990s. Thus, in the case of Britain, the category of art cinema may be seen to include not only the 'realism' of Ken Loach and Mike Leigh and the postmodern aesthetic experiments of Derek Jarman and Peter Greenaway, but also the aesthetically conservative 'heritage' cinema of Merchant-Ivory. In this last case, the 'art' of 'art cinema' derives not so much from the authorial presence of the director or the distance from classical narrational and stylistic techniques which such films display, as from the cachet of 'high art' which such films borrow from literary or theatrical sources.

For Crofts, art cinema is the prime example of a national cinema avoiding direct competition with Hollywood by targeting a distinct market sector. This model, he argues, aims 'to differentiate itself textually from Hollywood, to assert explicitly or implicitly an indigenous product, and to reach domestic and export markets through those specialist distribution channels and exhibition venues usually called arthouse'.[7] In this respect, the adoption of aesthetic strategies and cultural referents different from Hollywood also involves a certain foregrounding of 'national' credentials. The oft-noted irony of this, however, is that art cinema then achieves much of its status as national cinema by circulating internationally rather than nationally. While this means that art cinema (as in the case of Greenaway) may be as economically viable as ostensibly more commercial projects aimed at the 'popular' audience, it is also the case that successful British films have often done better outside Britain than within. A notorious example of this was Ken Loach's *Riff-Raff* which, at the time it won the European Film Award for Best Film in 1991, had been seen by more people in France than in the UK. Even in the case of the heritage film, it is international audiences, especially American, which have become a key source of revenues as well as prestige. As a result, it has become an attractive option to open such films in the United States before a release in Britain, as was the case, for example, with both *The Madness of King George* (1995) and *Sense and Sensibility* (1995).

In both these cases – the *cinéma d'auteur* which circulates in Europe and the heritage film which appeals to the US – it can be argued that the changed economic circumstances of the British film industry have led to a certain decline of 'national' cinema, in so far as the national address which earlier commercial British cinema appeared to have is no longer so evident. In this respect, much of the lamenting of the current state of the British film industry registers a sense of loss of the connection which it is assumed the British cinema once had with a national popular audience. There is a further twist to this argument, however. For, if the decline in domestic cinema audiences has made British film production increasingly dependent upon international revenues, it has also increased its reliance on television for revenues and production finance as well. The increasing inter-relationship between film and television which has resulted has had consequences for how film is consumed, and for the way it may be judged to be 'national'.

Audience

The changing character of British cinema in the 1980s may be explained, then, in terms of the new production strategies which emerged in the wake of declining cinema audiences. In 1946, annual cinema admissions reached an all-time high of 1,635 million, but then fell steadily until 1984, when they plummeted to 58 million. There has been a subsequent increase – admissions reached over 123 million in 1994, but this

Gregory's Girl *(Bill Forsyth, 1980). Gently subverting stereotypes of male and female roles.*

is still less than for any year before 1974. It is these figures which provide the backdrop to perceptions of cinema's declining national role. For if the British cinema of the Second World War is still regarded as a watershed in national cinema, it is not only as a result of the films which were then made but because of the size of the cinema audience which attended them. In 1940, admissions topped 1,000 million for the first time when, partly because of a lack of alternatives, films were the most popular form of entertainment. In this respect, wartime cinema is regarded as pre-eminently 'national', because of the size and range of its audience.

Even at its peak, however, the cinema audience was never fully representative of the nation. A survey of the British cinema audience in 1943, for example, revealed that 30 per cent of the population didn't go to the cinema at all, and that certain social groups were more likely to attend the cinema than others.[8] Women went to the cinema more than men, the manual working class and lower-middle class went more frequently than managerial and professional groups, town-dwellers more than country-dwellers. Most strikingly of all, the cinema audience was characteristically made up of the young rather than the old: the under-45s accounted for 85 per cent of the cinema audience but only 68 per cent of the overall population. Cinemagoing declined significantly with age, and 60 per cent of the over-65s are reported as never going to the cinema at all. The 'national' audience for British films, even during the 'golden age' of British cinema, was neither as homogeneous nor as socially representative of the nation as is sometimes assumed.

Audience factors are also relevant when considering the subsequent decline of the cinema. If the cinema audience has become a smaller proportion of the overall population and cinemagoing no longer occupies the central place in leisure activities which it once did, the social character of the audience and its cinema-watching habits have also changed.[9] Cinemagoing has become even more heavily concentrated amongst the young, particularly the 15–34 age group, which accounted for 78 per cent of cinema attendances in 1990 (but represented only 37 per cent of the population). By comparison, only 11 per cent of the over-45s attended the cinema despite representing 46 per cent of the population. The class basis of cinemagoing has also altered. Cinemagoing is no longer a predominantly working-class activity, and in 1990 social classes ABC1 accounted for 59 per cent of cinemagoers (while representing 42 per cent of the population).[10] One explanation for this is the growth of multiplexes, which since 1985 have been responsible for reviving the cinemagoing habit, especially amongst car-owners.[11] Multiplexes have also made the cinema more attractive to women, who, following a decline in attendance in the 1950s, have accounted for about 50 per cent of the cinema audience in the 1990s. From the 1950s onwards, the working-class cinema audience has been in decline and has been replaced by an increasingly young and more affluent audience; this reflects more general trends in cinemagoing which have seen an increase in the importance of the 15–24 age group (estimated to be as much as 80 per cent of the worldwide cinema audience for English-language films).[12] This audience demography is clearly significant for national cinema: what is most popular at the cinemas is not necessarily popular with a fully representative section of the 'nation', but only with a relatively narrow segment of it.

A further complication is that, while these trends are fairly clear with regard to cinemagoing, cinemas themselves are no longer the primary site for viewing films. Despite the global decline in cinema attendances, Douglas Gomery has argued that watching films is more popular than ever.[13] People may no longer watch films in the cinemas but they do watch in increasing numbers on television and video, especially in the UK where TV and video penetration is very high by world standards. Some comparisons are appropriate. In 1994, for example, total cinema admissions in Britain were 123 million; in the same year, video rentals (which are dominated by feature films) amounted to 194 million (a considerable drop, in fact, from 328 million the previous year) and there were 66 million video retail transactions.[14] In the case of television, the contrast is even more striking. There are considerably more films on TV than in the cinemas: in 1994, 299 features were released in UK cinemas, of which 35 were 'wholly' British,[15] but in the same year 1,910 films were screened on terrestrial TV, of which 413 were British productions.[16] Films on TV are also watched by considerably more people. In 1994 the viewing figures for the top ten films on TV alone matched the total audience for all 299 films shown in the cinemas. This also means that individual films, including British films, are seen by significantly more people on television than in the cinemas. The most popular 'wholly' British film of 1992, *Peter's Friends*, was seen by approximately four times as many people when it was shown on television in 1994 than in the cinema.[17] A commercially unsuccessful film such as *Waterland* was seen by nearly 34 times as many people when it was shown on television in 1994; if its television viewing audience of 3.3 million had been converted into cinema attendances, this would have put it in the box-office top ten for 1992.

Clearly, people watch more films on television and video than they do in the cinema; and the television/video audience is more representative of the 'nation' as a whole. The group which is over-represented in the cinemas – the 16–24 year-olds – is under-represented in the television audience, and those groups which are infrequent cinemagoers – the over-45s, social groups DE, country-dwellers – are much more likely to see films on TV.[18] While there are no precise figures, it does seem that many contemporary British films which are not regarded as especially 'popular' are nonetheless seen on television by as many people as 'popular' British films of the past. To put it provocatively, it may be that a British cinema which is generally regarded as being in decline is nonetheless producing films which are often seen by as many, and sometimes more, people as films made during the 'golden age' of British cinema.

There are provisos, of course. As has often been argued, the cinema experience and the television viewing experience are dissimilar: watching films on TV or video is characteristically less concentrated than in the cinema.[19] But it is also worth noting how habitual cinemagoing was in its heyday. Browning and Sorrell report that in 1946 nearly three-quarters of those who went to the cinema more than once a month did so whatever films were being shown and without choosing between cinemas.[20] Cinemagoing was only exceptionally an 'event' and, in a number of respects, television has taken over the cinema's former function of catering to the 'regular cinemagoer'. While this is true of most television scheduling of films, however, television can also use film as an 'event', breaking up the televisual flow and offering a 'special' experience. This commonly happens with the first screening of a Hollywood blockbuster but would also be true, for example, of Channel 4's heavily trailered first screening of *Four Weddings and a Funeral* in 1996, which attracted an audience of 12.38 million.[21]

Although films can achieve very high audience figures on television, other forms of drama (especially serial drama) achieve even higher figures. In this respect, the national reach of film is generally less than that of television drama. Indeed, John Caughie has expressed an anxiety that the growth in involvement of television in film production has led to an increased investment in drama on film aimed at the international market at the expense of more local forms of television drama. He contrasts the work of Ken Loach in the 1960s and the 1990s. '*Ladybird, Ladybird*,' he argues, 'circulates within an aesthetic and a cultural sphere which is given cultural prestige (and an economic viability) by international critics' awards, whereas *Cathy Come Home* circulated as a national event and functioned as documentary evidence within the political sphere.'[22] The point is well made but it sets up too stark an opposition. For if television drama circulates less as a 'national event' in the 1990s than it did in the 1960s, this is not simply the consequence of television involvement in cinema. It has more to do with the transformations which broadcasting as a whole has undergone, especially the increase in channels (both terrestrial and non-terrestrial), the rise of video (and its opportunities for alternative viewing and time-shifting), and the fragmentation of the national audience which has resulted. If the capacity of both television drama and film to function as a national event has lessened, this is partly because the national audience for television does not exist in the same way as it did in the 1960s and partly because neither individual television programmes nor films can lay claim to the same cultural dominance within the entertainment sphere that they once could. The national audience is in fact a series of audiences which are often addressed in different ways. At the same time, the representations which British cinema then makes available to them have themselves become much more complex and varied.

Representation

There is a scene in David Hare's *Strapless* (1988) which is suggestive in this regard. A doctor, working for the NHS, addresses a group of assembled hospital workers and speaks up on behalf of 'English values'. It is a scene with loose echoes of wartime movies such as *In Which We Serve* (1942) or *Henry V* (1944) in which morale-boosting speeches upholding traditional English virtues are delivered to an assembled group (in these instances, sailors and soldiers). There are, however, significant differences. In *Strapless*, the speech is delivered not by an Englishman but by an American woman, and the group she speaks to is not the homogeneous white male group of the earlier films but one which is differentiated by gender and ethnicity. By having an American defend the 'idea of Englishness', the film acknowledges the difficulty which such a speech presents for a contemporary British film and attempts to sidestep the irony which would, almost inevitably, have had to accompany its delivery by an English character (even so, there is still a hint of pastiche in the way the scene is realised). The difficulty of speaking for England is indicated, however, not only by the nationality of the speaker, but by the composition of the group she is addressing. Unlike in the earlier films, there is no confident assumption of who represents 'Englishness'.

Important works on British cinema by Jeffrey Richards on the 1930s, Charles Barr on Ealing and Raymond Durgnat on the post-war period have all uncovered in British films an effort to tell stories which invite audiences to interpret them in terms of ideas about the 'nation' and 'national identity'.[23] More recently, Andrew Higson has identified what he regards as a characteristic way of 'imagining the nation' as a 'knowable, organic community' in British films, which he links to a typically 'national style' characterised by episodic narratives involving multiple characters, a distanced observational viewpoint and a non-narrative use of space.[24] Clearly, there is a danger that such arguments underestimate the variety of British cinema and are too ready to make pronouncements about all British cinema on the basis of a selective sample of films (Higson's book deals with only five films in any detail). Nonetheless, it is equally evident that, if not all British cinema, then at least significant strands (such as wartime cinema and Ealing comedies) have evolved an aesthetic and a way of telling stories which clearly display a national-allegorical import.[25]

If this is so, then it is also apparent that the certainties concerning the nation upon which such films relied have, since the 1960s, increasingly dissolved. The strategy of national allegory, in this respect, has not so much been abandoned as refashioned to express a new sense of difference and even conflict. Films such as *My Beautiful Laundrette* (1987) and *Sammy and Rosie Get Laid* (1988) continue to employ, with a few postmodern embellishments, the stylistic features of British national cinema which Higson identifies, clearly inviting the individual stories of its characters to be read in terms of an 'allegory' of the 'state of the nation'. They do so, however, to project a much more fluid, hybrid and plural sense of 'Britishness' than was seen in earlier British cinema. Such films are responding to the more complex sense of national identity which has been characteristic of modern Britain. In this respect, the interests of the art film (which are often individual and subjective) may be seen to have merged with the preoccupations of public service television (which are characteristically more social and 'national' in scope). As a result, the alliance between film and television, which Caughie sees as lessening the local dimensions of *television*, may also be read as a strengthening of the local aspects of *cinema*.

Since the 1980s, it can be argued that not only has British cinema articulated a much more inclusive sense of Englishness than previously but that it has also accorded a much greater recognition to the differing nationalities and identities within Britain (including, for example, the emergence of a distinctive black British cinema). In this respect, British national cinema now clearly implies Scottish and Welsh cinema as well as just English cinema. Indeed, two of the most successful British films of the mid-1990s – *Shallow Grave* (1994) and *Trainspotting* (1995) – were very clearly Scottish. This has implications, not only for the inclusiveness of the representations of Britain which British cinema provides but also, as the example of *Gregory's Girl* indicates, for the way in which issues of national identity are then addressed.

Graeme Turner, writing of Australian cinema in the 1990s, has noted the suspicion which often accompanies discussion of both the nation and national cinema because of the socially conservative versions of national identity which these tend to imply. He argues that the post-colonial status of Australia means that its discourses of the nation are much less settled, and that it is possible for Australian films to provide 'a critical ... body of representations within mainstream Western cinema'.[26] In the same way, the peculiar historical circumstances of Scotland and Wales – which may have gained economically from the British colonial enterprise but which, culturally, encountered subordination – provide an opening for a more complex negotiation of the discourses around the 'nation' than English/British cinema has traditionally provided. *Trainspotting* is an interesting example in this regard. One of the most commercially successful British films of 1996, it was fully financed by the public service broadcaster Channel 4, and combines an interest in social issues (drug-taking, AIDS, poverty) with a determinedly self-conscious aesthetic style reminiscent of the French and British 'new waves'. In experimenting with cinematic style, however, it also plays with the inherited imagery of England and Scotland. Thus when the film's main character, Mark Renton (Ewan McGregor), arrives in London, the film cheerfully invokes the most clichéd images of London in an ironic inversion of the touristic imagery which commonly accompanies the arrival of an English character in Scotland.[27] In a similarly iconoclastic manner, the film escorts its main characters to the Scottish countryside, not to invoke the 'romantic' beauty of the Scottish landscape but to provide Renton with the occasion for a swingeing attack on 'being Scottish' ('We're the lowest of the fucking low... It's a shite state of affairs and all the fresh air in the world will not make any fucking difference'). So while *Trainspotting* may speak with a voice that is decidedly Scottish, it also does so in a way which avoids simple pieties concerning Scottish, or 'British', identity.

Conclusion

I have argued elsewhere that the idea of British national cinema has often been linked, virtually by definition, to discourses of nationalism and myths of national unity.[28] However, this formulation of a national cinema underestimates the possibilities for a national cinema to re-imagine the nation, or rather nations within Britain, and also to address the specificities of a national culture in a way which does not presume a homogeneous or 'pure' national identity. Indeed, as Paul Willemen has argued, the national cinema which genuinely addresses national specificity will actually be at odds with the 'homogenising project' of nationalism in so far as this entails a critical engagement with 'the complex, multidimensional and multidirectional tensions that characterise and shape a social formation's cultural configurations'.[29] In a sense, this is one of the apparent paradoxes that this essay has been addressing: that while British cinema may depend upon international finance and audiences for its viability, this may actually strengthen its ability to probe national questions; that while cinema has apparently lost its 'national' audience in the cinemas, it may have gained a more fully 'national' audience via television; and that while the British cinema may no longer assert the myths of 'nation' with its earlier confidence, it may nonetheless be a cinema which is more fully representative of national complexities than ever before.

Notes

1. Hugo Young, *One of Us* (London: Pan, 1990), p. 277.
2. *Cinematograph Films Act, 1927: Report of a Committee Appointed by the Board of Trade* (London: HMSO, 1936), p. 5.
3. *Screen Digest*, December 1993, p. 280.
4. Stephen Crofts 'Reconceptualizing National Cinema/s', *Quarterly Review of Film and Video*, vol. 14, no. 3, 1993, p. 50.
5. Alan Lovell, *The British Cinema: The Unknown Cinema*, BFI mimeo, 1969, p. 2.
6. David Bordwell, 'The Art Cinema as a Mode of Film Practice', *Film Criticism*, vol. 4, no. 1, Fall 1979.
7. Crofts, 'Reconceptualizing National Cinema/s', p. 51.
8. Louis Moss and Kathleen Box, *The Cinema Audience: An Inquiry made by the Wartime Social Survey for the Ministry of Information* (London: Ministry of Information, 1943).
9. In 'Cinemas and Cinema-Going in Great Britain', *Journal of the Royal Statistical Society*, vol. CXVII no. 11, 1954, p. 135, Browning and Sorrell indicate that in the years 1950–52 the cinema accounted for over 83 per cent of all taxable admissions on entertainment (including theatre, sport and other activities). In 1992, by comparison, spending on cinema admissions accounted for less than 6 per cent of household expenditure on entertainment. See Monopolies and Mergers Commission, *Films: A report on the supply of films for exhibition in cinemas in the UK* (London: HMSO, 1994), p. 90.
10. Karsten-Peter Grummitt, *Cinemagoing 4* (Leicester: Dodona Research, 1995), p. 1.
11. Between 1985, when the first multiplex was opened, and 1994 the number of multiplexes grew to 71 sites (incorporating 638 screens). By the end of 1993, about 40 per cent of all visits to the cinema were to multiplexes. See Monopolies and Mergers Commission, *Films: A report on the supply of films for exhibition in cinemas in the UK*, p. 96.
12. See the figures used by media consultant James Lee in *Movie Makars: Drama for Film and Television* (Glasgow: Scottish Film Council, 1993), p. 44.
13. Douglas Gomery, *Shared Pleasures: A History of Movie Presentation* (London: British Film Institute, 1992), p. 276.
14. These figures are taken from the *BFI Film and Television Handbook 1996* (London: British Film Institute, 1995), p. 34 and p. 47.
15. *Screen Finance*, 11 January 1995, p. 13. *Screen Finance* defines films as 'wholly' British when they were made solely by British production companies.
16. *Screen Finance*, 8 February 1995, p. 12.
17. Figures for box-office revenue come from *Screen Finance*, 24 February 1993, p. 9. I have estimated admissions for individual films by dividing 1992 box-office revenues by the average realised seat prices for that year, as identified in Monopolies and Mergers Commission, *Films: A report on the supply of films for exhibition in cinemas in the UK*, p. 102. Television viewing figures may be found in *BFI Film and Television Handbook 1996*, p. 57.
18. Patrick Barwise and Andrew Ehrenberg, *Television and Its Audience* (London: Sage, 1988), p. 29. The renting and buying of pre-recorded videos is also highest among the 'lower' social grades, especially the C2s. See BMRB International Report: CAVIAR 10, vol.3, *Report of Findings* (February 1993), p. 21.
19. As in the cinema the bulk of films watched by British audiences on television and video are American. But it is worth noting that television not only shows more British films than the cinemas but that, as the films it shows are from different periods, the circulation of British cinema for the modern audience also involves a sense of both its past and present. Thus in 1995, to take just one example, almost as many people watched Ken Loach's *Kes* (1969) as the same director's *Raining Stones* (1993). See *Screen Finance*, 24 January 1996, pp. 16–17.
20. 'Cinemas and Cinema-Going in Great Britain', p. 146.
21. These viewing figures made *Four Weddings and a Funeral* Channel 4's third most-watched broadcast ever. See *Broadcast*, 8 December 1995, p. 24.
22. John Caughie, 'The Logic of Convergence', in Hill and McLoone (eds.), *Big Picture, Small Screen* (Luton: John Libby University of Luton Press, 1996), p. 219.
23. See Jeffrey Richards, *The Age of the Dream Palace: Cinema and Society 1930–1939* (London: Routledge and Kegan Paul, 1984); Charles Barr, *Ealing Studios* (London: Cameron and Tayleur, 1977); and Raymond Durgnat, *A Mirror for England* (London: Faber and Faber, 1970).
24. Andrew Higson, *Waving the Flag: Constructing a National Cinema in Britain* (Oxford: Oxford University Press, 1995).
25. The idea of 'national allegory' has been employed, somewhat controversially, by Fredric Jameson in relation to 'third world' literature. See 'Third-World Literature in the Era of Multinational Capitalism', *Social Text*, 15, Fall 1986.
26. Graeme Turner, 'The End of the National Project? Australian Cinema in the 1990s', in Wimal

Dissanayake (ed.), *Colonialism and Nationalism in Asian Cinema* (Bloomington, Indiana University Press, 1994), p. 203.

27. The script refers to this interlude as a 'contemporary retake of all those "Swinging London" montages'. See John Hodge, *Trainspotting and Shallow Grave* (London: Faber and Faber, 1996), p. 76.

28. John Hill, 'The Issue of National Cinema and British Film Production', in Duncan Petrie (ed.), *New Questions of British Cinema* (London: British Film Institute, 1992).

29. Paul Willemen, 'The National', in *Looks and Frictions: Essays in Cultural Studies and Film Theory* (London: British Film Institute, 1994), p. 212.

Bibliography

Crofts, Stephen, 'Reconceptualizing National Cinema/s', *Quarterly Review of Film and Video*, vol. 14, no. 3, 1993.

Higson, Andrew, 'The Concept of National Cinema', *Screen*, vol. 30, no. 4, 1989.

Higson, Andrew, *Waving the Flag: Constructing a National Cinema in Britain* (Oxford: Clarendon Press, 1995).

Hill, John, 'The Issue of National Cinema and British Film Production', in Duncan Petrie (ed.), *New Questions of British Cinema* (London: British Film Institute, 1992).

Hill, John, McLoone, Martin, and Hainsworth, Paul (eds.), *Border Crossing: Film in Ireland, Britain and Europe* (Belfast: Institute of Irish Studies/London: British Film Institute, 1994).

Hill, John, and McLoone, Martin (eds.), *Big Picture, Small Screen: The Relations Between Film and Television* (Luton: John Libbey/University of Luton Press, 1996).

McArthur, Colin (ed.), *Scotch Reels: Scotland in Cinema and Television* (London: British Film Institute, 1982).

Richards, Jeffrey, 'National Identity in British Wartime Films', in Philip M. Taylor (ed.), *Britain and the Cinema in the Second World War* (Basingstoke: Macmillan, 1989).

Willemen, Paul, 'The National', in *Looks and Frictions: Essays in Cultural Studies and Film Theory* (London: British Film Institute, 1994).

Conclusion
A Short History of British Cinema

Robert Murphy

1. The Pleasure Garden

Trains rushing by; a wall being knocked down; a kiss; a cameraman being swallowed; a man being run over by a car; firemen putting out a fire; a burglar being chased: simple spectacles, naive tricks. British cinema was good at this sort of thing. Enterprising showmen like Walter Haggar, adaptable magic lantern men like Cecil Hepworth, ambitious photographers like James Williamson, took to the cinema like ducks to water. Britain had a tradition of optical entertainment, and for a dozen years or so British film-makers were as vigorous and popular and inventive as anyone. Charles Barr demonstrates the narrative sophistication of *Rescued by Rover* (Lewis Fitzhamon, 1905), but also points out that it was a small-scale, family affair.[1] While America created a major industry, Britain remained at the stage of small family businesses.

In the 1920s enterprising young entrepreneurs like Herbert Wilcox and Michael Balcon tried to update British film production by importing American stars for their films and seeking out co-production deals with German companies. The director they most relied on was Jack Graham Cutts, a proficient film-maker but an incessant intriguer who did his best to blight the prospects of two of his rivals, Adrian Brunel and Alfred Hitchcock. Brunel was easily shouldered aside and never did fulfil his early promise, but Hitchcock proved more formidable.

Hitchcock's first film, *The Pleasure Garden* (1926), was made at the Emelka studio in Munich and, like later Euro-puddings, has a strangely decentred feel about it. It is oddly structured and, as Raymond Durgnat comments, 'It's hard to tell now whether this unusual shape was a product of English primitivism or of Hitchcock's sophistication.'[2] Two sequences attest to Hitchcock's odd sensibility. The first, combining eroticism with comedy, occurs after Patsy (Virginia Valli), the stout-hearted heroine, offers to share her bed with Jill (Carmelita Geraghty), a provincial innocent she has rescued from lecherous stage-door Johnnies. Jill isn't as innocent as she pretends and she later develops into a ruthless *femme fatale*. As she kneels in her night-dress to say her bedtime prayers, Patsy's dog sniffs her out, distracting her by licking the soles of her feet. The second sequence, demonstrating Hitchcock's penchant for the macabre, comes after Patsy, spurned by Jill, accepts the marriage proposal of a dry, passionless man called Levet (Miles Mander). Her tearful wave to him as he sails off to the tropics to resume his colonial career dissolves into the frantically happy wave of a native girl (Nita Naldi) welcoming him back to a full-blooded, sensual relationship. When

Patsy follows him out, Levet discards his lover. Disconsolately she walks into the sea. Levet wades in after her. She turns, smiling, towards him, thinking he wants her after all. But no, he grabs her only to push her head under the waves, making sure she is well and truly drowned.

2. Rich and strange

The British film industry in the 1930s was a peculiar amalgam – talented refugees from Germany, Austria, Poland, Hungary rubbed shoulders with 'ace' technicians imported from Hollywood, British veterans from the silent period, and ambitious young men determined to grasp the opportunities offered by a new and expanding industry. The essays in this book by Sarah Street, Lawrence Napper, Linda Wood, Tom Ryall and Kevin Gough-Yates attest to an interest in the fully fledged industry of the mid-30s, with its flamboyant émigrés, its financial shenanigans and its contrasting modes of production. But the British cinema of the early 30s, the period between the coming of sound in 1929 and Korda's success with *The Private Life of Henry VIII* in 1933, remains neglected. Crackly sound, stagey acting, ridiculously plummy accents, make early sound films difficult to take, but once through these off-putting barriers one enters a fascinatingly unfamiliar world.

Hitchcock seemed to make a highly successful transition from silent to sound film, organising the shooting of *Blackmail* (1929) in such a way that it was possible to convert it quickly and release it as Britain's first sound film. His subsequent early sound films, however, share the neglect suffered by the whole of British cinema during this period. Thus a witty, revealing film like *Rich and Strange* (1931) comes as an agreeable surprise.

A huge clock hovers over the heads of serried ranks of clerks as they pack away their adding machines and make for the door. Crowds push and shove their way on to a tube train. Fred (Henry Kendall) stands out from the crowd because his umbrella won't open, his newspaper gets into a tangle and he wrecks a woman's hat. Arriving at his suburban home, he finds his wife busy with her sewing machine and has only an evening listening to the wireless ('Mr Baker will give his twelfth talk on accountancy in three minutes') to look forward to. 'The best place for us is the gas oven,' complains Fred, but escape from this purgatorial existence comes with the evening post. A rich uncle has decided to grant Fred his wish to see life, providing him with enough money to go on a world cruise.

Amid the sybaritic luxury of a sea cruise, Fred's marriage disintegrates. As he languishes, sea-sick, below deck, his wife Em (Joan Barry) emerges from under his shadow. She tells a pipe-smoking plantation owner on his way home back East, 'I can talk to you because you're just a man and not my husband.' But she finds she likes being listened to and treated with respect. Fred himself falls prey to an adventuress masquerading as a princess, and it seems that the couple must part. But when Em learns that the princess is a fraud and that her pompous, gullible, selfish husband will have to learn about life the hard way, she decides she must return to him. Ungracefully he accepts that he has been a fool and the couple find a bickering but more equal partnership as they make their hazardous way home to the now reassuring comforts of suburbia.

Tom Milne claims that Hitchcock is 'extraordinarily scathing about the timidity and emotional reserve of his central characters: innocence of the most banal and compromised kind confronts experience in the form of exotic strangers and risks, and responds by retreating further into its shell.'[3] But he misreads the tone of the film, which is gently rather than cruelly mocking, and comes from a man himself an innocent fascinated by the oddness of a real world which is unknowably rich and strange.

3. The Common Touch

Although the requisitioning of studios and recruitment into the armed services left the British film industry much depleted during the Second World War, this is still regarded as a period when British films flowered. Patriotic enthusiasm should not be allowed to obscure the fact that the war years produced nothing to equal the musicals, the comedies, the Hitchcock thrillers of the 30s, not to mention European-inspired experiments like Berthold Viertel's *The Passing of the Third Floor Back* (1935) or Lothar Mendes's *The Man Who Could Work Miracles* (1936). But the war films evoke values – bravery, self-sacrifice, social harmony, unselfish pulling together for the common good – which we have now lost. Documentaries like Harry Watt's *London Can Take It* (1940) and Humphrey Jennings's *Listen to Britain* (1941); feature films like Noël Coward and David Lean's *In Which We Serve* (1942) or the more ruggedly egalitarian *Millions Like Us* (Frank Launder and Sidney Gilliat, 1943) and *The Way Ahead* (Carol Reed, 1944) encapsulate an ethos which is moving and powerful. But the most plangent manifestation of wartime populism resides in the now almost forgotten films of John Baxter.

Baxter made a series of low-budget films in the 30s – *Doss House* (1933), *Say It with Flowers* (1933), *The Song of the Plough* (1933), *Music Hall* (1934), *The Song of the Road* (1937) – which dwell uniquely, if sentimentally, on the problems of the poor. When war broke out in 1939, Baxter formed an alliance with Lady Yule, a millionairess

Innocents fascinated by the oddness of the world. Henry Kendall and Joan Barry begin their journey in Rich and Strange *(Alfred Hitchcock, 1931).*

determined that her company, British National, should expand rather than abandon production. Baxter's contribution was a series of films (*Love on the Dole*, 1941; *The Common Touch*, 1941; *Let the People Sing*, 1942; *The Shipbuilders*, 1944) which pleaded for a post-war society where the evils of the past – unemployment, poverty, class conflict, injustice – would be banished.

If *Love on the Dole* is the most accomplished of these films, *The Common Touch* is the most bizarre. It is essentially a bigger-budget version of Baxter's earlier film, *Doss House*, where an undercover journalist investigates what it is like to be down and out in London. In *The Common Touch* a public schoolboy inherits his father's property company and decides it would be a good wheeze to find out about life in the shelter for down and outs which his managers want to demolish to make way for an ambitious new development. Tony Aldgate and Geoff Brown point out that in *The Common Touch* Baxter restores those elements – cabaret scenes, 'sex appeal' and a romantic sub-plot – which *Doss House* had won praise from the critics for leaving out.[4] Nonetheless, documentary film-maker Edgar Anstey, who had condemned his colleague Humphrey Jennings's *Listen to Britain* as 'the rarest piece of fiddling since the days of Nero', praised Baxter's 'curious and individual quality of fantasy and of lyricism' and concluded that 'the rich colour of its characterisation and the gusto of its symbolism gives the film some of the simple wisdom of a medieval allegory'.[5] Indeed Baxter's utopian populism is a cultural strand which might be traced back to John Ball and the Peasants Revolt.

4. I Know Where I'm Going

When the war ended in 1945 the British film industry seemed set to conquer the world. British films, once seen as something to be ashamed of, were now lauded by the critics for their realism and maturity. Production, at last, appeared to be organised on a sound financial basis with a large conglomerate – the Rank Organisation – big and powerful enough to challenge the American majors. And there seemed an abundance of talent – directors, producers, actors, technicians – capable of producing films as good as anything that Hollywood or Europe could offer.

The most successful and inventive of this new talent was distilled into a small company called The Archers, which worked under the umbrella of the Rank-financed Independent Producers. Its two leading lights, Michael Powell and Emeric Pressburger, had made a series of successful films – *The Spy in Black* (1939), *Contraband* (1940), *49th Parallel* (1941), *One of Our Aircraft is Missing* (1942) – and were given virtual *carte blanche* by Rank to make what they liked. They rewarded Rank's faith with *The Life and Death of Colonel Blimp* (1943) – which Churchill did his best to ban – and the audaciously eccentric *A Canterbury Tale* (1944).

Their next film, *I Know Where I'm Going* (1945), was quickly written by Emeric Pressburger and has the powerful simplicity of a fairy story. A bank manager's daughter travels up to Scotland to marry her boss. All her life she has been able to get what she wanted, but at the very last stage of her journey – a short trip across a strait of water to the island where her future husband awaits her – she is held back by the weather. Nonplussed that she cannot control the elements – her wish that the wind blow away the mist is answered by a storm which makes crossing even more hazardous – she is forced to recognise that what the fates have decreed for her is different from what she thought she wanted.

Kevin Gough-Yates stresses the film's concern with exile and cultural bewilderment.[6] But it is also an archetypal tale of love and destiny. The Scottish settings are real enough (much of the film was shot on the island of Mull), but Powell and Pressburger transmute them into a Brigadoon-like never-never land. The characters played by Pamela Brown, Captain Knight and Nancy Price, sharing their dim, ruined halls with dogs and eagles, belong as much to Gormenghast as to Scotland, but they are something more than picturesque eccentrics. Their lives, ruled by the elements, rooted in the landscape, represent a reality which is timeless and natural and implicitly more worthwhile than the busy, organised life of the Englishwoman, Joan (Wendy Hiller). Catriona (Pamela Brown), from her first appearance as she comes in out of the storm with a pack of huge Irish wolfhounds, haunts the film. With goddess-like dignity she gives up Torquil (Roger Livesey) to Joan and pushes him into the decisive action which will save her from drowning.

Britain's attempt on the world market failed, but *I Know Where I'm Going* and its successors – *A Matter of Life and Death* (1946), *Black Narcissus* (1947), *The Red Shoes* (1948) and *The Small Back Room* (1949) – make up a dazzling sequence of films that any national cinema would be proud of.

5. Reach For the Sky

Respectability, deference, caution, consensus marked the 50s, but beneath the tranquil surface lurked the dreadful but exciting events of the war. The Second World War, like most wars, was fought by very young men (the average age of Battle of Britain pilots was twenty-one), and for those who survived it was likely to be the most traumatic and dramatic period of their lives. War films allowed an opportunity to relive and come to terms with that experience. And for the generation who grew up surrounded by bomb sites and tales of the war, these films allowed a glimpse into a dangerous world which they had been too young to experience directly.

There is another reason for the popularity of British war films in the 50s. They were something the British film industry did well. Unlike musicals or Westerns or gangster films, war films didn't seem to be the exclusive preserve of Hollywood. Britain's role in winning the Second World War, though less significant than was believed at the time, was significant enough to fuel a body of often exciting and sometimes serious films. Like the horror films that began to emerge from Hammer studios after 1957, 50s war films constituted a genre. British Second World War films were very successful in commercial terms, but their stiff-upper-lip style proved unacceptable to later critics. Neil Rattigan sees them as evidence of a conspiracy: 'a reflection of the last ditch effort by the dominant class to maintain its hegemony by re-writing the history of the celluloid war in its own favour'.[7] And Andy Medhurst claims that:

> In the dominant, common-sense history of British cinema such films are seen as at best worthily dull, at worst the absolute epitome of the cinema of tight-lipped middle-class repression soon to be rightfully swept away by the social realist impetus of the late 1950s.[8]

Medhurst attempts a partial re-evaluation, finding much that is interesting in films like *The Cruel Sea* (Charles Frend, 1952), *Angels One Five* (George More O'Ferrall, 1952), and even *The Dam Busters* (Michael Anderson, 1955), but he draws the line at 'that seminal text of romanticised distortion', *Reach for the Sky* (Lewis Gilbert, 1956).

Reach for the Sky was the top box-office film of 1956, and unlike films such as *Scott of the Antarctic* (Charles Frend, 1948) and *The Magic Box* (John Boulting, 1951) which were devoted to honourable failures, it dealt with a successful British hero. Douglas

Bader's brand of cheery, dogged masculinity seems odd and unfashionable now, but it caught the public imagination in the 50s. Never again would Britishness be celebrated on the screen with such uncritical enthusiasm. By the end of 1956 British confidence had been shaken by the Suez debacle. War films – such as David Lean's *The Bridge on the River Kwai* (1957), Anthony Asquith's *Orders to Kill* (1958) and Val Guest's *Yesterday's Enemy* (1959) – became darker and more unsure of themselves.

The old guard at Pinewood themselves saw their authority and respect eroded as their ebullient certainties crumbled. The other phenomenal successes of 1956 were John Osborne's play, *Look Back in Anger*, Colin Wilson's book, *The Outsider*, and the low-budget American film, *Rock Around the Clock*. The Angry Young Men and rock and roll had arrived. Retrospectively, *Reach for the Sky* conjures up images of the band playing on the *Titanic* as the ship slips majestically beneath the water line. It is less for nostalgia (there are far more resonant war films than this) than as a record of a set of feelings and beliefs which have now almost completely disappeared that *Reach for the Sky* is invaluable.

6. Hell is a City

Crime films are an essential element of British cinema – country house whodunnits in the 30s, spiv movies and the huge array of non-generic crime films of the late 40s explored by Raymond Durgnat in this book, Scotland Yard investigation films in the 50s which prepared the way for popular television series like *Dixon of Dock Green, Z Cars* and *The Sweeney*. But as television took the middle ground, the cinema began to be more critical and adventurous. A key element in this process was the emergence of Stanley Baker as a major actor.[9] He played numerous minor roles in the late 40s and 50s before finding a satisfying screen persona as a tough but sensitive ex-convict trying to go straight in *Hell Drivers* (Cy Endfield, 1956).

The most significant of Baker's minor roles was in *The Cruel Sea*, as an officer who is not quite a gentleman and is soon removed from Jack Hawkins's efficient ship. Baker had a symbolic revenge by replacing Hawkins as Britain's leading screen detective in the late 50s. In Basil Dearden's *Violent Playground* (1957) he plays a detective unwillingly drafted into service as a community policeman; in Joseph Losey's *Blind Date* (1959) he is an up-from-the-ranks Scotland Yard detective bitterly aware that he has the wrong background and the wrong attitude to climb any further up the ladder; and in Val Guest's *Hell is a City* (1960), made for Hammer (in Hammerscope), he is an overworked policeman with an unhappy home life.

Guest, who had entered the industry in the 30s as a scriptwriter (responsible for films like Will Hay's *Oh Mr Porter*), is an uncelebrated director but he is idiosyncratic enough to qualify as an auteur. Between 1960 and 1964 he made four films – *Hell is a City, Jigsaw* (1962), *80,000 Suspects* (1963), *The Beauty Jungle* (1964) – shot mainly on location with cinematographer Arthur Grant (who had been John Baxter's camera operator in the 40s). All of them are flawed films in the sense that their elements don't quite gel, but they are also inventive, lively and quirky.

The title sequence of *Hell is a City*, with a police car rushing though night-time streets, seems to promise an American police thriller; the end, with Baker turning away from his chance of a loving relationship and wandering off into the rainy night, seems more like an angst-ridden European art movie. What is between is very English. Baker's Inspector Martineau tracks an escaped killer he's known since schooldays and eventually traps him on a rooftop. The chase is dogged and thorough rather than dangerous and exciting, but the incidental detail thrown up – a dodgy pub landlord and

A landmark on the road to gritty realism. Stanley Baker in Hell is a City *(Val Guest, 1960).*

his saucy, sensual barmaid; small-time crooks in their billiard halls and backstreet garages; the long-suffering bookie and his flighty wife; a pitch and toss game outside a Lancashire moorland village – jostle for attention in a vividly realised provincial world. Guest is never one to shun a cliché and he is hampered by a maladroitly cast villain, but *Hell is a City* is a landmark on the road from the staid but visually impressive Scotland Yard films of the 50s to the gritty realism of *Z Cars*.

7. The Reckoning

By the end of the 60s tawdriness and indulgence had descended on the British film industry. Some films have acquired a historical fascination as records of unlikely performances: Maureen Lipman as a loud-mouthed Battersea tart in *Up the Junction* (Peter Collinson, 1967), Joanna Lumley as a revolutionary LSE student in *The Breaking of Bumbo* (Andrew Sinclair, 1969), John Thaw as a Trotskyist activist in *Praise Marx and Pass the Ammunition* (Maurice Hatton, 1970). But what saved the cinema from the bathos of Swinging London was the infusion of talented television directors who brought a kind of realism back to British cinema.

Jack Gold's *The Reckoning* (1970) is a relentlessly flashy film, full of obtrusive camera movements and ugly close-ups, but it has a raw energy which makes it as compelling to watch as a Tarantino film. Nicol Williamson plays a working-class Liverpudlian who has got on in business and acquired a beautiful middle-class wife (Ann Bell) and a house in Virginia Water. The suspicious death of his father coincides with marital breakdown and a ruthless boardroom power struggle to throw his life into crisis.

261

The social rise of a working-class man is a key theme of 60s cinema. In *Room at the Top* (Jack Clayton, 1959), Joe Lampton (Laurence Harvey) finds the path to the top he no longer wants opened by the boss's daughter, whom he has made pregnant; in *Nothing But the Best* (Clive Donner, 1963), Alan Bates murders his aristocratic mentor when he threatens to expose him as a working-class chancer. Six years of a Labour government changed the ethos of British society. Though classlessness and equality of opportunity were far from fully realised ideals, *The Reckoning* reflects a world where doors to the top could be opened if they were given a sufficiently vigorous kick. This Williamson supplies with convincing gusto, employing a Machiavellian energy in using his friends and disposing of his enemies. Getting drunk, driving badly, indulging in adulterous relationships are cathartic releases of energy rather than fatal flaws, and he ends the film exultantly successful. As *The Reckoning* reminds us, the 60s wasn't just about peace and love.

8. Bad Timing

In 1977 the Rank organisation re-embarked on a £10 million film production programme. Unfortunately all but one of the films were marred by 'a fatal sense of un-adventurous orthodoxy'.[10] The exception, decried by one Rank executive as 'a sick film made by sick people for sick audiences', was *Bad Timing* (1980), the most unlikely Rank film since Powell and Pressburger presented a bemused J. Arthur Rank with *A Canterbury Tale* in 1944. With Art Garfunkel and Teresa Russell as Americans in Vienna, Harvey Keitel as an Austrian policeman and Denholm Elliott convincingly cast as a sad-eyed Czech, one could be forgiven for wondering if this is a British film at all, particularly as it confronts sex with un-English forthrightness. But it bears the unmistakable mark of its director, Nicolas Roeg.

Roeg's first film, *Performance* (1970), had been considered decadent, but it could be blamed on his co-director, Donald Cammel, an unstable figure compared to Roeg, a brilliant cameraman with a long apprenticeship in the industry. The films that followed – *Walkabout* (1970), *Don't Look Now* (1973) and *The Man Who Fell to Earth* (1976) – while quirky and sophisticated, were by no means outrageous. Hence *Bad Timing*, a disturbing tale of passion and sexual violence, with clean-cut Garfunkel smoothly evil as a concentration camp commander, shocked critics and audiences as well as Rank executives. Alex (Garfunkel), a successful academic working in Vienna, has an affair with Milena (Russell), a footloose young American. He is possessive and resentful of her friendships with other men, and when she refuses his offer of marriage he becomes increasingly brutal towards her. Answering her distress call after a drugs overdose, he rapes her while her life ebbs away.

As in *I Know Where I'm Going*, at the film's core there is a clash of values. In Powell and Pressburger's film, Joan has her busy, rational life disrupted, but her awakening to the beauty and terror of the world is untraumatic and she emerges as a more mature and whole person. In *Bad Timing*, Milena is spontaneous, natural, responsive to her environment, and she is destroyed by Alex's insistence on order and convention. This sexual obsession – concealed beneath a veneer of cool rationality – drives him to seek out the dark, unexplored nooks and crannies of her life, making her ever more defenceless and vulnerable.

Such a film was as welcome as a corpse at a children's party and the Rank Organisation refused to show it in its cinemas and abandoned film production for good.

9. High Hopes

The British film industry underwent unpleasant shock therapy under Thatcherism. The quota ensuring that all cinemas showed a percentage of British films was abandoned in 1982; the Films Act of 1985 abolished the Eady Levy and pulled the plug on the National Film Finance Corporation.[11] British films continued to be made but the infrastructure that ensured they reached an audience was kicked away. In Carlos Castaneda's *Tales of Power*, Don Juan explains that the Spanish invasion of Mexico was a disaster for the Indians but a marvellous opportunity for the sorcerers. All the energy that had found expression in the culture of Indian society was suppressed and channelled underground into sorcery.[12] Seventeen years of Tory rule have been similarly disastrous for the British film industry, but a clutch of films emerged which made a powerful riposte to the Thatcherite ideology of self-interest and materialism.[13] One of the most effective is Mike Leigh's *High Hopes*.

Despite his uniqueness as a perceptive, wryly humorous observer of British society, Leigh's refusal to work with a conventional script (his stories evolve out of extensive improvisation) barred him from most sources of film funding, and between *Bleak Moments* (1971) and *High Hopes* (1988) all his films were made on tiny budgets for television. *High Hopes*, largely funded by Channel 4 but released as a feature film, is not stylistically different from Leigh's television work. It centres upon three couples – Cyril and Shirley, Laetitia and Rupert, Valerie and Martin, and an old lady, Mrs Bender, who is Cyril and Valerie's mother and Rupert and Laetitia's next-door neighbour. Valerie and Martin are familiar Leigh stereotypes: they are vulgar, boorish, offensively loud and have more money than sense. Laetitia and Rupert are Thatcherite Yuppies. Cyril and Shirley are gauche, left-wing relics of an earlier era.

In most Mike Leigh films characters are combustible mixtures of the unspeakable and the winsome. Characters who appear as embarrassingly awful reveal, during a crisis, some touchingly human trait, and those who start out as sweetly reasonable show unexpected quirks and kinks. In *High Hopes*, Leigh allows a political dimension to creep in, encouraging us to feel unalloyed hostility to Laetitia and Rupert and to develop a close identification with Cyril and Shirley. In the sequence which brings these disparate characters together, Mrs Bender locks herself out and has to rely on the reluctant hospitality of Laetitia and Rupert while she waits for one of her offspring to arrive with a spare key. They make her pay for the privilege of sitting in their kitchen by subjecting her to a barrage of questions about the run-down state of her house and garden, revealing a set of values which exclude compassion, consideration and tolerance. No doubt these are qualities the rich have always lacked, but in British films they tend to be shown as cuddly eccentrics with hearts of gold, and Laetitia and Rupert's callousness comes as a shock.[14]

To balance this, there is a more definite resolution than Leigh normally allows. After a disastrous birthday party, Cyril and Shirley take Mrs Bender home with them. They are all slightly drunk. Cyril gives up his opposition to the idea of having a baby, and in the morning Mrs Bender seems to have emerged from her state of catatonic misery. This is not very high on the scale of human happiness, but it is enough to imbue the film with optimism rather than despair.

10. Riff-raff

Mrs Thatcher resigned in November 1990. The films released in 1991, though too early to connect with her political demise, nevertheless seemed to signify a new mood. In Alan Parker's adaptation of Roddy Doyle's *The Commitments*, Mike Leigh's *Life is*

Sweet, Hanif Kureishi's *London Kills Me*, there is a new concern with young people, and a feeling of trying to make the best of an absurd, unjust world. Ken Loach's *Riff-Raff* is unusual in that it endorses violent direct action, but it shares the same mood.

Given how much the cause of the working class had been set back by Thatcherism, *Riff-Raff* is remarkably cheerful. An insistence on the need to fight back, and not to be destroyed by the system, unites the two parts of the film: building workers converting what had been a hospital into luxury flats, and a relationship between one of the young workers and a girl whose illusions about life and reliance on drugs ill equip her to survive in the harsh world of the underclass.

Stevie (Robert Carlyle) is sharp, cautious, realistic – the extent of his high hopes is to have a market stall selling boxer shorts – but his decision to ditch his girlfriend, for fear of being dragged into the nightmare world of drug addiction, is shown as sad and painful rather than as a necessary and inevitable step on his path towards success. Her boldness in confronting him at the building site shows her to be something more than a pathetic deadbeat, and the loss of the warmth and sensuality of her company darkens Stevie's world and pushes him towards the cathartic revenge with which the film ends.

Riff-Raff's combination of comedy and tragedy, social criticism and concern for the lives of ordinary people sums up much of what is best in British cinema. There are other things which are absent from Loach's film – sexuality, mysticism, the struggle to uncover a meaningful national identity – and these too are an essential part of British cinema. One hundred years of British films has not produced the abundant crop of artistic masterpieces one would have hoped for, but they offer a unique insight into the process of cultural change in Britain in the twentieth century.

Notes

1. Charles Barr, 'Before *Blackmail*: Silent British Cinema', in this book, p. 11.
2. Raymond Durgnat, *The Strange Case of Alfred Hitchcock*, Faber and Faber, 1974, p. 67.
3. Tom Milne (ed.), *Time Out Film Guide* (Harmondsworth: Penguin, 1989), p. 501.
4. See Anthony Aldgate and Geoff Brown, *John Baxter* (London: British Film Institute, 1989), a modest attempt to rescue Baxter from obscurity.
5. Anstey's opinion of *Listen to Britain* quoted in Elizabeth Sussex, *The Rise and Fall of British Documentary* (Berkeley, CA and London: University of California Press, 1975), p. 144. Anstey's review of *The Common Touch* is quoted in Aldgate and Brown, *John Baxter*, p. 85.
6. Kevin Gough-Yates, 'Exiles and British Cinema', in this book, p. 103.
7. Neil Rattigan, 'The Last Gasp of the Middle Class: British War Films of the 1950s', in Wheeler Winston Dixon (ed.), *Re-viewing British Cinema* (New York: State University of New York Press, 1994), p. 150.
8. Andy Medhurst, '1950s War Films', in Geoff Hurd (ed.), *National Fictions* (London: British Film Institute, 1984), p. 35.
9. See Andrew Spicer, 'Male Stars, Masculinity and British Cinema', in this book, p. 139.
10. The judgment is Alexander Walker's. See his *National Heroes* (London: Harrap, 1985), pp. 204–8, a useful account of the Rank production venture. The films were: *Wombling Free* (Lionel Jeffries, 1977); *The 39 Steps* (Don Sharp, 1978), *The Lady Vanishes* (Anthony Page, 1979), *The Riddle of the Sands* (Tony Maylam, 1979), *Tarka the Otter* (David Cobham, 1979), *Eagle's Wing* (Anthony Harvey, 1979) and *Silver Dream Racer* (David Wickes, 1980).
11. The Eady Levy was, in part, a subsidy for British films calculated in relation to their box-office performance; the NFFC was a government film bank which nursed hundreds of British films into production throughout the 1950s, 60s and 70s.
12. Carlos Castaneda, *Tales of Power* (London: Hodder & Stoughton, 1975), p. 140.
13. See Lester Friedman, 'The Empire Strikes Out', in Friedman (ed.), *Fires Were Started: British Cinema and Thatcherism* (University of Minneapolis Press, 1993), pp. 10–11. 'British films of this period could not help being political (in the broadest sense of the word) as they charted the inexorably downward spiral of their homeland.... Though driven by their hatred of the present government, these visual artists still managed to tease the permanent out of the momentary. They

instinctively understood that Mrs Thatcher's ideology, her creation and re-creation of past and present history, must be matched by an alternative vision that offered a different version of this era.... Their pictures defined a turbulent era, revived the moribund British cinema, and froze a crucial moment in British culture.' See also, in the same book, the essay by Leonard Quart, 'The Religion of the Market: Thatcherite Politics and the British Film of the 1980s', pp. 15–34.

14. Compare, for example, *A Severed Head* (d. Dick Clements, 1970), where the world is seen from the point of view of a Rupert-like character.

Index

268

271

275

278